Who's #1?

Who's #1?

100-Plus Years of Controversial National Champions in College Football

Christopher J. Walsh

TAYLOR TRADE PUBLISHING
Lanham • New York • Boulder • Toronto • Plymouth, UK

Published by Taylor Trade Publishing
An imprint of The Rowman & Littlefield Publishing Group, Inc.
4501 Forbes Boulevard, Suite 200, Lanham, Maryland 20706

Distributed by NATIONAL BOOK NETWORK

Library of Congress Cataloging-in-Publication Data

Walsh, Christopher J., 1968-
    Who's #1? : 100-plus years of controversial national champions in college football / Christopher J. Walsh. — 1st taylor trade publishing ed. 2007.
        p. cm.
    ISBN-13: 978-1-58979-337-8 (cloth : alk. paper)
    ISBN-10: 1-58979-337-4 (cloth : alk. paper)
    1. Football teams—United States—History. 2. National Collegiate Athletic Association—History. I. Title.
    GV959.5.U6W35 2007
    796.332'63—dc22   2007022921

⊗™ The paper used in this publication meets the minimum requirements of American National Standard for Information Sciences—Permanence of Paper for Printed Library Materials, ANSI/NISO Z39.48-1992.

Manufactured in the United States of America.

To men and women of conviction like Pat Tillman,
and everything they stood for.

"I chose not to be a common man,
because it is my right to be uncommon, if I can."

FLOYD LITTLE, Syracuse University

Contents

Acknowledgments

ALTHOUGH Rick Rinehart at Taylor Trade Publishing and I had been talking about this project for a few months, the day he told me it was a go was January 3, 2007. It's permanently etched into my brain because my regular job is covering the University of Alabama football team and that was also the day the Crimson Tide hired Nick Saban away from the Miami Dolphins.

I'll never forget Rick calling and asking, "So, is anything going on?" He then told me that they wanted the book "yesterday." No pressure.

As always, my apologies to anyone I missed, but here are some people who especially come to mind:

- Thank you to my family for their love and support, and putting up with the fact that I all but vanished from their lives while writing this book. The same goes for my extended family around the country and world. You all know who you are, and how important you are to me (even when I was ignoring your e-mails, phone calls and instant messages).
- Thank you Rick Rinehart for green-lighting this project and to Lynn Weber and everyone at Taylor Trade who worked on it.
- Special thanks to every person who worked at the Tuscaloosa News since I was hired in 2004 (from Carla Jean Whitley to Edwin Stanton). This goes doubly so for Tim Thompson, Doug Ray, David Wasson and the entire sports staff.

Just to clarify something about the photos in this book, the absolutely most important factor for which ones were accumulated and used was simple availability. The decision was made from the start not to pay any rights or handling fees (which would have come out of the author's very limited pockets), which made acquiring some photos extremely difficult if not impossible. Having said that, I apologize to fans who are disappointed their favorite team isn't better represented, but hey, I tried.

However, some people who were incredibly helpful include Brad Green at the Paul W. Bryant Museum, Nicole O'Neil at the Tournament of Roses, John Heisler and Carol

Copley at Notre Dame, Greg Kinney from Michigan, Charles Bloom at the Southeastern Conference, Phil Marwill at the National Football Foundation, Bob Burda and Carmen Branch at the Big 12, and Victor (V.J.) Monzon-Aguirre from the Orange Bowl.

Additional thanks to Robert Sutton and Michelle Williams from the Tuscaloosa News for the nifty shots from Alabama at Florida in 2006, and to every school which answered my request for photos. It was, and still is, greatly appreciated.

Sources for this book would be too numerous to list, but some of the major ones include the *Official 2006 Division I and Division I-AA Football Records Book*, The Bowl Championship Series, National Football Foundation, College Football Hall of Fame, *ESPN College Football Encyclopedia*, the bowls, the conferences, the teams, and more media guides, Internet sites, press conferences, interviews, transcripts, and press releases than you could imagine.

Most of all, thank you fans. Keep the debate over "Who's #1?" going.

Introduction

THERE IS something to be said for wanting to be the best at something. About sacrificing to achieve, having the hunger and determination to persevere, and being rewarded with an accomplishment that no one can ever take away.

We love and celebrate our champions. We like to think they represent the best of ourselves, mark our accomplishments, and keep us striving for more.

To borrow the words of a football legend at another level, John Madden, "The only yardstick for success our society has is being a champion. No one remembers anything else."

It's therefore curious that there's nothing in American sports quite as controversial as college football's national championship, including the recently establishment-mandated Bowl Championships Series. This year, like just about every other year, the debate goes on about who should be the true national champion, and/or which teams should play for the all but mythical title.

Although the National Collegiate Athletic Association has never proclaimed a champion in Division I football, numerous others have done so since the first game between Princeton and Rutgers was played in 1869. Consequently, in only a handful of years has there been a clear-cut, undisputed champion like Yale in 1909 and Texas in 2005 (Note: Unless specifically stated otherwise, the years mentioned throughout this book relate to the season and not the bowl game. So even though Texas won the Rose Bowl in January 2006, it captured the 2005 national championship. Also, for simplicity, all rankings are from the Associated Press poll unless otherwise noted). Some seasons, four, five or even six schools have been named national champion by at least one ranking service or organization, leading to endless speculation, argumentation, and all-out second-guessing.

How is it that Arizona State, Nebraska, Notre Dame, Ohio State and Texas could all claim a share of the 1970 national championship 20 years after Kentucky, Oklahoma, Princeton and Tennessee could do likewise? Why is it that after so many years we're still experiencing split national titles and hearing regular complaints that the system isn't fair? Why has the Bowl Championship Series had as many failures as successes?

The list goes on and on, and while proponents of the system will argue that the lack of a true playoff makes college football unique, and garnishes extra attention year-round, others simply wonder how something as simple as a championship became so convoluted and complicated.

"Is it one guy, like the Wizard of Oz kind of thing?" Southern California coach Pete Carroll asked at a 2006 Rose Bowl press conference. However, he also once admitted that: "The fact that there's a controversy going on makes it all that much more interesting."

Although the NCAA declares annual champions in 88 sports, Division I-A (now known as the Football Bowl Subdivision) football is the only college title not definitively settled on the field through a tournament of some sort. Even Division I-AA (recently renamed the Football Championship Subdivision), Division II, and Division III football have season-concluding playoff systems. While the lack of an official declaration may help keep college football in the forefront of the American sports scene, it frequently creates as many questions as answers, if not more.

How this came to be is not easily explainable, but its continued lack of cohesion is clearly the result of one simple thing, money. Those who have it, and thus control the sport, don't want to give it up or share with those who don't.

But more about that later.

In the meantime, the NCAA continues to inch closer to a potential playoff while the process provokes everything from criticism and frustration to downright scorn, and the debate is far from reaching any sort of final resolution.

This is an effort to define, explain and fuel the discussion process, in addition to examining the BCS as a whole. While it will trace the history and evolution of college football championships, while focusing on the controversies, the aim is also to celebrate the game as a whole, both its individuals and teams, on and off the field. That goes for the champions as well as the spoilers, like Texas Christian in 1961, which finished 3-5-2, but tied No. 2 Ohio State (7-7), and beat No. 3 Texas (6-0), to ruin otherwise perfect seasons.

Perhaps no chance meeting explains college football better than the one Paul Bunker had in the Philippines, years after he played for Army and scored two touchdowns against rival Navy in 1902. It was when he ran into Navy back Ralph Strassburger, who had been on the losing end of that game.

"I hate you," Strassburger said. "Let's have a drink."

But before moving on to explore the teams and seasons which have left their mark over the years, homage must first paid to the coaches and the most important people in college football, the players themselves. What better way to do so than with a glimpse at a few of the sport's true characters, including some the brief biographies of those enshrined at the College Football Hall of Fame in South Bend, Indiana.

For example, did you know that when he wasn't coaching college football, John Heisman was a Shakespearean actor? Years later, Notre Dame had a standout halfback named William Shakespeare. Naturally, his teammates called him "The Bard." He excelled in special teams, set school career punting records, and went on to win four battle stars and the Bronze Star during World War II.

Northwestern end Edgar Manske (1931–33), nicknamed "Eggs," was the last man to play football without a helmet. His wife, the former Jane Fauntz, was a beauty queen and a medal winner in Olympic diving.

In 1934, the key game in Minnesota's national championship was against Pittsburgh. With time running out, the Golden Gophers had fourth down with four yards to go at the Pitt 17-yard line, when back Pug Lund took a lateral and instead of trying to gain the yards himself threw to end Bob Tenner for a touchdown and 13-7 victory.

"He was our spark plug," Coach Bernie Bierman said of Lund, considered an even better blocker than ball carrier. "He was battered and broken up, teeth knocked out, finger amputated, thumb broken, and through all that he carried on. Our opponents might break him in two, but they couldn't stop him."

Forrest Behm Jr. was badly burned in a brush fire when he was 5 years old and doctors wanted to amputate a leg. His father refused and with the parents' help he slowly regained use of all his muscles. In 1940, Behm was a tackle on Nebraska's Rose Bowl team, in addition to class president, ROTC Cadet Colonel, honor student, member of the college choir, and a recipient of a Harvard Fellowship for graduate study.

Alvin Wistert was a high school dropout who served in the Marines during World War II before entering college. He enrolled at Boston University and after a year transferred to Michigan, where he helped the Wolverines win three Big Ten titles and at age 33 became the oldest player named an All-American. Wistert and his brothers, Albert and Francis "Whitey," are all enshrined in the College Football Hall of Fame.

After enrolling at Notre Dame, quarterback Joe Theismann (pronounced THEES-man) was convinced by the sports information department to change the pronunciation of his last name to sound similar to the award he hoped to someday win, the Heisman Trophy. He compiled a 20-3-2 record while throwing for 4,411 yards and 31 touchdowns, set school records for passing yards in a game (526), in a season (2,429), and touchdowns in a season (16)—and as a senior, with the school promoting him as "Theismann, as in Heisman!" finished second in the balloting to Stanford's Jim Plunkett.

(FYI, Theismann went on to spurn the Miami Dolphins, who had selected him in the fourth round of the 1971 National Football League draft, with the Minnesota Twins also selecting him in baseball, to play for the Toronto Argonauts of the Canadian Football League. After the Washington Redskins secured his rights in 1974, he finally played in the NFL and led a Super Bowl victory against the Dolphins before eventually becoming a football commentator on television. He also once said: "Nobody in the game of football should be called a genius. A genius is somebody like Norman Einstein.")

Tackle Marvin Powell helped Southern California win the 1974 national championship, played professionally for 11 years, secured a law degree, wrote a newspaper column, and was elected president of the players' union. In an interview for a Southern California alumni publication, Powell said: "I was never afraid to set a lofty goal and then go for it. I didn't care what anybody thought. My father always encouraged me to shoot for everything. The key is striving to achieve a goal. If you fall short, so what? At least you went for it. As long as you want it and are willing to sacrifice for it, it doesn't matter whether you get there."

Other college football players and coaches obviously made much more significant contributions and sacrifices by also serving in the armed forces.

Joe Thompson was 18 when his parents moved from Ireland to the United States, and his football career began at Geneva College. While studying law at Pitt he helped the Panthers record their first undefeated season, 10-0, in 1904, and four years later took over the coaching duties (30-14-2). His 1910 team finished 9-0 and didn't yield a point. Thompson fought in Mexico and World War I, and while serving in France earned the Congressional Medal of Honor.

"Memphis Bill" Mallory, an All-American fullback who played at Yale from 1921-23, became an Air Force intelligence officer and rose to the rank of major during World War II. He devised "Operation Mallory," which was a tactical plan to cut 22 of 24 bridges spanning the Po River in Lombardy, thus helping to cut German supply lines into Italy. On his way home for discharge, Mallory was killed in 1945 when his plane crashed while taking off in Italy.

Florida coach James Van Fleet returned from World War I, where he had been wounded, with two Silver Stars and led the Gators to two winning seasons of 6-1-2 and 6-2-2. He returned to the military, and while in command of the 8th Infantry Regiment it spearheaded the landing of the 4th Infantry Division at Utah Beach on D-Day, June 6. He also led a division that relieved the Allies at the Battle of the Bulge, the last major offensive by the Germans in World War II, and was appointed Commanding General of the Eighth Army and United Nations troops in Korea (and drove the Chinese Army north until he was ordered to stop in hopes of an armistice).

Thomas Harmon won the Heisman Trophy while playing tailback, defensive back, kicker and punter, and was featured on the cover of *Life* magazine with the headline: "Michigan's Great Harmon." Against Cal in 1940, he returned the opening kickoff for a touchdown, returned a punt for a touchdown, ran in two more and passed for another for a 41-0 victory. He even successfully avoided a drunken fan who ran out of the stands and tried to tackle him on his 86-yard touchdown run. Harmon also eluded Pacific enemy forces after he was shot down and listed as missing twice during World War II. He won the Silver Star and Purple Heart before a short professional career with the Los Angeles Rams and a much longer stint as a sportscaster.

The playing career of Michigan halfback Bob Chappuis surrounded his time as a gunner in an Army B-25. On February 13, 1945, his bomber was shot down behind the German lines, and he parachuted into the Po Valley near Florence, Italy. An Italian family sympathetic to the Allies found him and hid him in their attic. At one point the German command moved its headquarters into the house next door, but Chappuis was never discovered and eventually freed when Allied troops liberated the town. He made several trips back to Italy to visit the family that saved him.

In October 1967, in dense jungle 40 miles northwest of Saigon, Major Don Holleder, a former All-American end at Army, was operations officer for a brigade of the First Infantry Division. When troops were ambushed by the Viet Cong, he went to their aid and while hacking a clearing for medical helicopters was killed by enemy machine-gun fire. Described an Army medic who was a witness: "What an officer. He went ahead of us, running in the point position."

Don Whitmire was an All-American tackle at Alabama and Navy, but as a rear-admiral directed the evacuation of Saigon at the end of the Vietnam War in 1975.

"Football taught me the virtue of team play and enhanced my leadership qualities," he said after being voted into the College Football Hall of Fame. "These traits have been most valuable in my Navy career. Football taught me to take hard knocks and come up fighting."

There are equally inspirational stories away from the military theaters as well.

In 1913, Fred "Duke" Slater told his father, a minister, that he wanted to quit high school to get a job. So his father got him one cutting ice on the Mississippi River. Not surprisingly, Slater quickly changed his mind. He eventually became an All-American tackle at Iowa, and in 1921 the Hawkeyes finished 7-0 including a 10-7 victory against Notre Dame. Slater played pro football with the Chicago Cardinals, but during the off-seasons earned his law degree. He was one of five starters from the 1921 Iowa team to become a lawyer and eventually named a Superior Court judge in Chicago.

Mal Stevens was a quarterback at Washburn College (1919–21) before joining Yale in 1923, and as a halfback contributed to an 8-0 season and corresponding scoring advantage of 230-38. At age 28, he was the youngest head coach at a major school in 1928, and three years later the younger president in the history of the American Coaches Association. Stevens coached at Yale through 1933, New York University from 1938–41, and in 1946 was the head coach of the Brooklyn Dodgers for a season. Stevens also obtained his medical degree at Yale and while coaching taught orthopedic surgery. The bone specialist rose to the rank of commander in the naval medical corps, served 13 years as a director of the Sister Kenny Foundation for Polio, and was a founder of the Aspen (Colorado) Medical Center.

In 1937, Colorado's Byron "Whizzer" White led the nation in scoring, rushing, total offense and all-purpose running. He averaged 246 yards a game in all-purpose running, a record until 1988. He was a Rhodes Scholar who studied at Oxford University in England in 1939, played professional football and at one point led the NFL in rushing, served in the Navy during World War II, and studied law at Yale, graduating first in his class in 1946. In 1962, White was appointed to the United States Supreme Court.

Boston College end George Kerr (1938-40) was known as the "Righteous Reject" and excelled as a guard despite his 155-pound frame. In addition to leading the Eagles to a 26-3-2 record during his three years including a victory against Tennessee in the Sugar Bowl, Kerr graduated at the top of his class. He subsequently entered the seminary and was ordained in 1945. Named a Domestic Prelate with the title of Right Reverend Monsignor of Pope Paul in 1964, Kerr served as chaplain of the Massachusetts

House of Representatives for 25 years. His legacy also included years of work with the Boston Association for Retarded Citizens and inner-city education.

Quarterback Joe Kapp led Cal to a Rose Bowl appearance and finished fifth in 1958 Heisman Trophy voting, but had even greater success with his philanthropic endeavors, especially the National Hispanic Scholarship Fund. In 1993, the City of Hope selected Kapp as its Sportsman of the Year and presented him with its prestigious "Spirit of Life" award.

Stanford end Bill McColl (1949–51) was a two-time All-American who was a standout with the Chicago Bears when he decided to retire to Korea, where the doctor dedicated himself to helping lepers and deformed children.

Penn State defensive tackle Mike Reid won the Outland Trophy in 1969, but was also a talented musician. After retiring from pro football, including two Pro Bowl appearances for the Cincinnati Bengals, he moved to Nashville to concentrate on music, and in 1983 received a Grammy Award for his composition "Stranger In My House." The following year he was named *Cash Box Magazine*'s "Songwriter of the Year" and in 1985 voted "Country Songwriter of the Year."

Notre Dame defensive end Alan Page went on to be the first defensive player to win the NFL's Most Valuable Player award, but also obtained a law degree at Minnesota. After his playing career concluded, Page became the assistant attorney general of Minnesota and in 1992 was elected to the state supreme court. In part due to his efforts to promote education with minority students, the NCAA presented him with its Silver Anniversary Award in 1991, and *Sports Illustrated*, in its "Amazing Americans" special edition in 1992, call him "a symbol of the best the world of sports can produce—a leader whose efforts and example have worthy impact beyond the athletic arena."

Perhaps it's only fitting that someone from Southern California found comparable success in Hollywood. Guard Aaron Rosenberg was known for motivating the highly-successful Trojans during the early 1930s, and gave the same effort as a director and producer. His box office hits included *The Glenn Miller Story*, *The Benny Goodman Story*, and *Mutiny on the Bounty*. In similar fashion, Trojans quarterback Irvine "Cotton" Warburton won an Oscar for film editing on *Mary Poppins*.

There have also been those who didn't necessarily enjoy the limelight, like Pitt's Hugh Green, the first defensive end to win the Maxwell Award, the Walter Camp Foundation's Player of the Year, and the *Sporting News* Player of the Year, and was a Heisman Trophy runner-up. When his football days ended, he simply returned to Natchez, Mississippi, and operated a farm.

Wisconsin standout Patrick John O'Dea was a highly-regarded rugby player in Australia before moving to the United States in 1896. Following his playing career, he briefly coached Notre Dame (14-4-2), Missouri and Stanford. He disappeared and was presumed dead in 1917, only to be discovered in 1934 in Westwood, California, using the assumed name Clarence Mitchell.

"I was tired of the football fame," he said.

Imagine a former Notre Dame coach attempting to do that today.

Those are just a handful of some of the unique individuals who participated in the sport at its highest level, and there are countless others. What follows are the teams and more than 100 years of arguments that continue to be heard long after those players left the locker rooms and playing fields across the country.

While the context of the disputes have changed as much as the game—in the early 1900s football had two 35-minute periods, a field goal was worth four points, a touchdown only five, the field was 110 yards, and there was no fourth down—college football's fueling passion has only intensified over time.

"Who's #1?" If only there was a simple answer to that question. . . .

PART I

How Champions Have Been Named

THE FIRST year that college football was played, 1869, there were only two teams in existence, and they played twice. Rutgers defeated Princeton 6-4, and in a rematch Princeton beat Rutgers 8-0. Years later, three services retroactively named Princeton the national champion, with one splitting the title between both schools ("Everyone's a winner!"). Thus, hindsight provided the first controversial title.

Although schools would occasionally self-proclaim themselves champions in general, or regional champions, etc., the notion of a national title really didn't begin to take hold until the 1920s, when college football really started to grow exponentially in popularity and the pool of teams went from single digits to 100-plus.

The first All-American team was named in 1889, while the first conference, which would eventually become known as the Big Ten, played its first organized season in 1896 (won by Wisconsin).

At the time, football was essentially a hybrid of rugby and soccer, only incredibly brutal. There was no neutral zone between teams at the line of scrimmage and few limits to what linemen could do to opposing players, or for that matter their own players as ball carriers could be picked up and thrown over the line. Gang tackling was the norm and, though extremely dangerous, most teams utilized the "Flying Wedge" formation in which teammates would link together—sometimes using a special belt equipped with handles— to form a "v" and charge into the opposition.

In 1905 alone, college football was credited with 18 deaths and 149 serious injuries. With the game at a crossroad and close to being banned, President Theodore Roosevelt, himself a fan of the sport, stepped in and during two White House conferences with collegiate athletic leaders made it clear that football would either be reformed or abolished.

Supposedly what prompted Roosevelt to step in was a newspaper photograph of Swarthmore guard Robert "Tiny" Maxwell, whose face was a bloodied mess after a game against Penn. Although team captain Robert Torrey was playing opposite Maxwell, Penn felt if it stopped Maxwell it could finish the season undefeated, and consequently double- and triple-teamed him throughout the game. Penn won 11-4, and later claimed the national championship, but football was never the same again.

In December of that year, Chancellor Henry M. MacCracken of New York University headed a meeting of 13 schools to initiate changes. It eventually led to the Intercollegiate Athletic Association of the United States (IAAUS), founded by 62 members. Within four years, it morphed into both a much stronger organization and different name, and thus the National Collegiate Athletic Association was born.

While the NCAA was able to organize, standardize and regulate the sport, it began the long (and continuing) struggle to enforce rules and curtail ringers, professionalism and rampant accusations of cheating. Despite its efforts, which wavered over the years, this era of bad feelings would have repercussions that are still seen and felt today.

For example, in 1906 Alabama's J.W.H. "Doc" Pollard unveiled a maneuver never seen before in the South against rival Auburn. His team had been secretly practicing the "Military Shift" (which he learned at Dartmouth and was described as every player except the center lining up on the line of scrimmage and joining hands, but then turning right or left to form an unbalanced line) and used it to record a 10-0 victory. Auburn coach Mike Donahue, who was generally known for his favorable demeanor, was so upset that he threatened to cancel the series. A year later, with the two schools also in dispute over expense money and referees, Pollard came up with another unique scheme, the "Varsity Two-Step" (which essentially was a much-more confusing version of the Military Shift) and used it to score the necessary touchdown for a 6-6 tie.

Alabama and Auburn, even though they were in the same state, and would play in the same conferences, refused to meet again until 1948, and still over the objections of Alabama and coach Frank Thomas. Not only did the Crimson Tide believe nothing could be gained by playing an inferior opponent that had never finished better than third in the Southeastern Conference since its inaugural season in 1933, but argued that brawls and other problems at rivalry games in Texas, Minnesota, Louisiana, Georgia, South Carolina, Maryland, Kansas and Tennessee made it undesirable. "We hazard nothing in saying that the game would not make a single constructive contribution to education in the state," the school's report from the Committee on Physical Education and Athletics argued. "The fundamental question is: Do the people of Alabama need a tranquil, sane kind of athletics in their two major institutions, or an irrational rabid kind?"

When state representatives threatened to hold back funding to both schools if they didn't annually meet on the football field, students gathered in Birmingham to bury a symbolic hatchet at Woodrow Wilson Park. On December 4, 1948, Alabama crushed Auburn 55-0, and the Tigers got even the following year, 14-13. The "Iron Bowl," which for years was played in Birmingham, is still considered one of college football's most fierce and intense rivalries.

By 1912, the specifics of the game itself, including points for scores, size of the field, and penalties etc., were uniform nationwide, but one crucial mandate the NCAA never handed down was how its Division I champion would be determined. Due to geographical limitations, with teams traveling by train, football was a mostly regional sport with cross-country contests rarely played. But with football continuing to grow at an alarming rate (an estimated 120,000 fans attended the Southern California vs. Notre Dame game at Chicago's Soldier Field in 1927), and campuses beginning to construct massive permanent stadiums in an effort to meet demand, it was only a matter of time before the game took its next steps.

The Rose Bowl

The first Tournament of Roses celebration was held in 1890 by members of Pasadena's Valley Hunt Club, who were mostly transplanted residents from the East and Midwest eager to showcase their new home's amazing year-round mild climate.

"In New York, people are buried in snow," Professor Charles F. Holder announced at a club meeting. "Here our flowers are blooming and our oranges are about to bear. Let's hold a festival to tell the world about our paradise."

However, that didn't necessarily translate immediately into hosting what became known as "The Granddaddy of Them All."

Initially, the attractions on the town lot (re-named Tournament Park in 1900) included ostrich races, bronco busting demonstrations and a race between a camel and an elephant (the elephant won). Reviewing stands were built along the parade route, and Eastern newspapers began to take notice. In 1895, the Tournament of Roses Association was formed to take charge of the festival, which had grown too large for the Valley Hunt Club to handle.

In 1902, the Tournament of Roses decided to host the first-ever postseason college football game, and nearby Stanford (3-1-2)—which included guard W. K. Roosevelt, second cousin of Theodore Roosevelt, who played despite a bone fracture in his leg—accepted an invitation to face Midwest powerhouse Michigan, which had compiled an impressive 10-0 record without giving up a single point. The game wasn't close as fullback Neil Snow scored five touchdowns and Fielding Yost's "Point-A-Minute" team crushed Stanford, 49-0, to finish the season with a scoring advantage of 555-0.

Unfortunately, the lopsided outcome, in addition to stampeding fans, temporarily soured organizers on football, and in 1903 they tried polo instead, which attracted only 2,000 people. That was followed by Ben-Hur-style chariot races, which remained the feature draw for 11 years. However, when the horses drew only 25,000 in 1915 and interest had clearly wavered, football was brought back, with organizers pairing Washington State against Brown for another exhibition.

In front of 7,000 fans, Carl Dietz, Benton Bangs and Ralph Boone combined for 289 yards as the Cougars won 14-0, in part due to a lackluster effort from the East Coast team. "We were over-confident and took the game as a lark, even attending the Rose Parade first," guard Wallace Wade said.

When Oregon (6-0-1) faced Penn (7-2-1) the following year, it attracted 26,000 fans, but a 14-0 upset put a big dent in the notion that East Coast football was vastly superior to that being played in the rest of the country (which would be supported later on by ranking services after retroactively applying their formulas to the previous years).

It helped open the door in 1917 to the first invitation issued to a Southern team as John Heisman's Georgia Tech squad finished 9-0, and outscored opponents 491-17. But instead of heading to Pasadena, the Tech players voted to decline so they could enroll into the military sooner.

With the game firmly established, its importance began to significantly grow after World War I, which officially ended with the Treaty of Versailles in June 1919, months before Harvard defeated Oregon 7-6 on Arnold Horween's extra point following a 13-yard touchdown run by Fred Church. William L. Leishman, the tournament's president in 1920, began the drive for a stadium similar to the Yale Bowl to be built in Pasadena's Arroyo Seco area, seating 57,000 and for a cost of $272,198.

Any doubt regarding the game's popularity was erased by the 1921 game, which drew a crowd of 42,000. In a matchup of unbeatens, California's "Wonder Team" coached by Andy Smith, defeated Ohio State and All-American Pete Stinchcomb, 28-0. Cal returned a year later still undefeated, but was outplayed by Washington & Lee with no completed passes and 49 rushing yards, only to salvage a 0-0 tie.

On January 1, 1923, 52,000 fans saw Southern California defeat Penn State, 14-3, and coaches "Gloomy Gus" Henderson and Hugo Bezdek nearly get into a fight after the Nittany Lions arrived late to the new stadium, dubbed the "Rose Bowl." The following year, Navy completed its first 14 passes only to see Washington come back and force a 14-14 tie.

By this point, the Rose Bowl was becoming synonymous with the best college football had to offer, which would soon be copied with the creation of the Sugar Bowl and Orange Bowl (both in 1935) and the Cotton Bowl (1937). The 1925 game, in particular, had the most hype yet with the Four Horsemen's final ride for Notre Dame (9-0), which was matched against Stanford (7-0-1). Among the numerous storylines were coaches Knute Rockne vs. Glenn "Pop" Warner and horsemen Elmer Layden, Jim Crowley, Harry Stuhldreher and Don Miller vs. Ernie Nevers, who was playing on injured ankles. Layden scored three touchdowns, while Nevers was stopped inches short at the goal-line, on controversial call by referee Ed Thorp. Stanford's late rally fell short, 27-10.

The 1926 game saw the emergence of Southern football to the national scene, only it nearly never happened. Even though Alabama had won the Southern Conference title with a 27-0 victory against Georgia, Rose Bowl Committee members on hand for the game left unimpressed with the Crimson Tide. Invitations first went to Dartmouth, Yale and Colgate, which were all facing pressure from the American Association of University Professors, who had issued a report unfavorable to the sport. After they all declined, Alabama was in and carried the hopes of the entire region. Even Auburn president Dr. Spright Dowell sent a telegram wishing good luck.

Despite the efforts of Washington running back George Wilson, who was knocked out of the game for a while with an injury, Johnny Mack Brown and "Pooley" Hubert led the Alabama rally after trailing 12-0 with three third-quarter touchdowns. The Crimson Tide won 20-19 and the players returned home as heroes, with scores of fans meeting their train from New Orleans on east. Alabama went back for the 1927 game and managed a 7-7 tie despite Stanford's advantage of 311 yards to 92, and Stanford returned a year later to edge 8-0-1 Pitt, 7-6.

Surprisingly, what gained the Rose Bowl its biggest notoriety nationally was one play during the 1929 game, between Georgia Tech (9-0) and Cal (6-1-2). When Cal center Roy Riegels recovered a fumble, he took off in the wrong direction only to be tackled by his own teammate, Benny Lom, at the 1-yard line.

"What am I seeing? What's wrong with me? Am I crazy? Am I crazy? Am I crazy?" broadcaster Graham McNamee said while calling the game on radio.

When Cal was unable to get a first down, Tech's Vance Maree blocked Lom's punt, resulting in a safety.

Supposedly, Riegels told his coach at halftime, "Coach, I can't do it. I've ruined you, I've ruined myself, I've ruined the University of California. I couldn't face that crowd to save my life."

"Roy, get up and go back out there. The game is only half over," Nibs Price replied.

Although Tech's "Stumpy" Thomason and Cal's Irvine Phillips later scored touchdowns, the buzz of the 8-7 game was the fumble, and Riegels said he simply got mixed up on which way to go. In attendance were 71,000 fans, but talk of "Wrong-Way Riegels" quickly went coast-to-coast.

Georgia Tech was considered the consensus national champion by most of the ever-growing services ranking teams, but a new debate was beginning to take hold, whether or not postseason games should count toward final rankings. At the time, the NCAA was against it.

The First Polls

With college football slowly becoming more of a national sport, rather than all but a regional one, but teams unable to frequently travel far to play top competition around the country, discussion began to grow regarding national supremacy.

In the early 1920s, Frank Dickinson, a professor of economics at the University of Illinois, began tinkering with a mathematical formula to rank teams and declare a national champion. In 1926, he unveiled it, and one of the first persons to become enamored with Dickinson's system was Notre Dame coach Knute Rockne, who asked him to backdate the last two years to 1924 when the Fighting Irish went 10-0 and won the Rose Bowl. With Notre Dame the clear and logical choice, it became the first "scientific" championship in college football.

Dickinson's formula weighed a team's wins based on the score and the quality of each opponent. However, while it may have been the first official ranking system, and the basis for awarding the Rissman National Trophy and later the Knute Rockne Intercollegiate Memorial Trophy, it wasn't long before others developed better reputations. For example, in 1925 when nearly every other service that went back to rank teams at season's end had 10-0 Rose Bowl–winner Alabama No. 1, Dickinson opted for Dartmouth (8-0). It only lasted until 1940.

Incidentally, Notre Dame gained permanent possession of the Rissman Trophy (named for Jack F. Rissman, a Chicago clothing manufacturer) after its third Dickinson title in 1930. Minnesota retired the Rockne Trophy after winning it for a third time in 1940.

A number of competing ranking systems were quickly devised and developed, beginning with the Houlgate System (1927–58), a mathematical rating developed by Deke Houlgate of Los Angeles. Like Dickinson, his rankings quickly became popular in newspapers, and also published in the annual Football Thesaurus (1946–58). Houlgate backdated his rankings to at least 1885.

In 1929, they were joined by the Dunkel Index, which is still one of the most respected mathematical ranking systems ever devised, with a formula that has remained unchanged. One of the unique aspects of the numerical ratings was that they could be used to predict the scoring differential of a game. The power index system, created by Dick Dunkel Sr., was one of the computer services used by the Bowl Championship Series (1999–2001) until organizers decided they didn't want scoring margins to factor into any of the computer calculations. Factoring into the index is strength of schedule, won-loss record, most-recent performances and upsets.

Another longstanding system was created by William Boand in 1930. Known as the Boand System, and/or the Azzi Ratem System, it appeared in newspapers and both the *Illustrated Football Annual* (1932–42) and *Football News* (1942–44 and 1951–60), and Boand went back and determined national champions from 1919–29.

The Williamson System, developed by New Orleans geologist Paul Williamson, who would later serve on the Sugar Bowl committee, began in 1932 and was syndicated throughout the South. For years, Williamson was the only system to rank teams and name its national champion after the completion of the bowl schedule.

By the time the Poling System, a mathematical rating system created by former Ohio Wesleyan player Richard Poling and published annually in the *Football Review Supplement*, came around in 1935 (and lasted until 1984), college football was ready for more bowl games and a significant change that would dramatically alter the national championship landscape, the creation of the Associated Press poll.

A New Age: Newspaper Polls

In 1935, Alan J. Gould, the sports editor of the Associated Press and described by *Time Magazine* as a "slight, bow-tied, cigar-chomping newsman," started ranking his own list of top 10 teams in his weekly column. For the record, his top three that year were Minnesota, Princeton and Southern Methodist. But Gould didn't clarify a No. 1 team, which didn't sit well with Minnesota fans, who were otherwise enjoying the consensus national championship ("East Coast bias!").

Gould knew he was on to something and in 1936 he created the Associated Press poll, with 44 sportswriters voting that first season. Even though Minnesota lost to Northwestern, 6-0, the Golden Gophers finished No. 1 and were the consensus choice ahead of LSU and Pittsburgh.

"It was a case of thinking up ideas to develop interest and controversy between football Saturdays," Gould later said. "Papers wanted material to fill space between games. That's all I had in mind, something to keep the pot boiling. Sports then was living off controversy, opinion, whatever. This was just another exercise in hoopla. Making it a top

10 was an arbitrary decision. It seemed logical to confine it to that number. It was tough enough to pick a top 10 in those days, let alone 15 or 20."

The Associated Press (or AP) poll, the first based solely on opinion, immediately became the foremost rankings in college football, and the most widely circulated. With the championship, a trophy has traditionally been awarded. In 1947, Notre Dame retired the Williams Trophy, which had been named after Minnesota coach Henry Williams and sponsored by the M Club of Minnesota. In 1956, Oklahoma retired the Reverend Hugh O'Donnell Trophy, named for the Notre Dame president and sponsored by Notre Dame alumni. The award was known as the AP Trophy from 1957–83, when it was renamed the Paul Bear Bryant Trophy.

The Associated Press poll has had two important fluctuations, the number of teams ranked and whether the final poll should be held before or after bowl games. Gould's first poll ranked 20 teams, but from 1962–67 only ten teams were listed. It finally expanded to 25 teams in 1989.

As for the postseason, bowl games were still essentially considered exhibitions, so the NCAA encouraged any final polling to take place at the end of the regular season. One notable exception occurred at the end of the 1947 season when Notre Dame didn't play in a bowl game and Michigan accepted an invitation to play No. 8 Southern California in the Rose Bowl. After the Wolverines won, 49-0, a special poll was conducted and voters changed their minds, selecting Michigan No. 1. However, the poll didn't supersede the final regular season poll.

In 1950, United Press news service, which was in direct competition with the Associated Press, decided it needed a poll of its own and created the coaches' poll, with 35 participants. Although United Press merged with International News Service (which had its own poll from 1952–57), becoming United Press International, the coaches' poll continues to exist today as the *USA Today*/ESPN poll (from 1982–96, it was the *USA Today*/CNN poll).

Naturally, that first year with two major polls resulted in a controversy, but not a split title. Both had Oklahoma No. 1 at the end of the regular season, but the Sooners subsequently lost to Paul W. "Bear" Bryant's Kentucky Wildcats in the Sugar Bowl, 13-7. It only took four years for the polls to select different champions. In 1954, the Associated Press sided with Ohio State, the coaches UCLA.

The first time a bowl game featured a No. 1 vs. No. 2 matchup was 1962, one year after Ohio State's faculty council voted 28–25 to turn down a Rose Bowl invitation, citing its discomfort with the school's overemphasis on sports. No. 2 Wisconsin scored three touchdowns and a safety in the fourth quarter to make a massive comeback against No. 1 Southern California, but ran out of time, 42-37. The following year also saw No. 1 play No. 2 in a bowl game, with top-ranked Texas defeating Navy, and Heisman Trophy-winning quarterback Roger Staubach, 28-6.

By 1964, the thinking that bowl games should only be considered exhibitions was changing. At the conclusion of the regular season, Alabama and Arkansas were both undefeated and both polls had the Crimson Tide No. 1. But after Arkansas defeated Nebraska in the Cotton Bowl, Alabama lost to Texas in the Orange Bowl.

The following year, the Associated Press pushed its final voting back until after the bowl schedule. At the end of the regular season, Michigan State (10-0), Arkansas (10-0) and Nebraska (10-0) were all undefeated, and UPI went ahead and crowned the Spartans its champion. Meanwhile, Bryant's Alabama team was No. 4 at 8-1-1, with its lone loss in the season-opener to Georgia considered controversial. When he figured out that there was still a way to finish No. 1 in the Associated Press poll and claim the national championship, the Crimson Tide turned down an invitation from the Cotton Bowl to face No. 3 Nebraska in the Orange Bowl.

When Michigan State lost to No. 5 UCLA in the Rose Bowl, 14-12, and Arkansas lost to LSU in the Cotton Bowl, 14-7, the Tide had its chance. Despite facing a much-bigger team, Alabama outgained Nebraska 518 to 377 yards to pull out an amazing 39-28 victory and defend its opportunistic, albeit controversial, title.

Due to pressure, the Associated Press went back to voting before the bowl games for two more years, before making the change permanent. The coaches stubbornly held out until after the 1973 season, when No. 1 Alabama (10-0), already named the UPI's national champion, lost to No. 3 Notre Dame (10-0) in the Sugar Bowl, 24-23.

The Military Exceptions

Before moving on to other ranking systems, there were some interesting and important developments during wartime.

During both World Wars, military bases were encouraged to field football teams, some of which were so prolific that they played a full season like their collegiate counterparts. Although the policy drew extensive criticism ("How can you play a game when there's a war on?"—especially since some teams included former All-Americans and some professionals depending on the base's policy), one of the biggest advocates for using sports as a training tool was Frank Knox, Secretary of Navy from 1940–44.

"This is a war where you kill or get killed," Knox was once quoted saying. "And I don't know anything that better prepares a man for bodily contact, including war, than the kind of training we get on the football field."

Additionally, schools like Duke, Michigan, and Purdue also benefited from on-campus Navy training programs that attracted college and pro athletes and let them play football during World War II. At one point, the Wolverines had an All-Big Ten backfield with Wisconsin's Elroy "Crazy Legs" Hirsch and Minnesota's Bill Daley.

While many schools suspended play during World War I, Georgia Tech (9-0) was considered the 1917 consensus champion, followed by Michigan (5-0) and Pittsburgh (4-1) receiving equal consideration following the abbreviated 1918 season.

However, none of those teams played in the Rose Bowl, which for the first time had a theme for the festivities at the end of the 1917 season, "Patriotism." With former Oregon coach Hugo Bezdek returning two years after defeating Penn, he again was victorious as the Mare Island Marines (5-0) defeated Camp Lewis Army (5-1-1), 19-7. Hollis Huntington was the star player, gaining 111 yards on 20 carries.

The Marines returned a year later with a 10-0 record, but couldn't stop former Northwestern halfback Paddy Driscoll, "The Wasp," who caught a touchdown pass, drop-kicked a 30-yard field goal and threw a 45-yard touchdown pass to George Halas (later the founder of the Chicago Bears). Halas was also stopped at the 3-yard line after returning an interception 77 yards. Great Lakes Navy (6-2) won 17-0, in front of 27,000 fans celebrating the theme "Victorious Peace."

"Nobody had a day like Driscoll," Halas said.

One nearly immediate consequence of Pearl Harbor and the start of World War II on December 7, 1941, was that the subsequent Rose Bowl, scheduled for approximately three weeks later, was moved as a wartime precaution. In the only Rose Bowl game played outside of Pasadena, Bob Dethman threw the game-winning pass to Gene Gray, as Oregon State defeated host Duke 20-16 before 56,000 fans. The loss ended any claims the Blue Devils (9-0 and ranked second) had on the national title, making Minnesota the clear, and consensus, national champion.

Military rivalries began to develop during World War II, and many bases took them as seriously as their collegiate counterparts. In 1942, Georgia Pre-Flight, coached by Alabama assistant coach Hank Crisp, posted an impressive 7-1-1 record with wins against Penn, North Carolina Pre-Flight, Duke, Jacksonville Naval Air Station, Auburn and Alabama, all of which finished above .500.

Meanwhile the Great Lakes Naval Air Station went 8-3-1 playing against Midwest teams like Iowa, Illinois, Michigan and Wisconsin. Iowa Pre-Flight finished 7-3 after playing the likes of Kansas, Missouri and Nebraska.

Both finished high in the 1943 Associated Press rankings, just ahead of Del Monte Pre-Flight. Highlighting the season was a No. 1 vs. No. 2 matchup between Notre Dame and Iowa Pre-Flight, with the Irish barely scraping out a 14-13 victory. A week later though, Great Lakes defeated Notre Dame, 19-14. Notre Dame finished first in the final poll, ahead of No. 2 Iowa Pre-Flight and No. 6 Great Lakes (10-2), but Great Lakes claimed the Service Team Title, which didn't sit well with Iowa Pre-Flight, nicknamed the Seahawks.

North Carolina Pre-Flight was ranked second in the first Associated Press poll of 1944, but fell out of the rankings by season's end. Instead, Randolph Air Force Base—which was coming off a 7-7 tie against Texas in the Cotton Bowl and 9-1 season under Coach Frank Tritico—went 10-0 and finished No. 3 in the final poll, before defeating 2nd Air Force 13-6 in the Treasury Bond Bowl in New York (both teams featured numerous pro players).

Meanwhile, able to essentially recruit star players away from other colleges, Army and Navy became football powerhouses. Army was the consensus national champion in 1944-45, with the 1946 title still in dispute with Notre Dame after the teams tied, 0-0. Navy finished No. 4 in 1944 and No. 2 in 1945.

It's no coincidence that two of Army's Heisman Trophy winners came during this time period, with the backfield of Doc Blanchard (1945) and Glenn Davis (1946). Blanchard enlisted after a year at North Carolina and appointed to West Point, and Davis was recruited out of high school.

The 27-0-1 run came to an end in 1947 when Army tied Illinois and Penn and lost to Columbia and Notre Dame, but it finished 8-0-1 in 1948. Ten years later, Army secured its third Heisman, won by halfback Pete Dawkins, who overcame polio and went on to have a distinguished military career, and was honored with the Legion of Merit, two

Bronze Stars, the Meritorious Service Medal, the Air Medal, and the Vietnamese Cross of Gallantry. As a Rhodes scholar at Oxford University in England, Dawkins earned both Bachelor and Master of Arts degrees, and added another graduate degree at Princeton following his service in Vietnam.

Other Ranking Systems

Naturally, as college football's popularity grew, more ways of ranking teams were developed. Here are many of them (in alphabetical order, with a little help from the NCAA Records Book, and 2006 final rankings if available):

Alderson System (1994–98): Unlike the mythical planet blown up in Star Wars, this was a mathematical rating system developed by Bob Alderson of Muldrow, Oklahoma. It was based on a point value system reflecting competition as well as won-lost record.

Anderson & Hester (1993–present): Otherwise known as the Seattle Times rankings, the mathematical rating system was devised by Jeff Anderson, a professor of political science at Air Force, and broadcaster Chris Hester. Strength of schedule is considered and teams are rewarded for beating quality opponents. It's currently used in determining Bowl Championship Series rankings. The 2006 final rankings were: 1. Florida; 2. Boise State; 3. Ohio State; 4. Louisville; 5. Southern California.

Berryman (1990–present): Clyde Berryman of Washington D.C. devised the Quality Point Rating System that takes into account strength of schedule, won-loss record, points scored and points allowed. It also balances each victory, so an early-season game figures as prominently as the last game of the season. It predated national champions from 1940–89. The 2006 final rankings were: 1. Florida; 2. Ohio State; 3. Southern California; 4. LSU; 5. Michigan. Undefeated Boise State finished 10th, behind Oklahoma, which it defeated in the Sugar Bowl.

Billingsley Report (1970–present): The mathematically based power rating system was developed by Richard Billingsley, whose work is published through his own company, the College Football Research Center. He also doubles as a college football historian. The main components in the formula are win-loss record, strength of schedule and recent performance. It also considers the game site and defensive scoring performance. It predated national champions from 1869-1969. The 2006 final rankings were: 1. Florida; 2. Ohio State; 3. Louisville; 4. Boise State; 5. Wisconsin.

College Football Researchers Association (1982–92): The organization was founded by Anthony Cusher of Reeder, North Dakota, and Robert Kirlin of Spokane, Washington. It determined its rankings by point system through a top-10 vote by membership. The champion was announced in its monthly bulletin. It predated national champions from 1919-81 through a poll conducted by Harry Carson Frye.

Colley Matrix (1992–present): Wes Colley is a graduate of Princeton and research scientist of astrophysical sciences at Alabama-Huntsville, and his rankings have been published in the *Atlanta Journal-Constitution*. His formula centers on the premise that a team's record is the most important factor in determining its ranking. It adjusts for strength of schedule by adjusting the wins of each team to an effective number of wins based upon the quality of its opponents. The adjustment is made again, based on the new, effective record of the opponents, and again, etc., until further adjustment no longer changes the effective win numbers. Also, it does not consider any preseason or past rankings. The Colley Matrix has been part of the BCS formula since 2001. The 2006 final rankings were: 1. Florida; 2. Southern California; 3. Louisville; 4. Ohio State; 5. Boise State. LSU, which finished fourth in the Associated Press and coaches' polls, was No. 7.

College Football News: The publication, which is now associated with Scout.com (better known as a leading recruiting site along with Rivals.com), not only ranks every team in the country, but just about everything else in college football from top teams of the 1990s to the 100 greatest finishes.

Congrove Computer rankings (1993–present): The rankings focus on strength of schedule, results and records. Organizers also keep a composite record dating back to its inception (through 2006, Florida State was the composite No. 1). The 2006 final rankings were: 1. Florida; 2. Boise State; 3. Ohio State; 4. Louisville; 5. Southern California.

Parke Davis (1933): The following is the direct explanation from the NCAA Records Book, which gives credit to Tex Noel (who has an interesting website called the College Football Resource): "The college football historian and former Princeton lineman went back and named the championship teams from 1869 through the 1932 season. He also named a national champion at the conclusion of the 1933 season. Interestingly, the years 1869-75 were identified by Davis as the Pioneer Period; the years 1876-93 were called the Period of the American Intercollegiate Football Association; and the years 1894-1933 were referred to as the Period of Rules Committees and Conferences. He also coached at Wisconsin, Amherst and Lafayette."

DeVold System (1945–present): The mathematical rating system was created by Harry DeVold, a former end at Cornell. DeVold was a writer, historian and handicapper for the *Football News*, where his rankings appeared, from 1955–91. He predated his rankings from 1939. Despite the national championship outcome, the 2006 final rankings were: 1. Ohio State; 2. Florida; 3. Southern California; 4. Boise State; 5. Louisville.

Eck Ratings System (1983–present): The mathematical point system was devised by Steve Eck, an aerospace worker with a master's degree from UCLA. The factors are game outcome, strength of opponent, location of the game and point spread. He also normalizes each team's rating to a common number of games to account for conference championships and preseason games.

Foundation for the Analysis of Competitions and Tournaments (FACT), (1968–present): The computerized mathematical ranking system was developed by the late David Rothman, a former defense and aerospace statistician and co-chair of the Committee on Statistics in Sports and Competition of the American Statistical Association in the 1970s. An important variable is the assigning of points based upon the winning margin along with strength of schedule. The rankings were an original component of the BCS formula. FACT's final rankings in 2006 were: 1. Florida; 2. Ohio State; 3. Southern California; 4. Louisville; 5. LSU.

Football News **(1958–02):** The publication held a weekly poll of its staff writers and named a national champion.

Football Writers Association of America (1954–present): The organization, which has more than 900 members, has a panel of 16 voters who represent the nation's football writers and rank the top 16 teams every week. The national champion is given the Grantland Rice Trophy (in the interest of full disclosure, the author belonged to this nonprofit organization as of this writing, but did not vote). The 2006 final rankings were: 1. Florida; 2. LSU and Ohio State (tie); 4. Boise State; 5. Southern California.

Helms Athletic Foundation (1941–82): Again from the NCAA Records Book: "Originally known by this name from 1936–69 and established by the founding sponsor, Paul H. Helms, Los Angeles sportsman and philanthropist. After Helms' death in 1957, United Savings & Loan Association became its benefactor during 1970–72. A merger of United Savings and Citizen Savings was completed in 1973, and the Athletic Foundation became known as Citizens Savings Athletic Foundation. In 1982, First Interstate Bank assumed sponsorship for its final rankings. In 1941, Bill Schroeder, managing director of the Helms Athletic Foundation, retroactively selected the national football champions for the period beginning in 1883 (the first year of a scoring system) through 1940. Thereafter, Schroeder, who died in 1988, then chose, with the assistance of a Hall Board, the annual national champion after the bowl games." In other words, they put together a panel to select champions and All-American teams. The Foundation also operated halls of fame for a number of sports, but not college football.

Litkenhous (1934–84): The difference-by-score formula was developed by Edward E. Litkenhous, a professor of chemical engineering at Vanderbilt, and his brother, Frank. The rankings were published in the *Knoxville News-Sentinel*.

Massey College Football Ratings (1995–present): Developed by Dr. Kenneth Massey, who earned his PhD at Virginia Tech and became a math professor at Carson-Newman College, the ratings system includes an overall team rating, offensive and defensive ratings, strength of schedule, even home-field advantage. The ratings have been part of the BCS since 1999, and the same formula is used for a number of other sports. The 2006 final rankings were: 1. Florida; 2. Ohio State; 3. LSU; 4. Boise State; 5. Southern California.

Matthews Grid Ratings (1966–present): The mathematical rating system was developed by college mathematics professor Herman Matthews, who teaches at Lincoln Memorial University. The rankings have appeared in numerous newspapers, Scripps Howard News Service and the *Football News*, and were part of the BCS formula until commissioners didn't want margin of victory to be considered (although there's a limit to how much running up the score can affect the grid ratings). The 2006 final rankings were: 1. Florida; 2. Southern California; 3. Louisville; 4. LSU; 5. Ohio State (undefeated Boise State was No. 17).

National Championship Foundation (1980–2001): Established by Mike Riter of Hudson, New York, the foundation has more than 120 chapters in 47 states, with a membership base of more than 12,000. It issued an annual report, and predated Division I-A national champions from 1869-1979.

National Football Foundation (1959–present): Established in 1947 to promote amateur athletics in the United States, and awards trophies to the national championship teams from Division I-AA, II, III and the NAIA champion at the annual Kickoff Luncheon for the American Football Coaches Association Convention. The NFF has more than 13,000 members, along with approximately 120 chapters. Along with the College Football Hall of Fame named its first national champion in 1959, which through 1990 was awarded the MacArthur Bowl. In 1991 and 1992, the NFF/HOF joined with United Press International to award the MacArthur Bowl, and in 1993, the NFF/HOF joined with *USA Today* to award the MacArthur Bowl to the team selected No. 1 in the final coaches poll. The National Football Foundation tabulates and releases the Bowl Championship Series standings.

New York Times **Computer Rankings (1979–2004):** The mathematical rating system accounted for the results, win-loss margin, quality of opponent and home-field advantage. Games later in the season counted more than earlier games, and bowls counted as one-and-half times more than a regular-season game.

Sagarin Ratings (1978–present): Jeff Sagarin was only 10 when he started ranking teams and his system is now used to rank everything from basketball to NASCAR and golf. The MIT mathematics graduate created a formula that considers strength of schedule, margin of victory and the location of the game. Sagarin's ratings have been published in *USA Today* since 1985, but his ELO-Chess formula, in which only winning and losing matter, is used to compile the Bowl Championship Series. His 2006 overall ratings were: 1. Florida; 2. Southern California; 3. LSU; 4. Ohio State; 5. Louisville (undefeated Boise State was No. 6).

Sporting News **(1975–present):** An opinion-based ranking determined by the staff of the St. Louis-based national publication.

Casper Whitney (1905–07): The sportswriter was one of the founders of the first All-American football team, which focused on Harvard, Princeton and Yale. He also selected polls for *Outing* magazine.

Peter Wolfe (1992–present): Not of the J.Giles Band or the English musician known as the Wolfman, Dr. Wolfe and Ross Baker developed a mathematically based power rating matrix, using what they described as a "maximum likelihood estimate." Margin of victory is not considered, but game location is. When not ranking football teams, Wolfe is an AIDS researcher at UCLA. The 2006 final rankings were: 1. Florida; 2. Ohio State; 3. Michigan; 4. Louisville; 5. LSU (followed by Southern California and Boise State).

If the reader hasn't figured it out yet, yes, there are more rankings systems than annual bowl games.

The Bowl Championship Series

In 1984, the entire landscape of college football became primed for major change thanks to what was symbolically an end zone spike by the United States Supreme Court.

In NCAA v. Board of Regents of University of Oklahoma and Georgia Athletic Association, the court was asked by the NCAA to overturn rulings made at the District Court and Court of Appeals levels that said the parent organization couldn't limit the number of televised football games. The litigation was triggered by the NCAA's response by the College Football Association, an organization of the more dominant football-playing schools and conferences, to develop an independent television plan (and in the process make a lot more money).

If this doesn't sound like a big deal, consider that cable television was still a relatively new concept at the time and college football was all but limited to a handful of games each weekend, if that.

The Supreme Court ruled that the NCAA was essentially regulating free trade and performing illegal price fixing. The court also rejected the NCAA's arguments that widespread broadcasts could curtail live attendance and that competition on the airwaves would be bad for the game.

Said the majority opinion delivered by John Paul Stevens, an expert in antitrust law: "Today we hold only that the record supports the District Court's conclusion that by curtailing output and blunting the ability of member institutions to respond to consumer preference, the NCAA has restricted rather than enhanced the place of intercollegiate athletics in the Nation's life. Accordingly, the judgment of the Court of Appeals is ... Affirmed."

(As far as we know, Justices Burger, Brennan, Marshall, Blackmun, Powell, Stevens and O'Connor did not high-five after the NCAA lawyers left the room, but some of their interns probably did.)

The deregulation sent every conference into a tizzy, looking for ways to maximize the financial potential. However, nearly all were already locked into a pre-existing bowl agreement, like the champions of the Big Ten and Pac-10 meeting every year at the Rose Bowl. The same year as the Supreme Court's ruling, No. 6 Ohio State played No. 18 Southern California in Pasadena, while the national championship came down to whether or not surprise No. 1 Brigham Young could defeat unranked Michigan in the Holiday Bowl (it did, 24-17).

Nevertheless, the building anxiety was somewhat similar, in a way, to the start of the Civil War in that everyone knew what was about to happen, but no one had a clue when and where the sparks would first fly, and what would remain afterward. It was the dawn of the superconferences and of the Bowl Championship Series, with the initial "shots" fired in the North and South.

The first of the big independents to join a conference was Penn State with the Big Ten in 1990. Not only did the Nittany Lions' addition give it a powerful presence in the East, but made one of the strongest conferences even stronger.

Meanwhile, commissioner Roy Kramer realized that the 10-school Southeastern Conference could take advantage of a loophole in NCAA rules to create an extra revenue-enhancing championship game, but in order to do so needed a membership of at least 12 teams. He asked, and received, unanimous permission from SEC presidents to begin interviewing potential candidates.

Rumors immediately swirled about potential additions, including Texas, Texas A&M, West Virginia, Florida State and Miami.

Somewhat surprisingly, it was Arkansas that first jumped at the opportunity, which simultaneously served as a death blow to the troubled Southwest Conference. In the late 1980s, SWC attendance plummeted, with the eight Texas schools playing before an average of 65 percent capacity at home, blamed mostly on the lack of winning programs and the success of the Dallas Cowboys and Houston Oilers of the National Football League. Attendance was also declining in men's basketball even though Arkansas was considered a national power under the direction of controversial coach Nolan Richardson.

With Title IX set to mandate a massive budgetary increase for women's sports, the SWC was hindered by a limited television market consisting of only two states (even if one of them was Texas). Coupled with sagging revenues, it also went through a litany of scandals, with seven of the nine schools placed on probation during the 1980s, and many top recruits electing to play elsewhere.

"It was like if you're not cheating, you're not trying to win," former Arkansas football coach Lou Holtz was quoted as saying.

On August 1, 1990, Arkansas' board of trustees, acting on recommendations from legendary athletic director Frank Broyles and the school's chancellor, accepted an invitation to join the SEC. It would soon be joined by South Carolina.

"I personally was concerned that [Texas] A&M and Texas would leave and not include us," Broyles said.

Texas flirted with the Pac-10 and Big Ten, but found both geographically undesirable. Texas A&M did ask about joining the SEC, but the conference would only accept both in a package deal.

Eventually, they ended up in the Big Eight, along with Texas Tech and Baylor in a partial merger, but again only after a major move by the SEC. Instead of adhering to a television contract extension with ABC and ESPN, negotiated with the College Football Association, the SEC signed a landmark five-year, $85 million deal with CBS, which had just lost the National Football League to Fox.

Days later, the Atlantic Coast Conference signed an $80 million deal with ABC and ESPN, and CBS quickly added the Big East, which formed in 1991, for $75 million, including basketball games. Florida State signed on with the ACC and Miami with the Big East (but later jumped to the ACC with Boston College and Virginia Tech).

As noted, the Big Eight evolved into the Big 12, signed a $100 million deal with ABC and Liberty Sports, and the SWC was officially no more. Meanwhile, Notre Dame, which had conveniently never signed its deal with the CFA, made an exclusive deal with NBC. The succession of moves would also eventually lead to the creation of Conference USA and Mountain West.

But college football had another, lingering problem, the championship. Over the previous 29 years, there had only been eight bowl games matching teams ranked first and second, with growing concern that Congress might soon intervene should some sort of playoff system not be implemented.

One of the fathers, if not the father, of the Bowl Championship Series was ACC executive Tim Mickle, who supposedly one day started scribbling down ideas for a new bowl format on a restaurant napkin. It grew into rotating a championship game between the major bowls. Among those instrumental in getting the major bowls to actually agree to it was Kramer.

Although it's been a financial windfall for all involved, it should be noted that Mickle's original intention was to move the bowl system a step closer to a playoff system, and in the meantime establish the potential for No. 1 to play No. 2 every year.

"Maybe I should have kept it to myself," Mickle told writer John Feinstein years later, after NCAA presidents used the BCS as a preemptive strike and excuse for not creating a playoff. By doing so, not only did they stay in control of the sport, but strengthen their grip on football revenues and bowl payouts.

Here's why:

While the NCAA men's basketball tournament might bring in more money, thanks to a huge exclusive contract with CBS (11 years, $6.2 billion, for an average of $565 per tournament), it has to be equally split between the 300-plus athletic departments.

With the Bowl Championship Series, only the conferences involved (six conferences, roughly 65 schools) split most of the revenues.

In terms of the 2005 bottom line, Alabama, for example, received $1.8 million in broadcast rights for men's basketball and an additional $1.8 million in NCAA/SEC distributions. Meanwhile, the football program took in $5.4 million in broadcast rights and $2.6 million in NCAA/SEC distributions.

University presidents are therefore adamant against a playoff system, which would almost certainly result in equal distribution across the board. During the 2004-05 school year, the NCAA took in more than $500 million in revenues, the bulk from television contracts. Of that, 95 percent was distributed among the member institutions.

To accentuate how times had changed following the Supreme Court ruling, in 1990 the 10 SEC schools shared $16.3 million in revenue. In 2002, when Kramer stepped down, the 12 split $95.7 million. In June 2006, the SEC announced it would distribute $116.1 million from the 2005-06 academic year.

The system has been extremely controversial and constantly tweaked, but here's a overly simplistic year-by-year look at the BCS:

1992: After a lengthy series of meetings, a number of conference commissioners along with Notre Dame and four bowl committees created the Bowl Coalition agreement. While it didn't alter any of the existing conference-bowl affiliations, it did create a selection process among the Cotton, Fiesta, Orange and Sugar bowls to improve the chances of a No. 1 vs. No. 2 matchup.

Specifically, it made it possible for the champions of the Big East or ACC, or Notre Dame, to play the champions of the Big Eight (Orange Bowl), SEC (Sugar Bowl) or SWC (Cotton Bowl). If the champions of the Big East or ACC, or Notre Dame had been ranked No. 1 or 2 at the end of the regular season, they would have met in the Fiesta Bowl for the national championship. In turn, the vacated spots in the Orange, Sugar or Cotton Bowls would have been filled from a pool of at-large teams made up of the second-place teams from the ACC, Big East, Big Eight, Pac-10 and Southwest conferences. To guarantee the at-large teams' postseason placement, the conferences contracted with the Gator and John Hancock Bowls to provide additional spots.

Despite the obvious holes, including conference-bowl ties and the non-participation of the Big Ten and Pac-10, the first year resulted in No. 1 Miami vs. No. 2 Alabama in the Sugar Bowl (the Crimson Tide won, 34-13).

1993: The coalition paired No. 1 Florida State (11-1) vs. No. 2 Nebraska in the Orange Bowl, but numerous other teams, including No. 3 West Virginia (11-0), believed they were deserving as well. Notre Dame defeated Florida State during the regular season, 31-24, and was considered the team to beat until it lost a week later to Boston College, 41-39. Despite Coach Lou Holtz's lobbying efforts, the Irish wound up in the Cotton Bowl, where they held on to beat Texas A&M, 24-21. The Seminoles won 18-16, while the Mountaineers were crushed by Florida in the Sugar Bowl, 41-7. If anything, calls for a designated championship game only intensified.

1994: The inevitable happened. Penn State in the Big Ten went 11-0 and automatically headed to the Rose Bowl to face Oregon. The best matchup the coalition could provide was No. 1 Nebraska vs. No. 3 Miami in the Orange Bowl. Nebraska and Penn State both won, and stayed 1-2 in the polls.

1995: With the coalition's three-year agreement expiring at the same time a number of existing conference-bowl affiliations concluded, the first significant change occurred with the creation of the Bowl Alliance.

Specifically, the new system allowed the champions of the ACC, Big East, Big Eight, SEC and SWC, along with an at-large team, to be matched in the three alliance bowls: Fiesta, Sugar and Orange. However, conference tie-ins to the three bowls were eliminated, and a team had to win at least eight games and be ranked in the top 12, or no lower than the lowest-ranked available conference champion, to qualify for an at-large spot.

Although the Big Ten and Pac-10 conferences were still not involved, among others, the new formula worked in its initial year, with No.1 Nebraska and No. 2 Florida, the two lone unbeaten teams, meeting at the Fiesta Bowl. The Cornhuskers crushed the Gators, 62-24.

1996: A second at-large team was added when the Big 12 Conference replaced the old Big Eight and Southwest Conference. However, there would be no 1 vs. 2 matchup. When No. 3 Nebraska lost to Texas in the first Big 12 Championship game, 37-17, there were clearly four top contenders. Due to previous obligations, No. 2 Arizona State met No. 4 Ohio State in the Rose Bowl. That left No. 1 Florida State playing a rematch against No. 3 Florida, which it had defeated in a No. 1 vs. No. 2 game in late November, 24-21.

When the Buckeyes defeated the Sun Devils, 20-17, it all but assured the winner of the Sugar Bowl would finish No. 1. This time, the Gators came through, 52-20.

1997: Again there was no 1 vs. 2 matchup even though there were only two unbeaten teams. No. 1 Michigan was destined for the Rose Bowl to face No. 8 Washington State, leaving No. 2 Nebraska to play No. 3 Tennessee in the Orange Bowl. However, when the Wolverines struggled to win, 21-16, and the Cornhuskers dominated, 42-17, the coaches bucked the system and voted Nebraska No. 1, resulting in a split title.

1998: The Big Ten, Pac-10 and Rose Bowl finally came into the fold with the Rose Bowl added to the championship rotation, and the conference champions guaranteed a spot in the Fiesta, Orange or Sugar Bowls if bumped by a national championship matchup. The agreement created what was initially called the "Super Alliance," later renamed the Bowl Championship Series.

Also, a new formula, the BCS standings, was created to determine participants of the four bowls. The components would be the Associated Press and coaches (*USA Today/ ESPN*) polls along with the average of three computer rankings (Sagarin, *Seattle Times* and

New York Times), the teams' records, and a strength-of-schedule index based on the records of a team's opponents and its opponents' opponents.

In addition to the six conferences, which would devour most of the BCS payouts and increasing television revenue thanks to a new contract with ABC, provisions were made to Notre Dame and any other school ranked sixth or higher in the BCS standings. Finally, unless the bowl was hosting the national championship, conference affiliations would apply to the specific bowls (Big Ten and Pac-10 to the Rose Bowl; Big 12 to the Fiesta Bowl; SEC to the Sugar Bowl; and ACC or Big East to the Orange Bowl).

The formula drew immediate criticism when Tennessee went 12-0 to emerge as the clear No.1 team, but Florida State, Ohio State, Kansas State, Arizona and UCLA all had one loss, with Kansas State and UCLA losing their last games to fall out of the top three. Thanks to its strength of schedule and higher ranking by the computers, Florida State was paired against Tennessee in the Fiesta Bowl. With a 23-16 victory, the Volunteers became the first BCS champion. However, Tulane, which went 11-0 and was ranked 10th in the final BCS rankings, was shut out and went on to defeat unranked Brigham Young in the Liberty Bowl, 41-27.

1999: Five more computer rankings were added, Billingsley, Dunkel, Massey, Matthews/Scripps Howard and Rothman, for a total of eight services comprising the computer section of the rankings.

Two teams, Florida State and Virginia Tech, went undefeated to finish 1-2 and met in the Sugar Bowl, while Nebraska (11-1) overcame a midseason loss to Texas to emerge as a solid No. 3, and undefeated Marshall (12-0) was 12th in the BCS standings. The Seminoles easily won, 46-29.

2000: The only change was that the National Football Foundation began compiling the BCS standings. Otherwise, college football was fixated on the debate on which team should play No. 1 Oklahoma in the Orange Bowl.

Similar to 1998, the Sooners were the lone undefeated team, with Miami, Florida State, Washington, Oregon State and Virginia Tech all with one loss. The writers and coaches liked Miami, which had lost to Washington in early September, 34-29. The computers preferred Florida State, which lost to Miami 27-24 in October. Only the *Seattle Times* rankings liked Washington, which had lost at Oregon, 23-16.

The computers won the argument, pairing Oklahoma against Florida State, with the Sooners winning, 13-2. Miami defeated No. 7 Florida in the Sugar Bowl, 37-20. Washington beat No. 14 Purdue at the Rose Bowl, 34-24, to finish No. 3.

2001: The Dunkel rankings and *New York Times* poll were replaced by rankings from Dr. Peter Wolfe and Wes Colley. Each team's highest and lowest scores were disregarded, with the other six comprising the computer segment of the rankings.

Also, further emphasis was placed on strength of schedule, with quality wins added to the formula. Teams with victories against opponents ranked in the top 15 of the BCS standings received bonus points.

Similar to the year before, Miami was the lone undefeated squad ahead of a host of one-loss teams including Oregon, Nebraska, Maryland and Illinois, while Colorado was third in the Associated Press poll despite two losses, and Florida fifth.

Again the writers and coaches preferred one school, in this case Oregon, only to be overruled by the computers. Miami played Nebraska in the Orange Bowl and won 37-14, while Oregon defeated Colorado at the Fiesta Bowl, 38-16. With all of the other one-loss teams coming up short in their bowl games, Florida finished third.

2002: After it was decided that margin of victory should not be a determining element, causing some teams to run up scores, the Matthews and Rothman rankings were removed and the *New York Times* returned. Only the lowest score was eliminated before averaging the computer rankings.

The changes resulted in Iowa (11-1), which was ranked third by both the writers and coaches, finishing fifth in the BCS standings, behind Georgia (11-1) and Southern California (10-2), which despite two losses moved up after playing the toughest schedule in the nation. Strangely enough, Iowa and USC met at the Orange Bowl (the Rose Bowl selected Oklahoma as a replacement for Ohio State, which was playing in the national championship), where the Trojans won, 38-14.

As the only two undefeated teams remaining, No. 1 Miami met No. 2 Ohio State at the Fiesta Bowl. For a change, the controversy was on the field with a questionable pass interference call, and the Buckeyes won in double-overtime, 31-24.

2003: The tweaking continued, but had no effect on the biggest controversy the BCS had seen yet. At the end of the regular season, no team was undefeated while three high-profile programs—Southern California, LSU, and Oklahoma—all had one loss.

Heading into the conference championships, Oklahoma was No. 1 in the Associated Press poll, but lost to No. 13 Kansas State in the Big 12 Championship game, 35-7. USC had lost to California earlier in the season, 34-31. LSU's loss was in early October to Florida, 19-7, but the Tigers defeated No. 5 Georgia in the SEC Championship game, 34-13.

Once again, computers were the determining factor. Although the writers and coaches both had Southern California No. 1, the computers had the Trojans third, as did the strength of schedule ranking. The pairings were LSU vs. Oklahoma, even though the Sooners didn't win their conference title, in the Sugar Bowl, with USC facing No. 4 Michigan in the Rose Bowl.

The Tigers won 21-14, but when the Trojans also won, 28-14, the writers thumbed their noses at the BCS and kept Southern California No. 1. It was another split championship, the very thing the BCS was created to prevent.

2004: Consider it the year of extensive change, and on numerous fronts.

First off, the commissioners requested that the coaches and Associated Press release their first polls after the season started. After they were thoroughly laughed at, they got down to some real alterations.

Among them was making it easier for a school not in one of the major conferences to qualify for a BCS game. Utah immediately took advantage and earned a spot in the Fiesta Bowl, where it defeated Pitt, 35-7, to finish 12-0 and ranked fourth in the final Associated Press poll.

Additionally, a fifth BCS bowl game, the National Championship Game, would be added beginning with the 2006 season, played on a rotating basis at the site of the Fiesta,

Sugar, Orange and Rose bowls, one week later (i.e. if the Rose Bowl was on January 1, then the championship game would be January 8).

As for the standings formula, it was adjusted so that the Associated Press poll, the *USA Today* coaches' poll and the computers all counted a third toward the rankings. The strength-of-schedule, team-record and quality-win components were removed, especially since they already factored into the computer rankings. The *New York Times* rankings were again out, and a team's highest and lowest computer scores would again be discarded in determining the computer poll average.

But that was nothing compared to the chaos that ensued that season, with Auburn, Oklahoma and Southern California all finishing undefeated at 12-0 (in addition to 11-0 Utah and Boise State). No matter what, one of the three teams was going to be on the outside looking in.

It wound up being Auburn, after the writers, coaches and computers all agreed the Tigers were No. 3, despite the popular notion that the SEC was the toughest conference in the country. USC crushed Oklahoma in the Orange Bowl, 55-19, to win the national championship, while Auburn squeaked out a 16-13 victory against No. 9 Virginia Tech in the Sugar Bowl to finish No. 2. Auburn fans still can't understand how the Tigers were ranked below the Sooners, even though Oklahoma played for the national championship the previous year and boasted the second- and third-place vote-getters for the Heisman Trophy, running back Adrian Peterson and quarterback Jason White (who won in 2003).

Also lost in the process was Texas coach Mack Brown lobbying for his No. 6 team to play in the Rose Bowl instead of No. 4 Cal, which happened, keeping the Bears out of the BCS (and from the corresponding bigger payout). Texas defeated No. 13 Michigan, 38-37, while Cal lost in the Holiday Bowl to No. 23 Texas Tech, 45-31.

2005: With writers having been thrust into the process, and thus making news instead of just reporting it (considered a conflict of interest), the Associated Press decided it would no longer allow its polls be used in the BCS standings, saying it had damaged its "reputation for honesty and integrity." It was replaced by the thusly created Harris Inter-active Poll, a panel comprised of more than 100 former players, coaches and administrators along with some media members, which represented all 11 Division I-A conferences and independent schools.

Southern California and Texas began the season ranked first and second, and despite the efforts of 11-1 Penn State, which was unranked in the preseason poll, finished the regular season there as well, both 12-0. The showdown at the Rose Bowl came down to a final fourth-down play, with quarterback Vince Young scoring an 8-yard touchdown with 19 seconds remaining for a 41-38 victory. Not only did it deny the Trojans a chance to claim a three-peat, but for once there was no doubt regarding the national champion.

However, in December, Congress expressed concern regarding the numerous controversies and called for a comprehensive review of the Bowl Championship Series. With the threat of an anti-trust investigation if the BCS kept hoarding revenue, Big 12 commissioner Kevin Weiberg, Big Ten commissioner Jim Delany, University of Mississippi president Robert Khayat and three bowl representatives appeared before a subcommittee of the House of Representatives Energy and Commerce Committee.

Even Rep. Tom Osborne, the former Nebraska coach, called for change and Sen. Joe Biden said, "It looks like a rigged deal."

"College football is not just an exhilarating sport, but a billion-dollar business that Congress cannot ignore," committee chairman Joe Barton said. "Too often college football ends in sniping and controversy, rather than winners and losers. The current system of determining who's No. 1 appears deeply flawed."

Congress had a mighty weapon that the commissioners desperately wanted to avoid as well. Due to the tie-in with education, all donations and revenues surrounding college athletics were exempt from federal taxes. That included television money and contributions, which could be used to upgrade facilities and build massive stadiums.

2006: With the addition of the fifth BCS game, two extra teams were added to the mix, which made it possible for No. 9 Boise State to receive an invitation to play No. 7 Oklahoma in the Fiesta Bowl. In one of the most memorable bowl games ever, the teams combined to score an astonishing 22 points in the final 86 seconds of regulation. Although Boise State blew an 18-point lead in the third quarter, it scored a last-second touchdown to send the game into overtime, when it won on a pair of trick plays, 43-42.

In hindsight Boise State (13-0) was able to argue it played in the wrong BCS game, but the biggest controversy was over the national championship pairing. For the first time in history, Michigan and Ohio State were both undefeated and ranked 1-2 heading into their annual showdown to close the regular season. When the Buckeyes won, 42-39, Michigan stayed No. 2, but only for a week. With Southern California thumping No. 6 Notre Dame, 44-24, the Trojans moved up, but also for only for a week due to the subsequent upset loss at rival UCLA, 13-9.

The debate was on between No. 3 Michigan and No. 4 Florida, which defeated Arkansas in the SEC Championship, 39-28, while the Big Ten had no title game. With Urban Meyer lobbying for his Gators and some voters clearly not eager for an Ohio State-Michigan rematch, Florida got in by a hundredth of a point in the Bowl Championship Series standings.

Specifically, the Gators had a BCS average of .944, and the Wolverines were just behind at .934. The teams were tied in the computer ratings, but Florida had a slim lead in both the Harris poll and coaches' poll. Michigan had to settle for playing USC in the Rose Bowl, where it lost, 32-18.

Taking full advantage of the opportunity, Florida, which was still celebrating the men's basketball championship from the previous March, won the national title by pounding Ohio State, 41-14. In the final Associated Press poll, the Gators received 64 first-place votes, while Boise State got one.

"No one gave us a chance at all," Florida receiver Dallas Baker said. "We came here with a chip on our shoulder and something to prove. Nobody gave us a chance, but finally we can throw up the No. 1."

Yet, the debate continues while the BCS continues to bend and weave an effort to remain in existence. Granted, the BCS had led to more controversies, it also resulted in more No. 1 vs. No. 2 postseason matchups:

Season	Bowl	No. 1 vs. No. 2 Outcome
1962	Rose	No. 1 Southern California 42, No. 2 Wisconsin 37
1963	Cotton	No. 1 Texas 28, No. 2 Navy 6
1968	Rose	No. 1 Ohio State 27, No. 2 Southern California 16
1971	Orange	No. 1 Nebraska 38, No. 2 Alabama 6
1978	Sugar	No. 2 Alabama 14, No. 1 Penn State 7
1982	Sugar	No. 2 Penn State 27, No. 1 Georgia 23
1986	Fiesta	No. 2 Penn State 14, No. 1 Miami (Fla.) 10
1987	Orange	No. 2 Miami (Fla.) 20, No. 1 Oklahoma 14
1992	Sugar	No. 2 Alabama 34, No. 1 Miami (Fla.) 13
1993	Orange	No. 1 Florida State 18, No. 2 Nebraska 16
1995	Fiesta	No. 1 Nebraska 62, No. 2 Florida 24
1998	Fiesta	No. 1 Tennessee 23, No. 2 Florida State 16
1999	Sugar	No. 1 Florida State 46, No. 2 Virginia Tech 29
2002	Fiesta	No. 2 Ohio State 31, No. 1 Miami (Fla.) 24 (2 OT)
2004	Orange	No. 1 Southern California 55, No. 2 Oklahoma 19
2005	Rose	No. 2 Texas 41, No. 1 Southern California 38
2006	BCS title	No. 2 Florida 41, No. 1 Ohio State 14

But specific to the 2006 games alone (actually played in January 2007), consider:

Approximately $2 million was paid by the Bowl Championship Series to Division I-AA conferences to support the sport as a whole. Another $100,000 was paid to Army, Navy and Temple for making their teams available to play in a BCS game if selected.

Nine percent of BCS revenues (approximately $9.27 million), was earmarked in aggregate to Conference USA, the Mid-American, Mountain West, Sun Belt and Western Athletic Conferences for their participation. With Boise State playing Oklahoma in the Fiesta Bowl, those conferences received an additional nine percent.

Notre Dame was guaranteed 1/66th of the net revenues after expenses, or approximately $1.3 million, but received $4.5 million as a participant for playing in the Sugar Bowl.

The approximate share to each conference with an annual automatic berth in the BCS (ACC, Big East, Big Ten, Big 12, Pac-10 and SEC) was $17 million. A second portion was awarded to the Big Ten and SEC for having second teams selected.

In 2004, Fox and the BCS finalized a four-year $320 million deal (or $80 million a year) for the broadcast rights to the Fiesta, Orange and Sugar bowls from 2007-10 and the national title game from 2007-09. That was up from the previous four-year $76.5 million deal with ABC, which has the rights to the Rose Bowl through 2014.

"This agreement does allow us to have increased revenue for distribution in our system," said Weiberg, the BCS coordinator at the time.

That's why there's no playoff in Division I-A college football.

PART II

The Teams

Chapter 1

The Perennial Powers

ALABAMA CRIMSON TIDE

Consensus national titles (1936–present): 1961, 1964, 1965, 1973, 1978, 1979, 1992
Other national titles: 1925, 1926, 1930, 1934, 1941, 1945, 1966, 1975, 1977

There's no such thing as a real University of Alabama football fan who doesn't know about the Rose Bowl at the end of the 1925 season.

After defeating Georgia, 27-0, to clinch the Southern Conference title, the Crimson Tide became the first Southern school to play in the Rose Bowl, essentially for the national championship. Although many initially thought the invitation to play heavily favored Washington a mistake, Johnny Mack Brown caught two touchdown passes in the third quarter to help Alabama pull off a dramatic 20-19 upset that changed the game and region forever.

At no other school does football transcend the boundaries of a field or stadium like the Crimson Tide. To quote ESPN's *College Football Encyclopedia*, "Perhaps no program has meant as much to the identity, even the self-esteem, of its home state as Alabama."

That was, in part, by design. When Dr. George Hutcheson Denny became president of the university in 1912, he was ahead of his time in that he saw football as a tool to build enrollment and gain notoriety. To give an example to how correct he was, when Denny arrived the campus had just 652 students and nine principal buildings. When he retired in 1936, there were more than 5,000 students and 23 major buildings, which still form the central core of the modern campus.

The Rose Bowl victory was just the first of six early Pasadena appearances for Alabama, with only one loss and one tie, despite being considered the underdog each time. Will Rogers referred to the Tide as "Tusc-a-losers" before the initial visit, but after one of the later victories said: "Stanford made a mistake in scoring first. It just made those Alabama boys mad."

The Tide claims 12 national titles, some obviously more legitimate and/or controversial than others, but its rich football heritage goes much deeper. Alabama has made the most bowl appearances with 54, and arguably had the game's greatest coach, Paul W. "Bear" Bryant, who could claim six national championships. As for the other titles,

Wallace Wade won three, Frank Thomas two and Gene Stallings one—the most recent in 1992.

"The best you can do is not enough unless it gets the job done," Wade said.

Although Alabama fans like to debate which team is the best in Tide history, it's hard to argue against Bryant's final title team, 1979, which outscored opponents 383-67 and finished a perfect 12-0. It came back from a 17-7 deficit to defeat Tennessee (27-17), beat LSU (3-0), and held off rival Auburn (25-18), before handing Arkansas a 24-9 loss in the Sugar Bowl to successfully defend its 1978 title.

That wasn't the only time the Crimson Tide enjoyed consecutive national championships. With the final polls of the 1964 season cast prior to the postseason, Alabama was No. 1 despite a 21-17 loss to Texas in the Orange Bowl. When the Associated Press switched the following year to voting after the bowl schedule was completed, the No. 4 Tide benefited from No. 1 Michigan State and No. 2 Arkansas both losing in their bowl games, and defeated No. 3 Nebraska in the Orange Bowl, 39-28, to finish first.

However, despite being the preseason No. 1 team in 1966, Alabama didn't finish there even after finishing as the only team with a perfect record, 11-0. Instead, voters had the Tide third behind Notre Dame and Michigan State, which tied in their mid-November meeting and neither played a postseason game. Alabama, which had yet to integrate the football team which many blamed for the snub, finished the highly controversial season with a 34-7 pounding of Nebraska at the Sugar Bowl.

Bryant's other unblemished season was 1961, when the Tide was the clear national champion with an 11-0 record. Led by linebacker Lee Roy Jordan, Alabama topped the campaign with a 10-3 victory against Arkansas in the Sugar Bowl, and just missed repeating with a 10-1 record in 1962 and 17-0 win against Oklahoma in the Orange Bowl (where Jordan made 30 tackles).

"He was one of the finest football players the world has ever seen," Bryant said about Jordan. "If runners stayed between the sidelines, he tackled them. He never had a bad day. He was 100 percent every day in practice and in the games."

Of late, Alabama is fresh off NCAA sanctions that included the loss of numerous scholarships, but stadium renovations have the Tide near the top of college football in home attendance. and after the 2006 season it drew Nick Saban away from the Miami Dolphins and signed him to the biggest contract in college football (roughly $4 million a year).

Alabama has so much history and tradition that it needs a museum to store and showcase it all. Named in honor of Bryant, it displays scores of title trophies, with many more in storage in the back rooms, and everything from Bryant's trademark houndstooth hat to photos of the all-time greats including 90 All-Americans.

They include Shaun Alexander, Cornelius Bennett, John Hannah, Dixie Howell, Pooley Hubert, Don Hutson, Lee Roy Jordan, Johnny Musso, Joe Namath, Ozzie Newsome, Derrick Thomas and DeMeco Ryans. However, somewhat surprisingly, Alabama has never won a Heisman Trophy, which some fans take as a compliment because to them it symbolizes that the team always comes first.

In the Yellowhammer State, they memorialize great plays in paintings, fans enjoy arguably the biggest rivalry game in the country (Auburn), and they dress up for games.

And they still pay homage to the man who after "Mama called," won 13 SEC titles, three coach of the year awards, and led a string of 24 consecutive bowl appearances. When he retired after the 1982 season, Bryant's 323 victories were a record among major colleges, but his iconic presence is still felt today.

"I ain't nothing but winner," he once said.

AUBURN TIGERS

Consensus national titles (1936–present): 1957

Other national titles: 1913, 1983, 1993

Although Auburn University won the 1957 national championship and has been one of college football's elite programs ever since, it could be argued that the Tigers are currently going through their greatest stretch ever.

Under Tommy Tuberville's direction, Auburn finished at least tied for first in the SEC Western Division five times from 2000-06. The Tigers ran the table with an impressive 13-0 record in 2004 and not only won the Southeastern Conference Championship game, but vied for the national title as well.

It's also a program that has earned two Heisman Trophies (quarterback Pat Sullivan in 1971, and running back Bo Jackson in 1985), two Outland Trophies (Zeke Smith in 1958, and Tracy Rocker in 1988), and had coaches like John Heisman (1895-99), Ralph "Shug" Jordan (1951-75) and Pat Dye (1981-92).

Some considered Jackson to be the greatest athlete of last century. He played center field for Auburn's baseball team, batting .401 one season, and was on the track team, posting 10.4 seconds in the 100 meters. He went on to be an all-star outfielder with the Kansas City Royals while simultaneously was an elite running back for the Los Angeles Raiders in the sport he described as his "hobby."

"When people tell me I could be the best athlete there is, I just let it go in one ear and out the other," Jackson once said. "There is always somebody out there who is better than you are."

"His greatest trait was the ability to inspire people," former Auburn director of athletics David Housel said. "His accomplishments came in the arena of everyday life. He became a living example of what a person can do if he sets his mind to do it. He came back to Auburn and finished work on his degree, a promise he had made to his mother. Money, fame, and acclaim do not motivate Bo Jackson. Values motivate Bo Jackson."

Prior to Dye's arrival, Auburn had won only one SEC title in 48 years. During his 12 seasons, the Tigers captured four SEC titles, including three straight from 1987-89.

"I don't believe in miracles. I believe in character," Dye once said.

There have also been a number of unsung heroes to the program as well, like wide receiver Terry Beasley. As Sullivan's favorite target, he finished eighth in Heisman voting in 1971. His career average of 17.8 yards per catch and his per-game average of 83.9 yards receiving were both SEC records, and he essentially re-wrote the receiving section of the Auburn record book.

"He was way ahead of his time," Sullivan said. "He was as fast as anyone playing the game. But the thing that really set him apart was that he was awfully, awfully, strong."

Nevertheless, for some reason the Tigers have never quite seemed to reach college football's version of utopia—like in 1971 when they won nine straight before losing to the Crimson Tide, or 1914 when Mike Donahue's team was undefeated and unscored upon, but finished 8-0-1 with a tie against Georgia (FYI, 9-0 Army was the consensus national champion).

In 2004, Auburn was the odd-team out of the Bowl Championship Series title game. When Terry Bowden coached the Tigers to an 11-0 finish in 1993, the Tigers were on NCAA probation. Even during the 1957 national championship season, Auburn was not bowl eligible due to recruiting violations.

It will also surprise some to learn that Auburn has won only six SEC titles in football, which among the 10 original schools remaining exceeds only Kentucky (two), Mississippi State (one) and Vanderbilt (zero).

Although Jordan's 1957 team gave up just 28 points, only seven of which were scored by an SEC opponent (Mississippi State), no team probably exemplifies Auburn better than the 2004 squad, which had four players—running back Carnell Williams, running back Ronnie Brown, quarterback Jason Campbell, and cornerback Carlos Rogers—selected in the first round of the subsequent National Football League draft.

The undefeated finish was even more remarkable considering that near the end of the previous season Auburn officials flew to Kentucky to offer Tuberville's job to Louisville coach Bob Petrino.

Ranked just seventeenth in the preseason, the Tigers defeated No. 5 LSU (10-9), No. 10 Tennessee (34-10), and No. 8 Georgia (24-6) to win the Western Division. During the rematch against Tennessee in the SEC Championship game, Campbell passed for a career-high 374 yards and three touchdowns to lead a 38-28 victory.

But with Southern California and Oklahoma first and second in the Bowl Championship Series rankings, they played for the national championship while Auburn was relegated to the Sugar Bowl, where it defeated feisty No. 9 Virginia Tech, 19-16.

Consequently, Tuberville became one of the biggest advocates for a playoff system to settle the national championship.

"I've about had it with this playoff deal," he said at SEC Media Days in 2006.

But even with titles and awards, the one thing that causes Auburn fans to scream "War Eagle" more than anything else is beating rival Alabama.

Many, if not most, of the Tigers' proudest moments have been in the annual season-ending grudge game tabbed the "Iron Bowl." For example, in 1969, Jordan, who had lost five straight to the Crimson Tide and Paul W. "Bear" Bryant, inspired his team with the following speech:

"Men, there is a time for everything," Jordan said prior to the 49-26 victory. "A time to live and a time to die; a time to love and a time to hate; a time for peace and a time for war; and gentleman, there's a time to beat Alabama. That time is now."

FLORIDA GATORS

Consensus national titles (1936–present): 1996, 2006

Other national titles: 1984, 1985

It's the program that Steve Spurrier built, not once, but twice.

The first time, of course, was as a player.

Against visiting Auburn on October 29, 1966, the quarterback essentially assured the school of its first Heisman Trophy when, facing fourth down in the closing moments, he waved the kicker off to attempt the 40-yard game-winning field goal himself.

Spurrier had thrown for 259 yards (and to give you an idea of how times have changed, he finished with 2,012 passing yards that season) and averaged 47 yards a punt. When he cleared the crossbar by about a foot, Coach Ray Graves could only smile. Auburn coach Ralph "Shug" Jordan called him "Steve Superior."

In 1990, Spurrier returned to Gainesville to be the "Head Ball Coach," as he would say, and turned the Gators into a national powerhouse.

Under Spurrier's direction, Florida became only one of six schools in major college football history, and one of two in SEC history, to win 100 games during a decade (100-22-1). The Gators were also the first team in the conference to win at least 10 games in six straight seasons, and the third school ever to be ranked for 200 consecutive weeks.

Spurrier even slapped the "Swamp" nickname on Ben Hill Griffin Stadium, saying "only Gators can survive a trip to the swamp." Easily one of the loudest stadiums in the country, with a capacity of 88,548, Florida was 68-5 there under his direction.

Perhaps amazingly, Spurrier didn't win a national coach of the year award, but did become the first Heisman winner to coach another Heisman winner–quarterback Danny Wuerffel in 1996.

"He was a little different," said Tommy Tuberville, who at Ole Miss and Auburn lost his first four games against Spurrier. "He was outspoken. You can be pretty much outspoken when you're kicking everybody's butt like he was."

"If people like you too much, it's probably because they're beating you," Spurrier said.

In 2006, Urban Meyer found out what that was like, when in his second year the Gators survived the toughest schedule in the country to win the SEC championship and, thanks to UCLA upsetting Southern California in the regular season finale, played Ohio State for the national title.

The game was a rout. Although the Buckeyes scored on the opening kickoff, the Gators crushed them, 41-14.

"Honestly, we played a lot better teams than them," defensive end Jarvis Moss said. "I could name four or five teams in the SEC that could probably compete with them and play the same type of game we did against them."

Although Meyer, who called himself an "organizational freak," brought with him a speed-based spread offense that was particularly difficult to counter, the secret of his success wasn't too difficult to figure out.

"Back as a player, I was always the hardest working guy," he said. "I would be so upset with myself if I wasn't. Was I the best? I was average, but I outworked everybody. As a coach, am I the smartest? No. But I believe that in a lot of areas I outwork a lot of guys."

So much for the program that cranked out the likes of Emmitt Smith (1987-89), Jack Youngblood (1968-70) and Wilber Marshall (1980-83), but for most of its existence was known more for its potential rather than big wins.

Alabama coach Paul W. Bear Bryant used to say that all Florida needed was the right person at the right time, and although the Gators made runs at the national championship in 1928, 1966 and 1969, all three efforts came up short.

Under Spurrier, who brought the Fun 'n Gun offense to the talent-rich Sunshine State, the Gators finally broke through with a national championship (1996), and captured six SEC titles. Incredibly, those were Florida's first conference championships in football.

Following the 2001 season, Spurrier left the Gators for the Washington Redskins (he's already back in the SEC at South Carolina), but similar fireworks are back at the Swamp, with the Meyer's spread offense helping make Florida once again a perennial power.

Now that's something for Gators fans to chomp about.

FLORIDA STATE SEMINOLES
Consensus national titles (1936–present): 1993, 1999
Other national titles: 1980, 1987, 1992, 1994, 1996

The name is Bowden, Bobby Bowden.

And he is unequivocally Florida State University football.

FSU, which until the late 1940s was a women's school, didn't start playing football until 1947, when Ed Williamson was appointed the first coach weeks before the inaugural season. With no stadium, no scholarships, no budgeted salaries and no nickname, FSU finished 0-5.

The program wasn't ranked in an Associated Press poll until 1964, when it lasted two weeks at No. 10 until a 20-11 loss at Virginia Tech. It occurred during Bill Peterson's reign, when from 1960-70 the Seminoles went 62-42-11 and played in four bowl games, including a 36-19 victory against Oklahoma in the 1965 Gator Bowl.

But in the three seasons before Bowden arrived from West Virginia in 1976, Florida State was 4-29, including a pathetic 0-11 in 1973 that prompted talk of dropping the program.

"I could think of only two jobs that would have been worse," Bowden wrote in his autobiography *Bound for Glory*. "Being elected mayor of Atlanta shortly after Sherman left town or being the general who volunteers to replace George Custer during the last siege of the Little Big Horn."

In 2005, the Birmingham native who initially considered Florida State a stepping stone and dreamed of someday coaching at Alabama or Auburn, celebrated both his 30th year at the helm, and having coached more than 1,000 Seminole players.

Not only do his 293 Florida State victories through 2006 easily outdistance the seven previous Seminoles coaches combined—FYI, he took over the FSU lead with win No. 63 in 1983—but his 366 career wins are the most in college football history among major programs.

Under Bowden's direction, FSU has captured two consensus national championships (1993 and 1999 after numerous near-misses), two Heisman Trophies (quarterbacks Charlie Ward and Chris Weinke in 1993 and 2000, respectively) and at least a share of 12 Atlantic Coast Conference titles.

The 1993 championship was controversial in that Florida lost a No. 1 vs. No. 2 regular-season meeting at Notre Dame, 31-24, a week before the Irish lost to Boston College, 41-39. Although West Virginia was undefeated (and went on to lose to Florida in the Sugar Bowl, 41-7), Florida State played Nebraska for the national championship at the Orange Bowl, and won 18-16. The final rankings had Florida State No. 1, and Notre Dame, which defeated Texas A&M at the Cotton Bowl, 24-21, No. 2.

In 1999, Bowden recorded his only perfect season when Florida State defeated No. 2 Virginia Tech in the Sugar Bowl, 46-29. Wide receiver Peter Warrick caught a 64-yard touchdown pass from Weinke in the first quarter, returned a punt 59 yards for another score in the second quarter, and made a sensational catch of a 43-yard bomb from Weinke with 7:42 left to put the game away.

"Right before that play, I asked the offense, 'Do you want me to finish them off?'" Warrick said. "They said, 'Yeah.'"

"We had to make a decision to win the game right here or sit on the ball," Bowden said. "He called about four guys over and he really said it to them."

Bowden's the only coach to ever lead his team to 10 or more wins over 14 straight seasons (1987-2000), during which the Seminoles finished in the top five of the Associated Press poll each year, which was unprecedented, and were the preseason No. 1 team five times. For the 1990s decade, Florida State finished 109-13-1 for a .890 winning percentage. Bowden also had an amazing 14-game unbeaten streak in bowl games (1982-95), though there was a 17-17 tie to Georgia in the 1984 Citrus Bowl.

"We've always told our players, 'You're the only team living in a dynasty,'" Bowden said prior to the 2001 Orange Bowl against Oklahoma, which was the national championship (the Seminoles lost, 13-2). "Bama was in a dynasty, Notre Dame was in a dynasty, Miami was in a dynasty, so-and-so was in a dynasty. We hope we keep it alive."

Tallahassee also became known as a breeding ground for pro talent. In 2005, Florida State had more active players in the National Football League than any other program.

One of the few FSU legacies that began before Bowden was Sod Cemetery, where chunks of the field from important road victories have been laid to rest in the corner of the Florida State practice field. The tradition began in 1962 when after an 18-0 win at Georgia, a piece of turf from Sanford Stadium was presented to Dean Coyle E. Moore. Each "burial" has a small tombstone listing the date and score of the game, and originally the markers were only added after upsets. As the Seminoles became more successful, the criteria changed, with bowl and landmark games, no matter who was favored, now also considered sod worthy.

Florida State also boasts the unlikely high-profile trio of Lee Corso, Burt Reynolds and Deion Sanders, along with legendary wide receivers Fred Biletnikoff and Ron Sellers.

"When those lights go on, it's prime time for me," Sanders once said. "It's like Jekyll and Hyde. When I have to put on a show, I put on a show."

But none of them have been honored with a bronze statue in front of the Moore Athletics Center. Bowden's was unveiled on September 24, 2004.

"At West Virginia, they sold bumper stickers that said 'Beat Pitt,'" Bowden said. "When I came to Florida State, they sold bumper stickers that said "Beat Anybody.""

GEORGIA BULLDOGS

Consensus national titles (1936–present): 1942, 1980

Other national titles: 1927, 1946, 1968

There's just something right about a bulldog named Uga.

Although Georgia's first mascot was a goat, the English bulldog with the spiked collar may be the most recognized mascot in all of college sports.

Uga has appeared on the cover of *Sports Illustrated*, had a cameo in the movie *Midnight in the Garden of Good and Evil*, and traveled with Herschel Walker to the Downtown Athletic Club in New York for the Heisman Trophy presentation. The first five Ugas are buried near the south stands of the football stadium, and flowers are placed on their graves before each game.

"Uga is the best mascot a team could have," receiver Clarence Kay once said. "He'll lay on you. He'll lick on you. Give him a bone and he'll love you for life."

The Bulldogs have won two consensus national titles (1942 and 1980, and voted No. 1 by various polls three other times), 12 Southeastern Conference championships and played in 49 bowl games. They've had two players win the Heisman—halfback Frank Sinkwich in 1942 and Walker in 1982—14 players inducted into the College Football Hall of Fame, and 24 players selected in the first round of the National Football League draft.

But when it comes to icons, like Uga, Georgia can compete with any college football program in the country.

It's a program that's been led by coaches Wally Butts and Pop Warner. It's "between the hedges" and "silver britches." It's ringing the chapel bell until midnight following Georgia wins and the historic arch that freshmen were told to avoid walking under. Before "How about them Cowboys?" was popularized by Dallas during its most recent Super Bowl run in the National Football League, "How 'bout them dawgs?" first caught on nationally after a victory against Notre Dame.

Georgia's first national title came in 1942, when the Bulldogs beat UCLA in the Rose Bowl, 9-0, to finish 11-1. That year also saw the South's first Heisman Trophy winner, Sinkwich, who had begged his coach to make him a fullback. The previous year, as a junior when Georgia finished 9-1-1, he established a national total-offense record of 2,187 yards, 1,392 through the air. In Georgia's 40-26 victory over Texas Christian in the Orange Bowl, he completed 9 of 13 passes for 243 yards and three touchdowns, and rushed for 139 yards and a touchdown, for 382 all-purpose yards.

When Sinkwich wasn't able to play against UCLA in the Rose Bowl, Charley Trippi made his first start and was named the game's most valuable player. Upon the conclusion of World War II, Trippi went back to Georgia and with John Rauch led the 1946 Bulldogs to an 11-0 season. Among the season's highlights was his decisive touchdown pass to Dan Edwards for a 20-10 victory against North Carolina in the Sugar Bowl, but Notre Dame was considered the consensus national champion.

Butts (140-86-9), made another title run in 1959, but at 10-1 had to settle for a top five finish. Frank Leahy called him "football's finest passing coach," and quarterback Fran Tarkenton said Butts "knew more football than any other man I ever met."

In 1968, Vince Dooley (201-77-10 and 20 bowl games over 25 years) and defensive end Bill Stanfill had Georgia receiving national title consideration (Ohio State was the consensus choice), but from 1980-83 the coach had an astonishing 43-4-1 record and won the 1980 championship.

Leading that team was Walker, who as a freshman accumulated 1,616 rushing yards, and in the Sugar Bowl had 150 yards for a 17-10 victory against Notre Dame and 12-0 finish. He went from third in Heisman voting to second and first, and in 33 regular season games had 5,259 rushing yards (an average of 159 per game) and scored 55 touchdowns. Also on the Bulldogs was All-American safety Terry Hoage, who as a junior in 1982 led the nation with 12 interceptions.

In 2001, the latest chapter in Georgia football opened when Mark Richt was hired as the program's 25th head coach. In addition to guiding Heisman quarterbacks Charlie Ward and Chris Weinke as a Florida State assistant coach, Richt had also been an outstanding quarterback prospect at Miami under Howard Schnellenberger.

"I figured I'd start my first year, be an All-American my second year, win the Heisman Trophy my third year, and then go pro after that," Richt said.

Instead, he spent most of his college career backing up future NFL Hall of Fame quarterback Jim Kelly, and during one season his teammates included Vinny Testaverde and Bernie Kosar.

In 2002, Georgia advanced to play in its first SEC Championship game, where it dominated Arkansas, 30-3, to win its first conference title in 20 years.

As part of the Bowl Championship Series, Georgia was paired against Florida State in the Sugar Bowl. Running back Musa Smith rushed for 145 yards, cornerback Bruce Thornton returned an interception 71 yards for a touchdown, and Billy Bennett kicked four field goals as the Bulldogs won, 26-13.

"To beat Florida State is a great feeling, since I have a great respect for the Florida State program," Richt said. "I'm so proud of these kids. They deserve to go out like this."

Another icon had been found in Georgia: Richt, the man who liked to say, "Finish the drill."

LSU TIGERS

Consensus national titles (1936–present): 1958, 2003
Other national titles: 1908, 1935, 1936, 1962

They've won a Heisman Trophy and two national championships, but when most people think of the Louisiana State Tigers usually the first thing that comes to mind are their fans.

Rowdy doesn't begin to describe the 90,000-plus people that jam into Tiger Stadium on Saturdays. Borderline insane might be a better description.

Said Brad Budde, a former All-American from Southern California: "Unbelievable, crazy. That place makes Notre Dame look like Romper Room."

Football is a little different in the bayou, where they sport bumper stickers that scream "Geaux Tigers," the mascot is a real live Bengal tiger named Mike, and most home games are played under the lights, giving fans all day to "rev" up. Usually that includes a lot more than jambalaya, gumbo and crawfish etouffee.

But there's little doubt that LSU's football history is as colorful as its purple and gold uniforms.

LSU's first national title came in 1958, when before unlimited substitution Paul Dietzel took advantage of a new rule that allowed any player, not just starters, to come off the field and go back in again once each quarter, to turn the Tigers into a three-platoon team.

The White Team, which played both ways, included Billy Cannon, who won the Heisman in 1959. The Go Team specialized in offense, and the third unit which concentrated on defense became known as the "Chinese Bandits"—borrowed from a "Terry and the Pirates" comic strip that referred to Chinese Bandits as the "most vicious people in the world."

The Tigers responded with a 10-0 regular season with only one opponent, Duke, able to score more than seven points. Although LSU defeated No. 6 Ole Miss 14-0, and survived a 7-6 scare against Mississippi State, the biggest game may have been against bayou rival Tulane. Inspired by Green Wave tailback Claude "Boo" Mason's statement, "We'll beat LSU because they'll choke," the Tigers scored 56 points in the final two quarters for an overwhelming 62-0 win, the most lopsided score in the series (since equaled in 1961 and 1965).

After being voted the consensus national champion at the end of the regular season (which was when the final polls were tabulated), LSU topped it off with a 7-0 victory against Clemson in the Sugar Bowl.

LSU was riding an 18-game winning streak in 1959 when its most famous play occurred on Halloween night against Ole Miss in a No. 1 vs. No. 3 matchup. Ahead 3-0 in the fourth quarter, the Rebels decided to punt on third-and-17 (which wasn't uncommon then) at their own 42. Cannon fielded the bouncing ball at the 11 and headed up the sideline, avoiding numerous tacklers en route to the end zone for a dramatic 7-3 victory.

Not only was it considered the play that secured Cannon the Heisman, but one of the greatest plays in college football history. However, LSU subsequently lost at Tennessee, 14-13, after Dietzel went for a victory instead of settling for a tie, ending any chance of defending the title, and Ole Miss got even in the Sugar Bowl, 21-0.

"We came to win, not to tie," Dietzel said. "If I had it to do over a hundred times, I would do the same thing."

LSU's other national championship came in 2003, when Nick Saban led the Tigers to the controversial Bowl Championship Series title by defeating Oklahoma in the Sugar Bowl, 21-14. Although the Sooners had Heisman Trophy winner Jason White and averaged 45.2 points and 461.4 yards per game, they were limited to just 154 yards on 70 plays from scrimmage.

"There's no doubt in my mind we're the best defense in the country," prison guard-turned-defensive tackle Chad Lavalais said after the game. "We made the plays when we needed to all year."

Perhaps fittingly, the decisive touchdown was a 20-yard interception return by defensive end Marcus Spears.

"We play in the (Southeastern Conference)," end Marquise Hill said. "We're used to playing smash-mouth football, real football. They weren't just going to come in here and blow it out on us. If they thought that, they were sadly mistaken."

But like everything else with LSU, it was anything but typical, as Associated Press voters placed Southern California first instead, resulting in a controversial split title.

It all comes with the territory for a team whose fans got so loud against Auburn in 1988 that the geology department's seismograph registered vibrations. Imagine what it might be like when Saban, who in 2007 was hired away from the Miami Dolphins by Alabama, returns for the first time on the opposing sideline.

"Baton Rouge happens to be the worst place in the world for a visiting team," legendary coach Paul W. "Bear" Bryant said. "It's like being inside a drum."

MIAMI HURRICANES

Consensus national titles (1936–present): 1983, 1987, 1989, 1991, 2001
Other national titles: 1986, 1988, 1990, 2000

They were the bad boys of college football, and proud of it.

From 1987-91, the Miami Hurricanes won three national titles, and missed a fourth by a point due to a controversial 31-30 loss to Notre Dame (not to mention the 34-13 loss to Alabama in the 1993 Sugar Bowl). During those five seasons, the Hurricanes went an incredible 56-4-0 and were considered the giants of the game.

"We played our way to this championship," Jimmy Johnson said after defeating No. 1 Oklahoma 20-14 in the Orange Bowl to finish 12-0 in 1987. "We have the best record versus anybody in the country .... We beat Oklahoma three in a row, Florida State and Notre Dame three in a row, Florida a couple ... What is sweetest is that we did it as a team. We lost starters and had other guys come in and played magnificently."

When Johnson left to coach the Dallas Cowboys, Dennis Erickson stepped in and won two titles. In 1989, the Hurricanes didn't allow a touchdown for one 10-quarter stretch during the regular season, held six opponents without a touchdown, and allowed just 9.3 points per game. Miami bounced back from a loss to Florida State to defeat No. 1 Notre Dame, 27-10, and defeated No. 7 Alabama in the Sugar Bowl.

Two years later, Miami benefited from "Wide Right I" to defeat No. 1 Florida State and went on to crush Nebraska in the Orange Bowl, 22-0, to finish 12-0 and split the national title with Washington, which finished No. 1 in the coaches' poll.

"To win one national championship is amazing," Erickson said. "For guys to win their second in three years, that hasn't been accomplished by many. That's what makes this championship special. And it came in a situation where we had not been picked to be that good. Some people said we'd be No. 3 in the state of Florida."

But even though it won three national championships from 1987-91, the outlaw reputation has at times caught up to Miami. The Hurricanes wound up on NCAA probation, it seemed that some players were mentioned in police blotters nearly as often as the sports pages, and *Sports Illustrated* even once called for the private school to banish the program. At heart of the cover story was the 1994 Pell Grant scandal in which an academic advisor pled guilty to helping more than 80 student athletes, 57 of whom were football players, falsify their grant applications in exchange for kickbacks.

After Butch Davis was hired in 1995 to revive the football program, which he did before leaving for the National Football League (and later returning to the college game at North Carolina), rookie coach Larry Coker won the 2001 national championship with a 37-14 victory against No. 2 Nebraska, and Heisman Trophy winner Eric Crouch, in the Rose Bowl. Highlighting the game was quarterback Ken Dorsey, who completed 22 of 35 passes for a career-high 362 yards and had touchdown passes to Andre Johnson (who had 199 receiving yards) and Jeremy Shockey.

"The entire team deserves to be MVP tonight," said Dorsey after he and Johnson shared the honor. "Our defense stepped up to the challenge and did a great job. Our offensive line, receivers, everybody did a great job against a great team."

Johnson added: "I felt like I had something to prove so I brought my 'A' game."

The Hurricanes just missed defending their title, losing 31-24 to Ohio State in double overtime at the 2003 Fiesta Bowl—remembered for the controversial pass interference call on Miami cornerback Glenn Sharpe—but set an NFL record when six players were selected in the first round of the 2004 draft.

"It's very painful," said Coker, who had won his first 24 games as Miami's head coach, about his first loss.

That completed the second of two great turnarounds in Miami history. The other came in 1979, when Howard Schnellenberger was hired. Over the previous 10 years, the Hurricanes had nearly as many coaches (six), as losing seasons (nine). After a 5-6 initial campaign under the coach, Miami had three winning seasons before going 10-1 in 1983 and shocking Nebraska in the Orange Bowl, 31-30, to win its first national championship.

After Schnellenberger left for the United States Football League, Johnson (52-9) and Erickson (63-9) followed, to continue one of the greatest runs in college football.

Miami has a rich tradition defensively—featuring linemen like Russell Maryland and Warren Sapp; linebackers Ray Lewis, Michael Barrow, Dan Morgan, and Jessie Armstead; and defensive backs Burgess Owens, Fred Marion and Bennie Blades. Defensive end Ted Hendricks, "The Mad Stork," also played for the Hurricanes from 1966-68. He compiled 327 tackles, averaging 109 per season, and in 1968 finished fifth in Heisman Trophy voting.

The program has also produced sensational running backs like Otis Anderson, Alonzo Highsmith, Edgerrin James, Willis McGahee and Clinton Portis. However, the Hurricanes are primarily known for their quarterbacks, starting with Jim Kelly, who had been recruited by Penn State as a linebacker.

Bernie Kosar, Steve Walsh, Craig Erickson, Gino Torretta and Dorsey all led Miami to a national championship, but Vinny Testaverde was the first player since Hendricks to have his number retired. Wearing No. 14, he completed 413 of 674 passes for 6,058 yards and 48 touchdowns, and in 1986 because the first Miami player to win the Heisman Trophy.

MICHIGAN WOLVERINES
Consensus national titles (1936–present): 1947, 1948, 1997
Other national titles: 1901, 1902, 1903, 1904, 1918, 1923, 1925, 1926, 1932, 1933, 1964, 1973, 1985

Even though the University of Michigan didn't reach the Bowl Championship Series title game at the end of the 2006 season, Wolverines fans feel like they did play for the title.

On November 18, Michigan and rival Ohio State met for the first time with both teams undefeated and ranked first and second in the Associated Press poll, with the Wolverines further inspired by the death of legendary coach Bo Schembechler.

Although the two defenses had allowed a combined average of 20 points per game that season, it turned into a surprising shootout with 900 yards of total offense. When the final big play was made, Ohio State quarterback Troy Smith, who won the Heisman Trophy, stood triumphant with a 42-39 victory.

"If this was boxing, they'd definitely get a rematch," Ohio State defensive back Brandon Mitchell said.

While Michigan initially held on to its No. 2 ranking, it didn't happen. Southern California leapfrogged it a week later, but when the Trojans were subsequently beaten by UCLA, and Florida won the SEC Championship, the Gators went to the title game and crushed the Buckeyes. After Michigan lost to USC in the Rose Bowl, 32-18, it finished No. 8.

Overall, there's a reason why the fight song is titled, "The Victors." Nearly everything Michigan does in college football is big, from the "Block M" on the east side of the bleachers, down to the maize and blue uniforms and winged helmets.

The Wolverines boast the most Division I victories (860 through 2006), the most Big Ten championships (42), and the largest college football stadium in the country, seating 107,501 (capacity is always listed with a final digit of 1 in honor of former coach Fritz Crisler, though the location of that seat remains a deeply guarded secret).

"There is no doubt this is my favorite place, to see four generations rise up and appreciate it, for the pageantry, the ambiance," said announcer Keith Jackson, who came up with the term "The Big House," for Michigan Stadium. "Michigan has such grandiosity. It has all those All-Americans. You can't go anywhere without finding a Michigan graduate."

Michigan claims 11 national championships, but has only three consensus titles since 1936 (the most recent in 1997), and only twice has been voted No. 1 by the Associated Press. However, it boasts a record 37 finishes in the top 10, and 52 in the top 20.

"Who are they that they should beat a Michigan team," said Fielding H. Yost (165-29-10 from 1901-23, 1925-26).

Although Crisler (1947), Bernie Oosterbaan (1948), Schembechler (1969), and Lloyd Carr (1997) were all named coach of the year, Yost's legacy is the strongest. He invented the linebacker position and was the first to use offensive motion as a decoy.

Some described his style of play as "punt, pass and pray," but from 1901-05 his "Point a Minute" teams went 55-1-1 with 50 shutouts and outscored opponents 2,821-42. Yost was credited (arguably, of course) with a share of eight national titles to go with seven Big Ten championships, even though the school dropped out of the conference for 10 years due to a rules dispute.

Yost also won the first Rose Bowl game, 49-0 against Stanford, to conclude the 11-0 1901 season having outscored the opposition 550-0 (incidentally, the next three years the Wolverines won by combined scores of 644-12, 565-6, 577-22). Fullback Neil Snow scored five touchdowns and halfback Willie Heston had 170 rushing yards on 18 carries.

Crisler's career (116-32-9) peaked during his final year of coaching, 1947, when the Wolverines put together a perfect 9-0 regular season and defeated Southern Cal, 49-0, to be the consensus national champion even though the Associated Press opted for Notre Dame (a special postseason poll was conducted and voters changed their minds in favor of Michigan, but it did not supersede the final regular season poll). Against the Trojans, who reached midfield only twice, Jack Weisenburger scored three touchdowns.

With former end Oosterbaan taking over and Pete Elliott still at quarterback (although in Michigan's single-wing attack it was primarily considered a blocking position), Michigan left no doubt to the title the following year by finishing 9-0. It shut out Oregon, Purdue, Northwestern, Navy and Indiana before closing the season with a 13-3 victory at Ohio State.

The other title came in 1997, under Carr's direction and aided by Heisman Trophy winner Charles Woodson, but it was a split championship. After quarterback Brian Griese completed 18 of 30 passes for 251 yards and three touchdowns, including 58- and 53-yard tosses to wide receiver Tai Streets, to lead the 21-16 victory against Washington State in the Rose Bowl, Associated Press voters selected Michigan by a wide margin. However, the coaches' poll picked Nebraska by a mere two votes.

Overall, Michigan has made 38 bowl appearances, including a consecutive streak dating back to the 1975 season, but it's always been the football factory of the north in turning out talented players.

The 27 inductees into the College Football Hall of Fame rank second only to Notre Dame. Michigan has had 76 consensus first-team All-Americans and more than 40 first-round selections in the National Football League.

Among its notable awards have been three Heisman Trophy winners—Tom Harmon (1940), Desmond Howard (1991) and Woodson (1997), whose primary position was cornerback. Although Woodson's versatility was highly praised, it was nothing compared to Harmon's. "Ol' 98" played tailback, defensive back, kicker and punter, and all with a mean streak. He twice led the nation in scoring.

Harmon's 98 is one of five jerseys the school has retired. The most recent was No. 48 during halftime of the 1994 Michigan State at Michigan game. It had belonged to the 1934 team MVP who earned the honor despite playing center, former President Gerald R. Ford.

NEBRASKA CORNHUSKERS
Consensus national titles (1936–present): 1970, 1971, 1994, 1995, 1997
Other national titles: 1980, 1981, 1982, 1983, 1984, 1993

Even though the school's colors are scarlet and cream, at the University of Nebraska they like to believe that real men wear black.

That's what the starting defensive players wear, with the practice jerseys ceremoniously awarded during the preseason.

"The thing could be a rag and you'd still look it as a shrine," Chad Kelsay a defensive end from 1995-98, said regarding the "Blackshirts."

Oh yeah, Nebraska has had three winners of the Heisman Trophy (Johnny Rodgers, 1972; Mike Rozier, 1983; and Eric Crouch, 2001) and seven different players have taken home the Outland Trophy as the nation's top collegiate interior lineman.

Although the program is currently in a bit of a transition phase under the direction of Bill Callahan, who replaced the traditional I-formation option attack for the more pass-oriented West Coast offense, its history can only be described as stellar.

For starters, Bob Devaney (101-20-2 from 1962-72), had a winning record all 11 seasons with nine bowl games, eight conference champions, a 32-game unbeaten streak, and back-to-back national championships in 1970 and 1971. In the previous 21 years, Nebraska had just three winning seasons.

In 1970, Nebraska came back from a 10-point deficit against Kansas to win 41-20, prompting the coach to tell his team, "You learned you can come back. Remember that. That is the lesson of life." The Cornhuskers went on to win the first of three consecutive Orange Bowls, 17-12 against LSU.

With Rodgers at halfback and Rich Glover leading the defense, the 1971 team was simply dominating, finishing 13-0 and scored 511 points. The marquee game that season was a 35-31 victory against Oklahoma, though Nebraska went to defeat Alabama in the Orange Bowl, 38-6.

Devaney was able to hand-pick his successor, Osborne, when he retired, only with mixed results at first. But after losing the first five rivalry games against Oklahoma, he did more than follow the legend, but exceed him with an incredible 255-49-3 record from 1973-97.

The Cornhuskers recorded 15 10-win seasons under his direction, and Osborne's worst season was 9-3-1 in 1976, when they "only" played in the Bluebonnet Bowl—a 27-24 victory against Texas Tech.

At its best, from 1994-97, Nebraska won three national championships, compiled a 49-2 record, and had nine All-Americans. The Cornhuskers won two Outland Trophies, one Lombardi, and a Johnny Unitas for best quarterback even though Nebraska had really never been known for its passing game.

(Note: The school yearbook once had a job description for the team's quarterback: "run fast, to dodge and twist through a broken field." That was in 1907.)

How's this for dominance? In the 1990s, Nebraska lost just three home games. While few programs have won 100 games in a decade, Nebraska is the only team in NCAA history to do it in consecutive decades.

After Byron Bennett's 45-yard field-goal attempt went wide left in the final seconds of the Orange Bowl, an 18-16 loss to Florida State, Nebraska came back in 1994 to win Osborne's first consensus title, though despite the 13-0 record it was anything from simple, or easy. Quarterback Tommie Frazier was sidelined after the fourth game by blood clot problems in his right knee, and replacement Brook Berringer was slowed by a partially collapsed lung. He still managed to lead a 24-17 victory against Miami at the Orange Bowl, and voters rewarded the Cornhuskers despite Penn State also finishing unbeaten at 12-0.

"We didn't just win this for ourselves, we won this for the whole state of Nebraska," co-captain Terry Connealy said.

With Frazier able to return, Berringer went back to the bench in 1995 when Nebraska was able to defend its title and no opponent could come within 14 points of the Cornhuskers. Tragically, Berringer died the following spring in a plane crash.

"The Brook I knew, there was nothing he could have done better," Osborne said. "The length (of his life) was not what you would have liked. But the quality couldn't have been better."

Thanks to a 42-17 victory against No. 3 Tennessee in the Orange Bowl, Osborne's final game, Nebraska was able to claim a split title after coaches leapfrogged it over Michigan in their final poll. Osborne called the squad "probably a little more talented than '94, certainly not near as controversial as '95. That was nice. So it was just kind of a nice way to go.

"Great leadership on the part of the players, and I didn't have to do much."

Between Devaney and Osborne, who in 2000 won a seat in the U.S. House of Representatives, Nebraska appeared in a record 35 consecutive bowl games (1969-2003), including 17 straight January bowl appearances (1981-1997).

To top it off, according computer analyst Jeff Sagarin, the best major college football team since 1956 was the 1995 Cornhuskers, led by Frazier, which won their regular-season games by an average of 38.7 points and destroyed Florida in the Fiesta Bowl for the national championship, 62-24. Second place was the 1971 team, which at 13-0 finished ahead of No. 2 Oklahoma and No. 3 Colorado. "We're the only undefeated team," Devaney said at the time. "I can't see how the Pope himself would vote for Notre Dame."

Nebraska had one other comparable stretch in terms of record, when E.O. Stiehm's teams went 35-2-3 from 1911-15. Leading the 1915 team was Guy Chamberlain, who moved from halfback to end after the 7-0-1 season in 1914. Contributing to the 8-0 campaign was a 20-19 victory against Notre Dame, with then-assistant coach Knute Rockne calling Chamberlain "the key to Nebraska's victory." In his final collegiate game, Chamberlain moved back to halfback and scored five touchdowns in a 52-7 victory against Iowa.

George Halas called him "the greatest two-way end in the history of the game."

NOTRE DAME FIGHTING IRISH

Consensus national titles (1936–present): 1943, 1946, 1947, 1949, 1966, 1973, 1977, 1988
Other national titles: 1919, 1920, 1924, 1927, 1929, 1930, 1938, 1953, 1964, 1967, 1970, 1989, 1993

The Gipper. The Four Horsemen. Rudy.

Ok, scratch that last one for Knute Rockne.

When it comes to college football, the University of Notre Dame *is* history. Not only is South Bend, Indiana, the home of the Golden Dome and Touchdown Jesus, but the location of the College Football Hall of Fame as well. That's fitting because Notre Dame has had more inductees, 41, than any other school, and by a wide margin (Michigan is second with 27).

To some people the Fighting Irish is college football, and the very definition of athletic tradition. Even the fight song, the "Notre Dame Victory March," is the most recognized song that sports has to offer.

Notre Dame is the place where they say, "Play like a champion today," which is also on a sign that each player touches on his way to the field before games. The Irish have backed it up with 11 consensus national championships, eight since the Associated Press poll came into existence in 1936, and seven Heisman Trophies (Angelo Bertelli, who only played six games before joining the Marines in 1943; quarterback John Lujack, 1947; end Leon Hart, 1949; halfback John Lattner, 1953; quarterback Paul Hornung, 1956; quarterback John Huarte, 1964; and wide receiver Tim Brown, 1987).

It says a lot when Joe Montana is not considered your best player (look up George Gipp's statistics sometime, the halfback is still high on the school's all-time rushing list with 2,341 yards and he also passed for 1,769 yards, scored 156 points, punted and returned kicks), or Ara Parseghian the best coach. Neither is Frank Leahy, who compiled an 87-11-9 record during his reign, and Dan Devine went 53-16-1 from 1975-80 with a national title during his six-year stint. Devine's .764 winning percentage among those who coached more than five seasons only ranks sixth.

Or how about Hornung's Heisman? It marked the only time the award has gone to a player on a losing team. He beat out Johnny Majors of Tennessee, Tommy McDonald and Jerry Tubbs of Oklahoma, Jim Brown at Syracuse, Ron Kramer at Michigan, John Brodie of Stanford and Jim Parker at Ohio State.

In short, Notre Dame is the New York Yankees of college football, and plays in a stadium that's the equivalent of Yankee Stadium, which is also fitting because both were built by Osborn Engineering Company of Cleveland. Not only does it ooze history, but some consider it a football shrine.

Opened in 1930, the stadium was designed by Rockne, who from 1918-30 compiled a 105-12-5 record, including five undefeated seasons. When he died at age 43, March 31, 1931 in a plane crash at Bazaar, Kansas, Will Rogers paid tribute: "Notre Dame was Knute Rockne's address, but every gridiron in America was his home." The gravesite a few miles west of campus simply reads: "Knute Rockne—Father."

Over the years, Notre Dame has enjoyed countless last-minute victories, but also a number of dips in the program, usually followed by claims that Notre Dame puts itself at a competitive disadvantage due to its rigorous admissions standards.

Arguably, the low point came in the early 1960s, when five straight sub-.500 seasons included records of 2-8 in 1960, and 2-7 in 1963. That led to Parseghian's hiring in 1964, and over the following 11 seasons the Irish went 95-17-4.

While there have been so many well-chronicled great moments in Notre Dame's history, there are also a large number which don't quite get the attention they deserve. For example, the 1929 team, with guard Bert Metzger, helmetless guard Jack Cannon and quarterback Frank Carideo, played every game on the road with Notre Dame Stadium still under construction. It finished 9-0, and then successfully defended its title in 1930 (10-0).

Creighton Miller led the nation in rushing with 911 yards in 1943 as 9-1 Notre Dame won the national championship. He also skipped every day of spring practice during his career to play golf. Leahy later admitted, "He was the best halfback I ever coached." (To provide an idea of how high praise that was, Leahy said of the 1949 team, which went on to win the national championship, "We'll have the worst team Notre Dame has ever had." About that same squad, Red Grange said, "It's the greatest college team I've ever seen." Of course, Rockne described his team's prospects in 1929 as "fair.")

The 1977 team was led in part by defensive end Ross Browner, who finished fifth in Heisman voting, with the Irish (11-1) securing the national title by snapping Texas' 30-game winning streak in the Cotton Bowl, 38-10. A year later, Montana, despite a nasty case of the flu, led a fierce comeback against Houston, rallying from 22 points down with eight minutes remaining to defeat Houston in the Cotton Bowl, 35-34.

More recently, the reins were turned over to Charlie Weis in 2005, who in his first year had Notre Dame in the Bowl Championship Series, but had title hopes dashed by Southern California's dramatic last-second controversial touchdown plunge by Matt Leinart midway through the season.

"People were pretty shocked and devastated," quarterback Brady Quinn said.

But should the Irish keep this up, Notre Dame will not just invoke images of golden helmets, green shamrocks and students dressed up as leprechauns (FYI, before 1965 the official mascot was an Irish terrier dog, usually named Clashmore Mike), rather South Bend will once again be the home to legends, the kind of which movies are made.

Like, for example, the 1924 team, which Rockne considered both his best and favorite. Notre Dame outscored the opposition 258-44 during its nine-game regular season and then crushed Stanford in the Rose Bowl, 27-10. It was the last bowl game the Irish would play for 45 years, but the team was best known for the backfield including Harry Stuhldreher, Don Miller, Jim Crowley and Elmer Layden.

"I think I sensed that the backfield was a product of destiny," Rockne said. "At times they caused me a certain amount of pain and exasperation, but mainly they brought me great joy."

For those that haven't made the connection yet, here's the more famous quote about the backfield: "Outlined against a blue, gray October sky, the Four Horsemen rode again," Grantland Rice wrote in the *New York Herald-Tribune* on October 19, 1924. "In dramatic lore, they are known as famine, pestilence, destruction and death. Those are only aliases. Their real names are Stuhldreher, Miller, Crowley and Layden."

OHIO STATE BUCKEYES

Consensus national titles (1936–present): 1942, 1954, 1957, 1961, 1968, 2002
Other national titles: 1933, 1944, 1969, 1970, 1973, 1974, 1975

Since 1936, they've punctuated home football games at Ohio State University the exact same way, with a bit of staccato.

After leading the "Skull Session" at St. John Arena, "The Best Damn Band in the Land," invades Ohio Stadium through the north tunnel and takes the field. When it finally performs its "Script of Ohio" formation, the roars of 100,000-plus fans reaches a crescendo when the high-stepping drum major points to a spot and the ceremonial dotting of the "i" is completed. The hat is doffed and the person bows in each direction.

Comedian Bob Hope once had the honor of dotting the "i," as did legendary coach Woody Hayes (1951-78), who was as animated on the sideline as he was successful.

Ohio State has won six national championships (1942, 1954, 1957, 1961, 1968 and 2002), and seven Heisman Trophies (Les Horvath, 1944; Vic Janowicz, 1950; Howard Cassady, 1955; Archie Griffin, 1974-75; Eddie George, 1995; and Troy Smith, 2006), including the only player to win the award twice.

Although he was just 5-foot-9, 180 pounds, Griffin accumulated 5,589 rushing yards, including 100 or more in 31 consecutive games, an NCAA record. Despite this, in 1975 Griffin cast the deciding vote among teammates to name quarterback Cornelius Greene the team's MVP.

Hayes, who once said "You win with people," called Griffin "a better young man than he is a football player, and he's the best football player I've ever seen."

FYI, Griffin is also the only player to start in four Rose Bowls and was named Big 10 MVP twice (1973-74), but not in 1975 when he won his second Heisman. As a sophomore in 1973, Griffin had 1,428 rushing yards (more than he had as a senior, 1,357) and finished fifth in Heisman voting behind winner John Cappelletti of Penn State, while teammate John Hicks, a tackle, was second.

The coach had a number of great players, including halfback "Hopalong" Cassady, who led the Buckeyes to the 1954 national title and won the 1955 Heisman Trophy (similar to Horvath, who behind tackle Bill Willis led Ohio State to the consensus national championship in 1942 and won the Heisman in 1944. He didn't play in 1943 due to a rule that prohibited him while in dentist school—it was quickly changed). Despite lining up both ways, he had 2,374 career rushing yards and scored 37 touchdowns. Hayes once said Cassady "was the most inspirational player I have ever seen."

Hayes' best team was probably the 1968 squad, despite starting five sophomores on offense and six on defense, including safety Jack Tatum, nicknamed "The Assassin." Ohio State upset No. 1 Purdue, 13-0, finished the regular season 9-0, and defeated Southern California in the Rose Bowl, 27-16, for the national championship. A total of 11 players from the team earned All-American standing during their careers and six because first-round draft selections.

During his 28 years, Hayes won 205 games, 13 Big Ten titles and three national championships. The former lieutenant commander in the Navy once said "All good commanders want to die in the field," but his emotions got the best of him at the 1978 Gator Bowl when he punched Clemson nose guard Charlie Bauman after his interception sealed the Tiger's 17-15 victory. Hayes was fired the next day.

Nevertheless, his legacy is still felt today, and will forever be a part of the program's lore. In 1974, when Hayes greeted President Gerald Ford, who played football at Michigan, at the Columbus airport, the photo caption in the newspaper read: "Woody Hayes and Friend."

At Ohio State, they ring the 2,420-pound Victory Bell, which hangs in the stadium's southeast tower, after wins. The final practice before the annual Michigan game is called "Senior Tackle," and has attracted more than 20,000 fans (when open to the public). The highlight is when each senior hits the tackling sled once.

They also paint Michigan's "M" in urinals throughout Columbus, and some people only refer to the rival as "that school up north." Hayes began that tradition, in part leading to the tall tale that he once pushed his car across the state border rather than purchase gasoline in Michigan.

The roots of another popular tradition go back to 1934, when in his pregame speech Francis Schmidt, who incidentally was famous for running trick plays, said: "Those fellows are human; they put their pants on one leg at a time." Ohio State won 34-0, and even though Michigan uncharacteristically finished 1-7 that season, the Pants Club was subsequently created. Membership goes to any Buckeyes player who takes part in a victory over the Wolverines.

Although many believe Michigan-Ohio State to be the best rivalry in college football today (something fans in Alabama rigorously dispute), before the No. 1 vs. No. 2 matchup in 2006, dramatically won by the Buckeyes 42-39, its heyday was from 1969-78, a period known as the "Ten Year War."

That particular stretch began when No. 1 Ohio State, which had destroyed its first eight opponents that season 371-69 and was riding a 22-game winning streak, lost at Michigan, and former Hayes assistant Bo Schembechler, 24-12.

Strangely enough, a loss to Michigan helped lead to Hayes' hiring. In 1950, the temperature in Columbus was 10 degrees with winds up to 40 mph that blew snow everywhere. When the athletic directors met before kickoff to discuss the idea of postponing the game, Michigan's Fritz Crisler supposedly said, "We're here and we're not coming back down next week." In front of 50,000-plus fans who managed to show up, the teams combined for 68 total yards, with Michigan scoring a touchdown and safety off blocked punts to pull out a 9-3 victory.

After going 0-3-1 against the Wolverines (but 21-10-2 against everyone else), Buck-eyes coach Wes Fesler was fired. Hayes lost his first game against Michigan 7-0, but was on the winning end of a 27-7 thumping in 1952.

John Cooper went 111-43-4 at Ohio State, but was fired after the 2000 season due to his 2-10-1 record against Michigan. Jim Tressel replaced him and has won four of five games against the Wolverines, but was also on the winning side of the dramatic 2003 Fiesta Bowl in which the Buckeyes pulled out a 31-24 double-overtime victory against Miami to dot each "i" in the words "national championship."

"We've always had the best damn band in the land," Tressel said. "Now we've got the best damn team in the land."

OKLAHOMA SOONERS

Consensus national titles (1936–present): 1950, 1955, 1956, 1974, 1975, 1985, 2000

Other national titles: 1915, 1949, 1953, 1957, 1967, 1973, 1978, 1980, 1986, 2003

Only at the University of Oklahoma could football fans sing the line, "When you say Bud, you said it all," and actually mean it.

To them, the King of the Sooners is actually a Minnesota native who was a former aircraft-carrier deck officer working for the family mortgage-trading business before join-ing Jim Tatum's staff in 1946.

The lack of excitement the office world provided was soon offset when just a year later, at the age of 31, Bud Wilkinson was promoted and unleashed his split-T formation on college football. The result was a new national powerhouse. The Sooners went 7-2-1 in his first season, followed by records of 10-1, 11-0 and 10-1, with Paul "Bear" Bryant's Kentucky Wildcats snapping the 31-game winning streak with a 13-7 victory at the 1951 Sugar Bowl. The 1949 team outscored opponents 364-88 and topped the season with a 35-0 victory against LSU in the Sugar Bowl.

During his 17 seasons in Norman, Wilkinson had an incredible record of 145-29-4. Oklahoma won national championships in 1950, 1955 and 1956, and from 1953-57 racked up a major-college record 47 consecutive victories (snapped by Notre Dame in 1958, 7-0) despite having stalwarts like Nebraska and Texas on the schedule. Center Jerry Tubbs was one of the players who after three varsity years finished his career without expe-riencing a single loss.

Additionally, the 1956 Sooners averaged 46.6 points per game, handing Texas its worst loss since 1908, 45-0, and pounded Notre Dame at South Bend, 40-0.

"Losing is easy," Wilkinson said. "It's not enjoyable, but easy."

Overall, Oklahoma has won seven consensus national titles, the most recent in 2000 when despite being a 10-point underdog to Florida State in the Orange Bowl, Heisman Trophy runner-up quarterback Josh Heupel led Bob Stoops' Sooners to a 13-2 victory.

"We wanted to be part of the comeback at Oklahoma," Heupel said after completing 25 of 39 passes for 214 yards. "It's not a Cinderella season. It's a dream come true. We're going to be on top for a long, long time."

"I think we can say it now, Oklahoma is back," Stoops said of Oklahoma's first consensus title in 15 years. "We weren't just happy to be here. We fully expected to win."

The program has enjoyed four Heisman Trophies (Billy Vessels, 1952; Steve Owens, 1969; Billy Sims, 1978; and Jason White, 2003), and won five Outland Trophies—the most notable of which was Lee Roy Selmon in 1975.

From 1967-69, Owens scored 56 touchdowns and had a string of 17 consecutive 100-yard games. His senior year, he led the nation with 1,523 rushing yards and 138 points. Sims won the award as a junior when he accumulated 1,762 rushing yards and 20 touchdowns. Although he led the nation in both categories again as a senior (1,506 and 22), Sims finished second to Southern California's Charles White for the Heisman.

Many consider Selmon the best player in program history. The youngest of nine children, two of his brothers also played for the Sooners and fans used to include "God bless Mrs. Selmon," in the pregame prayer. During his three years as a starter, Oklahoma went 32-1-1 and won two national championships. The education major was also named a National Football Foundation Scholar-Athlete in 1975 and devoted ten hours per week to volunteer projects. Selmon wound up being the first-overall selection of the 1976 National Football League draft by the Tampa Bay Buccaneers, and was eventually inducted into the Pro Football Hall of Fame.

Chuck Fairbanks revitalized the program (52-15-1 from 1967-72) and Barry Switzer (157-29-4) won national championships in 1974 and 1975 before numerous off-field issues kept the program in the national spotlight, but for all the wrong reasons. After numerous pleas, including one from former linebacker Brian Bosworth (who after rival Texas settled for a game-tying field goal in the 1984 game said that burnt orange "makes me puke"), Switzer stepped down in June 1989.

Regardless, Oklahoma has seemingly always had a rugged reputation. Its spirit group is called the Ruf/Neks, and the original Conestoga wagon and two Shetland ponies, Boomer and Sooner, which circle the field on game days, were donated in 1964 (although when the Sooner Schooner came on the field to celebrate an apparent field goal that had been nullified by penalty during the 1985 Orange Bowl, Switzer said "Those ponies didn't know what that yellow flag meant," after the subsequent attempt missed and Oklahoma lost to Washington, 28-17). But that image didn't really start to take hold until Wilkinson arrived.

"His teams dispelled the Dust Bowl Grapes of Wrath image of the Depression years," said former university president George Cross, who hired Wilkinson. "They made Oklahoma proud and called national attention to the state's potential."

PENN STATE NITTANY LIONS
Consensus national titles (1936–present): 1982, 1986
Other national titles: 1911, 1912, 1969, 1981, 1994

When it comes to Pennsylvania State University football, here are the answers to the three most commonly asked questions by outsiders:

Beaver Stadium, which opened in 1960, and Happy Valley are located in the heart of Pennsylvania's central valley, almost square between Pittsburgh, Philadelphia, Erie and Scranton, which are basically in the four corners of the state and each at least a 2½-hour drive.

The campus is in the shadow of Mount Nittany. It's believed that the word "Nittany" derives from a Native American term meaning "single mountain" (although some say it's named after Indian princess Nita-Nee). The Nittany Lion mascot dates back to 1907, when the baseball team adopted the lion part from Princeton. Mountain lions roamed central Pennsylvania until the 1880s.

Even with the large trifocals, white socks, black shoes and rolled up pant legs, it's not true that Joe Paterno was around to see the real lions.

When Paterno took over in 1966, Penn State was known as a good program, but hardly great. Primarily, its reputation centered around two successful time periods.

Coach Hugo Bezdek led the program from 1918-29, during which Penn State enjoyed a 30-game unbeaten streak with three ties from 1919-22. It peaked during this final season with an appearance in the Rose Bowl, a 14-3 loss to Southern California. Mike Palm and "Light Horse" Harry Wilson (the nickname stemmed from a comparison to Revolutionary War hero "Lighthorse Harry" Lee, father of Robert E. Lee) led the only scoring drive, a 20-yard drop kick by Palm. Other standouts for Bezdek included end Bob Higgins (who returned to coach Penn State and went 91-57-11 from 1930-48) and quarterback Glenn Killinger.

Rip Engle—who at age 14 drove a mule in a Pennsylvania coal mine and at 19 was a mine supervisor—compiled a 104-48-4 record from 1950-65, with two appearances in both the Gator and Liberty bowls. Among his standout players was "Riverboat" Rich Lucas, who finished second in voting for the 1959 Heisman Trophy behind LSU's Billy Cannon. He led the Nittany Lions in rushing (325 yards), completed 58 of 117 passes for 913 yards, punted 20 times for a 34.0 yard average, and as a safety returned five interceptions for 114 yards.

"I'll never forget the Illinois game," Engle said. "Illinois had a first down on the four, but four plays netted zero yards, with Richie making all four tackles, on both sides of the field, from his defensive halfback position."

During Engle's 16-year stint, Paterno, an English major from Brown University who initially said that he never wanted to coach football, was hired as an assistant. When he took over, Paterno talked of a "grand experiment" to prove a school could both educate players and win football games. At the time, it was seen as arrogant and self-righteous. Today he's simply viewed as being great.

During his 40-plus year reign, Paterno has recorded the second-most Division I victories with 363 though 2006, narrowly trailing only Florida State's Bobby Bowden. The Nittany Lions have won two national championships (1982 and 1986), recorded four unbeaten and untied seasons, and 22 bowl victories.

Under his direction, the school's string of consecutive non-losing seasons wasn't snapped until 1988 at 49. He's notched wins at the Orange, Cotton, Fiesta, Liberty, Sugar, Aloha, Holiday, Citrus, Rose, Hall of Fame, Outback and Alamo bowls, and Beaver Stadium's capacity was recently expanded to 107,282.

"I never thought I would get to 100," Paterno said during a press conference in 1998. "I never thought I would stay in coaching that long. Anybody who figures on staying in it as long as I have has got to be a little kooky, and maybe that explains it."

Paterno has had a Heisman winner with running back John Cappelletti in 1973 (1,522 rushing yards and 17 touchdowns), and other standout running backs like Franco Harris and Larry Johnson. But otherwise Penn State is known for being Linebacker U.

In 2005, junior Paul Posluszny joined an impressive group of All-Americans at that position, including LaVar Arrington, Greg Buttle, Shane Conlan, Jack Ham, Dennis Onkotz, Brandon Short and John Skorupan.

Ham helped lead Penn State to undefeated seasons in 1968-69, and finished with 251 career tackles, 143 unassisted.

"Jack Ham's career is a monument to the work ethic," Paterno said. "He was not a highly recruited athlete, but his exceptional intelligence and capacity for hard work made him an extraordinary football player. I don't think any of us knew then what an enormous talent we were getting. Jack Ham will always be the consummate Penn Stater."

Posluszny, who returned for his senior season in 2006, was also Paterno's 70th first-team All-American.

When the Nittany Lions posted losing records four out of five seasons from 2000-2004, many thought it was time for JoePa to retire. After all, when his coaching career began at Penn State, Harry Truman was president, the Dodgers were playing baseball in Brooklyn, and Paul W. "Bear" Bryant was just beginning to make a name for himself as a head coach ... at Kentucky.

(Incidentally, Paterno was on the winning side against Bryant and Alabama once as an assistant, 1959, but lost all four head coaching matchups. The Crimson Tide beat Penn State in the 1975 Sugar Bowl, 13-6, and the rematch to clinch the 1978 national championship, 14-7. Alabama also won at Penn State in 1981, 31-16, setting up Bryant's record-setting 315th win the following week at Auburn, and the Nittany Lions won the 1982 national championship despite a 42-21 loss at Alabama at Legion Field during Bryant's final season.

"He was obviously a great football coach and had a great presence about him," Paterno said about Bryant in 2000. "He was a real fun guy to be around one-on-one. He was a very, very competitive football coach who did a great job. Obviously, we didn't have much luck against him. He was a formidable opponent; there is no question about it.")

He disagreed, and in 2005 led Penn State to an 11-1 season, topped off by a 26-23 3OT victory against Bowden and Florida State in the Orange Bowl. The following year Paterno broke his shinbone and tore two ligaments in his left knee in a sideline collision during a loss to Wisconsin. He watched the next game from home, the first he'd missed since 1977, but saw both the season finale against Michigan State and the Outback Bowl against Tennessee from the press box. Penn State won both to finish 9-4.

"They need me like they need a hole in the head," Paterno said after the 20-10 victory against the Volunteers. "But I don't like it up there. It's not much fun."

That's because Paterno, who was born in 1926, thinks of himself as more old-school than anything, a perfect match to his team's simple dark blue uniforms and white helmets with a single stripe down the middle.

"I don't think our uniforms look that bad," Paterno once said. "I think they say something to kids about team-oriented play and an austere approach to life."

SOUTHERN CALIFORNIA

Consensus national titles (1936–present): 1962, 1967, 1972, 1974, 1978, 2003, 2004

Other national titles: 1928, 1929, 1931, 1932, 1933, 1939, 1976, 1979, 2002

Believe it or not, Southern California used to be known as the Methodists and the Wesleyans. But that was before 1912, when athletic director Warren Bovard asked *Los Angeles Times* sports editor Owen Bird to come up with a more appropriate nickname, eventually resulting in the uniquely titled Trojans.

Nowadays, the word most associated with the program under Pete Carroll's direction is "Dynasty."

Carroll told his team prior to the start of the 2003 season, "If you stay with me, I'll take you places you've never been," and he was correct. Since 2002, USC has compiled an amazing record of 69-6 and been in the title picture each and every year.

According to the Associated Press poll, it finished No. 4 in 2002, No. 1 in both 2003 and 2004, and No. 2 in 2005 and "slumped" back to No. 4 in 2006 after 11 players were selected in the previous National Football League draft. During that time period, it also had three Heisman Trophy winners with Carson Palmer (2002), Matt Leinart (2004), and Reggie Bush (2005).

That gives the program seven Heismans overall, matching its number of consensus national championships since 1936. Overall, the Trojans claim 11 national titles to go with 36 Pac-10 championships, and 30 Rose Bowl appearances.

Although USC won four national championships under Howard Jones from 1928-1939—including the 1931 team which boasted Hall of Famers John Baker, "Tay" Brown, Aaron Rosenberg and Ernie Smith on the line in front of the "Thundering Herd" backfield that featured Erny Pinckert—John McKay is viewed as the coach with the strongest legacy. From 1962-81, the Trojans won five national titles (the last under his popular replacement, John Robinson), played in 11 Rose Bowls and took home four Heismans, while McKay simultaneously emerged as one of college football's true characters.

"Well, gentlemen, I guess I wasn't so stupid today," McKay said after a 21-20 victory against UCLA in 1967. [Note: His most famous quote came while coaching the expansion Tampa Bay Buccaneers. When a reporter asked about the execution of his offense, McKay quipped that he was in favor of it. FYI, his quarterback in 1976 was Steve Spurrier.]

"He knew when to loosen a team up and he knew how to get after you," former USC quarterback Craig Fertig once said. "You'd never have to worry about him slapping a player. He could do it with his tongue."

From 1960-75, McKay compiled a 127-40-8 record, including just 17 conference losses during those 16 seasons. Over his last nine years, USC went 18-3 against its two biggest rivals, UCLA and Notre Dame.

The 1974 game against the Fighting Irish, dubbed "The Comeback," is still talked about in Los Angeles. Despite a 24-0 deficit in the second quarter, tailback Anthony Davis (with Ricky Bell at fullback before he had 1,875 yards the following year to finish second for the Heisman) sparked the Trojans with a 102-yard kickoff return to open the second half and USC went on to score 55 points in just under 17 minutes.

"We turned into madmen," Davis said.

The offensive onslaught was comparable to the 2005 Orange Bowl, when Leinart threw five touchdown passes to lead a 55-19 rout of No. 2 Oklahoma for the national championship in the first meeting of Heisman winners (Jason White was the 2003 recipient).

"I think they're great and they sure proved it," Sooners coach Bob Stoops said. "We just got whupped."

He and Bush nearly three-peated, only to be stymied by Heisman runner-up Vince Young and Texas in the Rose Bowl, 41-38, in what was called an instant classic.

"I still think we're a better team," Leinart said afterward. "They just made the plays in the end."

McKay coached offensive standouts like Pat Haden, Lynn Swann and Ron Yary, but it was under his direction that the "Tailback U" moniker emerged with the Trojans' trademark I-formation attack, beginning with Mike Garrett in 1965.

O.J. Simpson became the school's second Heisman winner in 1968 when he set the NCAA single-season rushing record with 1,709 yards. He also equaled or set 19 NCAA, conference and USC records before going on to establish the NFL single-season rushing record with 2,003 yards in 1973. In 1979, Charles White finished his career with 5,598 regular-season rushing yards, 6,245 including bowls.

"I don't remember ever playing against a tailback who can run like White," Paul W. "Bear" Bryant said after the running back had 199 rushing yards to lead a 24-14 victory against Alabama en route to the 1978 national championship.

White was followed by Marcus Allen, college football's first 2,000-yard rusher with 2,342 in 1981, averaging 212.9 yards per game. Setting another standard were Bush and LenDale White, when both exceeded 1,000 yards in 2005. Overall, a USC running back has recorded a 1,000-yard rushing season 26 times.

Other standouts have included Ronnie Lott, Tony Boselli, Mark Carrier, Jack Del Rio and Junior Seau.

It adds up to quite a program, one worthy of a conquering moniker.

"USC's not the No. 1 team in the country," Washington State coach Jim Sweeney on the 1972 national champion Trojans. "The Miami Dolphins are better."

TENNESSEE VOLUNTEERS

Consensus national titles (1936–present): 1938, 1951, 1998

Other national titles: 1940, 1950, 1956, 1967

When it comes to turning a Saturday afternoon in the fall into grand spectacle, the University of Tennessee is pretty tough to top.

There's the "T," the trademark bright orange, the crammed stadium seating more than 104,000, the Volunteer Navy which floats to games, the coonhound mascot named Smokey, the checkerboard end zone, and, of course, Rocky Top—even though it isn't the official fight song, but nonetheless played seemingly nonstop by the Pride of the Southland Band during games.

What Tennessee football is really about is General Robert Neyland, who transformed the Volunteers into a national power after taking the job in 1926.

Actually, that was only one of three stints for the West Point graduate who served in France during World War I. Twice he was called upon to leave the football team, for a peacetime tour in Panama followed by another tour of duty as a brigadier general in the Pacific theater during World War II. Twice he came back to the Volunteers.

Known for his discipline and hard-nosed approach, Neyland was originally hired to do something about Vanderbilt, to which Tennessee had lost 18 games out of 21. The turnaround was all but immediate, eventually prompting Dean Nathan Daugherty, the faculty chairman of athletics, to call Neyland's hiring the best move he ever made.

Led by quarterback Bobby Dodd, Tennessee went 27-1-2 from 1928-30. The *Atlanta Journal* may have called Dodd "the greatest football player ever developed in the South," but Tennessee fans referred to him warmly as "In Dodd We Trust."

During his three stints, Neyland compiled an amazing record of 173-31-12. In those 216 games, the opponent failed to score 112 times—including all ten regular-season opponents during the 1939 season, and his 71 consecutive scoreless quarters is still an NCAA record.

"If Neyland could score a touchdown against you, he had you beat," said Herman Hickman, one of Neyland's players who went on to join the original staff of *Sports Illustrated*. "If he could score two, he had you in a rout."

Despite missing four games and playing only a minute in the Rose Bowl due to an injury (a 14-0 loss to Southern California), one of the key players on the 1939 team was halfback George "Bad News" Cafego. Behind guards Ed "Big Mo" Molinski and Bob Suffridge, he accumulated 2,139 yards in total offense, averaging 6.1 yards every time he carried the ball. Neyland called him a "practice bum. On the practice field he couldn't do anything right, but for two hours on a Saturday afternoon he did everything an All-American is supposed to do."

Neyland's Volunteers were the consensus national champions in 1951, though they went on to lose to Maryland in the Sugar Bowl, 28-13. Various organizations also voted Tennessee the consensus champion in 1938 and its fans justifiably make a strong case for 1950 as well. Of course, UT's most recent title came in 1998—the first year of the Bowl Championship Series—under Phillip Fulmer, who was noted for saying: "Sometimes you've just got to win ugly."

Even though the Volunteers were ranked first heading into the title game at the Fiesta Bowl, No. 2 Florida State was favored. Wide receiver Peerless Price scored on a long touchdown pass and finished with 199 yards, but Tennessee's defense was the difference. Middle linebacker Al Wilson made nine tackles, cornerback Dwayne Goodrich returned an interception for a touchdown, and Seminoles standout Peter Warrick only had one reception, as Tennessee won, 23-16.

"You can't take anything away from Florida State's defense," Wilson said. "They were the No. 1 defense in the country. We wanted to show we had a pretty good defense as well. I think we did that."

Although Tennessee has never won a Heisman Trophy, it can boast of quarterback Peyton Manning (1994-97), defensive end Reggie White (1980-83), tackle Doug Atkins (1950-52), linebacker Frank Emanuel (1963-65), and halfback Beattie Feathers (1931-33).

Additionally, on opening day of 2006, Tennessee trailed only Miami (42) and Florida State (41) for most active players in the National Football League, with 40. That was the good news. The bad new that season was Tennessee's string of bowl appearances, dating back to 1988, was snapped in 2005. Even so, the Volunteers' 46 bowl appearances (tied with Texas) still only trailed Alabama's 54.

It was also against the Crimson Tide that Tennessee established itself as a national power. On October 20, 1928, Neyland approached Alabama coach Wallace Wade before their game in Tuscaloosa and asked if the game could end early if it got out of hand.

The gamesmanship worked. Halfback Gene McEver returned the opening kickoff 98 yards for a touchdown, and the defense frustrated heavily favored Alabama for a 15-13 victory. The two sides have been fierce rivals since.

Perhaps that's why Knute Rockne once called Neyland "football's greatest coach."

"The general was not the easiest guy to work with Monday through Friday, but on Saturday he was a fatherly figure," tailback Herky Payne said. "On Saturday, he was a warm man who gave you a lot of confidence."

TEXAS LONGHORNS
Consensus national titles (1936–present): 1963, 1969, 1970, 2005
Other national titles: 1914, 1941, 1968, 1977, 1981

Even though the University of Texas played its first football game in 1893, the program's biggest play didn't occur until 2005 at the Rose Bowl.

Down by five points with only seconds remaining, and the national championship at stake, the Longhorns had fourth down with 5 yards to go on the Southern California 8-yard line. All game long, the Trojans had struggled to stop quarterback Vince Young, who would finish with 200 rushing yards and 267 passing yards, yet still no one knew what to expect.

After taking the snap in shotgun formation, Young bounced on his toes while scanning the field for an open receiver. Finding none, he took off toward the right pylon and on its last offensive play of the season Texas won the title when the quarterback scored his third touchdown of the game.

"Do whatever it takes," Young said after the dramatic 41-38 victory.

But in addition to the title, the run also ended approximately 25 years of unfulfilled expectations for the Longhorns, who had developed a reputation for having a powerhouse program, with seemingly endless talent, that couldn't win big games.

For example, since 1998, Mack Brown's worst season still resulted in nine wins, and his teams had at least 10 wins in each of the four seasons prior to 2005. However, during that same time period, Texas played in only two Big 12 Championship games and lost both.

Although Texas has won two Heisman Trophies (Earl Campbell in 1977, and Ricky Williams in 1998), and used to all but dominate the Southwest Conference before it folded, the heart of its legacy stems from Darrell Royal.

After the former All-American quarterback took over the program in 1957, Texas quickly ascended to the top of the college football world, culminating in 1963 with an 11-0 record and 28-6 victory against Navy, and Heisman Trophy winner Roger Staubach, in the Cotton Bowl to win its first consensus national championship.

"Tune in your television to the Cotton Bowl and you'll laugh yourself silly," Pittsburgh sports journalist Myron Cope made the mistake of saying beforehand. "Texas is the biggest fraud ever perpetrated on the football public."

Royal's best team was probably the 1969 squad. A year after he and offensive coordinator Emory Ballard unveiled the wishbone (which Paul "Bear" Bryant would learn and incorporate into his offense at Alabama a couple years later), Texas' running game keyed on three All-Americans: halfback Steve Worster, receiver Cotton Speyrer and tackle Bobby Wuensch.

The result was a 10-0 regular season. Texas defeated Notre Dame 21-17 in the Cotton Bowl to win the national championship, and even though the Longhorns lost the rematch in 1970, 24-11, many organizations still voted Texas No. 1, giving Royal his third title in eight years.

Texas' first serious flirtation with the national championship began in 1914, when Dave Allerdice's team went 8-0 and outscored the opposition 358-21. Tackle "Bud" Sprague led the Longhorns to an 8-0-1 record in 1923, when Illinois was the consensus champion, to begin a long trend of outstanding players and coaches enduring near-misses.

Dana Bible (1937-46) went 55-13-2 in his last seven years, including three trips to the Cotton Bowl. Led by multi-talented end Mal Kutner, the 8-1-1 team in 1941 received national title consideration, and four years later the Longhorns finished 10-1 (the lone loss to Rice), and defeated Missouri 40-27 in the Cotton Bowl with quarterback Bobby Layne throwing six touchdown passes.

Layne came back in 1947, under Coach Blair Cherry, and led Texas to a 10-1 season, including a 27-7 victory against Alabama in the Sugar Bowl. Layne set 11 school records, but could muster only a No. 5 finish.

Halfback Chris Gilbert ran for 3,231 yards in 29 games for Texas from 1966-68, the last of which had the Longhorns knocking on another title door. He's believed to be the first player in NCAA history to record three 1,000-yard rushing seasons.

Although Campbell rushed for 4,443 yards during his career, a 38-10 loss to Joe Montana and Notre Dame in the Cotton Bowl, thanks to six turnovers, cost Texas the 1977 championship. The Longhorns went from first to No. 4.

Incidentally, Young had a near-miss himself, in 2004.

In the first-ever meeting against Michigan, he accumulated 372 yards of total offense, including 180 passing and 192 rushing, to account for five Texas touchdowns. It still came down to a 37-yard field goal by Dusty Mangum as time expired for a 38-37 victory. The Longhorns' final ranking? Fifth (fourth according to the coaches).

"There will never be a better game in the Rose Bowl," Brown said afterward. "You had two of the top four winningest programs and it should come down to two seconds left."

Chapter 2

The Contenders

ARIZONA STATE SUN DEVILS

Consensus national titles (1936–present): None

Other national titles: 1970, 1975

Over the years, Arizona State has played in three different conferences (and at times struggled with NCAA penalties), but still successfully made the transition from being known as a program with inflated accomplishments to a postseason staple.

Although the 1970 team finished 11-0, including a perfect 7-0 mark in the Western Athletic Conference and a 48-26 victory against North Carolina in the Peach Bowl (which still didn't get it into the top five of the Associated Press poll, but Poling rated Arizona State No. 1), the Sun Devils are primarily known for two standout seasons.

The first was 1975. Under the direction of Frank Kush (176-54-1, 1958-79), and led by cornerback Mike Haynes ("The best defensive back I've ever seen," Lou Holtz once said) and star wide receiver John Jefferson, the Sun Devils began the season with a 35-12 victory against Washington and didn't stop until they received an invitation to play in the hometown Fiesta Bowl against Nebraska.

Down 14-6 in the third quarter and quarterback Dennis Sproul out of the game with an injury, backup Fred Mortensen threw a 10-yard touchdown pass to Jefferson, followed by a successful two-point conversion. With 4:50 remaining, Danny Kush, the coach's son, kicked a game-winning 29-yard field goal to give Arizona State its biggest victory to date. Although Oklahoma was the consensus national champion, the National Championship Foundation had a split title and the *Sporting News* decreed the Sun Devils its No. 1.

"I treat my players all the same: terrible," said Kush, who in 22 years only had two losing seasons while the Sun Devils went from the Border Conference to the WAC, before finally landing in the Pac-10 in 1978.

The other team was the colorful 1996 squad, which was led by quarterback Jake "The Snake" Plummer, who finished third in Heisman Trophy voting and accumulated 8,827 career passing yards, along with offensive linemen Grey Ruegamer and Juan Roque, and linebackers Derrick Rodgers and Pat Tillman.

On September 21, Arizona State hosted Nebraska in a night game, with the defending national champions riding a 26-game winning streak and favored by 24 points. Additionally, Nebraska had pounded out a 77-28 victory in the previous year's meeting.

Coach Bruce Snyder's staff cheated a safety up toward the line of scrimmage and dared Nebraska to throw. Instead, the defense recorded three safeties en route to a stunning 19-0 upset.

After close wins against Southern California and UCLA (coming back from a 28-7 deficit in the first half), Arizona State seemed destined to win the national championship, but only if it could beat 10-1 Ohio State in the Rose Bowl. Ironically, the Buckeyes were coached by John Cooper, who led the Sun Devils to their first Rose Bowl win ever in 1986 (22-15 against Michigan).

Despite being sacked six times, Plummer rallied Arizona State and his 11-yard touchdown run with 1:40 remaining gave the Sun Devils a 17-14 lead. But Ohio State countered, driving 65 yards and scoring a touchdown with just 19 seconds left on the clock. The loss left the door open for Florida to win its first national championship, and Arizona State finished No. 4.

Although Arizona State's list of prominent athletes includes linebacker Ron Pritchard, quarterback Danny White and defensive end Terrell Suggs (not to mention Reggie Jackson, Barry Bongs and Phil Mickelson), Tillman may be the most beloved. At the height of his National Football League career, he and his brother Kevin, a former ASU baseball player, enlisted in the U.S. Army and became members of the elite U.S. Rangers. Pat was tragically killed by friendly fire in Afghanistan. His No. 42 has subsequently been retired.

"Pat is the most unique kid I ever coached," Snyder told the *Washington Times* in 2002. "The ancient Greeks talked about the combination of mind and body and, boy, this guy has it."

ARKANSAS RAZORBACKS

Consensus national titles (1936–present): 1964
Other national titles: 1977

Woooooo, Pig! Sooie! ... Woooooo, Pig! Sooie! ... "Woooooo, Pig! Sooie! Razorbacks!" Done correctly, the call starts with both hands in the air, fingers waving during the "Woooooo" part. Arms pump down on the word "Pig," and then back into the air for "Sooie."

If one person does it on his or her own, it can look a little silly. If 72,000 fans do it in unison at Donald W. Reynolds Razorback Stadium, it may not be a conspiracy (like Arlo Guthrie suggests in "Alice's Restaurant"), but will send a tingling sensation down your spine.

Naturally, Arkansas is known for more than just the Hog Call. There's Lance Alworth, Clyde "Smackover" Scott, Wear Schoonover, Darren McFadden, and legendary coach

Frank Boyles—who inherited a program with just five winning seasons over the previous 19 years and went 144-58-5 over the next 19 years with 10 bowl games and seven Southwest Conference titles.

If that's not enough name recognition, check out the 1964 national championship team, which was the first to don the Razorbacks logo on the helmets. Four men associated with the team, including, of course, Broyles, would coach national championship teams: Jimmy Johnson (Miami), Johnny Majors (Pittsburgh), and Barry Switzer (Oklahoma). Johnson and Switzer are the only coaches in history to win a college national championship and a Super Bowl, both with the Dallas Cowboys, owned by their former Arkansas comrade Jerry Jones. Jones and Johnson were both guards, Majors and Switzer were assistant coaches.

The 1964 team was also a bit of a surprise, especially after starting the season by struggling to victories against Oklahoma State (14-10), and Tulsa (31-22). It led to a showdown with defending national champion Texas, which had lost one regular-season game in four years. On October 19, the low-scoring game was decided by possibly the most exciting play in Razorbacks history, Ken Hatfield's 81-yard punt return for a touchdown thanks to some terrific blocks, including one by Jim Lindsey, en route to a 14-13 victory.

Arkansas, which posted five shutouts that season, didn't allow another point until Cotton Bowl, where Bobby Burnett's fourth-quarter 3-yard touchdown plunge capped an 80-yard drive to finish a 10-7 comeback victory against Nebraska.

The Razorbacks have made two other impressive runs at the title, but fell short.

The first was 1969, when Arkansas won its first nine games by a combined score of 317-51. With Ohio State, which was being touted by *Sports Illustrated* as possibly being the best team of all-time, losing to Michigan, all eyes were on the December 6 meeting between No. 1 Texas and No. 2 Arkansas, tabbed as both the "Big Shootout" and the "Game of the Century." With President Richard Nixon in the stands, Arkansas built up a 14-0 lead heading into the fourth quarter, when the Longhorns' James Street broke a 42-yard touchdown, and later put the game away on fourth-and-3 with a rare long pass resulting in a 44-yard completion to set up the winning score.

"They're a great team. They know how to win and they know how to lose," Nixon said outside the Arkansas locker room.

Texas went on to win the national championship, while 9-2 Arkansas finished third in the coaches' poll, but seventh according to the Associated Press after losing to Ole Miss in the Sugar Bowl, 27-22.

Arkansas was never No.1 in the Associated Press poll during the 1977 season, Lou Holtz's first coaching the Razorbacks, but after an impressive 10-1 season drew No. 2 Oklahoma, led by running back Billy Sims, in the Orange Bowl. With No. 1 Texas losing earlier in the day, the Sooners were playing for the title, but despite Holtz suspending his top two running backs and best receiver for disciplinary reasons, Arkansas crushed Oklahoma, 31-6.

"Your talent determines what you can do," Holtz wrote in his autobiography. "Your motivation determines how much you are willing to do. Your attitude determines how well you do it."

BOSTON COLLEGE EAGLES

Consensus national titles (1936–present): None

Other national titles: None

There may not be a college football fan in the country, if not the world, who doesn't think of quarterback Doug Flutie when Boston College is mentioned.

His miraculous touchdown as time expired to beat defending champion Miami in 1984, 47-45, was not only the signature moment of his career and the program, but arguably of college football in general.

"Some plays will last forever, and some plays, it seems, have a shelf life even longer than that," Flutie said years later.

Ok, the play was a big deal and Flutie went on to win the Heisman Trophy. The reason why the miracle pass gets mentioned here is because it was a key part of Boston College's best season.

The 1984 team also boasted offensive lineman Mike Ruth, who won the Outland Trophy the following season, and wide receiver Gerald Phalen, who helped the Eagles find ways to win. It began with a 38-31 victory against No. 9 Alabama on September 8, and derailed only by a 21-20 loss at West Virginia, and 37-30 defeat at Penn State.

"What that kid does is make people happy to watch football," Joe Paterno said after Boston College's 27-17 victory against Penn State the year before in 1983.

Against Miami, Flutie completed 34 of 46 passes for 472 yards and three touchdowns, compared to Bernie Kosar's 25 of 38 performance for 447 yards and two touchdowns. The icing on the cake was a 45-28 victory against Houston in the Cotton Bowl for a No. 5 final ranking, matching the school's best finish ever.

That occurred in 1940, with a team including future College Football Hall of Fame inductees center Chet "The Gentle Giant" Gladchuk, end Gene Goodreault, fullback Mike Holovak, guard George "The Righteous Reject" Kerr, and halfback Charlie O'Rourke. Before he went on to become a legend at that "other" Catholic school, Notre Dame, Frank Leahy guided Boston College to a 11-0 season, capped by a 19-13 victory against No. 4 Tennessee in the Sugar Bowl. Minnesota, the consensus national champion, and Stanford also finished undefeated, but when the Eagles returned home they were greeted by 100,000 fans in downtown Boston.

"To me, this is the best football program in the world," Leahy said.

Or, at least, thanks to Flutie, one that has no problems dreaming big.

BRIGHAM YOUNG COUGARS

Consensus national titles (1936–present): 1984

Other national titles: None

There's a reason why they call Brigham Young the quarterback factory. Over the years, it's churned out Virgil Carter, Gifford Nielsen, Marc Wilson, Jim McMahon, Gary Sheide, Steve Young, Robbie Bosco, Ty Detmer and Steve Sarkisian.

Between Wilson in 1978 and Detmer in 1991, BYU quarterbacks broke or tied 165 NCAA records. McMahon had the most with 71, but Detmer was the only one to win the Heisman Trophy after passing for 5,188 yards and 41 touchdowns as a junior in 1990.

"He had me running around like a chicken with my head cut off," Penn State linebacker Andre Collins said after the 1989 Holiday Bowl (a 50-39 victory for the Nittany Lions). "We didn't play that bad, Detmer is just that good."

Detmer also led BYU's first win against a No. 1-ranked team, 28-21 against visiting Miami in 1990, but it was Bosco who quarterbacked the biggest victory in school history.

It came at the Holiday Bowl, where the Western Athletic Conference champion was obligated to play on December 21, 1984. The undefeated Cougars didn't reach the top of the polls until they were 11-0, and were far from a unanimous choice, but nevertheless had 6-5 Michigan as its final test.

Bosco was sidelined by a knee injury in the first quarter, but returned in the second, while the Wolverines were able to grind out a 17-10 lead. With 10:51 remaining, the quarterback led the Cougars on an 80-yard drive to tie the game, and with 1:23 left connected with running back Kelly Smith for the game-winning points.

"You're the greatest BYU team that's ever been," LaVell Edwards (1972-2000, 257-101-3) told them after the game.

Prior to his arrival in 1972, the program had won just 173 games with 16 winning seasons out of 47, and been shut out 72 times. That happened only once under Edwards, whose offense averaged 32 points in 361 games. During his 29 years, BYU won 20 WAC titles, with 13 bowl appearances.

One of the primary reasons for the struggles pre-Edwards was due to the school's affiliation with the Church of Jesus Christ of Latter-day Saints, because male students frequently went on two-year missions for the church. Edwards made it easier for them to return and play football.

Outside of 1984, BYU has twice finished in the Associated Press' top 10—No. 7 in 1983, and No. 5 in 1996 after the Cougars (14-1) defeated Kansas State in the Cotton Bowl, 19-15.

"In the South there's Bear Bryant, Darrell Royal and Frank Boyles," ESPN analyst Lee Corso once said. "In the East there's Joe Paterno. In the Midwest there's Bo Schembechler, Woody Hayes and Tom Osborne. And in the West, there's John McKay and LaVell Edwards. He's a legend, and as good a football coach as he was, he's a better man and he did it the right way. He's known throughout the country as a legend."

CALIFORNIA GOLDEN BEARS
Consensus national titles (1936–present): None
Other national titles: 1920, 1921, 1922, 1923, 1937

Cal is one of the few programs best known for a single play, even though it was made by a team that finished just 7-4, and didn't play in a bowl game.

It was the kick return in the final four seconds against John Elway and rival Stanford, the one in which the Golden Bears razzle-dazzled their way not only through the opposing team, but its marching band as well.

For the record, the rugby-style play went Kevin Moen to Richard Rodgers to Dwight Garner (whose knee may have touched the ground) to Rodgers to Mariet Ford to Moen, who took it into the end zone and slammed into trombonist Gary Tyrrell.

"And the Bears ... the Bears ... have won, the Bears have won!" radio announcer Joe Starkey called. "Oh my God! The most amazing, sensational, dramatic, heart-rending, exciting, thrilling finish in the history of college football!"

You really can't blame Starkey, especially since 1952 he could count the number of back-to-back winning seasons on one hand—a string that continued until Jeff Tedford took over in 2002 and returned Cal to the top of the Pac-10.

But that doesn't mean the Golden Bears have never been a national power; far from it. After compiling a record of 24-13-3 during his first four seasons, things really clicked for Andy Smith's squads. The Wonder Teams, with standout "Babe" Horrell at center, went 44-0-4 between 1920 and 1924, including a consensus national championship in 1920.

Cal went 8-0-0 that season, giving up just two touchdowns (one during a 79-7 victory against Nevada) while scoring 510 points, and capped it off with a 28-0 drubbing of Ohio State in the Rose Bowl. It went back the following season and tied Washington & Jefferson, 0-0, for a 9-0-1 finish, and the Golden Bears didn't experience another loss until a 15-0 decision against the Olympic Club in 1925.

"Horrell was about 50 percent of the psychological effect of the Bears," St. Mary's coach Slip Madigan said. "He could get his men together better than any football captain I ever saw. Andy Smith could have stood the loss of five good men better than the graduation of Horrell."

Although Pappy Waldorf's teams finished in the top five three straight years (1948-50), Cal's best team after the creation of the Associated Press poll came the following year, 1937. Coached by Leonard "Stub" Allison, the "Thunder Team" allowed only 33 points and shut out seven opponents, including No. 4 Alabama in the Rose Bowl, 13-0. Although the Bears had numerous standouts like halfback Sam Chapman, center Bob Herwig, and end Harold "Brick" Muller, halfback Vic Bottari may have been the toughest to stop.

"This California team was tough and that Bottari, oohh," Alabama coach Frank Thomas said. Although Cal (10-0-1) did receive some national acclaim, Pitt (9-0-1) was considered the consensus national champion. The Bears finished No. 2.

"Alabama has a pass and a prayer," Mark Ehllinger wrote in the *San Francisco Examiner* after the Rose Bowl. "California had the pass and the necessary power, they didn't need the prayer."

CLEMSON TIGERS
Consensus national titles (1936–present): 1981
Other national titles: None

It's all about a rock, and a hill.

The hill has always been there. When Clemson University's Memorial Stadium was built in time for the 1942 season, seating 20,000, the quickest way to the field was through a gate at the top of the hill beyond the east end zone. It was tabbed "Death Valley" by Lonnie McMillan, coach of Presbyterian (nicknamed the Blue Hose), which from 1930-57 opened every season at Clemson and won only once.

Meanwhile, in the mid-1960s, S.C. Jones, Class of 1919, made a trip to California and upon his return presented Frank Howard with a white flint rock he picked up in Death Valley. Years later, while cleaning out his office, the coach asked Gene Willimon to basically get rid of it.

Instead of throwing the rock away, Willimon, who was the executive secretary of a booster organization, had it mounted and placed at the top of the hill. During its debut game, Clemson came from 18 points down with 17 minutes left to play to defeat Virginia 40-35, thanks, in part, to a 65-yard pass from Jimmy Addison to Jacky Jackson.

A year later, players began to rub the rock as part of their pre-game ritual before running down to the field. Howard supposedly told his players before a 23-6 victory against Wake Forest, "If you're going to give me 110 percent, you can rub that rock. If you're not, keep your filthy hands off."

That's how traditions are born.

Nowadays, the ritual, which includes cannons and the band playing "Tiger Rag," is called "the most exciting 25 seconds in college football from a color and pageantry standpoint." The stadium seats 81,473.

Clemson's rise to prominence began in 1900, when John Heisman led the Tigers to a 19-3-2 record over four seasons. The Tigers have won the most Atlantic Coast Conference titles, and as the only undefeated team in 1981 were the consensus national champions after defeating Nebraska in the Orange Bowl, 22-15. With that, Danny Ford became the youngest coach to ever win the national title at age 33.

Clemson also boasts a booster base nearly as big and wide as former defensive tackle William "The Refrigerator" Perry appeared on the field. He received the nickname from teammate Ray Brown after they tried to get into an elevator together. Brown said Perry took up as much room as a refrigerator.

"Even when I was little, I was big," Perry once said.

But Howard's name is the one synonymous with Clemson, not only for his 165-118-12 record, but his down-home attitude that endeared him to fans. He said that he left his hometown, Barlow Bend, Alabama, "walking barefoot on a barbed-wire fence with a wildcat under each arm." Howard attended the University of Alabama on an academic scholarship and after graduating went to Clemson.

"My first title was line coach, but I also coached track, managed ticket sales, recruited players and had charge of equipment," Howard said. "In my spare time I cut grass, lined tennis courts and operated the canteen while the regular man was out to lunch."

COLORADO BUFFALOES
Consensus national titles (1936–present): 1990
Other national titles: None

It could be argued that no program in college football has experienced such highs and lows—and occasionally at the same time.

Colorado has won a Heisman Trophy with Rashaan Salaam in 1994, won a national championship, and experienced one of greatest clutch plays in history.

On September 24, 1994, the Buffaloes had the ball at their own 15-yard line, with 14 seconds showing on the clock and no times outs. Amazingly, quarterback Kordell Stewart heaved a ball more than 70 yards into the end zone where wide receiver Michael Westbrook caught it off a deflection to beat host Michigan.

"Better than Doug Flutie!" cornerback and wide receiver T.J. Cunningham declared, as Colorado had been down 26-14 with four minutes remaining.

However, the program has also endured numerous scandals—including allegations of sexual assault and a slush fund for athletic department officials—resignations and investigations.

It's been about as steady as the buffalo named Ralphie rumbling on to the field at home games, or the lifestyle of prospectors who originally settled the region.

Nothing demonstrates the whirlwind nature of Colorado football than the reign of Bill McCartney, who was hired away from Michigan, where he had been Bo Schembechler's defensive coordinator, at the age of 42 in 1981.

His first three seasons resulted in a 7-25-1 record, but in 1985 he switched the offense to the wishbone. By the end of the decade the Buffaloes would be playing for the national championship.

"I've never wanted just part of the package, part of the prize," McCartney said. "I want it all."

Colorado finished the 1989 regular season 11-0 and went into the Orange Bowl ranked No. 1. The offense averaged 6.1 yards per rush and 41 points per game, and had dedicated the season to quarterback Sal Aunese, who had died during the offseason.

But the offense sputtered early against Notre Dame, while the Fighting Irish proved to be opportunistic, taking a 14-0 lead in the third quarter and then chewing up the clock with a 17-play, 82-yard drive that all but finished off the 21-6 victory.

The 1990 season didn't start any better as Colorado opened with a tie against Tennessee, barely squeezed out a 21-17 victory against Stanford and then lost at Illinois, 23-22. After close wins against Texas and Washington, the Buffaloes benefited in the epic "fifth down" controversy at Missouri, when officials mistakenly gave Colorado an extra down in the closing seconds, and it used it to score the game-winning touchdown.

Colorado was ranked 12th going into the game, and Associated Press voters knocked it down to No. 14. But against the toughest schedule in the nation, the Buffaloes didn't lose again and eventually rose back to No.1 when they were invited to play a rematch against No. 5 Notre Dame in the Orange Bowl.

At halftime, things looked bleak. Quarterback Darian Hagan and defensive end Kanavis McGhee had both been knocked out of the game, and in the third quarter Notre Dame built up a 9-3 lead. But two substitutes stepped up. Linebacker Paul Rose recovered a fumble and quarterback Charles Johnson sparked the offense, with running back Eric Bienemy's 1-yard touchdown providing a 10-9 lead.

As if to make it more gut-wrenching for both sides, Raghib Ismail appeared to return a punt 91 yards for a last-minute touchdown, but a clipping penalty nullified the play—a call the Irish still dispute.

McCartney won three Big Eight titles during his 13 years and finished No. 3 in 1994, but from 1986-89, 24 players were arrested for various reasons. In a surprise move, McCartney resigned on November 19, 1994, and helped start the evangelical Christian group Promise Keepers.

Colorado's other title run came in 1971 under Eddie Crowder, but it couldn't overcome losses to Nebraska and Oklahoma, as the three teams finished 1-2-3 in the final Associated Press poll.

DUKE BLUE DEVILS
Consensus national titles (1936–present): None
Other national titles: None

There used to be a time when Duke wasn't known as a basketball school, and, in fact, had a stronger reputation in football. Granted, the Blue Devils went a 25-year stretch without a bowl appearance, and have played one postseason game since 1990, but there's a lot more to the program than being the first place Steve Spurrier was a head coach.

Duke has played in all four traditional major bowl games, won 18 league championships between the Southern and Atlantic Coast conferences, and, back when it was known as Trinity College, played in the first football game south of the Mason-Dixon Line (defeating North Carolina 16-0 in 1888).

The pride and joy of the program is the 1938 team, led by Robert O'Mara. Known as the Iron Dukes, the unbeaten and untied team didn't give up a single point during the regular season, an accomplishment that only Tennessee has matched since, in 1939.

Highlighting the regular season, when Duke outscored opponents 114-0 (and won five games by the score of 6-0 or 7-0), was the finale against No. 4 Pitt, played in a snowstorm. Duke's Eric Tipton punted 16 times, 14 of which pinned the Panthers inside their 20-yard line. Bolo Perdue's blocked punt recovered in the end zone was the only score of the game.

However, Duke lost in the Rose Bowl on a touchdown pass by a fourth-string quarterback with 40 seconds remaining, giving Southern California a 7-3 victory.

"I hated to see the boys lose it when they played such a great game," Coach Wallace Wade said. "We did well as long as they used only two teams, but when they put in those third and fourth teams, they were too much for us."

While the Iron Dukes finished No. 3 in the final Associated Press poll, the 1941 team came in one spot higher at No. 2 behind Minnesota (the Gophers were the consensus national champions, but Alabama and Texas also received consideration). Duke hosted the subsequent Rose Bowl, played in Durham due to West Coast safety concerns during World War II, but lost to Oregon State, 20-16. It remains the only time the Rose Bowl was not played in California.

GEORGIA TECH YELLOW JACKETS
Consensus national titles (1936–present): 1990
Other national titles: 1917, 1928, 1951, 1952, 1956

If you ever want to find out whether someone is a serious Georgia Tech fan, ask him or her if they know George P. Burdell. If they've never heard of the mythical person band members page at away games, and was actually listed on 1927 class rosters, they're a fair-weather fan at best.

Otherwise, Georgia Tech's history is as solid as can be ... except the legendary story about end/tackle Bill Fincher (1916-20). During a game a Davidson player hit Fincher and then ran off the field telling his coach how he had knocked his eye out. Fincher later admitted that he removed his porcelain eye before every game.

One of the early Southern powers, Georgia Tech was the first school to win all four traditional major bowls—Rose, Orange, Sugar and Cotton—all under the direction of Bill Alexander (134-95-15).

"Bill gets more out of nothing than any coach in America," Knute Rockne once said, and it was hard to argue. For example, Alexander called halfback Buck Flowers "pound for pound, my greatest player." In 1920, Flowers was listed at 5-foot-8, 152 pounds, "but I weighed only 117 my first year of college ball," he later admitted.

Its first full-time coach was none other than John Heisman, who from 1904-17 compiled a 102-29-7 record and won the school's first national title in 1917 (a rare unanimous choice). In comparison, previous to Heisman's arrival the team had a record of 9-32-5 (1892-1903).

The program's other legendary coach is Bobby Dodd, who from 1945 to 1966 went 165-64-8, including a 31-game unbeaten streak from 1950-53. The 1951 campaign produced an 11-0-1 record which included a regular-season 14-14 tie with Duke and a 17-14 victory over Baylor in the Orange Bowl, and could only be surpassed by the subsequent 1952 season, when the Rambling Wreck was the first in program history to finish 12-0 and also post four shutouts.

"I never compare teams, but I repeat, this team could play in any league," Army coach Red Blaik said after a 45-6 loss.

The Yellow Jackets boasted six first-team All-Americans—center Pete Brown, halfback Leon Hardeman, end Buck Martin, tackle Hal Miller, defensive back Bobby Moorhead and linebacker George Morris—and finished the season with a 24-7 victory against Ole Miss in the Sugar Bowl (Alabama nearly spoiled the perfect mark, but a Morris fumble recovery deep in Crimson Tide territory led to a touchdown and 7-3 victory). But it still had to settle for a No. 2 finish in the Associated Press poll because Michigan State, which was coming off its second-consecutive unbeaten season, was the consensus national champion despite not playing in a bowl game.

Although Dodd said the 1952 team was the best he ever coached, he called the 1962 victory against Alabama and quarterback Joe Namath his biggest win. It snapped the Crimson Tide's 26-unbeaten streak and was decided by a failed two-point conversion for a 7-6 final.

The most legendary season for the Yellow Jackets and Rambling Wreck—both nicknames are acceptable—came in 1990, two years removed from a 3-8 season. Unranked in the preseason, Georgia Tech started to receive serious national attention with a narrow 21-19 victory against Clemson, and, two weeks after a 13-13 tie at North Carolina, dramatically won at No. 1 Virginia, 41-38. In that game, No. 16 Tech trailed 13-0 and 28-14, only to score the winning points with seven seconds remaining.

When it defeated Nebraska in the Florida Citrus Bowl, 45-21, Georgia Tech finished No. 1 in the coaches' poll, while controversial Colorado (11-1-1) topped the Associated Press poll.

Georgia Tech had only 10 coaches in the 1900s, and in terms of individual accomplishments saved its best for last. Quarterback Joe Hamilton was the runner-up for the Heisman Trophy in 1999, when he passed for more than 3,000 yards and ran for 734 more (at the time the most ever by a Division I-A quarterback). For his career, Hamilton threw for 8,882 yards and 65 touchdowns.

ILLINOIS FIGHTING ILLINI

Consensus national titles (1936–present): None
Other national titles: 1914, 1919, 1923, 1927, 1951

Although the idea of homecoming is believed to have originated with Illinois, conceived by students C.F. "Dab" Williams and W. Elmer Ekblaw for the 1910 season, the program is better known for three individuals: Red Grange, Dick Butkus and George Halas.

Although Grange stood just 5-foot-10, 170 pounds (but incredibly muscular from working on an ice truck), the Galloping Ghost was the sport's first true superstar. In 20 games over three years at Illinois he amassed 2,071 rushing yards, 575 passing yards and scored 31 touchdowns.

In 1924, he scored the first four times he touched the ball against Michigan, which coming in had a 22-game winning streak, for a total of 265 yards during a span of 12 minutes. He then sat to rest until the third quarter when Grange came back to score twice more. A year later, he gained 363 yards and scored three touchdowns at Eastern power Penn.

"This man Red Grange of Illinois is three or four men and a horse rolled into one," Damon Runyon wrote.

Grange helped Illinois win the 1923 national championship, Robert Zuppke's third, but it probably wasn't the best team in program history. That distinction goes to the 1914 squad, which went 7-0, outscored opponents 224-22, and shared the title with Texas and consensus choice Army. While the defense posted four shutouts, the offense was led by halfback Bart Macomber and guard Ralph Chapman.

Although Zuppke also won a title in 1927, perhaps his biggest victory came against Minnesota in 1916. While Illinois was 2-2, Minnesota was a 40-point favorite with five All-American candidates.

With Halas out due to an injury, Illinois used only 11 players, went up 14-0, and held on for the 14-9 win. The headline of the *Chicago Herald* said: "Hold on tight when you read this!"

"I am Louis XIV, and you are my court," Zuppke said in his pregame speech. "After us, the deluge. Let them eat cake today, we'll live on bread."

Actually, that comment was pretty tame for Zuppke, who was the innovator of the "pocket" and "screen" passing, "strategy maps" for quarterbacks, and was the first coach to use the 5-4-2 defense. According to the College Football Hall of Fame, seven well-known "Zuppkeisms" are:

> Never let hope elude you; that is life's biggest failure.
> The greatest athlete is one who can carry a nimble brain to the place of action.
> Moral courage is the result of respect from fellow men.
> A good back should keep his feet at all times and never lose his head.
> Men do their best if they know they are being observed.
> Alumni are loyal if a coach wins all his games.
> Advice to freshmen: don't drink the liniment.

Coach Pete Elliott once said that Butkus, "never took a loafing step," and the center/linebacker made an interception to seal the 17-7 victory against Washington at the end of the 1963 season at the Rose Bowl, where fullback Jim Grabowski had 125 rushing yards to be named the game's most valuable player.

Another character from Illinois was lineman Alex Agase (1941-43, 1946, while in 1944-45 he served in the Pacific and was in the battles of Iwo Jima and Okinawa), who scored two touchdowns against Minnesota in 1942. On the first, he stole the ball from Bill Daley and ran 38 yards to the goal line. On the second, he recovered Vic Kulbitski's fumble. Agase, who blocked for 5-5 halfback Buddy Young, was also the Big Ten's most valuable player in 1946.

Since the Associated Press poll was created in 1936, Illinois has finished in the top five three times, including 1951, the most recent undefeated season. The Illini outscored opponents 220-83 with only a scoreless tie against Ohio State preventing the perfect season. By scoring 34 unanswered points in the second half against Stanford, for a 40-7 victory, Illinois received title consideration, but finished No. 4 in the final Associated Press poll.

Otherwise, Illinois has played in one Rose Bowl since 1964, when wide receiver David Williams helped key a 10-game winning streak in 1983.

IOWA HAWKEYES

Consensus national titles (1936–present): None

Other national titles: 1921, 1956, 1958, 1960

One of the most interesting people to ever play college football was 1939 Heisman Trophy winner Nile Kinnick, who was as versatile off the field as on. He led the conference in scoring, total yards, first downs, rushing, passing and pass-completion percentage, and the nation in kickoff-return yardage and tied for the lead in interceptions. He scored 107 of the team's 130 points in eight games, and was named the nation's Outstanding Male Athlete ahead of Joe DiMaggio and Joe Louis.

"This country is okay as long as it produces Nile Kinnicks," Bill Cunningham wrote in the *Boston Globe*. "The football part is incidental."

After college football, Kinnick enrolled in law school, but one year later enlisted in the Naval Air Corps reserve. In 1943 he was flying above the Gulf of Paria in the Caribbean Sea, but instead of attempting to land his oil-leaking plane on to the USS Lexington, which could have endangered planes spotted for takeoff, he ditched it into the sea, and was never found.

At 6-1-1, Iowa was ranked No. 9 in the final Associated Press poll in 1939; one of 11 times it would finish in the top 10.

Although Hayden Fry is the coach most associated with Iowa, the Hawkeyes never finished better than 10-1-1 during his 19-year reign that resulted in a 143-89-6 record and three Rose Bowl appearances (all losses)—although the 1985 team was led by quarterback Chuck Long, who was runner-up to Bo Jackson for the Heisman Trophy by the slimmest margin in the award's history (1,509-1,464).

Actually, Iowa had its greatest success under Forest Evashevski, and his wing-T offense, in the 1950s. His first four games in 1952 were all losses by a combined score of 129-54, when No. 16 Ohio State visited for homecoming. He installed a new offense and new defense, and the Buckeyes never got a sniff of the end zone. Iowa scored in the final minutes for an 8-0 victory.

The following season, 1953, Iowa played a part in the controversial national championship with its season-ending 14-14 tie at Notre Dame, causing voters to bump the Fighting Irish down to No. 2 behind Maryland.

It challenged for the title again three years later in 1956. A 17-14 loss to Michigan proved to be the only blemish, and when Iowa rebounded with a 7-0 win against No. 6 Minnesota, and 6-0 victory against No.6 Ohio State, the Hawkeyes found themselves at No. 3. But even with a 48-0 trashing of Notre Dame, they couldn't move up, and the final polls had Oklahoma first and Tennessee second, both 10-0. It turns out they got it right, because the Volunteers lost to Baylor in the Sugar Bowl, 13-7.

Iowa beat No. 10 Oregon State 35-19 in the Rose Bowl at the end of the season, and in 1958 went back with arguably the best team in program history. With All-American quarterback Randy Duncan throwing to a group of ends dubbed the Gluefingers Gang, Iowa won the Big Ten title despite a loss to Ohio State, and behind Bob Jeter's 194 rushing yards drilled Cal in the Rose Bowl, 38-12.

Unfortunately for the No. 2 Hawkeyes, LSU went 10-0 and defeated Clemson in the Sugar Bowl, 7-0.

Iowa's first two title chases came under Howard Jones, who compiled a 42-17-1 record from 1916-23. The 1921 and 1992 squads both went 7-0 (the 1921 team outscored opponents 225-36 and snapped Notre Dame's 20-game winning streak), but the Hawkeyes didn't play in their first bowl game until the 1956 season, when they defeated Oregon State in the Rose Bowl.

One of the key players on the team was Alex Karras, who in 1957 won the Outland Trophy as the nation's best interior lineman and was runner-up to John David Crow (Texas A&M) for the Heisman Trophy. He's also known as "Mongo" in the movie "Blazing Saddles," and for other acting roles.

KANSAS STATE WILDCATS
Consensus national titles (1936–present): None
Other national titles: None

When Bill Snyder took over the program in 1989, it was about as bad as any in the country. Since 1937, the Wildcats had only four winning seasons, compared to 27 with eight losses or more. The highlights had been one conference championship (in 1934), one bowl appearance (a 14-3 loss to Wisconsin in the Independence Bowl), and linebacker Gary Spani (1974-77), the first Wildcat to be inducted into the College Football Hall of Fame.

"Watching Spani play was like watching a falcon hunt for small prey," his defensive coach, Dick Selcer, said. "Gary's precision to dissect a play and then wreak havoc was incredible to watch. His instinct as a linebacker is the best I've ever seen or coached."

Among the major lowlights was a 30-game winless streak—including 27 failed attempts at the program's 300th all-time win—still ongoing when Snyder was hired. Director of athletics Steve Miller told him that not only is Kansas State "flat on its back," but, "You may have heard it's one of the toughest jobs in the country. It's not. It's the toughest."

Snyder still took the job, and finished 1-10 that first season. In 1993, Kansas State went to the Copper Bowl and defeated Wyoming, 52-17. From 1997-2003, the Wildcats won at least 11 games and finished in the Associated Press top 10 five out of seven seasons.

In 1998, Kansas State defeated Nebraska for the first time in 30 attempts (after being outscored 1,234-337 in the previous 29 losses), and the Wildcats reached No. 1 in the coaches' poll (No. 2 in the Associated Press poll) for the first time in program history. Quarterback Michael Bishop finished second in Heisman Trophy voting, but the Wildcats blew a 27-12 lead against Texas A&M in the Big 12 Championship game, and subsequently lost to Purdue in the Alamo Bowl, 37-34.

In 2003, Kansas State turned the tables on Oklahoma, which was being praised as potentially the best Sooners team ever. The Wildcats won the Big 12 Championship game in a 35-7 rout.

In addition to Bishop, Kansas State has inducted quarterbacks Lynn Dickey (1968-70) and Steve Grogan (1972-74) into its ring of honor, which is highlighted by Veryl Switzer, an All-American from 1951-53 who sill ranks in the program's top five in single-season and career punt-return yards (in 1953 he averaged 31.0 yards per punt return).

LOUISVILLE CARDINALS
Consensus national titles (1936–present): None
Other national titles: None

Although Louisville only has two finishes in the Associated Press' top 10, the first came in 2004, and the other when the Cardinals were just a loss against resurgent Rutgers away from possibly playing the 2006 national championship—but still participated in the Bowl Championship Series.   ·

Previously, the program's highlights were few and far between, with Louisville best known for quarterback Johnny Unitas in the 1950s.

During his 22 years coaching Louisville, Frank Camp led the 1957 team to the program's first bowl appearance, a 34-20 victory against Drake in the Sun Bowl.

Howard Schnellenberger revived the program after his days in Miami, and in 1990 quarterback Browning Nagle passed for 451 yards for a 34-7 upset of Alabama in the Fiesta Bowl. The Cardinals finished the season 10-1-1, but were only ranked No. 14 in the final Associated Press poll.

Before John L. Smith came aboard in 1998, Louisville had played in just five bowl games. In five seasons under Smith, the Cardinals received bowl invitations each year and won two conference titles. The 2001 team finished 11-2, topped by a 28-10 victory against Brigham Young in the Liberty Bowl. It still only led to a No. 17 ranking.

In 2004, only a 41-38 loss to No. 3 Miami kept the Cardinals from a perfect regular season. Instead, Louisville, which led the nation in scoring by averaging 49.8 yards per game (along with total offense and passing efficiency), had to settle for a 44-40 victory against Boise State in the Liberty Bowl.

Bobby Petrino's team finished No. 6, the best finish in program history. But when he matched it in 2006, the coach left for the NFL's Atlanta Falcons.

MARYLAND TERRAPINS
Consensus national titles (1936–present): 1953
Other national titles: 1951

If a road was like Maryland football, it would probably stretch from Death Valley to Mount Everest and touch every point imaginable in between.

Paul W. "Bear" Bryant coached there one year (1945), as did Lou Saban (1966). From 1963-71, Maryland didn't have a winning season, including a stretch of nine wins over five years, until Jerry Claiborne ended the streak. Beginning in 1973, his teams played in six consecutive bowl games and the 1976 squad finished 11-1. From 2001-3, Maryland posted three consecutive 10-win seasons for the first time.

Maybe it's only fitting that the Terrapins were involved in the biggest comeback in NCAA history.

It happened in 1984, when Maryland was being crushed 31-0 by No. 6 Miami at halftime. Bobby Ross inserted quarterback Frank Reich, who did more than just spark the Terps. While the defense limited the Hurricanes to just three points until the final moments of the game, Reich completed 12 of 16 passes for 260 yards and three touchdowns as Maryland pulled off a stunning 42-40 victory and went on to defend its Atlantic Coast Conference title.

Incidentally, Reich engineered a similar accomplishment for the Buffalo Bills in the 1992 National Football League playoffs. Down 35-3 early in the second half to the Houston Oilers, Reich came in for injured Jim Kelly (who ironically played for Miami in college), and threw for 289 yards and four touchdowns (three to Andre Reed) to pull off an amazing 41-38 victory in overtime.

Maryland's history includes the likes of defensive lineman Randy White and quarterbacks Boomer Esiason and Jack Scarbath, who finished second in 1952 Heisman Trophy voting. But its heyday came under the direction of "Big" Jim Tatum, who from 1947-55 compiled a record of 73-15-4.

Although Maryland finished the 1949 season 9-1, it didn't enter the national title picture until two years later, when in the midst of a 22-game unbeaten streak the Terps finished a perfect 10-0 and defeated Tennessee in the Sugar Bowl, 28-13.

"We were soundly beaten by a superior team," Tennessee coach Bob Neyland said.

But the co-champions (with Virginia Military Institute) of the Southern Conference, whose presidents wanted to boycott bowls that year, were only No. 3 in the final Associated Press poll, held at the end of the regular season, behind Tennessee and Michigan State.

Maryland would be on the flip side in 1953, when it was led by tackle Stan Jones. While outscoring opponents 298-31, the Terps' split-T attack averaged 359.5 yards per game, which ranked sixth in the nation. When it defeated Alabama, 21-0, and No. 1 Notre Dame tied Iowa 14-14, Maryland (10-0) made the jump to No. 1 in the final poll and was awarded the national championship.

In its first year of existence the Atlantic Coast Conference had a contract to send its champion to the Orange Bowl, to be paired against the Big Seven champion. Twice the Terps had first down inside the Oklahoma 10-yard line, but couldn't score, and the Sooners held on for a 7-0 victory.

MICHIGAN STATE SPARTANS
Consensus national titles (1936–present): 1952, 1965
Other national titles: 1951, 1955, 1957, 1966

When the program was founded in 1896, school president Jonathan L. Snyder was quoted as saying, "If we must have football, I want the kind that wins." Michigan Agricultural College did find success in those early years—except against rival Michigan, against which it went 2-23-3 in the first 28 meetings—but it wasn't for another 50 years before Michigan State was at the pinnacle of college football.

When it comes to Spartans' history, you primarily need to know two names, both coaches: Clarence "Biggie" Munn and Hugh "Duffy" Daugherty. Although Jim Crowley (one of Notre Dame's legendary Four Horsemen) and Charlie Bachman were instrumental in turning a fledgling team into a nationally respected program, Munn made the Spartans a regular contender for championships, which Daugherty continued through 1972.

Munn's first game was a 55-0 loss at Michigan, topped off with the Spartans' locker room being flooded by overflowed toilet water. His team went on to finish the 1947 season with a 7-2 record, but he vowed to do whatever it took to get the upper hand on the Wolverines. It took a couple more tries, and losses, but from 1950-69 Michigan State went 14-4-2 in the series.

The 1950 season saw the breakthrough. Even though the Spartans lost to Maryland, 34-7, a week after beating Michigan, 14-7, they still went 8-1 to finish No. 8 in the final Associated Press poll. For an encore, the Spartans compiled a 27-1 record over the next three seasons, and in 1952 were the consensus national champion (9-0).

The winning streak ended with a 6-0 loss to Purdue in 1953, but No. 3 Michigan State went on to defeat UCLA in the Rose Bowl, 28-20 (the final polls were cast at the end of the regular season. No. 1 Maryland lost to No. 4 Oklahoma in the Orange Bowl, 7-0, but 8-0-1 No. 2 Notre Dame was idle).

After Munn (54-9-2) became Michigan State's athletic director, the personable Daugherty stepped in and began compiling a 109-69-5 record, with seven top 10 finishes in the Associated Press poll.

The 1955 team went 9-1 and earned a trip to the Rose Bowl, a 17-14 victory against UCLA, and the 1957 squad followed suit with an 8-1 record, but neither won the Big Ten title.

However, the 1965 and '66 teams, which included linebacker George Webster and massive defensive end Bubba Smith, sparked another impressive run, 19-1-1, with the 1965 team finishing No. 1 in the coaches' poll despite a 14-12 loss to UCLA in the Rose Bowl. The lone tie, 10-10 in 1966, was to Notre Dame in the controversial "Game of the Century" (FYI, both Spartan teams finished second in the final Associated Press polls).

Michigan State hasn't finished with at least a share of the Big Ten title since 1990, when it scored four late touchdowns to upset No. 1 Michigan, 28-27. It did, however, finish second in 1999 under Nick Saban, who was hired away by LSU, where he won a national championship.

MINNESOTA GOLDEN GOPHERS
Consensus national titles (1936–present): 1936, 1940, 1941, 1960
Other national titles: 1904, 1934, 1935

Nowadays, some people best know Minnesota as originating cheerleading in 1898, and not only creating the idea of a trophy game, but taking it to unheard of heights. When Michigan left behind a water jug following a 6-6 tie in 1903, Minnesota athletic director L.J. Cooke told the Wolverines they would have to win it back.

In addition to the Little Brown Jug, the Golden Gophers also play Iowa for the Floyd of Rosedale, Wisconsin for Paul Bunyan's Axe (although originally it was the Slab of Bacon trophy), and Penn State for the Governor's Victory Bell. The problem is, Minnesota's never held all four trophies at the same time (FYI, the Victory Bell only began in 1993—the Gophers last had the other three simultaneously in 1967).

Of course, it hasn't always that way. Long before Minnesota moved off campus and into the Hubert H. Humphrey Metrodome (as of this writing, a new outdoors stadium on campus was in the works to open in 2009), the Gophers were a national powerhouse initially built by Henry Williams, with a history as rich as any other program.

For example, ever heard of Bronko Nagurski? The All-American fullback and tackle became a legend after cracking a transverse vertebra in his back against Iowa in 1928, but didn't leave the game. In the season finale, while wearing a special brace for his ribs and back, Nagurski had three interceptions, knocked down a pass at the goal-line and caused the fumble that led to the only touchdown of a 6-0 victory that cost Wisconsin the Big Ten title.

One of the players who influenced Nagurski was fullback Herb Joesting, a three-time All-American from 1925-27, who gained 1,850 yards in 24 games. Notre Dame's Knute Rockne said to his team about the "Owatonna Thunderbolt," "I'll buy a new suit for the guy who can throw Joesting for a loss." No one did in the 7-7 tie and Minnesota went on to finish 6-0-2.

"I play each game for all it's worth," Joesting said. "No more can be asked of an athlete than that he goes all out in every situation."

Under the direction of Bernie Bierman, who served as a Marine during World War I and II, the Gophers were a dynasty from 1934-41, when they went undefeated five times, won six Big Ten titles and three national championships.

"If I found that four or five plays were doing the job, we stuck with them," the low-key Bierman said. "Still, we probably had more plays than our opponents. I always figured that ball control with good execution is the best thing you can have."

Arguably, the best team was "Bierman's Monsters" of 1934. Led by players like Bill Bevan, the last Big Ten player not to wear a helmet, and future Oklahoma coach Bud Wilkinson, the Gophers averaged 33.7 points while allowing just 4.8 points and 103 yards a game.

Highlighting that season was a 48-12 victory at Iowa in which all 514 offensive yards came on the ground, and destroying Wisconsin in the season finale, 34-0, after the Badgers gave up just 50 points all season.

Minnesota recorded another perfect season in 1940 for another national championship, and was the preseason No. 1 team heading into 1941, when coming off narrow wins against No. 3 Michigan (7-0), and No. 9 Northwestern (8-7), the Gophers were bypassed in the Associated Press poll by Texas, which was enjoying its 34-0 victory against No. 20 Southern Methodist. But a week later when Texas only managed a 7-7 tie against Baylor, Minnesota, led by Heisman Trophy winner Bruce Smith and halfback George "Sonny" Franck, was back on top and, after finishing 8-0, the undisputed champion.

Incidentally, Bierman was also a standout ball carrier himself, and, along with end Bert Baston and Pudge Wyman's passing, helped lead Minnesota to a 6-0-1 record in 1915, and a 6-1 season in 1916, when the Gophers averaged 49.7 points a game. His coaching career began in 1919 at Montana, and along with stints at Mississippi State, Tulane and Minnesota compiled a 146-62-12 record. Some of his other top players included Pug Lund, Leo Nomellini, Clayton Tonnemaker, Ed Widseth and Dick Wildung, who are all in the College Football Hall of Fame.

Under Murray Warmath's direction, the Gophers won another national title in 1960 (despite being unranked in the preseason poll), earned a Rose Bowl trip and returned the following year, and won Minnesota's most recent Big Ten title in 1967. Guard Tom Brown, known as the "Rock of Gibraltar" finished second in 1960 Heisman Trophy voting.

But those two Rose Bowl teams were also known for something else: The Gophers were the first major college team to have a black All-American quarterback (Minnesota had the first black player in the Big Ten with Bobby "Rube" Marshall from 1904-6, when the Gophers went 13-0, 10-1 and 4-1, and outscored opponents a combined 1,238-63). Warmath, originally from Tennessee and the former coach at Mississippi State, started recruiting black players in the 1950s before national pressure began to mount.

"I was going to be more than a Big Ten quarterback who was black," Sandy Stephens said. "I was going to be a Big Ten quarterback who took his team to the Rose Bowl."

OLE MISS REBELS
Consensus national titles (1936–present): 1960
Other national titles: 1959, 1962

Ole Miss is known for "The Grove," John Vaught and Chucky Mullins' No. 38, which used to be awarded to the team's top defensive player in honor of the courageous standout who was paralyzed during the 1989 homecoming game and died two years later.

Former quarterbacks Archie Manning and his son Eli are considered the pride and joy of the program. Archie passed for 4,753 yards and ran for 823 during his career (1968-70), and is the only player in Ole Miss history to have his jersey retired, No. 18. When he concluded his career in 2003, Eli Manning had passed for 10,119 yards. But neither won a Heisman Trophy, nor a championship.

Ole Miss does have one consensus national title to its credit, and naturally, it came with controversy—especially considering that the Rebels have never finished a season atop the Associated Press poll.

In 1960, the final Associated Press rankings were released on November 28, with Minnesota No. 1 ahead of Ole Miss. The Gophers subsequently lost to Washington in the Rose Bowl, 17-7, while the Rebels beat Rice in the Sugar Bowl, 14-6. A numbers of services awarded Ole Miss the title, including the Football Writers, DeVold, Dunkel, Football Research, National Championship Foundation and Williamson.

In similar fashion, the 1959 Rebels were No. 1 according to the Berryman and Dunkel services, and the 1962 team was both the Billingsly and Litkenhous national champion. However, the 1959 team was named the SEC Team of the Decade in an Associated Press poll, and when *USA Today*'s Jeff Sagarin computed his list of the highest-rated teams from 1956-95, the 1959 Rebels were No. 3 behind two Nebraska squads (1995 and 1971).

That Ole Miss team, which finished No. 2 to Syracuse and future Heisman Trophy winner Ernie Davis, led the nation in scoring defense by allowing just 2.1 points per game, with eight shutouts. No opponent scored more than seven points, including LSU, which managed to pull out a 7-3 victory thanks to Billy Cannon's epic punt return for a touchdown which all but secured his Heisman.

The Rebels were able to avenge the loss in the Sugar Bowl, 21-0, by allowing just six first downs and 74 yards total offense, but had squandered a rare opportunity. Since then, they've won six Southeastern Conference titles (but none since 1963), all under Vaught.

"I'll do anything for Ole Miss," he once said.

During his career (1947-70, 1973), Vaught compiled a 190-61-12 record, for a .745 winning percentage, and 18 bowl appearances. He preached diligence and preparation, and was the coach when the 1962 race riots broke out following enrollment of the school's first black student. The football program didn't add black players until 1972.

"If it hadn't been for football, they probably would have closed Ole Miss," Vaught later reflected.

MISSOURI TIGERS
Consensus national titles (1936–present): None
Other national titles: 1960

Although Missouri's history includes numerous bowl appearances, an all-time record well above .500, and tight end Kellen Winslow (1975-78), the word most closely associated with Tigers' football is heartache.

The first 45 years of the program, Missouri had 23 head coaches. From 1930 to 1934, the Tigers won only six games, and were shut out 24 times. Recently, Missouri endured a 25-year losing streak to Nebraska, which was finally snapped in 2003.

In terms of competing for a national title, there's a clear-cut example, the 1960 team which many Missouri fans thought would be the one to break through.

The roll of victories was impressive: Southern Methodist, Oklahoma State, Penn State, Air Force, Kansas State, Iowa State, Nebraska and Colorado, before a lopsided 41-19 win at Oklahoma vaulted the Tigers to No. 1 for the first time in school history. All Missouri had to do to close out the Big Six championship was beat rival Kansas at home in the regular season finale.

The Jayhawks jumped out to a 17-0 lead and held on for a 23-7 victory. Soon after, the conference ruled that Kansas had to forfeit two games, including the Missouri victory, for using an ineligible player. With the damage already done, Missouri went to the Orange Bowl, where it defeated Navy, 21-14, but the final Associated Press ranking was No. 5. It's the only time the Tigers have ever finished that high.

Coach Don Faurot came close twice. In 1939, the Tigers were 8-1 until they lost to Georgia Tech in the Orange Bowl, 21-7. Two years later, Missouri had the same record heading into the Sugar Bowl, but was rebuffed by Fordham, 2-0.

Leading the 1939 team was quarterback Paul Christman, a St. Louis native who was known more for his arm than his feet, and set Missouri passing records that stood for almost 30 years.

"I knew I was awkward," Christman said. "Coach Faurot knew I had to be able to run to make my passing effective, so he spent hours in the offseason, working with me on quick starts and short sprints. I actually improved my speed."

With Christman gone, Faurot turned to his backfield of Harry Ice and Bob Steuber, who would run behind center Darold Jenkins in 1941, and created the split-T formation in an effort to free them up. Missouri didn't lose a conference game through the 1942 season, and Steuber went on to set numerous school records including season points (121), career points (222), season touchdowns (18), and career touchdowns (32).

Missouri's best team might have been the 1969 squad, coached by Dan Devine, which went 9-1 in the regular season thanks to impressive victories against Kansas, Michigan, Nebraska, and a 44-10 pounding of Oklahoma. Ranked sixth, the Tigers received an invitation for the Orange Bowl to play Penn State, which was riding a 29-game winning streak. Although the game was marred by nine turnovers, Missouri's final drive came to an end at the Penn State 14-yard line, resulting in a 10-3 loss. The final ranking was No. 6.

Incidentally, that was also the most recent time Missouri played in a January bowl. It faced Arizona State in the 1972 Fiesta Bowl on December 23, but that was 10 years before the bowl was played in January.

Since then, the closest Missouri has come to being involved in a controversy regarding the national championship was 1990, when it hosted the famous "Fifth Down" game. In the final seconds, officials inexcusably gave Colorado an extra down near the goal-line, which it used to score the winning touchdown—Missouri also disputes that quarterback Charles Johnson made it to the end zone—and win 33-31. Colorado went on to split the national title with Georgia Tech, but Missouri fans still consider it the best goal-line stand in program history.

NORTH CAROLINA TAR HEELS
Consensus national titles (1936–present): None
Other national titles: None

Although North Carolina has never won a national championship in football, it's come close more than once and can boast of some of the best players to ever put on a uniform including a slew of running backs like Don McCauley, Mike Voight, Derrick Fenner, Ethan Horton, Amos Lawrence and Natrone Means.

Topping that list is triple-threat quarterback Charlie "Choo-Choo" Justice, who ran, passed, punted and played special team from 1946-49, leading the Tar Heels to three major bowl appearances including its only Cotton Bowl trip. During his career, which began at age 22 after four years in the Navy during World War II, North Carolina went 32-7-2 as he scored 234 points, passed or ran for 53 touchdowns, and accumulated 2,634 rushing yards.

Justice also has the distinction of twice being the runner-up for the Heisman Trophy, to Doak Walker of Southern Methodist in 1948, and Leon Hart of Notre Dame in 1949. Additionally, a book, "Choo Choo," and a song, "All the Way with Choo Choo" by the Benny Goodman band, were composed in his honor.

A big reason why Justice is still revered today in the region is that it was during the 1948 season that North Carolina made its only appearance at No. 1, and just for a week. North Carolina had opened the season with a 34-7 victory against Texas and followed it up with a 21-14 win at Georgia, where Justice scored all three touchdowns, one on an 84-punt return.

Even though North Carolina had yet to lose, it was passed in the Associated Press poll by Michigan, which went on to win the national championship, and Notre Dame. It kept pace with them with victories against LSU and at Tennessee, but a 7-7 tie at William & Mary was as damaging as a loss.

North Carolina came back with an impressive 49-20 victory against Maryland to finish third in the final poll, but then lost to No. 5 Oklahoma in the Sugar Bowl, 14-6. Still, it's the best showing in program history.

The 1980 team, which featured outside linebacker Lawrence Taylor, also made a run up the rankings with a 7-0 start that had the Tar Heels at No. 6. But the only loss of the season, 41-7 to Oklahoma, was hard for voters to forget, and even with a 16-7 win against Texas in the Bluebonnet Bowl the Associated Press had 11-1 North Carolina 10th at season's end.

Coach Mack Brown (1988-97) never won an Atlantic Coast Conference title before he left for Texas, but had eight consecutive winning years, including back-to-back seasons with 10-plus victories in 1996-97.

North Carolina appeared to be well on its way to a Fiesta Bowl bid in 1996, only to blow a 17-3 lead in the final 10 minutes against Virginia, and had to settle for the Gator Bowl—a 20-13 victory against West Virginia for a No. 10 final ranking.

A 20-3 decision to Florida State was the only loss in 1997, and after crushing Virginia Tech in the Gator Bowl, 42-3, the Tar Heels were rewarded with a No. 4 finish in the coaches' poll, No. 6 according to the Associated Press.

OREGON DUCKS

Consensus national titles (1936–present): None
Other national titles: None

Before Nike co-founder Phil Knight began inserting vast sums of money into the program and Oregon started improving its facilities, the Ducks weren't much of a blip on the college football radar. The biggest contributions came from names like Dan Fouts, John McKay, Norm Van Brocklin, Mel Renfro, George Shaw, Bill Musgrave, and two early Rose Bowl appearances.

Walter Camp's Bulldogs outscored their opponents 698-0 en route to a 13-0 record in 1888. End Amos Alonzo Stagg is on the far left, and guard William W. "Pudge" Heffelfinger is at the top. Courtesy of Yale University.

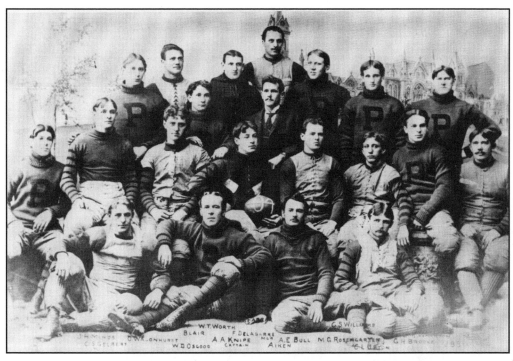

Even though Penn finished 12-0 in 1894, it wasn't the consensus national champion, which was instead Yale. However, Penn came back the next season to shut out its first 10 opponents en route to a 14-0 record and first consensus national title. Courtesy of the University of Pennsylvania.

The 1899 Tigers finished 12-0 and outscored their opposition 322-10, but what really set the team apart was defeating five opponents in six days all on the road at Texas, Texas A&M, Tulane, LSU, and Ole Miss. Courtesy the University of the South.

The 1914 Illinois team coached by Bob Zuppke, center, finished 7-0 and outscored opponents 224-22. Although Army's considered the consensus national champion, Illinois and Texas also received consideration. Courtesy of Illinois Sports Information Archives.

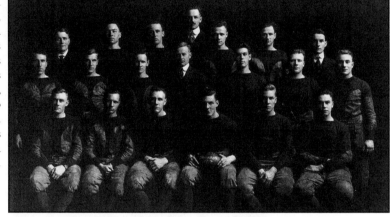

Army finished 9-0 and outscored opponents 235-36, but Pittsburgh was considered the consensus national champion in 1916. Two years previous, Army held that honor after finishing 9-0 with a scoring advantage of 219-20. Courtesy of the United States Military Academy.

Led by the legendary backfield known as the Four Horsemen, Notre Dame was 10-0 in 1924 and outscored the opposition 285-57. Courtesy of the University of Notre Dame.

Although none of them stood taller than six foot, or weighed more than 162 pounds, Notre Dame's Four Horsemen of quarterback Harry Stuhldreher, left halfback Jim Crowley, right halfback Don Miller, and fullback Elmer Layden, might have been the greatest backfield ever. Courtesy of the University of Notre Dame.

Johnny Mack Brown, with helmet, comes around for a reverse while Pooley Hubert steps forward to be his lead blocker in the 27-0 victory against Georgia in 1925. Courtesy of the Paul W. Bryant Museum.

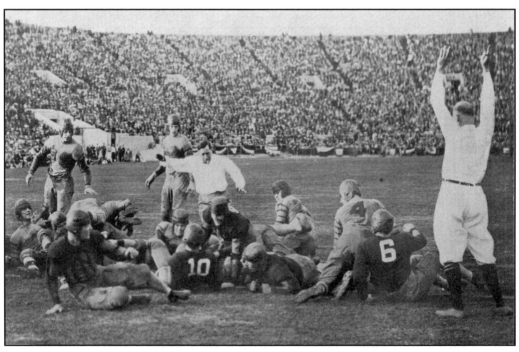

Pooley Hubert scores Alabama's first touchdown in the 1926 Rose Bowl after five consecutive carries. Alabama went on to defeat Washington, 20-19. Courtesy of the Paul W. Bryant Museum.

Knute Rockne's Fighting Irish went 9-0 in 1929, one of five undefeated seasons the coach enjoyed. From 1918 to 1930, his teams went 105-12-5, and Rockne won his final 19 games resulting in back-to-back national championships. Courtesy of the University of Notre Dame.

Alabama captain "Foots" Clement, left, meets the Washington State captain, believed to be Elmer Schwartz, during the 1931 Rose Bowl festivities. Alabama (10-0) won 24-0, though Notre Dame was considered the consensus national champion. Courtesy of the Paul W. Bryant Museum.

Notre Dame Stadium was dedicated on October 4, 1930, and celebrated with a 20-14 victory against Southern Methodist. The Fighting Irish went 10-0 to defend its national title. Courtesy of the University of Notre Dame.

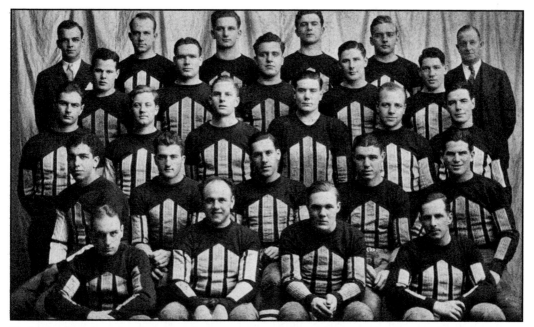

Under the direction of Andy Kerr, Colgate went 9-0 and didn't allow a single point in 1932. However, the Rose Bowl extended an invitation to 8-0-2 Pitt, which was promptly crushed by Southern California, 35-0. Provided by the Colgate Athletic Communications Office.

The 1935 SMU-TCU game became known as the Game of the First Half of the Century, when the Mustangs came back from a 14-point deficit to win 20-14. With the victory, SMU was named national champion by more than one service and received an invitation to the Rose Bowl. Courtesy of Southern Methodist University.

Stanford All-American tackle Bob "Horse" Reynolds and coach C.E. Thornhill meet with Alabama coach Frank Thomas and All-American halfback Millar "Dixie" Howell before the 1935 Rose Bowl. Led by its passing game, Alabama won 29-13. Courtesy of the Paul W. Bryant Museum.

After defeating Stanford in the 1935 Rose Bowl, the Crimson Tide (10-0) was able to make a claim on the national title, although Minnesota was the consensus choice. Courtesy of the Paul W. Bryant Museum.

Only a last-second field goal by Alabama kept the 1937 Commodores, led by All-American center Carl "Iron Man" Hinkle, the SEC's most valuable player, out of the 1938 Rose Bowl. Courtesy of the Southeastern Conference.

Heisman Trophy winner Glenn Davis is quickly stopped on this carry against Notre Dame in 1946. Although Army moved to within the Irish 30-yard line six times, it never scored, resulting in a legendary 0-0 tie. Courtesy of the University of Notre Dame.

Heisman Trophy winner Johnny Lujack completes a pass to end Leon Hart to help lead a 27-7 victory against Army in 1947. Although the Associated Press voted Notre Dame No. 1, most considered Michigan the national champion after its 49-0 pounding of Southern California in the Rose Bowl. Courtesy of the University of Notre Dame.

The 1948 season was one of the few in which there was practically no doubt which team was the national champion, Michigan. Led by All-American quarterback Pete Elliott, the Wolverines finished 9-0 and outscored opponents 252-44. Courtesy of the Bentley Historical Library (photo BL001327), the University of Michigan.

General Robert Neyland twice left the Volunteers to serve in the military, but compiled an amazing 173-31-12 record. The 1939 team shut out 10 consecutive opponents and the 1950 team finished 11-1 to earn national title consideration. He followed that up with a 10-0 regular season and consensus national title, though Tennessee lost to Maryland 28-13 in the 1952 Sugar Bowl. Courtesy of the University of Tennessee.

Kentucky coach Paul W. "Bear" Bryant and Oklahoma's Bud Wilkinson go "bowling" prior to the 1951 Sugar Bowl. Although the Sooners had already been proclaimed national champions, the Wildcats won 13-7. Courtesy of the Paul W. Bryant Museum

Under the direction of Red Sanders, here pictured from his days at Vanderbilt, UCLA led the nation in 1954 both in scoring, averaging 41 points per game, and scoring defense. Courtesy of the Southeastern Conference.

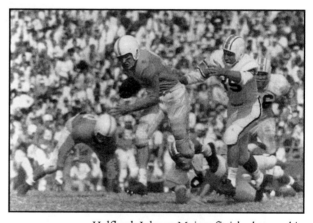

Halfback Johnny Majors finished second in 1956 Heisman Trophy voting to Notre Dame's Paul Hornung, and after a 10-0 regular season Tennessee finished No. 2 in the final polls as well. Courtesy of the Southeastern Conference.

Ralph "Shug" Jordan's Tigers finished 10-0 for a No. 1 ranking in the 1957 final Associated Press poll, but voted No. 2 by the coaches. Auburn shut out six opponents and never gave up more than seven points, but had been banned from playing in a bowl game due to recruiting violations. Courtesy of the Southeastern Conference.

Although the 1959 LSU team, including the high-profile Chinese Bandits, went 11-0 to win the national championship, Billy Cannon's 89-yard punt return against Ole Miss is considered one of the greatest plays in college football history and might have secured his Heisman Trophy. Courtesy of Louisiana State University.

In 1959, Syracuse led the nation in both total offense and total defense, and outscored opponents by an average score of 39-5. Topping the season was a 23-14 victory against No. 4 Texas at the Orange Bowl. Leading the team was No. 44 Ernie Davis (fourth row of players, second from the right), who in 1961 became the first black player to win the Heisman Trophy. Courtesy of Syracuse University Athletics.

Although John Vaught's 1959 team may have been better, the No. 2 Rebels were 10-0-1 after they defeated Rice in the Sugar Bowl, 14-6, while No. 1 Minnesota (8-1) lost to No. 6 Washington in the Rose Bowl. Courtesy of the Southeastern Conference.

Paul W. "Bear" Bryant's first national championship with the Crimson Tide came in 1961 after a 10-0 regular season and 10-3 victory against No. 9 Arkansas in the Sugar Bowl. Alabama shut out its last five opponents of the regular season. Courtesy of the Paul W. Bryant Museum.

Quarterback Joe Namath shakes hands with Ray Perkins during the 1964 season when at 10-0 Alabama was awarded the national championship by the Associated Press prior to its controversial 21-17 loss to Texas in the Orange Bowl. Courtesy of the Paul W. Bryant Museum.

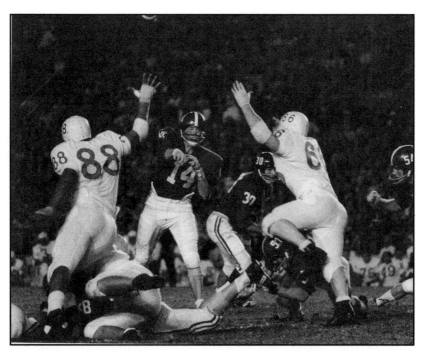

Quarterback Steve Sloan throws a 32-yard pass to Ray Perkins for the opening touchdown as Alabama defeats Nebraska in the 1966 Orange Bowl, 39-28. The victory clinched the national championship with the Associated Press voting after the bowl games for the first time. Courtesy of the Paul W. Bryant Museum.

Paul W. "Bear" Bryant sized up the competition, in this case Nebraska coach Bob Devaney, prior to the 1966 Rose Bowl. With No. 1 Michigan State and No. 2 Arkansas both losing, No. 4 Alabama won the national title by defeating No. 3 Nebraska, 39-28. Courtesy of the Orange Bowl Committee.

Nick Eddy (No. 47), here making a move with Rocky Bleier just below him (No. 28), was Notre Dame's leading rusher in 1966 and finished third in Heisman Trophy voting, but didn't play in the biggest game of the year, the 10-10 tie against Michigan State. He slipped getting off the train at East Lansing and aggravated his shoulder injury. Courtesy of the University of Notre Dame.

The first came in 1916, when despite facing a team with two losses, Penn (7-2-1), Oregon (6-0-1) was considered an underdog primarily because the Northeast was still considered the dominant region of college football. Led by versatile tackle John Beckett (who went on to serve in the Marines for 50 years and reached the rank of brigadier general), brothers Hollis and Shy Huntington, and receiver Lloyd Tegert, it pulled off the 14-0 victory, which was viewed as a win for the entire West Coast.

The other was at the end of the 1919 season, when Harvard (8-0-1) made its lone bowl appearance ever. Oregon (5-1) had field goals by Bill Steers and 128-pound Skeets Manerud, but Manerud narrowly missed the game-winner as Harvard won, 7-6.

Prior to 1990, Oregon had been ranked a total of 28 weeks since the Associated Press poll was created in 1936, but only once at the end of a season, No. 9 in 1948, when it also went on to lose to Southern Methodist in the Cotton Bowl, 21-13. From there, the bowl appearances were limited to the 1958 Rose Bowl (a 10-7 loss to Ohio State), the 1960 Liberty Bowl (a 41-12 loss to Penn State), and the 1963 Sun Bowl (a 21-14 win against Southern Methodist).

A 27-24 victory against Tulsa in the 1989 Independence Bowl ended the 26-year bowl drought, and signaled the program's resurgence. Although Rich Brooks returned the Ducks to the Rose Bowl, losing to Penn State, 38-20, to cap a 9-4 1994 season, Mike Bellotti's team in 2001, coming off its first 10-win season (and subsequent No. 7 ranking), provided the most exciting season in program history.

For example, in the season opener against Wisconsin, the lead changed hands six times before quarterback Joey Harrington managed to finish off a 31-28 victory. Harrington threw 27 touchdowns that season as Oregon won five games by seven points or less, and despite a 49-42 loss to Stanford won the Pac-10 title.

At 10-1, the Ducks were in the mix to play for the national championship, only the computer polls had Oregon ranked lower than their human counterparts, which instead allowed Nebraska to square off against Miami in the Rose Bowl (and lose, 37-14).

Instead, Oregon played Colorado in the Fiesta Bowl, an interesting matchup of contrasting styles. While the Ducks were viewed as being relatively free-wheeling, Colorado was a physical, run-first team that had pounded Nebraska, 62-36. Oregon stacked the line and forced Colorado to beat it in the air. With Harrington passing for 350 yards and the offense topping 500 yards, Oregon won 38-16 to prove it belonged with the more traditional powers.

"We dominated," linebacker Kevin Mitchell said. "It's not a secret. It's not a fairy tale. It's a fact."

PITTSBURGH PANTHERS
Consensus national titles (1936–present): 1937, 1976
Other national titles: 1910, 1915, 1916, 1918, 1929, 1931, 1936, 1980, 1981

There are few college programs that can boast the kind of name recognition and football personalities as the University of Pittsburgh.

"Iron" Mike Ditka, Tony Dorsett, Dan Marino, Hugh Green, Johnny Majors, Joe Schmidt and Marshall Goldberg.

Or, more recently, Curtis Martin, Ruben Brown, Bill Maas, Tony Siragusa, Marty Schottenheimer, Bill Fralic, Mark May, Larry Fitzgerald, Antonio Bryant and coach Dave Wannstedt, who was a graduate assistant in 1975-76.

"We were in a staff meeting and I'm sitting at the far end of the table—it was the '76 year, the year we won the national championship—and I think my job that day was to make the coffee," Wannstedt said. "I'm looking at Coach Majors and I said to myself, 'Someday I will be the head coach at the University of Pittsburgh.'"

Majors had been hired in 1972 to rescue the program, which had lost 56 of the previous 72 games. His first year, Pitt went to the Fiesta Bowl, and his strategy of over-recruiting the roster helped lead to NCAA legislation limiting scholarships.

Pitt claims nine overall national championships, including consensus titles in 1937 and 1976. The latter came after a 27-3 dominating performance against Georgia in the Sugar Bowl (the Panthers' defense caught more pass attempts by the Bulldogs, four, than the Georgia receivers, three), even though Majors had already announced he was leaving for his alma mater, Tennessee. Despite that, Pitt subsequently made two more strong bids for a championship, finishing No. 2 in 1980 and No. 4 in 1981 according to the Associated Press, with the extremely talented line including Jim Covert, Fralic and May blocking for Marino (7,905 career yards and 74 touchdowns).

However, Pitt's best line was probably on the 1936 team which featured Ave Daniell—who blocked for Marshall Goldberg two years before he moved to fullback in the "Dream Backfield" with John Chickerneo—Harold Stebbins and Dick Cassiano.

From 1890 to 1990, Pitt was considered one of the country's strongest independents until the Panthers became a charter member of the Big East in 1991. Its coaching legacy includes both Glenn "Pop" Warner (60-12-4 from 1915-23) and "Jock" Sutherland (111-20-12, 1924-38), who had a winning percentage of .818 and guided Pitt to four Rose Bowls, but declined the invitation after a 9-0-1 season in 1937.

Warner didn't lose a game until his fourth season at Pitt and claimed three national titles (Georgia Tech was the consensus choice in 1917). The first, in 1915, featured the unique war cry from center Bob Peck: "When Peck fights, the team fights!" Warner called the 1916 team Pitt's best. It went 8-0 including wins against Navy, Syracuse, Penn and Penn State, and didn't give up a point. Fullback George "Tank" McLaren returned to lead Pitt to a 10-0 record in 1917 and established single-season school records with 13 touchdowns and 782 rushing yards. Herb Stein took over at center in 1918, when Pitt began another impressive run of 21-6-4.

However, Joe "Mugsy" Skladany (1931-33) may have the best name in Pitt history. As a senior, the 190-pound end held Pitt opponents to a net minus-6 yards around his right side, and was known for punishing hits. During his three seasons, Pitt went 24-3-2.

Dancer/actor Gene Kelly also went to Pittsburgh, but never showed the kind of footwork Dorsett did at Pitt Stadium (the team recently started playing at Heinz Field).

Not only is Dorsett the school's lone Heisman Trophy winner (1976—he had 6,082 career yards and went from 11th to 13th and fourth in voting before he won), but he and

Marcus Allen are the only people to have a resumé including a college national championship, Super Bowl victory, and both the college and pro football halls of fame.

"I look at him with a football, and it's about as beautiful as football is ever supposed to look," Coach Joe Paterno of rival Penn State said about Dorsett. "I think that's part of why it's hard to tackle him. He's so elegant, it would be like tackling Fred Astaire."

PURDUE BOILERMAKERS
Consensus national titles (1936–present): None
Other national titles: 1931

Although it has won only one Big Ten title outright (1929, with seven shared championships), there might not have been a conference at all if it wasn't for Purdue president James H. Smart. In 1895, he gathered school presidents from Chicago, Illinois, Michigan, Minnesota, Northwestern and Wisconsin together to address abuses in the game, including the paying of professionals and players enrolling in a single class to be eligible.

The proposed faculty control of all athletics led to the creation of the Western Conference, which was later renamed the Big Ten.

Purdue's best run in the conference came during the four-year stretch from 1929-33, when it compiled an overall record of 36-4-2. James Phelan was the coach for the 1929 season, when the Boilermakers went 5-0 in the Big Ten and 8-0 overall, before leaving for the University of Washington. Led by the Four Riveters—quarterback John White and running backs Ralph Welch, Glen Harmeson and Alex Yunevich—and tackle Elmer Sleight, the team outscored opponents 187-44, and posted a rare victory against Michigan, 30-16.

Noble Kizer replaced him and posted records of 9-1 in 1931, and 7-0-1 in 1932, but his reign would be shortened by a kidney ailment diagnosed in 1937. He died three years later.

Although Purdue has finished in the top 10 of the Associated Press poll five times, it's essentially made two strong runs at the national championship.

The first was in 1943, when coming off a 1-8 season coach Elmer Burnham pieced together a team made up of 26 Marines, nine Navy men and nine civilians (in fairness, many schools didn't play the 1943 season due to World War II). The Boilermakers went 9-0 and finished the season ranked fifth.

The other was 1968, two years after Purdue made its first appearance in the Rose Bowl. At the time, Big Ten rules prevented any team from representing the conference in consecutive years. In 1966, a 41-20 loss to Michigan State cost Purdue the Big Ten championship, but the Spartans had visited Pasadena the season before so the honor fell to the Boilermakers. Led by quarterback Bob Griese (who in 1965 led a 25-21 victory against No. 1 Notre Dame), Purdue finished the regular season with four straight wins, outscoring the last three opponents 90-6. It was outgained by Southern California, but fullback Perry Williams scored two touchdowns while the Trojans failed on a late two-point conversion, as the Boilermakers won 14-13.

Despite being unable to make a return trip, Purdue still managed one of four straight 8-2 seasons in 1967 and shared the Big Ten title with Indiana. It resulted in a preseason No. 1 ranking in 1968, and averaged 41.3 points in impressive wins against Virginia, Notre Dame and Northwestern. But the Boilermakers ran into the young, tough Ohio State Buckeyes, ranked fourth, who pulled out a 13-0 victory. Purdue finished No. 10 and Leroy Keyes was the second of three Boilermakers to place second in Heisman Trophy voting over a four-year period (Griese in 1966 and Mike Phillips in 1969).

"We just got clobbered, that's all," said Jack Mollenkopf, Purdue's all-time winningest coach at 84-39-9.

SOUTHERN METHODIST MUSTANGS
Consensus national titles (1936-present): None.
Other national titles: 1935, 1981, 1982

One of the most unfortunate aspects to the National Collegiate Athletic Association issuing the death penalty, which abolished the football program in 1987 and after returning two years later has since floundered, is that much of Southern Methodist's history disappeared from the public landscape.

SMU has won its share of national championships, boasts a Heisman Trophy winner, and was involved in the Game of the First Half of the Century.

It occurred in 1935, when No. 2 SMU and No. 1 Texas Christian were both 10-0. All-SWC back Harry Shuford was sidelined with an injury, but Bobby Wilson scored two touchdowns for a 14-0 lead, only to see Sammy Baugh lead TCU back to tie the game in the fourth quarter.

On fourth-and-4 at the TCU 39, first-year coach Madison "Matty" Bell thought his players would try and punt the ball out-of-bounds near the goal-line, only they called for a fake (at the time, coaches designated a player on the field to call plays, in this case Jack Rabbit Smith). When quarterback Bob Finley, who was also the team's punter, broke the huddle Wilson grabbed him and said, "Throw it as far as you can. I'll be there."

"Wilson was out wide," Finley later said. "I made as if to kick the ball, and the line slowed down. Then I backed up and threw it, and I was buried. I heard the people scream, and when I got up, I saw Wilson in the end zone, jumping up and down."

What he missed seeing was Wilson catching the ball at the 4 between two defenders, and dive into the end zone. With the victory, SMU won the Southwest Conference title, was named the national champion by more than one service, and received an invitation to play in the Rose Bowl—where it lost to Stanford, 7-0.

"When I was coaching at Texas A&M we played Tulane's 1931 Rose Bowl team, and I never forgot the ice-water poise they had in the unexcited way they went about their business," Bell once recalled. "I told myself that if I ever had a great team I'd try to keep them in the same frame of mind."

However, he also said about the Stanford loss: "What I should have done was to have banned banquets, abolished autographs and taken the team into the desert until the day of the game."

Even with the Rose Bowl loss, the SMU-TCU game helped launch the Southwest Conference into the upper echelon of college football.

SMU's other great title runs were led by Eric Dickerson, who from 1979-82 accumulated 4,450 rushing yards. Coming off a heartbreaking 46-45 loss to Jim McMahon's BYU Cougars in the Holiday Bowl, the 1981 team finished 10-1 with the lone defeat to Texas, 9-7, to finish No. 5 in the final Associated Press poll.

Behind Dickerson and fellow running back Craig James, the 1982 Mustangs finished 10-0-1, topped off by a 7-3 victory against Pitt in the Cotton Bowl, thanks to option quarterback Lance McIlhenny's clutch touchdown. Known as the Pony Express team, No. 2 SMU received title consideration, but 11-1 Penn State, which won a 1 vs. 2 matchup with Georgia in the Sugar Bowl, was the consensus choice.

As for the Heisman, Doak Walker was the first player to win the award as a junior. In 1948, the running back had 108 carries for 532 yards and eight touchdowns, completed 26 of 46 passes for 304 yards and five touchdowns, and caught 15 passes for 278 yards and two touchdowns. On defense, he had three interceptions and returned them for 75 yards, and on special teams he returned 10 punts for 169 yards and a touchdown, returned five kickoffs for 161 yards, kicked 22 of 29 extra points and averaged 42.1 yards per punt in 35 attempts.

"Some called it luck, others called it destiny, but Doak had a natural knack for pulling off great deeds," Bell said.

According to Texas lore the second deck of the Cotton Bowl was added due to demand to see Walker play. Since 1990, the Doak Walker Award has been given to college football's best running back.

SMU is the only school in NCAA history to receive the death penalty for recruiting violations and 13 players allegedly receiving more than $61,000 from boosters, lies and non-cooperation by the school and players, and the continuation of payments even while the school was serving a two-year probation handed down in 1985. In addition to the 1987 season being cancelled, school officials also wiped out the 1988 season. The program was docked 60 scholarships and banned from bowl games and television until the 1990 season.

Despite the 2000 opening of Gerald F. Ford Stadium (32,000 capacity and could easily be expanded), which is not named for the former president Gerald R. Ford but an alumnus and bank CEO who donated $20 million, the stigma continues to be felt. Since the penalties were issued, SMU has had one winning season, 6-5 in 1997 under Mike Cavan, with five one- or no-win seasons.

STANFORD CARDINAL
Consensus national titles (1936–present): 1940
Other national titles: 1926

Since 1982, Stanford has been best known for the final play against Cal, when the Golden Bears' Kevin Moen scored after five laterals and slammed into trombonist Gary Tyrrell in the end zone.

But the Cardinal (called the Indians until 1972) played in the first Rose Bowl game, won a national title in 1926 (and received consideration in 1940), and earned a Heisman Trophy, awarded to quarterback Jim Plunkett in 1970.

Its very impressive stable of legendary coaches includes Fielding Yost, Glenn "Pop" Warner, John Ralston, Bill Walsh and Walter Camp, who actually coached both Yale and Stanford in 1892. He led Yale to a 13-0 season and then took over Stanford, where the season started in December. The team finished 2-0-2, and Camp returned for the 1894-95 seasons (10-3-1) to close his coaching career.

Among those who have suited up for the Cardinal include quarterbacks John Elway (who in four years completed 774 passes for 9,349 yards, and in 1982 finished second in Heisman voting) and John Brodie and fullbacks Bobby Grayson and Ernie Nevers, who in 1962 was named by *Sports Illustrated* the greatest football player ever. Against Notre Dame's Four Horsemen in the 1925 Rose Bowl, he played on two heavily braced ankles fractured earlier in the season to gain 114 rushing yards on 34 carries, but was stopped inches short on a disputed goal-line call, with the Irish winning 27-10.

The title Stanford claims was in 1926, before the Associated Press poll existed, when it topped the power rankings computed by Frank Dickinson, a University of Illinois economics professor. Led by All-American end Ted Shipkey and sophomore fullback Clifford "Biff" Hoffman, Stanford finished 10-0-1. The tie came in the Rose Bowl against Alabama, despite out-gaining the Crimson Tide 305 yards to 98, thanks mostly to a blocked punt. Shipkey had a 23-yard end-around and five receptions to go with two fumble recoveries on defense.

Fittingly, Frankie Wilton, who had the blocked punt, wound up being the hero a year later when Stanford retuned to the Rose Bowl and edged Pittsburgh, 7-6. Although Pitt scored on a Wilton fumble returned by Jimmy Hagan for a touchdown, Walt Heinecke blocked the extra point. When Stanford's Bob Sims lost the ball at the Pitt 2-yard line, Wilton grabbed it and scored.

Under the direction of C.E. Thornhill, Stanford made three consecutive appearances in the Rose Bowl beginning with the 1933 season. Known as the "Vow Boys" because a group of freshmen the year before promised never to lose to rival Southern California (they didn't and also beat Cal three straight times), Stanford lost to Columbia, 7-0, and the following year to Alabama, 29-13, but finally came through against undefeated Southern Methodist, 7-0. Quarterback Bill Paulman scored the lone touchdown on a short run.

The 1940 season saw perhaps the greatest turnaround in college football history. Coming off a 1-7-1 season, Stanford hired Clark Shaughnessy, the "Father of the T Formation," as head coach.

"If Stanford wins a single game with that crazy formation, you can throw all the football I ever knew into the Pacific Ocean," Warner proclaimed.

Shaughnessy moved Frankie Albert, who was said to be a master at the bootleg, from tailback to quarterback, and aided by halfback Hugh "Duke" Gallarneau and guard Chuck Taylor led Stanford to a 10-0 season, including a 21-13 victory against Nebraska in the Rose Bowl. Gallarneau scored two touchdowns, a 10-yard carry and a 40-yard reception, while Pete Kmetovic had 141 rushing yards and returned a punt for a touchdown.

Stanford has returned to the Rose Bowl only four times since. At the end of the 1951 season, with Taylor as coach, it lost to Illinois, 40-7. But Ralston guided Stanford to consecutive appearances at the end of the 1970 and 1971 seasons. In the first, against 9-0 Ohio State, Plunkett outperformed Rex Kern and rallied Stanford back from a 17-13 deficit in the fourth quarter. A touchdown catch by Randy Vataha and Jackie Brown's clinching touchdown run, set up by a Bob Moore reception, resulted in a 27-17 upset. Plunkett, who chose Stanford so he could be near his blind parents, went 22-8-2 over his three years, but called the Ohio State victory his best game.

A year later, quarterback Don Bunce helped lead Stanford's 13-12 win against 11-0 Michigan, with Rod Garcia hitting a 31-yard field goal as time expired.

SYRACUSE ORANGE

Consensus national titles (1936–present): 1959

Other national titles: None

Even though it's been decades since the Northeast was considered the hotbed of American football, there was a time when Syracuse was almost exclusively known as a football school.

When Ben Schwartzwalder was hired in 1949 (FYI, he was a paratrooper in World War II, rose to the rank of major and awarded the Silver Star, Bronze Star, Purple Heart, four Battle Stars and Presidential Unit Citation), Syracuse had won only nine games over the previous four seasons, and hadn't enjoyed more than a six-win season since 1931.

"The alumni wanted a big-name coach," Schwartzwalder once told the Syracuse *Post-Standard*. "What they got was a long-name coach."

In 1959, Syracuse won the region's lone national championship after finishing the regular season a perfect 10-0, and outscored opponents by an average of 39-5. By defeating No. 4 Texas in the Cotton Bowl, 23-14, it was the nation's lone undefeated team. The Orangemen (the nickname before the "men" was dropped), led the nation in offense, averaging 451 yards per game, and defense, allowing an average of 193 yards over 10 games.

The team was also guided by arguably the best player in the program's history—and it wasn't Jim Brown, who finished fifth in 1956 Heisman Trophy voting before rewriting the record book in the National Football League (not to mention also lettering in basketball and track, and was considered the nation's best lacrosse player).

Instead, it was another No. 44, sophomore Ernie Davis, who broke Brown's rushing record and in 1961 became the first black player to win the Heisman. He finished his career with 2,386 rushing yards, 3,306 all-purpose yards, and 220 points including 35 touchdowns.

"Winning the Heisman Trophy is something you just dream about," Davis said. "You never think it could happen to you."

Against Texas, after Syracuse had already been awarded the national title, Davis scored an 87-yard touchdown reception on the third play from scrimmage and later added a 1-yard touchdown run on fourth down. On defense, his interception keyed the final touchdown to put the game out of reach.

Tragically, Davis died from leukemia in 1963, after the Cleveland Browns traded for his rights as the No. 1 pick of the 1962 NFL Draft with the intention of having him in the same backfield with Brown.

"Some people say I'm unlucky," Davis said. "I don't believe it. When I look back, I can't call myself unlucky."

Incidentally, another player to wear No. 44 was Floyd Little, who broke both Brown's and Davis' records and in 1965 led the nation in all-purpose yards, averaging 199 per game. In 30 regular season games from 1964-66, he averaged 5.4 yards per carry, 20 yards on punt returns, and 29 on kickoff returns, scored 46 touchdowns, caught 50 passes and threw one.

"God gave you two ends: One to sit on, one to think with. Heads you win, tails you lose," Little later said as a public speaker.

There have been 11 players to wear No. 44 since Brown first did in 1954, but those three were the only ones to receive All-American honors.

Schwartzwalder, who also recruited fullback Larry Csonka and Jim Nance, retired in 1973 with a record of 153-91-3. During his coaching reign, Syracuse enjoyed 22 consecutive .500 seasons or better and finished in the top 20 of either the Associated Press or coaches' poll nine times.

Although Paul Pasqualoni led Syracuse to back-to-back 10-win seasons in 1991-92, including New Year's Day bowl victories against Ohio State (24-17, Hall of Fame Bowl) and Colorado (26-22, Fiesta Bowl), the school's other serious run at the national title came under the direction of Richard MacPherson in 1987.

After finishing the regular season 10-0 as an independent, including wins against Maryland, Virginia Tech, Missouri, Penn State, Pittsburgh, Boston College and West Virginia, No. 4 Syracuse was paired against No. 6 Auburn in the Sugar Bowl. After it played to a 16-16 tie, Syracuse stayed at No. 4, but even with a victory probably would have only moved up to No. 3 behind 12-0 Miami, which beat Oklahoma in the Orange Bowl to displace the Sooners at No. 1, and Florida State, which heading into its 31-28 victory against No. 5 Nebraska in the Fiesta Bowl, was ranked third.

As for Csonka, he too set numerous records despite being a bruising fullback. He accumulated 2,934 yards, a school record that lasted 14 years, averaged 4.9 yards per carry, had 14 100-yard games and an incredible 43 carries against Maryland in 1967.

"I had my own body-building program," he said. "I grew up on a farm. I picked corn, shoveled dirt, baled hay, milked cows, and every day I ran two miles home for supper."

TEXAS A&M AGGIES
Consensus national titles (1936–present): 1939
Other national titles: 1919, 1927

At Texas A&M, they serve warning to the newcomers, especially those who might be squeamish about something like the building moving.

"Welcome to Kyle Field," the weekly press notes reads. "For those of you visiting for the first time, please do not be alarmed. The press box will move during the Aggie War Hymn."

If national championships were determined by the sheer number of traditions, then Texas A&M would be a perennial power.

It's the home of "The 12th Man," Midnight Yell Practice (with more than 20,000 contributors), Silver Taps and Muster. Football games feature the close marching of the Aggie Band, the cadets get kisses from their girlfriends after scores, and the mascot is an American collie named Reveille.

As for the Hymn, fans and students lock arms and sway, causing the upper deck to noticeably move. The movement can be nearly as intimidating as the deafening cheers. Before "Mama called" for his return to Alabama, Paul W. "Bear" Bryant said "10 Aggies can yell louder than a hundred of anybody else."

It makes one wonder how they find the time to play football, but the Aggies have certainly done that as well.

Dana X. Bible (1917, 1919-1928) never had a losing year, with two undefeated seasons (1919 and 1927), and Texas A&M's first postseason appearance, a 22-14 victory against Centre in the Dixie Classic, the forerunner of bowl games in the Southwest, on January 2, 1922.

But Bryant was the program's most high-profile coach, and in the nine years after he left the Aggies never won more than four games a season (25-59-6 from 1958-66). He also had one of the program's two top five finishes, 1956, when led by linebacker Jack Pardee, Texas A&M went 9-0-1, with the tie at Houston, 14-14.

A famous story involving Bryant and his star player, John David Crow, occurred in 1955 against Southern Methodist. Crow a sophomore, took a punt at his own 40 and promptly lost 30 yards trying to find a way around the defenders. A few plays later, Crow lost another five yards on a sweep. When he returned to the sideline, Bryant merely informed him, "John, our goal is that-away."

Two years later, Crow won the Heisman Trophy.

Texas A&M's lone national championship came in 1939, under the direction of Homer Norton, who had gone 22-23-6 during his first five seasons.

According to local legend, in 1936 Norton told trainer Lilburn Dimmitt to make a list of the best players in the state, and the school subsequently enrolled 37 of the "Wanted 40." The defense yielded only 18 points during the 10-game championship run, compared to A&M scoring 198, and the Aggies came from behind to edge Tulane in the Sugar Bowl, 14-13.

Of one of the key players on that team, aggressive guard Joe Routt, legendary sportswriter Grantland Rice once wrote: "He was a glutton for hard, all-afternoon play and was at his best when the going was toughest. Routt used a system of stacking up a whole side of the opposing line, thereby breaking up a play and allowing a teammate to make a tackle."

Texas A&M also won the Southwest Conference title in both 1940 and 1941, proving a three-year conference reign that would take 40 years to match by Jackie Sherrill, and another 10 for R.C. Slocum.

Although A&M has as many Big 12 championships—which began play in 1996—as Heisman Trophies (although fullback "Jarrin" John Kimbrough finished second in 1940 and many believe was a better athlete than Crow). In the Sugar Bowl victory over Tulane he had 152 rushing yards on 26 carries and scored two touchdowns), it proudly boasts its state records and all accomplishments against that unmentioned school around campus otherwise known as "UT."

TEXAS CHRISTIAN HORNED FROGS

Consensus national titles (1936–present): 1938
Other national titles: 1935

Texas Christian's initial rise to prominence began under Francis Schmidt, who in his first year guided the team to its first unbeaten season at 9-0-1 in 1929, and over five seasons went 46-6-5.

But L.R. "Dutch" Meyer, who many credit for introducing the spread offense to college football and had a knack for pulling major upsets, brought the program to national prominence and won three conference titles in addition to two national titles (one consensus).

"Fight 'em 'til hell freezes over, then fight 'em on the ice," Meyer once said.

The first came in 1935, when the Horned Frogs, a nickname that dates back to 1897, had a 10-0 record heading into a showdown with rival Southern Methodist, which had the same record, and they were generally considered the best two teams in the country (the first Associated Press poll occurred a year later, in 1936). It would later be called the Game of the First Half of the Century.

While TCU was led by quarterback Sammy Baugh, SMU had Bobby Wilson, who scored two touchdowns for an early 14-0 lead. But Baugh brought the Frogs back, and tied the game at 14 with a touchdown pass in the fourth quarter. The deciding play came on fourth-and-4 at the TCU 37 when SMU lined up to punt, only quarterback Bob Finley instead threw a pass with Wilson's over-the-shoulder catch at the 4 resulting in a touchdown and 20-14 victory.

With the victory, SMU received $85,000 to play in the Rose Bowl, which it used to help pay off then-new SMU stadium, and was named the national champion by many services along with Minnesota. But SMU lost to Stanford in the Rose Bowl, 7-0, while Texas Christian recovered to edge LSU in the Sugar Bowl, 3-2. The Williamson System, which at the time was the only service to rank teams after bowl games, had TCU No. 1.

Three years later, in 1938, TCU put a bigger stamp on college football when it ran the table (11-0) and defeated No. 6 Carnegie Tech in the Sugar Bowl, 15-7—after trailing at halftime for the first time all season, 7-6. Led by quarterback Davey O'Brien, Texas Christian scored on its first possession of the second half to take the lead for good. Overall, the Frogs outscored their opponents that season 269-60.

However, the title was somewhat controversial due to Tennessee also finishing undefeated and beating No. 4 Oklahoma in the Orange Bowl, 17-0.

Despite being 5-foot-7, O'Brien was the first player to win the Heisman, Water Camp Award and Maxwell trophies all in the same year. Today, the Davey O'Brien National Quarterback Award is an annual trophy given to the best college quarterback in the nation.

"Baugh was a better all-around player than O'Brien, and a better passer, but as a field general Davey has never been equaled," Meyer said. "He was the finest play selector I've ever seen."

Incidentally, a center for both star quarterbacks was Ki Aldrich, who replaced All-American Darrell Lester. Meyer once said of Aldrich, "That boy wanted to play football more than anyone I ever knew. He liked it rough." Baugh, called him "the toughest player I ever knew." In 1938, *Life* magazine described him as "probably the greatest linebacker in history."

Although Abe Martin coached TCU to four bowl appearances in the 1950s, including two with "Mr. Defense" tackle Bob Lilly, and two with halfback Jim Swink, who in 1955 was second to Howard "Hopalong" Cassady of Ohio State in Heisman voting, the program fell on hard times. It bottomed out in the 1970s when it had one winning season and Coach Jim Pittman collapsed during the Baylor game and soon after died. It didn't have another winning season until 1984 under Jim Wacker, but encountered a rebirth under Dennis Franchione (25-10, 1998-2000), and Garry Patterson (54-19 his first six seasons), and in 2000 finished a season ranked for the first time since 1959.

Running back LaDainian Tomlinson had 2,158 rushing yards to lead the nation for the second straight season, but finished fourth in Heisman voting behind Florida State's Chris Weinke, Oklahoma's Josh Heupel, and Purdue's Drew Brees.

"It lets me know that it's almost impossible for a guy from TCU to win the Heisman," Tomlinson said at the time.

Instead, he went on beat Brees for National Football League MVP honors in 2006.

UCLA BRUINS

Consensus national titles (1936–present): 1954

Other national titles: None

Although the University of California-Los Angeles had captured 99 NCAA team titles heading into the 2006-07 school year, it had a grand total of zero national championships when it came to football.

Sort of.

In 1954, under the direction of Red Sanders and led by All-Americans Bob Davenport, Jack Ellena, and Jim Salisbury, UCLA finished the regular season 9-0. It defeated defending national champion Maryland, 12-7, led the country in scoring and scoring defense, and outscored opponents by a staggering 367-40.

And the Bruins did not finish No. 1 in the final Associated Press poll.

Even though UCLA closed its regular season with a 34-0 victory over rival Southern California, the Trojans played in the Rose Bowl because at the time the Pacific

Coast Conference had a no-repeat rule. No. 17 USC subsequently lost to No. 1 Ohio State, 20-7.

Regardless, the final Associated Press poll that season was cast on November 29, before the Rose Bowl, with UCLA second. The Bruins were named No. 1 by the United Press International coaches' poll, but have never been named the AP's national champion. Consequently, in the All-Time Final Associated Press Poll, devised by former SEC Assistant Director of Media Relations Chris Woodroof, UCLA is the highest-ranked team, 17th, to have never won the AP national championship.

Instead, the Bruins have finished in the Associated Press' top five nine times (even with seven consecutive bowl wins from 1982 to 1988 under Terry Donahue, considered the winningest coach in Pac-10 history), including at least once each decade since the 1940s. Sanders did it three straight years, 1953-55, with a No. 6 finish in 1952 while compiling a 49-10 record.

Although its legacy includes players like Troy Aikman, Kris Farris, Kenny Easley, Cade McNown, Billy Kilmer, Donn Moomaw, Jonathan Ogden, Jerry Robinson, Kenny Washington, and walk-on quarterbacks Rick Neuheisel and John Barnes, the program is best known for two individuals in particular.

Before he broke the color barrier in baseball, Jackie Robinson was a four-sport standout at UCLA (football, basketball, track and baseball). He led the nation in punt returns in 1939 and 1940, and his 18.8-yard career average still ranks fourth in National Collegiate Athletic Association history.

The other was quarterback Gary Beban, who over three seasons helped the Bruins go 24-5-2, and won the Heisman Trophy in 1967. When Beban was a sophomore in 1965, a Rose Bowl berth was at stake against USC, when he led an incredible comeback from down 16-6 with four minutes remaining. After his 34-yard touchdown pass and the subsequent two-point conversion made it 16-14, linebacker Dallas Grider recovered the onside kick and Beban connected with Kurt Altenberg for a 52-yard game-winning touchdown.

In the rematch from the season opener against No. 1 Michigan State (a 13-3 loss), UCLA took a 14-0 lead, when the Spartans came back and scored in the final minute to pull within 14-12. But fullback Bob Apisa was stopped on the two-point conversion by Grider and safety Bob Stiles, who was knocked out on the play.

The result, coupled with No. 2 Arkansas losing to LSU, opened the door for Alabama to leap from No. 4 to No. 1 with a win against No. 3 Nebraska in the Orange Bowl. The final rankings were: 1. Alabama (9-1-1); 2. Michigan State (10-1-0); 3. Arkansas (8-2-1); 4. UCLA (8-2-1); and 5. Nebraska (10-1).

As for coaches, Donahue compiled a 151-74-8 record from 1976-95, and was in six Rose Bowls, one as a player, one as an assistant coach and four as a head coach. His mentors were Tommy Prothro, whom he played for at UCLA in 1964-66; Pepper Rodgers, whom he served as assistant at Kansas and UCLA; and Dick Vermeil, whom he also served as assistant at UCLA.

"Prothro made me believe in the value of fundamentals," Donahue said. "Rodgers was brilliant in his way of teaching technical features. Vermeil taught me the value of organized drills and hard work."

VIRGINIA TECH HOKIES

Consensus national titles (1936–present): None

Other national titles: None

Whenever Virginia Tech plays an opponent for the first time, it's usually only a matter of minutes before the obvious question is asked.

"What on earth is a Hokie?"

According to the school, the term goes back to the 1800s, when a "Hokie" was a verbal form of providing encouragement or approval. In 1896, when Virginia Agricultural and Mechanical College changed its name, a contest was held to create a new cheer. Senior O.M. Stull won for his "Hokie" yell, which is still used today.

So in other words, we really don't know either. However, opposing fans will get a kick out of knowing that the burnt orange and maroon colors were selected by a committee to replace the striped black and gray which invoked images of prison uniforms.

Virginia Tech has been around since 1892 and has five inductees in the College Football Hall of Fame—Hunter Carpenter, Carroll Dale, Frank Loria, Andy Gustafson and Jerry Claiborne. Carpenter, a halfback, was the first great player in school history, and in 1905 led the team to a 9-1 record, including victories against Army, North Carolina, South Carolina and Virginia. The loss came to Navy, 12-6, but Tech outscored the opposition 305-24, and Carpenter totaled 82 points.

However, the program is still known for three people in particular, all fairly recently. That's what happens when the first time you finish a season ranked in the Associated Press poll was 1954, and the second 1986.

Before he went on to terrorize quarterbacks in the National Football League, Bruce Smith was an All-American in 1983-84, with his career concluding with Virginia Tech's fifth-ever bowl appearance (a 23-7 loss to Air Force in the Independence Bowl).

After Frank Beamer took over for Bill Dooley in 1987, it took a few years for things to click, but in 1993 the program began an impressive run of bowl games. It peaked over the 1999-2000 seasons, when Virginia Tech went 22-2 and came within a sniff of a national championship.

The game that served notice to the nation that the Hokies were for real was a nationally televised Thursday night contest against Clemson, which Virginia Tech won 31-11. The buzz regarding quarterback Michael Vick only grew louder with a 62-0 win against No. 16 Syracuse, and a 43-10 win vs. powerhouse Miami, ranked 19th.

"No one can tell this team any longer that it doesn't belong," Beamer said after a 38-14 victory against Boston College.

At 11-0, the No. 2 Hokies earned a place in the national championship game and had a 29-28 lead after three quarters, but were subsequently outscored 18-0 by No. 1 Florida State in the Sugar Bowl, for a 46-29 final.

Virginia Tech came back to match the 11-1 record in 2000, and was making another title run in 2002 when a 28-21 comeback win by Pitt began a three-game tailspin that knocked the Hokies out of the Bowl Championship Series. In 2004, it returned to the Sugar Bowl, a 16-13 loss to Auburn, but had become a regular title contender.

WASHINGTON HUSKIES

Consensus national titles (1936–present): 1991
Other national titles: 1960, 1984, 1990

There may be no more picturesque setting in college football than Husky Stadium, which sits on the shores of Lake Washington and has an upper-deck view of Mount Rainier. When things are going well for the Huskies, they're the equivalent of that view to fans and the darlings of the Seattle area. Consequently, a number of teams will forever be fondly remembered throughout the region.

That includes the Warren Moon-led 1977 squad which overcame a 1-3 start to reach and win at the Rose Bowl, the 1994 squad which ended Miami's 58-game home winning streak, and the 1959 team, led by one-eyed quarterback Bob Schloredt, which pulled off a 44-8 upset of Wisconsin in the Rose Bowl.

Overall, there have been two great eras of Washington football.

The first began under the direction of ruthless coach Gil Dobie, whose teams went 58-0-3 from 1908-16. But with the heart of college football still in the Northeast, Washington received little national recognition until Enoch Bagshaw's team in 1923, which at 10-1 received an invitation to play Navy in the Rose Bowl. Even with fullback Elmer Tesreau playing with a broken leg and Les Sherman kicking two conversions despite a broken toe, halfback George Wilson rallied Washington to a 14-14 tie.

The Huskies returned to the Rose Bowl in 1925, where Wilson—who played his entire senior season with a stomach ailment that curtailed his food intake—gained 134 yards on 15 carries to help Washington take a 12-0 lead. But after he was knocked out of the game, Alabama scored three touchdowns in the third quarter and held on for a 20-19 victory that helped turned the South into a football-crazed region.

Under the direction of Don James, the Huskies played in the Rose Bowl six times from 1977-92, winning four. The 1984 team went 11-1 and with a 28-17 victory against Oklahoma in the Orange Bowl finished No. 2, but the 1991 squad was unequivocally Washington's best.

Led by defensive tackle Steve Emtman, who finished fourth in Heisman Trophy voting, and quarterback Billy Joe Hobert, the Huskies ran the table and then punctuated the season with a 34-14 victory against Michigan in Pasadena, where Heisman winner Desmond Howard only had one reception. The result was a split national title, with Associated Press voters selecting Miami, but coaches opting for Washington.

But the Huskies have also had their fair share of turmoil. For example, after running back Hugh McElhenny's college career ended in 1951, he joked that he only took about a $3,000 pay cut in the NFL. It helped lead to a two-year bowl ban and probation from the Pacific Coast Conference (which existed from 1915-59).

In 1992, James' career unraveled after the *Seattle Times* reported that Hobert had accepted an improper $50,000 loan. When the National Collegiate Athletic Association also discovered that players had worked some easy summer jobs for money along with bookkeeping errors regarding expense money for recruits, Washington was quickly penalized by the Pac-10, including a two-year bowl ban, the loss of 20 scholarships and one year of television revenue. James resigned in protest over the severity of the penalties with a 150-60-2 record.

Finally, in 2003 Rick Neuheisel, who in four seasons compiled a 33-16 record and made four bowl appearances, including a 34-24 victory against Purdue in the Rose Bowl to cap an 11-1 season in 2000, was forced to resign after admitting to winning a March Madness basketball pool, with school officials alleging he lied to NCAA investigators. Neuheisel sued for wrongful termination and after a compliance memo authorizing participation in pools outside of the athletic department surfaced, he received a $4.5 million settlement.

WEST VIRGINIA MOUNTAINEERS
Consensus national titles (1936–present): None
Other national titles: None

West Virginia boasts names like Sam Huff, Darryl Talley, Renaldo Turnbull, Aaron Beasley, Major Harris, Jeff Hostetler (who passed for 321 yards and four touchdowns in his first start to beat No. 9 Oklahoma, 41-27, in 1982), Bruce Bosley, Marc Bulger, Joe Stydahar, Adrian Murrell, and so on. Among coaches, Bobby Bowden led the Mountaineers for six years (1970-75), compiling a 42-26 record with two Peach Bowl appearances before moving on to Florida State.

However, the biggest name associated with the program is Don Nehlen, who in 1980 inherited a 5-6 team and two years later beat Florida in the Peach Bowl to finish 9-3. By the end of the decade the Mountaineers were challenging for national championships.

In 1988, West Virginia went on a rampage, beating teams like Maryland, 55-24, and rival Pitt, 31-10, before a three-week run against Boston College (59-19), Penn State (51-30), and Cincinnati (51-13), all but forced a postseason showdown with No. 1 Notre Dame in the Fiesta Bowl. For the first time, a defense was able to contain mobile quarterback Harris, who was limited to 166 passing yards and one touchdown, and the Fighting Irish secured the national championship with a 34-21 victory. UWV was fifth in the final Associated Press poll.

The 1993 season was almost an exact repeat. Although the scores weren't as dominating, West Virginia survived the Big East season unblemished at 11-0, and proved that the conference wasn't just Miami and a bunch of second-tier programs with a 17-14 victory against the Hurricanes. The Mountaineers climbed to No. 3, but subsequently lost to Florida in the Sugar Bowl, 41-7, to drop out of the top five.

With Nehlen's departure in 2000 (149-93-4), spread-offense innovator Rich Rodriguez was handed the reins and in 2005 returned West Virginia to the top five. The 11-1 season culminated with Steve Slaton rushing for 204 yards to lead the 38-35 upset of Georgia in the first Sugar Bowl played outside of New Orleans, relocated to Atlanta due to Hurricane Katrina damage.

"I think we took to heart some of the criticism of our league and the fact that no one was predicting us to win," Rodriguez said. "Basically, we were playing in their home environment, their home state."

"It was just our speed," Slaton said. "They couldn't match up with us."

West Virginia had two other strong periods. The first came around World War I, when fullback Ira "Rat" Rodgers, whom Grantland Rice once dubbed the "finest all-around football player in the land," led the Mountaineers in 1915-17 and 1919. During his final season, he accounted for 147 points, which is still a school record, and led a high-profile 25-0 victory against Princeton by passing for 162 yards and two touchdowns. Coach Clarence Spears continued the winning ways, going 30-6-3 from 1921-24, highlighted by the 10-0-1 season of 1922 which concluded with the program's first postseason appearance, a 21-13 victory against Gonzaga at the East-West Bowl played in San Diego.

The other was under the direction of Art "Pappy" Lewis, who from 1952-57 guided the Mountaineers to a 44-13-1 mark, including 30 consecutive wins in the Southern Conference and an appearance in the 1954 Sugar Bowl (a 42-19 loss to Georgia Tech).

WISCONSIN BADGERS
Consensus national titles (1936–present): None
Other national titles: 1942

In the 1820s, lead miners in the state of Wisconsin burrowed tunnels into hillsides in an effort to survive the winters, causing people to say they "lived like Badgers."

Almost 200 years later, the University of Wisconsin's football team keeps that spirit alive, priding itself on playing with a tough, physical style that has been labeled a blue-collar ethic.

Most of its pronounced success came under the direction of Barry Alvarez (1990-2005), who during his 16 years led the Badgers to 11 bowl games including three Rose Bowl appearances. Additionally, nine Badgers were first-round selections in the National Football League draft: Troy Vincent, Aaron Gibson, Ron Dayne, Chris McIntosh, Jamar Fletcher, Michael Bennett, Wendell Bryant, Lee Evans and Erasmus James.

In 2005, Camp Randall Stadium also completed a four-year, $109 million renovation that included new FieldTurf, suites and club seats, new scoreboards, offices, and increased capacity to 80,321. Over the years, the stadium has become a must-visit for die-hard fans in a football-crazy state. Win or lose, a fifth quarter celebration is held, and the press box has been known to sway during games (especially when the song "Jump Around" is played after the third quarter).

Although the Badgers' lone claim to a national title is 1942, when the Helms Athletic Foundation named Wisconsin its champion even though Ohio State was the consensus No. 1 ahead of Georgia, it's had impressive flashes of greatness.

But the Badgers might have squandered their best chance at a national championship in 1912, when it plowed through its schedule, including impressive wins against Northwestern (56-0), Purdue (41-0), Arkansas (64-7), and Minnesota (14-0), to finish 7-0. Unfortunately, the team, led by tackle "Butts" Butler, never got a chance to see how it stacked up against an Eastern power due to the faculty blocking plans for a meeting with Yale. Instead, Harvard wound up the consensus national champion.

Wisconsin's first glory years were 1896 to 1901, when under the direction of Phil King the Badgers went 51-6-1, including 9-0 in 1901. They outscored opponents 1,622-110 during those six seasons, with 44 shutouts.

As for the 1942 team, the Badgers went 8-1-1 and knocked off national champion Ohio State, 17-7. Scoring all 17 points was fullback Pat Harder, who inspired cheers of "Hit 'em again, Harder! Harder! Harder!" and also in the backfield was halfback Elroy "Crazy Legs" Hirsch, who got the nickname after a 62-yard touchdown run against the Great Lakes Naval Training Center team. "I must have looked pretty funny," Hirsch said. "I've always run kind of funny because my left foot points out to the side and I seem to wobble."

Wisconsin finally played the Rose Bowl at the end of the 1952 season, and returned in both 1959 and 1962, but didn't win in Pasadena until 1993, when it thumped UCLA, 21-16, in front of 101,237 fans dressed predominantly in red.

"We certainly didn't get the feeling we were playing on our home field," said UCLA coach Terry Donahue, though he still might have been in shock from the six Bruins turnovers.

The program also boasts two Heisman Trophy winners, running backs Alan Ameche (1954) and Dayne (1999), whose names are displayed on the façade of the second deck at Camp Randall. Incidentally, Ameche is also known for scoring the winning touchdown in the legendary 1958 overtime championship game for the Baltimore Colts.

Other Notable Teams

Air Force: While the school was only founded in 1954, it dominated the Commander-in-Chief's Trophy, which goes to the best service academy team, 16 of the first 32 years after it was created in 1972. Despite strict admissions policies and restrictions (like pilots had to be small enough to fit into a cockpit), the Falcons have twice finished a season ranked in the Associated Press poll—No. 6 in 1958, and No. 8 in 1985. That 1958 team, led by tackle Brock Strom, tied Rose Bowl-bound and heavily favored Iowa, 13-13, and tied Texas Christian in the Cotton Bowl, 0-0, to finish 9-0-2. Strom went on to serve in Southeast Asia and was decorated with two Distinguished Flying Crosses, two Bronze Stars and three Air Medals. He served as Deputy of the Space Defense Systems in Los Angeles, responsible to the Secretary of the Air Force for the entire U.S. Space Defense Program. Each player at Air Force is adopted by a flying squadron and sent a flight scarf bearing the squadron's patch, and after he was a consensus All-American defensive tackle and academic All-American, Chad Hennings won three Super Bowls with the Dallas Cowboys and flew an A-10 tankbuster during the Persian Gulf War in 1991.

Arizona: The Wildcats' two best seasons came under the direction of Dick Tomey, who won 95 games over 14 seasons. In 1993, 9-2 Arizona was paired against Miami in the Fiesta Bowl, but the defense (dubbed Desert Swarm by Tomey to honor the U.S. Desert Storm offensive in the Gulf War) limited the Hurricanes to just 182 yards for a 29-0 victory. "They just kicked the living tar out of us," Miami coach Dennis Erickson said. In 1998, Arizona went 12-1, but missed out on the Rose Bowl due to a tiebreaker. Led by quarterbacks Keith Smith and Ortege Jenkins (who had the play of the year against Washington when he somersaulted off a hit and landed in the end zone for a 31-28 victory), running back Trung Canidate, linebacker Marcus Bell and cornerback Chris McAlister, the Wildcats defeated Nebraska 23-20 in the Holiday Bowl to finish No. 4. Although he didn't lead Arizona to a bowl appearance in his first year, 1973, Jim Young's team shared the Western Athletic Conference title with Arizona State.

Baylor: Conference titles have been few and far between for the Bears, but Grant Teaff won two in the Southwest Conference and posted 128 wins from 1972-92. He also gave one of the most famous pregame speeches in history. Two days before playing Texas he told a joke about two Eskimos ice fishing and one was catching all the fish. The other one asked how he was doing it and the fisherman took a worm out of his mouth and said, "You have to keep the worms warm." Before taking the field, Teaff said, "The game is yours, but there's one thing I'll do for you, I'll keep the worms warm," and popped a live worm into his mouth (he waited until the players left and spit it into the trash). Baylor destroyed heavily favored No. 9 Texas, 38-14. Baylor's best finish was No. 9 in 1951, when it went 8-2-1 and was invited to its first major bowl, a 17-14 loss to Georgia Tech in the Orange Bowl. Its best player, arguably, has been linebacker Mike Singletary, who broke 16 helmets during his career, 1977-80. Coach Morley Jennings (83-60-6 from 1926-40) also deserves mention, especially after nine of his players were killed in a bus accident. Baylor went from 2-7-0 in 1927, to 8-2-0 (with the losses 14-0 to Arkansas and 6-0 to Texas), and enjoyed the start of guard Barton Koch's career, Baylor's first All-American.

Boise State: The Broncos have played on its trademark blue field since 1986 and made the jump to Division I-A in 1996. In 2001, Boise State knocked off No. 8 Fresno State on national television, 35-30, and in 2004 a 44-40 loss to Louisville in the Liberty Bowl snapped a 22-game winning streak. In 2006, it played its way into the Bowl Championship Series, to face traditional power Oklahoma in the Fiesta Bowl. After Boise State blew an 18-point lead in the third quarter, the two teams had a wild finish and combined to score 22 points in the final 86 seconds—featuring a 50-yard hook-and-ladder by the Broncos on fourth-and-18—to send the game into overtime. After the Sooners scored on their first play, Boise State answered with a trick play, wide receiver Vinny Perretta's fourth-down touchdown pass to Derek Schouman, and won with another. On the two-point conversion, first-year coach Chris Petersen called for the Statue of Liberty, quarterback Jared Zabransky faking a throw to his right while handing the ball behind his back to tailback Ian Johnson, who reached the end zone untouched and topped the evening by asking his cheerleader girlfriend to marry him. "Yeah, another day at the office, huh?" Petersen said. His 13-0 team was ranked fifth in the final Associated Press poll.

Houston: The Cougars' three biggest seasons all concluded in the same place, Dallas. In 1976, Houston joined the Southwest Conference and stunned the field by defeating Baylor, Texas A&M, Southern Methodist and Texas Christian before crushing Texas, 30-0, with the Longhorns accumulating just 24 rushing yards. Even though the Cougars, under Bill Yeoman (160-108-8 from 1962-86), were co-conference champions, they were heavy underdogs against No. 5 Maryland in the Cotton Bowl. Houston jumped out to a 21-0 lead in the first quarter and accumulated 320 rushing yards for a 30-21 victory and No. 4 final ranking. Houston went back to the Cotton Bowl two years later only to see Notre Dame, with quarterback Joe Montana, tally 23 points in the final 7:37, with the final touchdown scored with no time remaining, for a 35-34 victory. Its finest season, though, was 1979, when Houston won 11 games and faced Nebraska on January 1. While the Cornhuskers managed just 227 offensive yards, half their average, the game came down to one play, fourth-and-goal from the 6 with 19 seconds remaining. Quarterback Terry Elston found Eric Herring for the touchdown and 17-14 victory. Houston also won a Heisman Trophy in 1989 with quarterback Andre Ware, who in 11 games passed for an amazing 4,699 yards and 46 touchdowns. When Ware left for the National Football League after his junior year, he had 8,202 career yards with 75 touchdowns and had set 26 National Collegiate Athletic Association records.

Indiana: The program's only outright Big Ten championship came in 1945 when it added two All-Americans to the roster following the season-opening 13-7 victory at Michigan. Howard Brown was granted a 60-day leave from the military and returned from Europe to play, and Pete Pihos was given permanent leave. Playing fullback, he wound up eighth in Heisman Trophy voting. After Northwestern managed a 7-7 tie, Indiana won eight straight games and outscored opponents 279-56. The final three wins were 49-0 at No. 20 Minnesota, 19-0 at Pitt, and 26-0 vs. No. 18 Purdue. The Hoosiers matched the No. 4 finish in 1967, which was even more impressive considering that they were coming off a 1-8-1 season. Although Indiana lost to Minnesota, 33-7, to fall from No. 5 to out of the top ten, Terry Cole had 155 rushing yards on 15 carries the following week to lead a 19-14 upset of Purdue and secure the program's first bowl bid (a 14-3 loss to No. 1 Southern California in its lone Rose Bowl appearance). Only one coach in 1920, Bo McMillin (63-48-1, 1934-47), finished his career with a winning record, but Bill Mallory won more games, 68, and led the Hoosiers to six bowls over an eight-year stretch (1986-93). Lee Corso guided the Hoosiers to the 1979 Holiday Bowl, a 38-37 victory against Brigham Young, and Sam Wyche coached Indiana for one season (3-8, 1983). Running back Anthony Thompson, who had 5,299 rushing yards from 1986-89, was the runner-up for the 1989 Heisman Trophy.

Kansas: The Jayhawks have won only five conference titles, and just one since 1947. It came in 1968, when quarterback Bobby Douglass and fullback John Riggins got Kansas off to a 7-0 start and No. 3 ranking. However, a 27-23 home loss to unranked Oklahoma knocked the Jayhawks out of the national-title picture and they subsequently lost to No. 3 Penn State in the Orange Bowl, 15-14. Adding to the disappointment was that after a long gain a botched substitution resulted in Kansas having 12 men on the field for five plays, including the key touchdown for the Nittany Lions. When Penn State went for the two-point conversion and failed, officials noticed the extra player and called the penalty. With another chance, it scored the game-winning points. The "Wichita Whiz," halfback James Bausch, led Kansas to its first Big Six conference title in 1930 after transferring from Wichita State (with Wheatshocker fans accusing the Jayhawks of tampering). The 1960 team went 7-2-1 and won the Big Eight title, but had to forfeit two games due to ineligible players, including the 23-7 victory against rival Missouri which was No. 1 entering the game. But it did keep the Tigers from winning the national title. Although he didn't win the Heisman Trophy, running back Gale Sayers is widely considered the best football player in Kansas history.

Kentucky: The Wildcats have the distinction of being the first team to go from a winless year to a bowl in successive seasons (1982-3 under Jerry Claiborne), but Kentucky was once on the doorstep of being a perennial football power with arguably the greatest college football coach ever, who had eight straight winning seasons to go with appearances in the Orange, Sugar and Cotton Bowls from 1946-53. When Paul "Bear" Bryant, who won six national championships and 13 SEC titles at Alabama, realized that contrary to promises basketball would remain the top priority of the athletic department, he quit despite having a 12-year contract. His 60 wins over eight years remain the school record. Bryant's 1950 team, which finished 11-1 and featured quarterback Babe Parilli and lineman Bob Gain, is considered the best in Kentucky history. In the coach's fifth season, the only loss was 7-0 at Tennessee in the regular-season finale played in cold and snow. With Kentucky 5-1 in Southeastern Conference play and Tennessee only 4-1 (thanks to an early-season 7-0 loss at Mississippi State), the Wildcats were awarded their first SEC championship. As a reward, Kentucky, ranked No. 7, was invited to play powerhouse Oklahoma in the Sugar Bowl. Bud Wilkinson's team had won 31 straight games and already been awarded the national championship (final polls were conducted before bowl games then), but Kentucky won, 13-7. Years later, *USA Today*'s Jeff Sagarin's retrospective computer rankings had the Wildcats finishing No. 1.

Miami (Ohio): The "other" Miami has been around a lot longer (1809), and accumulated many more victories than the school in Florida. While Dick Crum is the only one to have three 10-plus winning seasons, the coaching fraternity features an incredible list of names including Paul Brown, Weeb Ewbank, Sid Gillman, Woody Hayes, Ara Parseghian, George Little, Paul Dietzel, Bo Schembechler and Jim Tressel. Although Parseghian went 39-6-1 from 1951-55, the program's best stretch was from 1973-75, when Miami went 32-1-1, and won three consecutive Mid-American Conference titles and subsequent Tangerine Bowls to finish with Associated Press rankings of 15, 10 and 12. The lone loss was 14-13 to Michigan State, which was riding a 24-game unbeaten streak. To put that further into perspective, Miami has only finished a season ranked five times. The most recent was

No. 10 in 2003, when quarterback Ben Roethlisberger shattered the school passing record with 4,486 yards and had a 165.8 passer rating. Before leaving a year early for the National Football League, he had 10,829 yards and 84 touchdowns, compiled a 27-11 record and took Miami to its first bowl game in 17 years, a 49-28 victory against Louisville in the GMAC Bowl. "I can't wait to play them when he's gone," Bowling Green coach Gregg Brandon said after Roethlisberger passed for 440 yards against his team.

Mississippi State: In 1939, The Bulldogs were picked to finish 11th in the Southeastern Conference under first-year coach Allyn McKeen, only they opened the season with three straight shutouts and wound up 8-2. The program earned its first national ranking the following year, recorded its only unbeaten season, 10-0-1, and notched its first bowl victory with a 14-7 win against Georgetown in the Orange Bowl. Although ranked only No. 9, the Associated Press named Mississippi State the "undisputed king of football in the Deep South." McKeen's team came back in 1941 to win the Bulldogs' lone SEC title (8-1-1). McKeen (65-19-3) coached MSU until 1948, when he was fired after losing to Ole Miss in consecutive seasons. The two biggest wins in program history were both major upsets. The first was a 13-7 victory against powerhouse Army in 1935, the other in 1980 when Mississippi State snapped the 28-game winning streak of defending national champion Alabama. In 1998, Mississippi State was recovering from NCAA penalties for recruiting violations when late-season wins against Alabama, Arkansas and Ole Miss landed the Bulldogs in the SEC Championship game. MSU led 14-10 in the fourth quarter before Tennessee, which went on to win the national championship, pulled out a 24-14 victory. Coach Jackie Sherrill's team received an invitation to play Texas in the Cotton Bowl but lost 38-11. The following season, the Bulldogs won their first eight games before sustaining back-to-back losses to Alabama and Arkansas, but still finished 10-2 after defeating Clemson in the Peach Bowl, 17-7, to finish No. 13 in the final Associated Press poll. Three coaches who had brief stays in Starkville before winning the national championship elsewhere were Bernie Bierman (1925-26), Murray Warmath (1952-53), and Darrell Royal (1954-55).

North Carolina State: Although quarterback Roman Garbriel, halfback Jack McDowall, and center Jim Ritcher (his coach, Bo Rein said: "He was strong and quick. His talent enabled us to outline certain plays we wouldn't have considered with normal players. He would be a star at any position except quarterback or wide receiver") are considered the pride of the program, it was halfback Dick Christy who led the Wolfpack to its first Atlantic Coast Conference title in 1957. The clinching game was a 29-26 victory against South Carolina, even though the teams were tied in the final seconds. When South Carolina was called for pass interference, N.C. State had one final play at the 30, and Christy asked Coach Earle Edwards if he could attempt a 46-yard field goal even though it would be the first attempt of his career. "Man, I was stunned," Christy said. "But oh, it felt good." The 7-1-2 team was No. 15 in the final Associated Press poll. N.C. State rose to No. 3 in 1967, thanks to sweeping rivals Duke, Maryland, North Carolina and Wake Forest for the first time along with upsets of Florida State and Houston. Although it lost close games to Penn State (with a pass intercepted in the end zone and the offense was also stopped on fourth-and-goal from the 1) and Clemson, the Wolfpack came back to defeat Georgia in the Liberty Bowl, 14-7, for a 9-2 finish. Under the direction of Lou Holtz, N.C. State went 33-12-3 from 1972-75, including 20-1-1 at home, and made four bowl appearances. Of them, the 1974 team tied Houston in the Bluebonnet Bowl, 31-31, to finish 9-2-1 for the program's best finish, No. 11. Chuck Amato's team in 2002 came close to topping that, with a program-best nine-game winning streak, leading to an 11-3 record and No. 12 conclusion.

Northwestern: Most of the program's history is rather dismal, including six winless seasons since 1955 and a streak of 23 consecutive losing seasons lasting from 1972-94. But the Wildcats have a number of gems, including halfback Otto Graham, who was discovered in an intramural football game and went on to break every Big Ten passing record. He was also an All-American basketball player before serving in World War II, and then helping the Cleveland Browns dominate professional football. Under Dick Hanley, Northwestern was co-Big Ten champions in 1930 and 1931, and won the conference title outright in 1936 (to finish No. 7), after it upset defending national champion Minnesota, which was riding a 28-game unbeaten streak, 6-0. The Wildcats also played in the Rose Bowl at the end of the 1948 season and beat undefeated California, 20-14. Earlier that year, Northwestern was down 16-0 to Minnesota when team captain Alex Sarkisian, also the center, called the players together and said, "We are going to win. Anyone who doesn't think so can get off the field right now." The Wildcats did win, 19-16. In his second season at Northwestern, coach Ara Parseghian went 0-9 in 1957, but had winning seasons five of the next six years. In 1962, the Wildcats got off to a 6-0 start and were No. 1 for two weeks behind the passing combination of Tom Myers to Paul Flatley, before they stumbled against Wisconsin and Michigan State. Northwestern also beat Notre Dame for the fourth straight time, and after the 1963 season the Fighting Irish hired away Parseghian. The Wildcats also enjoyed a brief, but amazing resurgence under Gary Barnett. Coming off a 3-7-1 year, they opened the 1995 season with a shocking 17-15 victory against Notre Dame, its first win in the series since 1962. "I do not want you to carry me off the field after this game," Barnett told his players beforehand despite Notre Dame being favored by 28 points. "I want you to act like you've been here before." Inspired by the offseason death of Marcel Price, linebacker Pat Fitzgerald and running back Darnell Autry led Northwestern to a 10-1 record, conference title and Rose Bowl bid—a 41-32 loss to Southern California, resulting in a No. 8 final ranking.

Oklahoma State: While the program appears to be undergoing a rebirth, thanks in part to huge donations by alumnus Boone Pickens which have been used to upgrade the athletic facilities, Oklahoma State has been known for a lot more than knocking rival Oklahoma out of the national-title picture like it did in 2001 (when the defending national champion Sooners were 10-1 and ranked fourth). Over the 1944-45 seasons, the Cowboys lost only one game, and enjoyed dominating performances in major bowls. Under "Smiling" Jim Lookabaugh, they came off wins against Texas (13-8) and Oklahoma (28-6) to pound Texas Christian in the Cotton Bowl, 34-0. In 1945, Oklahoma State didn't allow an opponent to score more than 14 points, to finish 9-0. Behind offensive All-Americans Neill Armstrong and Bob Fenimore, it handed Oklahoma its worst defeat to that point, 47-0, and landed its only top five finish in the Associated Press poll. The Cowboys wouldn't finish another season ranked until 1976, which contributed to a 15-year stretch when coaches Jim Staley (1973-78), Jimmy Johnson (1979-83) and Pat Jones (1984-94) guided them to eight bowl appearances. Highlighting this era were two running backs, with Thurman Thomas setting the school's all-time career rushing record only to see it shattered by his former backup, Barry Sanders. When Sanders rushed for 2,628 yards and 39 touchdowns, both National Collegiate Athletic Association records, he won the school's lone Heisman Trophy in 1988. Because the Cowboys (10-2) had scheduled their season finale against Texas Christian in Tokyo, Japan, Sanders had to accept the award via satellite transmission, and insisted his offensive linemen join him for the presentation.

Oregon State: While most people know the Beavers for coaches Mike Riley and Dennis Erickson, who after a 35-year bowl drought had Oregon State in the postseason five of six seasons from 1999-2004, it came after 28 consecutive years of losing football. Oregon State has won five Pac-10 titles, two outright, and in 1962 Terry Baker won the Heisman Trophy (in addition to the Maxwell Award, and also named *Sports Illustrated*'s Sportsman of the Year before helping lead the basketball team to the Final Four). At the end of the 1941 season, Oregon State traveled to Duke for the only Rose Bowl played outside of Pasadena (as a wartime precaution). Bob Dethman threw the game-winning pass to Gene Gray for a 20-16 victory. With respect to the recent coaches, Tommy Prothro is considered the program's best coach and from 1955-64 compiled a 67-37-2 record and two Rose Bowl appearances (losing both). In 1967, Oregon State defeated No. 2 Purdue, 22-14, and tied No. 2 UCLA, 16-16, both on the road. "I'm tired of playing these No. 2 teams," said Coach Dee Andros, who was nicknamed "The Great Pumpkin." "Bring on No. 1." The Beavers, known as the Giant Killers, won that game too, 3-0, even though O.J. Simpson had 188 rushing yards on 33 carries for Southern California, which would still go on to win the national championship. At 7-2-1, Oregon State finished No. 7. The only top five finish came under Erickson in 2000. Despite having a walk-on quarterback, Jonathan Smith, and a small running back (Ken Simonton, who accumulated 5,044 rushing yards), the Beavers also featured wide receiver Chad Johnson and All-American center Chris Gibson. An early 33-30 loss at Washington didn't faze Oregon State too much, which capped the 10-1 regular season with a 23-13 victory against rival Oregon, and went on to crush No. 10 Notre Dame in the Fiesta Bowl, 41-9.

Rice: In 2006, Rice was coming off a 1-10 year and opened the season with four straight losses, including back-to-back defeats to Texas and Florida State by a combined score of 107-14. But when the Owls put together six straight Conference USA wins, they made the first bowl appearance since 1961. During his 27-year coaching stint, Jess Neely won four Southwest Conference titles and three of six bowl games while compiling a 144-124-10 record. In 1946, Rice beat No. 7 Tennessee in the Orange Bowl, 8-0, with a 9-2 record and a No. 10 final ranking. The 1949 Owls, who passed more than usual with quarterback Tobin Rote and Foggy Williams, went 10-1 and defeated North Carolina in the Cotton Bowl, 27-13, for the program's highest season-ending ranking, No. 5. Rice appeared in the Cotton Bowl in 1953 and 1957, defeating Alabama (remembered for the Crimson Tide's Tommy Lewis jumping off the bench in the middle of a play and tackling Dick Maegle. He was credited with the touchdown and finished with 265 yards on 11 carries) and losing to Navy, respectively, and came up short in the 1961 Sugar Bowl, a 14-6 defeat to Ole Miss. In terms of name recognition, Tommy Kramer passed for 3,317 yards and finished fifth in 1976 Heisman Trophy voting, and Trevor Cobb won the 1991 Doak Walker award as the nation's top running back. John Heisman was Rice's first full-time coach, though it was his last coaching job. He had a record of 14-18-3 from 1924-27 and led the first victory against behemoth in-state rival Texas, 19-6, in 1924. Rice's last win in the series was 1994, snapping a 28-game losing streak. "Why does Rice play Texas?" President John F. Kennedy said at Rice Stadium in 1962. "We choose to go to the moon. We choose to go to the moon in this decade and do all the other things, not because they are easy, but because they are hard."

Rutgers: The Scarlet Knights have played football longer than all but one college program in the country (Princeton, which it defeated in the first game in 1869, 6-4), yet didn't leave the state of New Jersey to play in a bowl game until 2005, when they lost to Arizona State in the Insight Bowl, 45-40. But it set up an amazing run in 2006, when Greg Schiano's team was the buzz of college football. Going into a showdown with No. 3 Louisville, Rutgers was 8-0, but had only five wins ever against teams ranked higher than 15th in the Associated Press poll. Down 25-7 in the first half, the Scarlet Knights came back and erased the deficit before kicking a field goal with 13 seconds remaining to send New Jersey into pandemonium. With the victory, Rutgers was in place to secure a spot in the Bowl Championship Series, only it lost the following week to Cincinnati, 30-11, and the regular-season finale to West Virginia, 41-39 in triple-overtime. Rutgers closed the year with a 37-10 victory against Kansas State in the Texas Bowl, and at No. 12. "We've tasted it, tasted the water and it's a great feeling," said Ray Rice, who ran for 170 yards and a touchdown in the program's first bowl victory. The first bowl appearance was in 1978, two years after being shut out of the postseason despite an 11-0 finish and No. 17 ranking under Frank Burns. Rutgers played Arizona State in the first Garden State Bowl, and lost 34-18 at Giants Stadium. Previously, one of the few points of football pride was Paul Robeson, only the third black man to receive a Rutgers scholarship, who from 1915-18 helped the Scarlet Knights compile a 22-6-3 record and outscore opponents 944-191. Walter Camp called him "the greatest end to ever trod the gridiron." Robeson went on to record the song "Ol' Man River" and star in movies and plays. *Ebony* magazine tabbed him "one of the ten most important black men in American history."

South Carolina: Since 1892, the Gamecocks have won no national championships, one conference title, and just four bowl games. Yet Williams-Brice Stadium consistently attracts more than 80,000 fans. The program's best finish came in 1984, when Joe Morrison's team got on an unprecedented roll, defeating Georgia, Pittsburgh, Kansas State, Florida State, and even won at Notre Dame for a No. 2 ranking behind Washington. However, South Carolina surprisingly slipped at Navy, a game that was rescheduled on the road so the Gamecocks could have an extra home date the following season. Doubling the disappointment was that Washington lost on the same day, depriving South Carolina of its first No. 1 ranking. It went on to rally from an 18-point deficit to defeat rival Clemson, 22-21, only to lose 21-14 to Oklahoma State in the Gator Bowl to finish No. 11. Although Lou Holtz transformed South Carolina from a Southeastern Conference doormat that went 1-10 in 1998 into a top 20 program that finished both the 2000 and 2001 seasons with New Year's Day wins against Ohio State in the Outback Bowl, two names are synonymous with the program's past and future. The first is running back George Rogers, who rushed for 1,894 yards in 1980, including back-to-back 140-plus yards in consecutive road games against Southern California and Michigan, to win the Heisman Trophy. The other is Steve Spurrier, who won a national championship at Florida. "I know our history is not the greatest in the world as far as winning the conference, but we've got everything here," Spurrier said. "I'd like to borrow a phrase from the Boston Red Sox, 'Why not us?' Why can't we get to the top of the SEC? Certainly that's going to be my dream." During his first season in 2005, South Carolina lost three of its first five games, but won five of the final six including against No. 23 Tennessee and No. 12 Florida. He came back in 2006 to lead the Gamecocks to a 44-36 win against Houston in the Liberty Bowl, and then turned down overtures to coach Alabama. "Some of you might not like me, but you're stuck with me," Spurrier told his team.

Texas Tech: Throughout most of its existence, Texas Tech has played second fiddle to in-state powers Texas and Texas A&M, but the Red Raiders have significantly closed the gap. Although the program has enjoyed bits of success—like Pete Cawthon leading seasons of 10-2 in 1932, 10-1 and a Cotton Bowl berth in 1938, and 9-1-1 in 1940; Dell Morgan's 9-2 season in 1941; and the 11-1 1953 season that was capped by a 35-13 victory against Auburn in the Gator Bowl—the turnaround began in 1961 under J.T. King. Despite budget limitations his teams made back-to-back bowl trips in 1964-65, and beat Texas in both 1967 and 1968. With the foundation in place, Jim Carlen led Tech to four bowl games in five years, including a 28-19 victory against Tennessee in the Gator Bowl to finish 11-1 and No. 11 in 1973. In 1976, the Red Raiders lost to Nebraska in the Bluebonnet Bowl, 27-24, but finished 10-2. The program dipped in the 1980s, but Spike Dykes started to build it back up in the 1990s, highlighted by an appearance in the 1995 Cotton Bowl, and a 9-3 record the following season with a 55-41 victory against Air Force in the Copper Bowl. Coach Mike Leach's passing attack helped make Texas Tech a top 25 program again and led to quarterbacks Kliff Kingsbury and B.J. Symons setting or tying 32 National Collegiate Athletic Conference records. But even when not ranked, the flamboyant (or eccentric depending on your point of view) coach and the Red Raiders have been equally entertaining. "I ought to have Mike's Pirate School," Leach once said. "The freshmen, all they get is the bandana. When you're a senior, you get the sword and the skull and crossbones." At the 2006 Insight Bowl, the Red Raiders came back from a 31-point deficit in the third quarter to pull off a 44-41 overtime victory against Minnesota (which led to Glen Mason's firing).

Tulane: The Green Wave has had a tumultuous history with everything from title runs to scandals, and administrators nearly disbanding the program. For 33 years, Tulane competed in the Southeastern Conference, and despite three SEC titles the small private school couldn't keep up with the competition and withdrew in 1965. That came after Clark Shaughnessy (who in 1915 was hired at age 23) posted two of the best years in program history. After a 17-1-1 record over the 1924-25 seasons Tulane received an invitation to play in the Rose Bowl, but school president Dr. A.B. Dinwiddie wouldn't approve the trip. A year later, Shaughnessy left Tulane for neighboring Loyola. Nevertheless, from 1929-31 Tulane went 28-2 under Bernie Bierman and nearly won a national championship. Led by halfback Bill Banker, receiver Jerry Dalrymple and a defense that shut out eight opponents during the regular season, Tulane was riding an 18-game winning streak and paired against Southern California in the Rose Bowl. USC jumped out to a 21-0 lead, but despite outgaining the Trojans the Green Wave could pull no closer than 21-12, helping make Southern California the consensus national champion. Featuring halfback Monk Simons, Tulane played in the inaugural 1935 Sugar Bowl, a 20-14 victory against Temple, and Red Dawson returned the Green Wave to the Rose Bowl at the end of the 8-1-1 1939 season. In 1998, only one team, Louisville, came within seven points of Tulane, which finished a perfect 12-0, including a 41-27 victory against Brigham Young in the Liberty Bowl—Tulane's first bowl victory in 28 years. Due to the setup of the Bowl Alliance, the Green Wave didn't have the opportunity to play in a major bowl game and was ranked No. 7 in the final poll. Since then, quarterbacks Shaun King, Patrick Ramsey, and J.P Losman have all landed in the National Football League.

Utah: Although Urban Meyer's 2004 team was the first non-Bowl Championship Series school to play in a BCS game, Ike Armstrong is the coach best associated with the Utes. During his 25 years, Utah went 141-55-15 and had just two losing seasons. In addition to winning 12 conference championships (most in the Rocky Mountain conference), he beat rival Brigham Young 18 times, but never landed a season-ending ranking. No one did until 1994, when Kevin Dyson caught the game-winning touchdown of the Freedom Bowl on fourth down for a 16-13 victory against Arizona. The program's first 10-win season came in the middle of Ron McBride's six bowl appearances from 1992-2001, and resulted in a No. 10 finish. Meyer inherited a 5-6 team and immediately posted a 10-2 season to win the Mountain West title in 2003, highlighted by regular season wins against California, Oregon and Brigham Young, and a 17-0 victory against Southern Miss in the Liberty Bowl. Led by quarterback Alex Smith, who was fourth in Heisman Trophy voting, the high-flying Utes averaged 45.3 points, and no opponent finished within 14 points in 2004 when Utah finished 12-0. After it crushed Pitt in the Fiesta Bowl, 35-7, Associated Press voters had Utah at No. 4.

Virginia: Although Virginia enjoyed initial success and didn't have a losing season until 1916, the program's first postseason game didn't occur until 1984, when it defeated Purdue in the Peach Bowl, 27-24. Before George Welsh arrived in 1982, the Cavaliers had managed two winning seasons over the previous 29 years. Through 2000, his teams went 134-86-3, won two Atlantic Coast Conference titles and played in 12 bowl games. In 1990, Virginia's 20-7 victory against Clemson was Virginia's first win in the series in 30 attempts, and first victory against a top 10 team. Led by wide receiver Herman Moore, the Cavaliers were 7-0 and ranked No. 1 for the first time in school history when they hosted unbeaten Georgia Tech for homecoming. Virginia led 28-14 at halftime, but lost on a field goal in the final seconds, 41-38. Georgia Tech went on to earn a share of the national championship, while Virginia stumbled to an 8-4 finish following a 23-22 loss to Tennessee in the Sugar Bowl. Welsh's teams played in bowls 10 of his last 12 years, but the most memorable game during that span may have been the 1995 meeting with No. 2 Florida State, which had won 29 straight conference games since joining the ACC. Quarterback Danny Kanell led the Seminoles on their final drive down to the Cavaliers' 6-yard line with four seconds remaining, but running back Warrick Dunn was stopped inches short of the goal-line on the final play. Virginia finished 9-4 after a 34-27 victory against Georgia in the Peach Bowl. Other standouts include twins Ronde and Tiki Barber, Bill Dudley (who finished fifth in 1941 Heisman Trophy voting but won the Maxwell Trophy), and Tom Scott.

Wake Forest: Bowl berths have been few and far between for the Demon Deacons—in fact there's only been seven—but in 2006 they were among the biggest surprises of the college football season by winning 11 games to secure the Atlantic Coast Athletic title and qualify for a Bowl Championship Series game. Although Wake Forest lost to No. 5 Louisville, 24-13, it was still arguably the best season in program history. "We felt like we could do this, but nobody else did," defensive tackle Jamil Smith said. "So it was great to prove people wrong." Previously, that distinction belonged to the only other Deacon Demon team to win the ACC, 1970, even though it finished 6-5. After a 0-3 start against Nebraska (which went on to win the national championship), South Carolina and Florida State, all on the road, Wake Forest went 5-1 in the conference with the final two losses against No. 9 Tennessee and at Houston. With Wake Forest having defeated unbeaten Duke and North Carolina State, a Duke loss against North Carolina clinched the conference title for the Demon Deacons. The 1992 team had a comparable year after a 1-3 start, but won six straight games and capped the season with a 39-35 victory against Oregon in the Independence Bowl. Additionally, the 1945 team nearly matched the 2006 squad for the highest finish in the Associated Press poll, No. 19 (compared to No. 18), and the 1946 squad upset No. 4 Tennessee, 19-6.

Washington State: The Cougars have finished in the top 10 four times, but their history has had its fill of ups and downs. For example, an invitation to the 1981 Holiday Bowl (a 38-36 loss to Brigham Young) ended a 50-year postseason drought, and the 67-year absence in the Rose Bowl ended in 1997. Coach Mike Price was the architect of that 10-2 team, which lost to Michigan in Pasadena, 21-16, but still served as the benchmark for the program. Coming off a 5-6 season, quarterback Ryan Leaf engineered wins against

Southern California and UCLA, and went on to eclipse many of Drew Bledsoe's passing records. The Cougars closed the regular season with a 41-35 victory against Washington, even though wide receiver Chris Jackson promised beforehand that they would "kill" the Huskies. He backed it up with eight catches for 185 yards and two touchdowns. Washington State went back to the Rose Bowl at the end of the 2002 season, but lost to Oklahoma, 34-14. The program's first trip to the Rose Bowl came at the end of the 1930 season, thanks to a key interception by Glen Edwards against Oregon State. But Washington State lost 24-0 to Alabama, ironically the program Price left for but would never coach a game at due to an off-field incident. At the time, Washington State was coached by Orin "Babe" Hollingbery, who never attended college, but over 17 years compiled a 93-53-14 record and had only two losing seasons.

Chapter 3

The Former Greats

ARMY BLACK KNIGHTS

Consensus national titles (1936–present): 1944, 1945, 1946

Other national titles: 1914, 1916

It was a 17-word telegram wired to West Point upon the completion of the 1944 undefeated season, including a 23-7 victory against Navy.

"The greatest of all Army teams—STOP—We have stopped the war to celebrate your magnificent success. MacArthur."

Obviously, the World War II reprieve didn't last long, but the United States Military Academy was just getting started on one of the most impressive runs in college football history.

From 1944-46, Army went 27-0-1, and won the national championship all three years, although the 1946 controversial title is disputed due to a high-profile tie with Notre Dame.

The 1944 team averaged 56 points per game, while yielding a total of 35, thanks in part to four shutouts. It also boasted six first-team All-Americans, which caused Earl Henry "Red" Blaik to once proclaim that the best game he saw his team play that season was a practice scrimmage. The depth chart was so deep the Cadets actually had two offensive units.

Blaik inherited a 1-7-1 team, but compiled a 121-33-10 record from 1941-58. Among his assistants, 15 of whom went on to become head coaches, were Sid Gillman (line coach, 1948) and Vince Lombardi (backs coach, 1949-53).

However, he was also the head coach during the cheating scandal that resulted in the dismissal of 90 cadets, including 37 football players. Among them was Blaik's son, Bobby, who was also Army's quarterback. Blaik had to be talked out of resigning by General Douglas MacArthur, who said "Don't leave under fire."

Blaik rebuilt the program and then retired after the 8-0-1 season in 1958. Among his other accomplishments, he was awarded the Presidential Medal of Freedom from President Reagan in 1986, wrote the book "You Have to Pay the Price" with sportswriter Tom Cohane (foreword by MacArthur), and Blaik wrote a syndicated newspaper column, published twice a week during football season with the proceeds earmarked to graduate scholarships for football players.

Army has had three Heisman Trophy winners: Doc Blanchard (1945), Glenn Davis (1946), and Pete Dawkins (1958). While in the same backfield, Blanchard and Davis were known as Mr. Inside and Mr. Outside. Ed McKeever, while coaching Notre Dame during the 1944 season, said: "I've just seen Superman in the flesh. He wears number 35 and goes by the name of Blanchard."

From 1920-65, Army's record of 299-110-26 gave it a winning percentage of .717. That trailed only Notre Dame (.755), Tennessee (.733) and Alabama (.733). Since then, Army's had a losing record, but the traditions and legacy remain unblemished. For example, Michie Stadium was named after the cadet who in 1890 accepted a challenge from Navy students to play a football game.

BROWN BEARS
Consensus national titles (1936–present): None
Other national titles: None

Although Brown did play in the 1916 Rose Bowl, a 14-0 loss to Washington State before the game's appeal began to really grow, its impact on the game has been more far-reaching.

For example, Joe Paterno and John Heisman both played for Brown, as did Fritz Pollard, who in 1916 became the first black to play football in the Rose Bowl. The following season, he led Brown to an 8-1 season and became an All-American with Walter Camp calling him "one of the best runners these eyes have ever seen." In 1921, Pollard became the first black head coach in National Football League history when he was hired by the Akron Pros.

Incidentally, in 1905 Pollard's sister Noami became the first black woman to graduate from Northwestern and his brother Leslie was on the 1908 Dartmouth football team. Pollard went on to own coal companies in Harlem and Chicago, operate a movie studio, publish a weekly paper in New York, found the nation's first African-American investment company, and operate a booking agency.

Brown has won two Ivy League championships, but its best years occurred before the league was created in 1956 (in fact, from 1959-72 it averaged less than one Ivy League win a season).

In 1910, it knocked off defending national champion Yale, 21-0, and went on to finish 7-2-1 under E.N. Robinson. During three different stints, Robinson accumulated 140 victories.

The 1926 team was called the Iron Men, and during a four-week stretch they defeated Yale 7-0, Dartmouth 10-0, Norwich 27-0, and Harvard 21-0. Colgate managed a 10-10 tie, as Brown, under D.O. McLaughry, finished its only undefeated season 9-0-1.

The 1932 squad was known as the Cinderella Bears, when they won seven consecutive games against an undefeated team. The eighth game, against 8-0 Colgate, which had outscored opponents 243-0, proved to be too much, resulting in a 21-0 loss before a record crowd of 33,000. Brown's final record was 7-1.

CARLISLE INDIAN SCHOOL
Consensus national titles (1936–present): None
Other national titles: None

Undoubtedly the best college football program most people have never heard of, Carlisle was the first federally supported school of Native Americans to be established off a reservation, in Carlisle, Pennsylvania. Over 25 years, before the school was closed in 1918, it compiled a record of 167-88-13, thanks in part to eight future inductees into the College Football Hall of Fame.

The program's most notable player was Jim Thorpe, considered by many to be the greatest all-around athlete the United States has ever had. As a halfback in 1907-08, and again in 1911-12, he played 44 games with 53 touchdowns and 421 points. According to the College Football Hall of Fame, statistics for 29 of the games show he averaged 8.4 yards per carry. In 1912, he had 29 touchdowns and 224 points, which led the nation.

"Thorpe was the greatest athlete of his time, maybe of any time in any land," Red Smith once wrote, and with good reason. At the 1912 Olympics in Stockholm he won the pentathlon and decathlon. Thorpe went on to play Major League Baseball (1913-19), pro football (1915-28), and was said to excel in every sport he tried, including golf, tennis, lacrosse, field hockey, riding, rowing, gymnastics, archery, bowling, darts, billiards, basketball, swimming, boxing and wrestling.

Thorpe's coach was Glenn Warner, more commonly known as "Pop" Warner, who was at Carlisle from 1899–1903, and 1907–1914. Actually, the entire coaching staff consisted of Warner and an Oneida Indian named Wallace Denny, the trainer, who doubled as Carlisle's night watchman. The team often played as many as 10 games in six weeks. In 1912, Warner's team went 12-1-1 and scored 504 points. The following year it finished 11-2-1 with 295 points.

CENTRE COLONELS
Consensus national titles (1936–present): None
Other national titles: 1919

Centre, a small liberal arts college in Danville, Kentucky, which now plays in Division III, has a football history that dates back to 1880, when the Colonels participated in the first football game played south of the Ohio River, in Lexington, against Kentucky University (Transylvania). It lost by the unusual score of 13¾ to 0.

The program's high point, before the college began to deemphasize the sport in the 1930s and later ceased awarding athletic scholarships, was from 1917-24, when the "Praying

Colonels" went 57-8-2 while playing much bigger schools. For example, during the 9-0 season of 1919, Centre defeated Indiana, Virginia, West Virginia and Kentucky. No opponent scored more than seven points, and the Colonels outscored the opposition 485-23.

Leading the team was quarterback Alvin "Bo" McMillin, who followed his coach, "Chief" Robert L. Myers, from Northside High School in Fort Worth along with teammates Matty Bell, Bill Janee, Sully Montgomery and Red Weaver. In 1919, McMillin (who went on to coach Centenary 1922-24, Geneva 1925-27, Kansas State 1928-33, and Indiana 1934-47, where his 1945 team won the Hoosiers' first Big Ten championship, for a record of 146-77-13) was named first team All-American by Walter Camp despite playing at a school with an enrollment of 270 students.

Although Centre defeated Texas Christian (9-1) at the Fort Worth Classic, 63-7, at the end of the 1920 season (8-2, outscoring teams 532-62), its biggest victory came in 1921, when the small school from the South traveled to Cambridge to face Harvard, which had not lost a game since 1918 (and played in the Rose Bowl at the end of the 1919 season, where it defeated Oregon, 7-6).

On October 29, Centre stunned Harvard, 6-0. McMillin scored the lone touchdown after breaking a tackle, on a 35-yard run. It's still considered one of the biggest upsets in college football history.

Centre also defeated Clemson, Virginia Tech, Kentucky, Auburn, Washington & Lee and Tulane for a 9-0 record, before agreeing to play two postseason games. The first was against Arizona in the San Diego East-West Christmas Classic, played on December 26. Centre won, 38-0.

The team then traveled to Dallas to play Texas A&M in the Dixie Classic, the precursor of the Cotton Bowl, on January 2. Centre had allowed only six points all season, but lost, 22-14.

The game was also the start of the Aggies' famous 12th Man tradition. With the team sustaining numerous injuries during the first half, Dana X. Bible had student E. King Gill (a former player on hand to help out as a spotter), put on a uniform and be ready to play if Texas A&M ran out of healthy players. Today, students stand throughout home games in case they are needed to go in and play.

CHICAGO MAROONS
Consensus national titles (1936–present): None
Other national titles: 1905, 1913

Even though the University of Chicago dropped football in 1939 (it restarted the program for Division III in 1968), it won a national championship in 1905 and seven Big Ten titles from 1899-1924.

Jay Berwanger was the first winner of the Heisman Trophy in 1935, and subsequently the first selection in the first National Football League draft (he never played pro ball, but is one of nine Chicago inductees into the College Football Hall of Fame). Although the program featured quarterback Walter Eckersall (1903-06) and guard Bob "Tiny" Maxwell (1902, 1904-5)—for whom both the Maxwell Club and Maxwell Trophy are named, and in 1902 he helped lead the Maroons to an 11-1 record—the name most associated with Chicago is coach Amos Alonzo Stagg.

"The Grand Old Man of the Midway," who was at Chicago from 1892-1932, invented the end-around, hidden-ball trick, fake punt, quick-kick, man-in-motion, double reverse, huddle, backfield shift, Statue of Liberty play, padded goal posts, and having numbers on players' backs. Incidentally, he also invented the batting cage for baseball and the trough for overflow in swimming pools.

"All football comes from Stagg," said Knute Rockne, whose football hero as a kid was Eckersall.

In 1913, 7-0 Chicago was led by All-American center Paul Des Jardien, who was said to respect Stagg, but couldn't help occasionally make light of his numerous training rules and restrictions: "Watch your diets!" he mockingly quoted him as saying. "Keep the hot-dogs in the stands where they belong.

"I never ate one in my life."

COLGATE RAIDERS

Consensus national titles (1936–present): None
Other national titles: 1875, 1932

One of the more notable stories about Dick Harlow has to do with the 1924 squad that finished 5-4, but shut out four opponents. Before the start of one game the coach had a druggist make up some harmless sugar pills which he brought to the locker room and said, "Men, these tablets are made from an old Indian formula that I found during my wanderings in Pennsylvania. They're compounded from the glands of a buffalo and give you abnormal strength." The players took them and won the game, and then demanded the pills before each game. When they finally lost, Harlow told them, "Football is all in the mind," and the following season Colgate finished 7-0-2.

The Raiders have twice been briefly ranked in the Associated Press poll, No. 9 in 1942 and No. 20 in 1977. They also shut out five opponents and scored 107 points against Rensselaer Polytechnic Institute en route to a 5-1 record in 1915.

But the program's best run came under Andy Kerr (1929-46), who emphasized the downfield lateral (which most coaches now frown upon).

"The public likes razzle-dazzle, but I use laterals mostly as whip-crackers beyond the scrimmage line, not behind it," Kerr said. "It serves to keep tacklers off-balance."

During Kerr's first three years, the Raiders went 25-3-0 and held 19 of their 28 opponents scoreless while out-pointing them 925-80. Among the teams Colgate defeated were Brown, Michigan State, New York University, Penn State and Syracuse.

The 1932 team was Kerr's best, which went 9-0, didn't yield a single point, and defeated Penn State 31-0, Syracuse 16-0 and Brown 21-0. However, even though Pitt was

8-0-2, the Rose Bowl extended an invitation to the Panthers, who were subsequently crushed by Southern California, 35-0.

Kerr's subsequent teams went 6-1-1 and 7-1, with the lone loss in 1934 to Ohio State, 10-7. But like most programs that eventually wound up playing in Division I-AA, Colgate couldn't keep up with the bigger schools.

In 1986, running back Kenny Gamble led the nation in all-purpose yards (2,425) and rushing yards (1,816). In 1987, he led in all-purpose yards (2,097) and was second in rushing yards (1,411), to win the Walter Payton Award as the nation's best player in Division I-AA. Running back Jamaal Branch won the award in 2003.

COLUMBIA LIONS
Consensus national titles (1936–present): None
Other national titles: None

When Lou Little received a call from the West Coast inviting his Lions to play in the 1934 Rose Bowl, he thought someone was playing a prank on him—especially since Columbia (7-1) had been soundly defeated that season by Princeton, 20-0. When he realized the invitation was legit, he said yes and began preparing to play highly touted Stanford, which was heavily favored.

The game featured only one score, a 17-yard touchdown run by fullback Al Barabas on essentially a hidden-ball option play titled KF-79, for a 7-0 final. Quarterback Cliff Montgomery, who had called the play, was named the game's most outstanding player, and he finished his career with a 22-3-2 record.

Little—who told a group of alumni when he was hired, "I did not come to Columbia to fail"—was nearly lured away by Yale in 1949, but another coaching non-move has Lions fans still wondering: "What if?" After a 5-3-1 season in 1924, Columbia offered to make Knute Rockne the highest paid coach in the country and more than double his salary. When the story broke before Rockne could finalize his release from Notre Dame, he had no choice but to stay put.

Columbia is also known for All-American quarterback Sid Luckman, who couldn't lead the Lions to a winning record in 1938, but beat Yale, 27-14, and Army 20-18 (he returned a kickoff 85 yards for a touchdown, threw two touchdown passes and kicked an extra point), and halfback Walter Koppisch. Coach Percy Haughton said of him, "He's the best back I've ever coached," and one of Koppisch's blockers was none other than future baseball legend Lou Gehrig.

Before becoming known as the "Miracle Worker" at Rutgers, George Sanford began his coaching career at Columbia (1899-1901) and was given the task of reviving the program, which had been abandoned after the 1891 season. His 1899 team defeated Yale for the first time ever, and unveiled the famous "Flying Hurdle Play" which saw 5-foot-10 Harold Weekes catapulted over the scrimmage line only to land on his feet and run away from the stunned defenders for a 55-yard gain and score the decisive points.

Nowadays, Columbia, which has won only one Ivy League title (1961), is better known for its losing ways. In 1988, when the Lions upset Princeton to snap a 44-game losing streak, fans stormed the field and tore down the goalposts.

CORNELL BIG RED

Consensus national titles (1936–present): None

Other national titles: 1915, 1921, 1922, 1923, 1939

In addition to Campbell Soups using the same color scheme on its cans due to controller and general manager Herberton Williams being impressed with the football team's new bright red uniforms after attending a home victory coached by Glenn "Pop" Warner in 1898, Cornell has the distinction of having the Ivy League's last serious contender for a consensus national title, and its last legitimate Heisman Trophy contender.

The player was running back Ed Marinaro, who as a senior in 1971 led the nation in rushing, all-purpose yards and scoring, but was edged in voting by Auburn quarterback Pat Sullivan. After six years in the pros, Marinaro became familiar to another generation as police officer Joe Coffey on the popular television series "Hill Street Blues."

The team was the 1939 squad, which defeated Syracuse (19-6), Penn State (47-0) and Ohio State (24-14), and rose to No. 3 in the Associated Press poll trailing only Texas A&M and Tennessee. At 8-0 under the direction of Carl "The Gray Fox" Snavely (the first coach to use game film), Cornell was set to play in the Rose Bowl against Southern California, only school president Edmund Ezra Day decided the season had gone long enough and wanted players to concentrate on academics. The Big Red never made the trip and USC went on to defeat Tennessee.

The decision echoed the sentiment of Andrew Dickson White, who as president in 1873 shot down a trip to Cleveland to play Michigan: "I refuse to allow 40 men to go 400 miles merely to agitate a bag of wind."

One of the players who would have been highlighted in Pasadena was All-American end Jerome "Brud" Holland, who worked his way through Cornell as a dishwasher and furnace-tender.

"I was born with slightly deformed legs," he once said. "My grandmother, Julia Bagby, massaged my legs daily, and they became normal."

Holland graduated with highest honors in 1939, obtained a master's degree at Cornell in 1941, and PhD at the University of Pennsylvania in 1950. His later titles included: president of Hampton Institute, president of Delaware State, U.S. ambassador to Sweden (1970-72), chairman American Red Cross, chairman Salvation Army, chairman Planned Parenthood, and the first black director of the New York Stock Exchange. Among his awards was the Medal of Freedom, the nation's highest civilian award, issued in 1985.

Cornell stakes a strong claim to three national championships, the first under Al Sharpe in 1915. The key game was a 10-0 victory against Harvard, which was riding a 33-game unbeaten streak, with the lone touchdown scored by Charley Barrett.

Looking to capitalize on the program's success, Gil Dobie was hired from Washington, where he had accumulated a record of 58-0-3. From 1920-35, his teams went 82-36-7 including a 26-game winning streak that fully encompassed the 1921-23 seasons, during which the Big Red gave up a total of 81 points (or 3.1 per game) while scoring 1,134.

Following a 41-0 victory in the rain against Penn in 1921, during which Eddie Kaw scored five touchdowns, the *New York Times* correspondent wrote: "There was only one thing more slippery than the mud, and that was the open field running of halfback Eddie Kaw, who was far ahead of any other player on the field. ...

"[Kaw] skipped over the ooze and water as if he were running on a cinder track, side-stepping a small lake and a Penn tackler with one and the same motion."

Also in the same backfield was quarterback George Pfann, who during three seasons never lost. Pfann went on to earn his law degree, become a Rhodes Scholar at Oxford University in England, and was decorated with seven battle stars as a lieutenant colonel on the staff of General George Patton in World War II.

Dobie—who was nicknamed "Gloomy Gil" due to his pessimistic predictions about his teams—came close to another undefeated season in 1931 (at 7-1, Cornell's only loss was to Dartmouth, 14-0), but with academic standards at the school rising he had his first losing season, 2-5 in 1934, and went winless in 1935 before leaving Cornell. He instead finished his career at Boston College.

"You can't win games with Phi Beta Kappas," Dobie once said.

DARTMOUTH BIG GREEN
Consensus national titles (1936–present): None
Other national titles: 1925

Dartmouth has the distinction of being the last team from the Ivy League to finish a season ranked. In 1970, the Big Green didn't allow a point over the final four games to finish a perfect 9-0. Amazingly, Bob Blackman's team yielded only 42 points all season and finished the year No. 14 in the Associated Press poll (FYI, Dartmouth's best finish in the polls was No. 7 in 1937 after Earl Blaik's team went 7-0-2). When Joe Paterno suggested a matchup against 7-3 Penn State for Northeast supremacy even though Ivy League schools weren't allowed to play postseason games, Blackman couldn't help himself by saying, "I'd prefer to play a team with a better record."

From 1956-70, Dartmouth went 104-37-3 under Blackman (whose playing career at Southern California ended before it started due to polio), including a 79-24-2 mark in Ivy League play. The only comparable stretch came in the 1920s under Jesse Hawley, who during his first three years went 23-1-1 and outscored opponents 767-114. The last of those three teams, 1925, was the best, going 8-0-0, with five shutouts. Cornell scored the most points of all opponents, 13, but gave up 62, and Harvard lost 32-9.

When Dartmouth, then called the Indians because it was founded in 1769 in part to educate Native Americans, won its season finale at Chicago, 33-7, two services (Dickinson and Parke Davis), had it No. 1, while everyone else opted for Alabama.

"Dartmouth, football champion of the East, is also champion of the world!" Damon Runyon said.

FORDHAM RAMS

Consensus national titles (1936–present): None

Other national titles: None

The Rams were a powerhouse of the 1930s behind its high-profile line dubbed the "Seven Blocks of Granite." Ed Franco and Alex Wojciechowicz were two key members of that unit who went on to be inducted into the College Football Hall of Fame, along with future legendary National Football League coach Vince Lombardi.

In 1935, the Rams posted a 6-1-2 record with five shutouts, and the 1936 team only lost one game. The 1937 squad, which didn't yield a single touchdown, had the best finish of any Fordham team, No. 3 in the season's final Associated Press poll. At 7-1, the Rams received an invitation to play in the 1941 Cotton Bowl (a 13-12 loss to No. 6 Texas A&M), and the following year they turned down an opportunity to play in the Rose Bowl due to a previous agreement to appear in the Sugar Bowl. No. 6 Fordham defeated No. 7 Missouri, 2-0.

On December 15, 1954, Fordham cut the football program, mostly due to financial reasons. A club was established in 1964, and Fordham was back playing Division III football in 1970. It's competed at the Division I-AA level since 1989.

GRAMBLING TIGERS

Consensus national titles (1936–present): None

Other national titles: None

Over 56 years, Eddie Robinson had an amazing record of 408-165-15, with 17 Southwestern Athletic Conference titles and a string of 27 consecutive winning seasons. When he retired in 1997, the College Football Hall of Fame waived the requirement that a coach be out of the game for at least three years before being considered for enshrinement.

You want to talk about respect, Baton Rouge, home of Grambling's biggest rival Southern, named a street in Robinson's honor.

Robinson's best team might have been during his second year, 1942, when Grambling went 9-0 despite having only 67 men enrolled (33 of which were on the team), although the 1961 team with future NBA player Willis Reed won the NAIA championship.

The Tigers' best stretch was from 1971 to 1980, when they won or shared eight SWAC championships and were named the back college national champion five times. Topping the list of impressive players are Willie Brown, Buck Buchanan (the first black college player taken as a No. 1 overall draft pick), Willie Davis, James Harris, Ernie Ladd, Doug

Williams (the first black quarterback to win the Super Bowl), Gary Johnson and Tank Younger.

On September 28, 1985, Grambling defeated Oregon State 23-6 for Robinson's victory No. 323, tying Paul W. "Bear" Bryant for the all-time coaching record. He got No. 324 on October 5 against Prairie View, 27-7.

HARVARD CRIMSON

Consensus national titles (1936–present): None

Other national titles: 1874, 1875, 1890, 1898, 1899, 1901, 1908, 1910, 1912, 1913, 1919, 1920

Constructed in 1903, Harvard Stadium was the largest fully reinforced concrete structure in the world and modeled after a Roman amphitheater. But it indirectly also helped make one other huge contribution to the sport of football.

In 1906, President Theodore Roosevelt called together representatives of the sport to make it clear that due to the brutality of the game it would either be reformed or abolished. One change Roosevelt, who was a fan of football, suggested was widening the field 40 yards, but his former school balked because the stadium's structure couldn't be altered to fit the new configuration. Instead, another idea was agreed to, the forward pass.

In the early years of college football, winning a national championship wasn't very difficult due to the simple fact that there weren't many teams. Harvard's first two "titles," in 1874 and 1875, came at the end of four-game seasons in which it played Montreal's McGill University three times in 1874 (although the two sides had a vast difference of opinion on the rules), and a Canadian All-Star team twice in 1875.

The first game against rival Yale was also in 1875, when approximately 2,000 fans paid 50 cents each in New Haven to watch the visiting team win, 4-0. By 1891, "The Game" had already grown to the point that scalpers were arrested, and three years later it attracted 25,000 fans.

"Gentlemen, you are now going out to play football against Harvard. Never again in your life will you do anything so important," Yale coach Tomas A.D. Jones said before the 1923 meeting. Yale won, 13-0.

However, in 1915, Harvard's 170-pound fullback Eddie Mahan scored four touchdowns and kicked five conversion points to hand Yale its worst defeat in the first 44 years of football at the school, 41-0.

"The" game of "The Game" was in 1968 when both teams were undefeated for the first time since 1909. Although Brian Dowling, who finished his college career with a 65-0-1 record, led Yale to a 29-13 lead in the fourth quarter, the Bulldogs fumbled deep in Harvard territory with 3:34 remaining, and the Crimson scored two touchdowns in the final minute for a 29-29 tie. Dowling is still remembered, and honored, as the character B.D. in the comic "Doonesbury."

During Harvard's first 50 years playing football, it had only one losing season (1-2 in 1878), compared to 15 with 10 wins or more even though some years it didn't play that many games. From 1908-16, Percy Haughton's teams compiled a 71-7-5 record, including a consecutive winning streak of 22 games, and won three national titles with teams that finished 8-0-1 (1910), 9-0 (1912) and 9-0 (1913)—the last two of which were led by back Charles Brickley, who still holds the school career record for points with 215 (23 touchdowns, 25 field goals and two extra points).

Just before he died in 1924, after briefly coaching Columbia, Haughton's last words were: "Tell the squad I'm proud of them." Also, in his book "Football and how to watch it," he wrote: "Football is a miniature war game played under somewhat more civilized rules of conduct, in which the team becomes the military force of the school or university it represents."

Although Harvard received consideration from one ranking service in 1920, its true last national championship came in 1919, with perhaps its best team. Robert T. Fisher's squad shut out seven opponents in the regular season, with Princeton managing a 10-10 tie, to receive an invitation to play in the Rose Bowl.

In its only bowl appearance ever, Eddie Casey made two receptions to set up Fred Church's 12-yard touchdown, and Arnold Horween made the deciding extra point to beat Oregon, 7-6. Skeets Manerud made two field goals for Oregon, but barely missed what would have been the game-winner.

NAVY MIDSHIPMEN

Consensus national titles (1936–present): None
Other national titles: 1926

At every Naval Academy home game, the 4,000 members of the Brigade of Midshipmen march on to the field. With every score, students throw their caps into the air, a cannon is fired, and freshmen do a pushup for each point.

There's also Bill the Goat, who always faces the direction the offense is going. Navy tried everything including a carrier pigeon, a cat and a dog, but a goat has held the job since 1904. Since then, there have been 33 Bill the Goats, and each one's success has been measured by the team's success against rival Army.

As of this writing, Navy had as many representatives in the College Football Hall of Fame, 20, as Ohio State. The best known is quarterback Roger Staubach, who in 1963, when he won the Heisman Trophy, had the distinction of being on the cover of *Time* in his football uniform and *Sports Illustrated* in his military uniform.

During his three years leading Navy, Staubach completed 292 of 463 pass attempts for a 63 percent completion rate, and only 19 interceptions. However, he isn't Navy's lone Heisman winner. Halfback Joe Bellino first won the award in 1960.

"My first step was at top speed," said Bellino, whose name literally translates into "little beauty." "I could hit the hole as fast as anyone, then quickly get outside."

Of course, most Midshipmen never play football again after the academy. Even Staubach, who went on to lead the Dallas Cowboys to two Super Bowl victories, first served four years in the U.S. Navy.

Guard Steve Eisenhauer (1951-53) was also an academic All-American, and added a graduate degree in aeronautical engineering in 1964 and a master's degree from George Washington University in 1971. He served as an operations officer in Vietnam and flew

120 combat missions. After he retired with numerous honors, he became an executive with the Head Start Program, which assists children, and served as consultant to the Naval Academy on military and missile programs.

Halfback Fred "Buzz" Borries, who scored the touchdown to beat Notre Dame in 1933, won a Bronze Star during World War II. Aboard the carrier *Gambier Bay*, the commander was able to launch all the ship's aircraft while the vessel was sinking and under heavy fire, and helped save the lives of 200 crew members.

Tackle Slade Cutter (who won a national flute competition in high school), commanded a submarine during World War II, the Sea Horse, which sank 19 Japanese ships. He served as director of athletics at the U.S. Naval Academy 1957-60, and later curator of the Naval War College Museum.

"There is a grapevine in the ranks of all the services," Cutter said in 1957. "The men make it their business to find out who their officers are. There is a special respect for those who would carry the ball on a football field, throw a wicked block, or make a dead-stop tackle."

Navy's lone claim at a national title was in 1926, when in his first year coach Bill Ingram guided the Midshipmen to a 9-0-1 record (although most rankings had 9-0-1 Alabama No. 1). While Navy, led by quarterback and future admiral Tom Hamilton and tackle Frank Wickhorst, defeated Michigan 10-0 before 80,000 fans in Baltimore, it only tied rival Army, 21-21.

Incidentally, Jonas Ingram, a ruthless fullback for Navy in 1904 and 1906, was known as the "One-Armed Admiral" for repeatedly making the claim: "I'd give my right arm to win this ball game." Serving in both World Wars, he was awarded the Medal of Honor, the Navy Cross and the Distinguished Service Cross, and served as Commander-in-Chief of the U.S. Atlantic Fleet in 1944.

After a 3-30 stretch from 2000-02, Paul Johnson helped revive the winning ways and in 2006 the Midshipmen (9-4) won the 107th meeting against Army, not only securing Navy's fourth straight Commander-in-Chief's Trophy, but the senior class was the first ever to finish a perfect 8-0 against Army and Air Force.

"The program didn't get the way it is overnight, and it's not going to change overnight," Johnson said. "But I am confident that you can win here. If I didn't believe that, I would have never accepted the job."

But Navy is obviously known for so much more.

When Lou Holtz, then coaching William & Mary (1969-71), looked at the list of battles the Navy had fought, documented on the Memorial Stadium façade, he said, "Now that's a tough schedule."

PENN QUAKERS

Consensus national titles (1936–present): None

Other national titles: 1894, 1895, 1897, 1904, 1908, 1924

Penn began playing football in 1876, but had limited success until E.O. Wagenhurst guided it to 11-3 and 11-2 seasons in 1890 and 1891, respectively. When former Yale guard George Woodruff (124-15-2 over 10 years, outscoring opponents 1,777-88 points) was hired in 1892, Penn all but destroyed the competition, beginning with a 15-1 record the first year, with the only loss to Woodruff's former school.

From 1894-98, Penn compiled a 67-2 record, including a 12-0 season in 1894 to receive national title consideration (Yale was the consensus choice as the two teams didn't play), and was the obvious choice the following year after shutting out the first 10 opponents and finishing 14-0. One standout was fullback George Brooke, who was described by sportswriter and author Casper Whitney as, "A very hard man to stop. He strikes the line with almost irresistible force." Keying his line was oversized guard Buck Wharton (6-foot-3, 210 pounds) while on the other side of the center was another Hall of Fame guard, Charlie Gelbert, who weighed only 170 pounds (the "Miracle Man" was also the father of Charles M. Gelbert, a shortstop for the Cardinals, Reds, Tigers, Senators and Red Sox from 1929-40).

Penn was even more dominating in 1897, when led by four All-Americans including tackle/halfback John Outland, for whom the Outland Trophy for best lineman is named (he had been outspoken that interior linemen should receive more recognition and in 1946 the Football Writers Association of America agreed), it finished 15-0 and outscored opponents 443-20, with 12 shutouts.

After a 12-0 finish and allowing just four points under Carl Williams, Penn essentially split the 1904 title with Michigan, and was again the consensus choice in 1908 when, in his only season, Sol Metzger guided Penn to an 11-0-1 record with the 6-6 tie to Carlisle and Jim Thorpe (11-1 Penn received some title recognition in 1907 even with a 26-6 loss to Carlisle). The 1904 squad, which outscored the opposition 222-4, was led by quarterback Steve Stevenson (he went on to become a crewman on trans-oceanic oil tankers, which were the primary targets for German submarines during World War I), while Metzger's star players in 1908 were end Hunter Scarlett (who became a renowned eye surgeon) and halfback Bill Hollenback (who once played a game with a leg fracture, dislocations of both shoulders, shin splints and hip bruises).

"He's one of college football's greatest ends," Hollenback said of his fellow All-American. "He's a superlative defensive end, quick to get down-field on punts and an exceptional diagnostician."

Even though Penn had losses to Swarthmore and Pitt, and a tie against Dartmouth during the 1916 season, it was invited to play in the Rose Bowl. Penn was favored, and led by future Columbia coach Lou Little at tackle and All-American fullback Howard Berry, but couldn't keep up with the Huntington Brothers, Hollis and Shy, who led Oregon to a 14-0 victory.

Other notable names in Penn football include Chuck Bednarik, who before becoming the first offensive lineman to win the Maxwell Award was a 20-year-old veteran of World War II (a highly decorated aerial gunner with 30 combat missions over Germany); Al Bagnoli, who in his first 15 seasons compiled a 109-39 record and won six Ivy League championships; and George Munger, an alum who was teaching math and sacred studies at Episcopal Academy when he was hired in 1939 at age 28 and over sixteen seasons went 82-42-19 to win outright or share nine Ivy League titles.

One of Munger's star players was Francis "Reds" Bagnell, who went from being the team's water boy to team captain in 1949 and named an All-American halfback. In 1981,

President Ronald Reagan made him a member of the Battle Monuments Commission, charged with preservation of U.S. military cemeteries on foreign soil. He was elected president of the Maxwell Club in 1976 and president of the National Football Foundation in 1990.

Incidentally, fullback Jack Minds, 1894-97, is first credited with kicking conversion points with the aid of a holder, instead of via drop kicks, which weren't nearly as accurate.

PRINCETON TIGERS

Consensus national titles (1936–present): None

Other national titles: 1869, 1870, 1872, 1873, 1874, 1875, 1877, 1878, 1879, 1880, 1881, 1884, 1885, 1886, 1889, 1893, 1894, 1896, 1898, 1899, 1903, 1906, 1911, 1920, 1922, 1933, 1935, 1950

Princeton played in the first collegiate football game in 1869, due to a challenge issued by the school originally chartered as Queen's College, Rutgers, after it lost in baseball 40-2, and lost in the new sport as well, 6-4. But it came back a week later to win the rematch, 8-0, thus, in essence, securing its first national championship. It won its only game in 1870 to defend its "title," and for the most part did the same in 1872-73 (there were no football games played in 1871), before having to win a total of two games in both 1874 and 1875.

For years, Princeton was at the forefront of football, regularly adding innovations like the power sweep, the spiral punt (performed by Alex Moffat), and fake punts, believed to be first executed by fullback Knowlton "Snake" Ames, a member of the first All-America team in 1889 who enjoyed a four-year record of 35-3-1.

"He was clever at spinning, changing direction and faking the tackler," Yale's Pudge Heffelfinger said. "It was fatal to go for his knees or legs. They wouldn't be there."

In one game alone Ames returned a punt 70 yards for a touchdown, returned another kick 50 yards, and ran 105 yards from scrimmage (football was played on a 110-yard field then). He still holds nearly all Princeton scoring records, with 730 points, 62 touchdowns, and 176 points after touchdowns. He scored 60 points in a game against Penn.

Princeton boasted numerous standouts in its early years, like quarterback Hobey Baker, who was an even better hockey player (college hockey's equivalent to the Heisman Trophy is the Hobey Baker Award), end Arthur Poe (one of six brothers who tormented Yale and was the great nephew of Edgar Allan Poe), and end Gary Cochran. As captain, the team was known as "Cochran's Steamrollers," and in 1896 Princeton crushed rival Yale, 24-6, to finish 10-0-1. Over the next two seasons, it went 21-1-1. One of the guards on those teams was "Big Bill" Edwards, who in 1910 tackled and subdued would-be assassin James J. Gallagher, who had attempted to take the life of William Gaynor. The mayor of New York City was shot in the neck from point-blank range and seriously wounded, but survived. Edwards sustained a flesh wound in the arm and was later awarded the Carnegie Medal for Heroism.

By 1922, Princeton had won 15 national championships, which were significantly aided by the fact that for the first 10 years there were fewer than 10 programs in existence (and for nearly 20 years there were less than 20).

Of all the teams and championships, the one most revered by Tigers fans is the 1922 "Team of Destiny," coached by Bill Roper (89-28-17 during three different stints, 1906-8, 1910-11, 1919-30). With only three returning starters, Princeton was picked to finish behind Harvard and Yale, but opened the season with shutout victories against Johns Hopkins, Virginia, Colgate and Maryland. The true test came on the road at Chicago, coached by Amos Alonzo Stagg, which had an 18-7 lead late in the game. Howdy Gray recovered a fumble and returned it 40 yards for a touchdown, and Harry Crum scored on fourth-and-goal from the 1-yard line for a 21-18 lead. Chicago had time for a final drive, but was stopped by a goal-line stand.

Princeton, which scored only 127 points all season, but held the opposition to just 34, returned to the East Coast to beat Harvard, 10-3, and Yale, 3-0, to finish 8-0 and win the national championship.

A pair of 9-0 seasons under Fritz Crisler, the father of two-platoon football, meant national-title consideration in 1933 and 1935, and in 1945 Team of Destiny member Charlie Caldwell returned to try and win another title. During one stretch his teams won 24 consecutive games and 33 of 34 games.

Princeton was the last Ivy League program awarded a national championship by any service when both Boand and Poling systems had the 9-0 Tigers No. 1 in 1950 (Oklahoma was the consensus choice).

The Tigers matched the record and No. 6 final ranking in the Associated Press poll in 1951, but took home another honor. Running Princeton's single-wing offense Dick Kazmaier won his last 22 games to finish his career with 35 touchdown passes, 20 rushing touchdowns, and 4,354 all-purpose yards. After his senior season, which included an incredible performance against No. 12 Cornell—14 of 17 passes for 236 yards and three touchdowns, 124 rushing yards and two more touchdowns, and scored a safety on defense—for a 53-15 victory, Kazmaier won the Heisman Trophy.

"I thought it was nice, and then I went back to class," he said.

SANTA CLARA BRONCOS
Consensus national titles (1936–present): None
Other national titles: None.

Like its biggest rival, St. Mary's, which it used to play annually in "The Little Big Game," Santa Clara has abandoned its football program, but more than made its mark on the game, particularly on the West Coast.

Santa Clara had its greatest success under the direction of Buck Shaw, a former Notre Dame tackle who first joined the Broncos as an assistant coach in 1929, and was promoted in 1936. Over seven seasons he compiled a 47-10-4 record and enjoyed two 16-game winning streaks. Among the big-name programs Shaw's teams defeated included Auburn, Arizona, Arkansas, California, Michigan State, Oklahoma, Oregon State, Purdue, Stanford, Texas A&M and UCLA.

The 1936 Broncos defeated Stanford (13-0), Auburn (12-0), San Francisco (15-7), Loyola (13-6), Portland (26-0), and San Jose State (20-0), and snapped a 13-year losing streak to St. Mary's en route to a Sugar Bowl invitation to play heavily favored No. 2 Louisiana State. Ranked sixth and led by quarterback Nello "Flash" Falaschi, Santa Clara didn't blink and pulled out a 21-14 victory.

"That was a day I'll never forget," Shaw later said. "LSU was supposed to have the greatest team in its history and we were such underdogs that hardly any odds were posted."

Santa Clara finished 8-1, with the only loss against Sammy Baugh and Texas Christian, 9-0. It backed it up with a 9-0 season, in which the defense allowed only nine points in nine games and 25 rushing yards per game, both NCAA records. When the Sugar Bowl scheduled a rematch with LSU, No. 9 Santa Clara won again, 6-0. The only score was a 4-yard pass from Bruno Pellegrini to Jim Coughlin.

Santa Clara's other major bowl appearance came at the end of the 1949 season, when, during his final year with the Broncos, Len Casanova led an 8-2-1 season that included an invitation to the Orange Bowl to face Paul W. Bryant's Kentucky Wildcats. Up 7-0, Kentucky threatened to take a commanding lead after quarterback Babe Parilli completed a 45-yard pass to Bill Leskovar for a first down at the Santa Clara 3-yard line. But two running plays failed to reach the end zone as time ran out for the half, and the Broncos came back to score two touchdowns, one on a quarterback sneak by John Pasco, in the third quarter for a 21-13 victory. Bryant later called it one of the biggest errors of his coaching career.

ST. MARY'S GAELS

Consensus national titles (1936–present): None
Other national titles: None.

When "Squirmin" Herman Wedemeyer left Hawaii to attend St. Mary's in Moraga, Calif., near San Francisco, enrollment was 142 men, of which 41 played football. Yet, some games attracted more than 80,000 fans. Its best team was in 1945, under the direction of Jimmie Phelan, Wedemeyer was third in the nation in total offense, fourth in passing, fourth in punting, and fourth in the Heisman Trophy vote.

"I can't find a way to stop him," Southern California coach Jeff Cravath said. "You never know if he's going to skirt the end, pass, hit the line or punt."

St. Mary's went on to play in the Sugar Bowl, a 33-13 loss to Oklahoma State, but finished seventh in the season's final Associated Press poll, its lone top 10 result. The following year, Wedemeyer (who was an actor on the television show "Hawaii Five-O" and later elected to the state legislature), led the Gaels to the Oil Bowl in Houston, a 41-19 loss to No. 11 Georgia Tech.

Edward "Slip" Madigan, who played at Notre Dame, was the person responsible for building the program up and challenging much bigger schools on a regular basis. From 1921-39, he compiled 117 victories, compared to 45 losses and 12 ties. Led by lineman

Larry Bettencourt, St. Mary's recorded 19 shutouts and went 33-5-2 from 1924-27. The Galloping Gaels upset Stanford in 1927, 16-0, and Southern California in 1931, 13-7, both Rose Bowl-bound teams. In 1938, St. Mary's was invited to play in the Cotton Bowl, and upset No. 11 Texas Tech, 20-13.

The program was abandoned for 16 years (1951-66), and on March 3, 2004, the school discontinued the Division I-AA program.

"This difficult decision is the result of thoughtful and lengthy discussions over recent years about the competitive and financial realities confronting all higher educational institutions of our size," college president Brother Craig Franz announced. "Based on recommendations made to our Board of Trustees by an Athletics Review Task Force on the best way to optimize our athletic resources, the Board of Trustees voted unanimously earlier today to discontinue the Saint Mary's football program, and to reallocate those resources to our 14 other intercollegiate sports programs."

UNIVERSITY OF THE SOUTH, SEWANEE TIGERS

Consensus national titles (1936–present): None
Other national titles: None

Although the Purple Tigers were a charter member of the Southeastern Conference in 1932, they withdrew in 1940 having never won a conference game.

However, the 1899 team has gone down in history as one of the South's best, thanks to the greatest road trip ever taken by a football squad. Under the direction of Billy Sutter, and led by halfback Henry "Ditty" Seibels, the "Iron Men" went 12-0 and outscored the opposition 322-10.

The famous trip featured five opponents in six days, all at different locations, adding up to 2,500 miles round-trip from the Tennessee school located in the mountains:

November 9 at Austin: Sewanee 12, Texas 0.

November 10 at Houston: Sewanee 10, Texas A&M 0.

November 11 at New Orleans: Sewanee 23, Tulane 0.

November 13 at Baton Rouge: Sewanee 34, LSU 0.

November 14 at Memphis: Sewanee 12, Ole Miss 0.

John Heisman's Auburn squad was the only team to score against Sewanee, which also defeated Georgia, Georgia Tech and Tennessee by a combined score of 90-0. After it beat North Carolina in Atlanta, 5-0, Sewanee declared itself the Southern football champion. Who could argue?

"While there are some who would swear to the contrary, I did not see the 1899 Sewanee football team play in person," Penn State Joe Paterno said. "Winning five road games in six days has to be one of the most staggering achievements in the history of the sport. If the Bowl Champions Series had been in effect in 1899, there seems little doubt Sewanee would have played in the title game. And they wouldn't have been done in by any computer ranking."

Nevertheless, with the focus of football still in the Northeast, Sewanee didn't receive serious consideration for the national title, which went to 10-0-1 Harvard.

VANDERBILT COMMODORES

Consensus national titles (1936–present): None
Other national titles: None

Vanderbilt has never won a conference championship, or, obviously, a modern national title. It's played in only three bowl games and has become a perennial cellar-dwelling program in the Southeastern Conference, bottoming out in the 1960s when the Commodores averaged less than two wins per season (15-60-5) from 1960-67.

However, before bowl games became vogue, the Commodores were a national power that others desperately tried to emulate. When Tennessee hired legendary coach Robert Neyland, it was with the primary objective of beating Vanderbilt, which dominated their early series and from 1915-35 enjoyed 21 consecutive winning seasons.

The man Neyland was hired to try and best was Dan McGugin, who led the Commodores from 1904-34 (though spent 1918 fulfilling military duty), compiling an incredible record of 197-55-19. His first team, which might have been his best team, went 9-0 and outscored opponents 474-4 (and that's not a typo). The 1906 and 1911 teams both received national title consideration even though both lost to Michigan and coaching nemesis Fielding Yost, who just happened to be his brother-in-law. McGugin didn't experience his fourth loss until his fifth season, and all were to the Wolverines. Needless to say, during a 25-4-5 run from 1919-22, which included two unbeaten seasons and 19 shutouts, Michigan was on the schedule only once, a 0-0 tie in 1922 when the Commodores outplayed the Wolverines and outscored everyone else 177-16. Overall, McGugin's 30 teams outscored opponents 6,673-1,668.

Football historian Fred Russell described McGugin as: "sensationally successful, winning glorious intersectional victories ... responsible, more than any other man, for Southern football gaining national recognition."

Arguably Vanderbilt's last two dominating seasons under McGugin's direction came in 1929 and 1930, finishing 7-2 and 8-2, respectively. But by the time the SEC came into existence in 1933, many of the other programs had caught and/or surpassed the Commodores. In 1935, when Ray Morrison replaced McGugin, who retired after 30 seasons due to health reasons (he died in 1936 at the age of 56), the team's second-place finish (7-3 overall, 5-1 SEC) set a mark in the league standings that the Commodores have been unable to equal since.

Led by the "Iron Man" Carl Hinkle, who was named the SEC's Most Valuable Player despite playing center, Vanderbilt posted a 7-2 record in 1937 and barely missed a Rose Bowl invitation. With the bid on the line against Alabama in the season finale, a field goal propelled the Crimson Tide to a 9-7 victory. Although Hinkle missed out on Pasadena, during World War II he served as a pilot and won the Distinguished Flying

Cross with two Oak Leaf Clusters, the Air Force Medal of Commendation, France's Croix de Guerre and a Presidential Citation Unit with Oak Leaf Clusters.

Before he went to UCLA, Red Sanders returned to his alma mater in 1940 and no coach since has been able to surpass his eight-win seasons of 1941 and 1948. One of his assistant coaches, in charge of the offensive line, was Paul W. "Bear" Bryant, who was on the Commodores' sideline for one of their biggest upsets, against national powerhouse Alabama.

Vanderbilt was also the home to maybe the greatest college football writer ever, Grantland Rice, who coined numerous phrases, including "It's not whether you win or lose, it's how you play the game."

WASHINGTON & JEFFERSON PRESIDENTS

Consensus national titles (1936–present): None

Other national titles: 1921

The small liberal arts college near Pittsburgh, with an enrollment of approximately 1,350 students, is now known as a Division III power, but in 1921 Washington & Jefferson was a serious contender for the national championship.

Coached by Greasy Neale after he finished the baseball season with Cincinnati Reds (in 1919 he was the leading hitter for the Reds in the World Series and then coached Marietta, where he only had one loss), the Presidents finished the regular season 10-0 and received an invitation to play in the Rose Bowl.

Neale's team never made a single substitution while outplaying favored Cal (9-0) in the mud, with the Bears unable to complete a pass and limited to 49 rushing yards. The final result was a scoreless tie.

John Heisman coached the Presidents in 1923, as did Andy Kerr from 1926-28, while All-American tackle Wilbur "Pete" Henry was a charter member of the College Football Hall of Fame in 1951. Fellow offensive lineman Edgar Garbisch played four years at the school and was the team captain in 1920 before moving on to play four more years with Army (and had the distinction of facing Notre Dame five times) due to his military exception. He served 20 years in the Army Engineers, worked on procurement of engineering materials for the North Africa and Normandy invasions in World War II, and retired at the rank of colonel.

WASHINGTON & LEE GENERALS

Consensus national titles (1936–present): None

Other national titles: None

Football at the liberal arts school in Lexington, Virginia, dates back to 1873 when the Generals played Virginia Military Institute in the first game ever played in the South. From 1912-15, Washington & Lee went 32-3-1, and the 1914 team coached by Jogger Elcock finished undefeated (9-0), while outscoring opponents 324-12.

Although it would be another 20 years before the Generals won another Southern Conference title, they tied Vanderbilt at 4-1-1 in 1923 thanks to an inspired victory against rival Virginia. Team captain Eddie Cameron wasn't in uniform for the first half after attending his mother's funeral in Pennsylvania the day before. After traveling overnight by train, he ran on to the field for the second half to key a 7-0 victory. Generals coach Jimmie DeHart called it the greatest performance by a fullback he had ever seen.

The program's best season was 1950, when Washington & Lee finished 8-2, but 5-0 in Southern Conference play to win the league title. Led by quarterback Gil Bocetti and linebacker/fullback Walt Michaels, the offense averaged more than 30 points per game, with the losses to Virginia and Tennessee (which was outgained but scored three touchdowns on returns).

Ranked 18th in the final Associated Press poll, Washington & Lee was paired against undefeated Wyoming in the Gator Bowl, for its only postseason bowl appearance. But without Michaels, out due to appendicitis, the Generals lost, 20-7.

The 1951 season was essentially the last hurrah against top competition, when Washington & Lee upset Virginia, 42-14. Despite facing No. 1 Tennessee, No. 3 Maryland, played at Miami (Florida), and against Louisville quarterbacked by Johnny Unitas, the Generals finished 5-1 in the Southern Conference and 6-4 overall. Three years later, school officials abolished the practice of awarding athletic scholarships. Washington & Lee currently plays in Division III.

YALE BULLDOGS

Consensus national titles (1936–present): None

Other national titles: 1872, 1874, 1876, 1877, 1879, 1880, 1881, 1882, 1883, 1884, 1886, 1887, 1888, 1891, 1892, 1893, 1894, 1895, 1897, 1900, 1901, 1902, 1905, 1906, 1907, 1909, 1927

When Knute Rockne, perhaps college football's most famous football coach, was once asked about a backfield alignment and where the idea came from, he said, "Where everything else in football came from, Yale."

Although Princeton and Rutgers played the first college football game in 1869, Yale joined in a few years later and proved to be a quick study. From 1876-1909, Yale's worst season was 7-2-1 in 1899.

Walter Camp played at Yale from 1877-82 and was the program's first football coach, compiling a 68-2 record from 1888-92. Among his many notable achievements was to standardize the game's rules, thus becoming known as the "Father of American Football." He created the line of scrimmage, the 11-man team, signal-calling, the quarterback position, and was the originator of the rule whereby a team had to give up the ball unless it had advanced a specified distance within a set number of downs.

Yale, and that other school it regularly plays (Harvard), have given us "The Game," which commanded $50 seats from scalpers during the depression. Today, that might get you a seat cushion.

Yale has won 27 national championships (give or take), 13 Ivy League championships, had 100-plus consensus All-Americans, and two Heisman Trophy winners—Larry Kelley in 1936 and Clint Frank the following year. They also helped lead Yale to two of its four season-ending rankings in the Associated Press poll, both at No. 12.

The 1888 team, including legendary guard William W. "Pudge" Heffelfinger and end Amos Alonzo Stagg, outscored opponents 698-0 to finish 13-0, contributing to a 37-game winning streak. With players like guard "Wild" Bill Hickok and end "Silent" Frank Hinkey, from 1891-94 Yale outscored opponents 1,730-25. The 1894 Bulldogs, coached by William Rhodes, finished 16-0 and gave up just 13 points. End Tom Shevlin captained the 1905 team that finished 10-0 and outscored the competition 227-4 (Princeton scored the only points) as Yale all but split the national title with Chicago. The 1909 championship team, featuring six All-Americans including fullback Ted Coy, didn't give up a single point, with the closest game an 8-0 victory against Harvard.

Guard Gordon "Skim" Brown captained the 1900 squad dubbed: "The Team of the Century." The Bulldogs finished 12-0, including 10 shutouts, and outscored the opposition 336-10. In the final game of the season, Yale rushed for 555 yards in a 28-0 win over Harvard. Seven of the 11 starters were named All-Americans.

The program's effects are even felt today in the South. When the University of Georgia was founded by Yale graduates, it adopted the same bulldog "Handsome Dan" as its nickname and image (although at Georgia he's named Uga).

On October 12, 1929, when Georgia dedicated Sanford Stadium—which was built for $360,000 and seated an unseemly 30,000 fans—it invited Yale to join in on the celebration, and then proved to be a lousy host. The sophomore-laden home team pulled off a 15-0 shocker (FYI, when the Yale Bowl, which inspired the Rose Bowl design, was dedicated in 1914, it lost to Harvard, 36-0).

Among those invited to attend was Chief Justice William Howard Taft, who had wanted to play football for Yale but his father refused to give him permission because it was "not a gentlemen's sport." He had to settle for crew, wrestling and watching baseball (FYI: Contrary to popular belief, Taft did not create the seventh-inning stretch, but was the first president to throw the ceremonial first pitch at a baseball game in 1910).

Some of the things that the 27th President of the United States was quoted as saying about the game included:

"The stadium overshadows the classroom."

"Athletics have a dollar sign in front of them."

"Menace to our whole American educational system."

Some things don't change, but you have to wonder what Taft would have said had Yale won.

Incidentally, Yale hasn't ventured South again since the loss.

PART III

The Controversies

Chapter 4

More Than a Century of Issues

IT ACTUALLY all began with a baseball game in 1866 between Princeton (known as the College of New Jersey until 1896), and Rutgers, with the future Ivy League school winning by a humbling 40-2 score. In response, William Leggett, a Rutgers student, issued a challenge for a best-of-three rematch in another sport, which would evolve into football.

The first game, played on November 6, 1869, had 25 men to a side, a round ball, and two goalposts set 100 yards apart. Players could kick or hit the ball, but were not allowed to pick it up and run with it. The first team to score six goals would be the winner. The only thing to distinguish the players were scarlet scarves the Rutgers players wrapped around their heads like turbans. It eventually helped lead to the school's nickname, the Scarlet Knights.

Princeton lost 6-4, but won the rematch 8-0, and the lone meeting in 1870, 6-2.

History does not record who the first person was to come up with the idea of a national champion, but chances are he or she certainly had no idea what they instigated. As noted elsewhere, the first formal opinion poll, by the Associated Press, didn't occur until 1936, but the origins of determining champions started well before that. The first conference (the future Big Ten) was organized in 1896, the first All-American team was named in 1889, and Frank Dickinson's mathematical rankings were first used in 1926.

Although numerous rankings have gone back and named champions for those early years, it really wasn't too difficult to do considering there were so few teams and, consequently, games played.

For years, schools outside of the Northeast received little or no national attention primarily because teams were limited by travel, but also because with all the East Coast teams playing one another those games were considered the benchmark for the sport as a whole. Consequently, there were few real controversies about who had the best team because most of the programs involved scheduled each other and it was therefore frequently settled on the field. An exception was when Princeton and Yale would play to a tie, but otherwise finish unbeaten, which occurred in 1877, 1879, 1880, 1881, 1886 and 1906.

Even the consensus All-American teams reflected this, dominated by players from programs like Harvard, Penn, Princeton or Yale, which took decades for other regions and schools to overcome, until teams from the rest of the country could prove that they were at least comparable, if not better. A good example was in 1937, when halfback Clint Frank of Yale won the Heisman Trophy, but Colorado's Byron "Whizzer" White led the nation in scoring, rushing, all-purpose yards and total defense, to guide the Buffaloes to an 8-0 season. Colorado lost to Rice in the Cotton Bowl, but more importantly White went on to become a Rhodes Scholar and Supreme Court Justice.

Although Purdue (8-0), and Minnesota (5-0), both finished undefeated in 1892—and the following year Maryland (6-0), Minnesota (6-0), Stanford (8-0-1), and Texas (4-0) did so as well—Michigan was really the first non-Eastern school to be considered a national power, with Fielding Yost's point-a-minute teams.

Actually, Yost's first undefeated season came at Kansas (10-0) in 1899. The only opponent to score more than six points was Nebraska, which still lost, 36-20. Chicago had an impressive season finishing 12-0-2, but Midwest football was still considered inferior, thus Harvard (10-0-1) was considered the game's best team that year.

Things slowly began to change in 1901, when Michigan destroyed Stanford at the subsequent Rose Bowl, 49-0. The first real controversial national champion came two years later in 1903, when despite a tie with Minnesota (14-0-1), Michigan essentially split the national title with Princeton, which finished 11-0. The following year, the Wolverines (10-0) were again tied with Minnesota (13-0) atop the Big Ten, but shared the national honors with Penn (12-0), which due to popular belief was considered the top team in the region over Pitt (10-0), while Vanderbilt (9-0) emerged as a true power in the South approximately 20 years before Alabama earned its first Rose Bowl victory.

As the regional differences slowly began to dissipate, and more conferences were organized, other programs began to emerge.

For example, Bennie Owen, who was Yost's quarterback at Kansas (and lost an arm in a hunting accident) took over at Oklahoma in 1905. Over 22 years he compiled a 122-54-16 record including four impressive seasons that failed to result in a No. 1 ranking. His 1911 team went 8-0 and outscored opponents 282-15. Led by passing fullback Forest Geyer in 1914, Oklahoma went 9-1-1 and led the nation in scoring with 435 points. The 1915 Sooners finished 10-0 and again topped the nation in scoring with 370 points. The 1918 team finished 6-0, with a scoring edge of 278-7.

By 1919, when Harvard (9-0-1), Illinois (6-1), Notre Dame (9-0), and Texas A&M (10-0) could all claim to be the nation's best, demand for postseason games began to grow. In addition to the Rose Bowl, a smattering of exhibitions were played including the Fort Worth Classic, Dixie Classic, San Diego East-West Christmas Classic, and Los Angeles Christmas Festival, but did little to quiet the growing debate on which programs could legitimately call themselves No. 1. In 1921, California (9-0-1), Cornell (7-0), Iowa (7-0), Lafayette (9-0), and Washington & Jefferson (10-0-1) could all make a claim, and, not surprisingly, came from different regions.

Alabama essentially won the national championship outright, and scored a huge moral victory for Southern football, with the Rose Bowl victory at the end of the 1925 season, and its tie with Stanford a year later resulted in split honors. Despite Alabama's 10-0 season, including a victory over Washington State in the Rose Bowl, Notre Dame was considered the consensus champion in 1930, and Southern California followed suit the next two years. Colgate didn't give up a point during the 1932 season and crushed the likes of Penn State, Syracuse, and Brown (which had defeated seven unbeaten teams before playing Colgate) en route to a 9-0 record. However, the Rose Bowl opted for 7-0-2 Pitt, which was subsequently crushed by the Trojans, 35-0, to be considered the consensus national champion.

Naturally, the discussions and disputes only grew stronger and louder with the creation of the Associated Press poll in 1936.

Pittsburgh was the consensus champion in 1937 after finishing 9-0-1, with the tie against No. 3 Fordham (for the third straight year they played to a 0-0 result), and high-profile wins against Notre Dame and Nebraska. However, Cal had the same record (its 0-0 tie came against Washington), and defeated No. 4 Alabama in the Rose Bowl, 13-0.

A good debate could still be held over which team deserved the 1942 championship, Georgia or Ohio State. Coached by Paul Brown, the Buckeyes finished 9-1, with the lone loss to No. 6 Wisconsin, 17-7. Meanwhile, Georgia, led by Heisman Trophy winner Frank Sinkwich, stumbled against rival Auburn, 27-13, before redeeming itself somewhat with shutout victories against No. 5 Georgia Tech (34-0), and UCLA (9-0 in the Rose Bowl).

The Associated Press opted for Ohio State, but the mathematical rankings split roughly 50-50. Meanwhile, teams that blew golden opportunities were Wisconsin and Boston College. A week after beating the Buckeyes, the Badgers lost to Iowa 6-0, and finished third in the final poll just ahead of Missouri Valley champion Tulsa (10-0, but lost to Tennessee in the Sugar Bowl, 14-7). After Georgia lost, Boston College replaced it at No. 1, only to endure a shocking 55-12 loss to Holy Cross in its regular season finale. The Eagles went on to lose to No. 10 Alabama in the Orange Bowl, 37-21.

In 1943, after the advent of the Associated Press poll, Notre Dame finished 9-1, losing only to the Great Lakes Naval Station, 19-14, in the final 30 seconds of play on a 46-yard touchdown pass from Steve Lach to Paul Anderson. Although the defeat came in Notre Dame's final game of the season, it retained the No. 1 status and the national championship, in large part due to the Fighting Irish having played seven teams ranked in the top 13 spots in the final Associated Press poll (FYI, No. 2 was Iowa Pre-Flight, which lost to Notre Dame the week before, 14-13). Quarterback Angelo Bertelli, who only played six games before joining the Marines, won the Heisman Trophy.

Two years later, Alabama, which wasn't able to field a team in 1943 due to the decimated lineup from World War II, pieced together a rag-tag group of players, including quarterback Harry Gilmer, nicknamed the "War Baby Tiders." Coach Frank Thomas somehow guided them to the Sugar Bowl, and in 1945 Alabama came back to go 10-0 and end Southern California's eight-game winning streak in the Rose Bowl, 34-14. At No. 3, the Tide had the best non-military team in the country behind Army and Navy, and just ahead of No. 4 Indiana (9-0-1).

In 1984, voters were looking for reasons to dock undefeated Brigham Young, which didn't play an opponent that finished ranked in the top 20 at season's end, but couldn't find a suitable alternative to the high-flying Cougars. When No. 6 Oklahoma defeated No. 1 Nebraska, 17-7, and No. 2 South Carolina lost to Navy, 38-21, both on November 17, BYU took over the top spot in the weekly poll and only needed to beat 6-5 Michigan in the Holiday Bowl to secure the championship. With Boston College quarterback Doug Flutie winning the Heisman Trophy, it was considered the year of the underdogs.

The 1986 national championship was also controversial, but not because of what happened on the field. With Penn State and Miami both undefeated and not obligated to play in a particular bowl, they were basically able to auction the first No. 1 vs. No. 2 showdown between independents since Army vs. Notre Dame in 1946, to the highest bidder. The Fiesta Bowl, in conjunction with NBC, won by agreeing to double the payments to both teams to $2.4 million each, and the game was moved from New Year's Day to January 2. Although the Hurricanes were clear favorites, the game lived up to its billing. Penn State intercepted five passes by Heisman Trophy-winning quarterback Vinny Testaverde for a 14-10 victory.

But in terms of controversy, none of those can compare with the ones in the next chapter.

Chapter 5

The 10 Most Controversial National Champions

10. Slippery Rock's No. 1! (1936)

It shouldn't surprise anyone that the first Associated Press poll in 1936 brought about the first controversy (talk about an obvious foreshadow) when Minnesota was declared the national champion, completing a very unusual season for the Golden Gophers.

With Bernie Bierman wanting to beef up the schedule, Minnesota was set to open against Washington in Seattle, a four-day trip by train. Bierman scheduled two practices along the way, but while staying overnight at the Florence Hotel in Missoula, Montana, the players were forced to flee at approximately 3 a.m. due to the building being on fire. No one was hurt, but most of the hotel was destroyed. With Julian Alfonse intercepting three passes at the goal-line, Minnesota also escaped the Huskies with a 14-7 victory, and went on to post impressive wins against Nebraska, Michigan, Purdue, Iowa, Texas and Wisconsin.

Heading into a Halloween showdown with Northwestern, which many thought would likely determine both the conference and national championship, Minnesota was No. 1, the Wildcats ranked third. Played in wind and driving rain, the Gophers, who hadn't lost since the season finale of the 1932 season to Michigan, a streak of 28 games, couldn't reach the end zone while Northwestern punched in a touchdown for a 6-0 victory. Fullback Steve Toth scored from the 1-yard line on third down shortly after reserve Don Geyer had fumbled with Minnesota tackle Ed Widseth penalized for punching Geyer during the scramble for the loose ball.

However, after sitting atop the poll for three weeks, Big Ten champion Northwestern was pounded by Notre Dame, 26-6, and would finish seventh in the final poll.

Even with the one loss, voters put Minnesota back up to No. 1, ahead of LSU (9-0-1), Pittsburgh (7-1-1), and Alabama (8-0-1), and with the regular season complete the Gophers secured the consensus national championship. Three services: Boand, Football Research and Houlgate, proclaimed Pitt their national champion. LSU lost to No. 6 Santa Clara in the Sugar Bowl, 21-14, Pittsburgh beat Washington in the Rose Bowl, 21-0, and Alabama didn't play in a bowl.

Also controversial that year was Arkansas being snubbed for the Cotton Bowl, even though it was the Southwest Conference champion. Instead, Texas Christian received the invitation because it would be quarterback Sammy Baugh's final collegiate game. The Horned Frogs beat Marquette, 16-6.

Finally, one sportswriter came up with a unique winner of the mythical title, and after backtracking the season's results made a case for Slippery Rock in an article that was reprinted throughout the country.

Here's why: Slippery Rock beat Westminster, which defeated West Virginia Wesleyan, which beat Duquesne, which upset Pittsburgh, which defeated Notre Dame, which beat Northwestern, which beat Minnesota.

That's why you'll still occasionally hear an announcer or broadcaster mention a Slippery Rock score.

9. What Game Was He Watching? (2002)

The 2002 national championship game between Miami and Ohio State at the Fiesta Bowl was one of the most exciting title games ever if for no other reason than it went to double-overtime. However, Hurricanes fans are still calling foul.

Miami forced overtime when Todd Sievers made a 40-yard field goal on the final play of regulation for a 17-17 score. The play everyone remembers, though, occurred in the first extra frame. On fourth-and-3 and the 5-yard line, Buckeyes quarterback Craig Krenzel threw into the right corner of the end zone where Chris Gamble was being defended by corner-back Glenn Sharpe. As Gamble reached for the ball, he got his hands on it, but couldn't pull in the reception. Moments later, with fireworks prematurely going off and Miami beginning to celebrate, field judge Terry Porter threw the flag to call pass interference. With the first down, Ohio State scored three plays later and the game went to a second overtime.

Buckeyes freshman tailback Maurice Clarett scored on a 5-yard run for the final 31-24 score.

"It feels unreal," Miami fullback Quadtrine Hill said. "After the game was over, it felt like we had one play left. It can't be over. It's something I never want to feel again."

It was arguably the most controversial call in a title game since the Rose Bowl at the end of the 1978 season. Bo Schembechler had returned Michigan to its perennial power-house status, except for one thing: The Wolverines had lost all four Rose Bowl appearances (and at the Orange Bowl too) under the coach, who would go on to win 13 Big Ten titles.

The high-profile matchup was No. 3 Southern California (11-1), coached by John Robinson, against No. 5 Michigan (10-1). Aided by interceptions by defensive backs Ronnie Lott and Dennis Smith, USC was able to take an early lead and hold on for a 17-10 victory. However, even with Michigan scoring a third-quarter touchdown, a 44-yard pass from Rick Leach to tailback Roosevelt Smith, the deciding touchdown was one that the Wolverines believe shouldn't have counted.

It occurred in the second quarter on a 3-yard run by Charles White. However, just as he was crossing the goal line, the standout running back was stripped of the football by linebacker Ron Simpkins, with linebacker Jerry Meter recovering the ball at the 1-yard line. Even though the line judge ruled that White had reached the end zone before losing control, many observers thought that White may have crossed the goal line, but the ball did not.

With the victory, Southern California was able to claim half of the split national championship with Alabama (11-1), which defeated No. 1 Penn State in the Sugar Bowl, 14-7. The thinking behind the coaches vaulting the Trojans to No. 1 was that they defeated the Crimson Tide in an early-season matchup, 24-14. When USC subsequently lost to Pac-10 newcomer Arizona State, it dropped down in the polls below Alabama, with both running the table thereafter. Incidentally, it was the first of two years the Associated Press poll finished: 1. Alabama; 2. Southern California; 3. Oklahoma.

But in terms of questionable calls, that wasn't nearly as controversial as what happened in 1953.

No. 1 Notre Dame was 7-0 heading into a late-season meeting against No. 20 Iowa (5-3). The Hawkeyes led 7-0 when an official stopped the clock with 1 second remaining in the first half because a Fighting Irish player appeared to be injured. With the extra play quarterback Ralph Guglielmi threw a 12-yard touchdown pass to Dan Shannon to tie the game.

Again Iowa took the lead, 14-7, when with less than a minute remaining in the game two more official timeouts were called due to apparent Notre Dame injuries. Guglielmi found Shannon for another touchdown, this time 9 yards and with 6 seconds remaining.

Although the season-ending game finished in a 14-14 tie, Iowa left South Bend furious, and the following day Hawkeyes coach Forest Evashevski told a pep rally that they had been "gypped."

But Iowa also got the last laugh. Notre Dame, which had been ranked No. 1 all season, was being hailed nationwide as the "Fainting Irish" and in the subsequent Associated Press poll was bumped down to No. 2 in favor of 10-0 Maryland. That's how the final polls had it at the end of the regular season, only to see Maryland lose to Oklahoma in the Orange Bowl, 7-0.

Not surprisingly, both schools claim the title.

8. The Bear Did It (1950)

Although the first Associated Press poll was in 1936, the debate on whether or not to move the final tabulation until after the bowl games didn't start to heat up until 1950, in part because there were so few bowl games—not to mention that they still had the air of being exhibitions.

That year, Oklahoma was already declared the national champion when it arrived at the Sugar Bowl to face Paul W. "Bear" Bryant's No. 7 Kentucky Wildcats. Naturally, the Sooners, riding a 31-game winning streak, were considered heavy favorites and no one seriously thought that Bud Wilkinson wouldn't find a way to win convincingly.

But led by linemen Walt Yowarsky and Bob Gain, the Wildcats lived up to their No. 2 national ranking defensively. Wilbur Jamerson scored two touchdowns, including a 14-yard touchdown pass from Babe Parilli, and Yowarsky was named game MVP as Kentucky won, 13-7.

Had voting taken place after the postseason, a number of teams would have certainly received title consideration, including 11-1 Tennessee (which defeated No. 3 Texas in the

Cotton Bowl, 20-14, and was the only top five team to win a bowl game), 9-1-1 California (despite a loss to Michigan in the Rose Bowl, 14-6), 9-0 Princeton, 8-1 Michigan State (which had just joined the Big Ten and was two years away from being eligible to play in the Rose Bowl), 10-1 Oklahoma, and 8-1 Army (which lost its finale against Navy, 14-2). The guess here is that the final rankings would probably have been: 1. Tennessee; 2. Kentucky; 3. Oklahoma; and either Army or Texas.

Over the following three years, there were two more times in which the team ranked No.1 in the final poll went on to lose its bowl game—Maryland 28, Tennessee 13 in the Sugar Bowl at the end of the 1951 season, and Oklahoma 7, Maryland 0 in the Orange Bowl after the 1953 season. Both results might have given Michigan State the title under different circumstances (although Notre Dame was No. 2 and Oklahoma fourth when it defeated Maryland).

The 1960 season had a similar result. Despite an 8-1 record, thanks to a 23-14 loss to Purdue, Minnesota was No. 1 ahead of No. 2 Ole Miss, which was 9-0-1 due to the 6-6 tie against LSU. Minnesota lost to No. 6 Washington in the Rose Bowl, 17-7, while Ole Miss defeated Rice in the Sugar Bowl, 14-6. It's an obvious change that the benefit of hindsight surely would have corrected.

Bryant, who had moved on to Texas A&M and then Alabama, was able to take advantage of the changing times and attitude after the 1964 season, when Arkansas posted four less-than inspiring wins before shocking No. 1 Texas and then going on an epic roll, outscoring the final five opponents 116-0.

The Associated Press ranked only 10 teams at the time, so coming off a 5-5 year Arkansas was essentially a preseason afterthought. Even after defeating the Longhorns, the Razorbacks were still behind the Crimson Tide in the polls, and when both finished the regular season it was: 1. Alabama; 2. Arkansas.

However, the Crimson Tide lost 21-17 to Texas in the first Orange Bowl played under the lights (which came down to a controversial call at the end of the game on fourth down when one official signaled that quarterback Joe Namath had dove into the end zone, only to be overruled by another official), while the Razorbacks defeated No. 6 Nebraska in the Cotton Bowl, 10-7.

Ranking services waiting until after the bowls to declare their champions, including the Football Writers Association of America and the Helms Athletic Foundation, had Arkansas No. 1 instead of Alabama. Consequently, the Associated Press changed its procedure the following year, but only for the 1965 season. Almost unbelievably, it worked to Alabama's advantage again.

After beating LSU 31-7, and Auburn 30-3, Alabama was ranked fourth and turned down an opportunity to play in the Cotton Bowl to meet No. 3 Nebraska in the Orange Bowl and keep its dim national championship hopes alive. Bryant's thinking was that if No. 1 Michigan State lost to UCLA in the Rose Bowl, and No. 2 Arkansas had its 22-game unbeaten streak snapped by LSU in the Cotton Bowl, the Crimson Tide would have a chance to defend its title against No. 3 Nebraska.

That's exactly what happened.

Despite being outsized, Alabama outgained Nebraska 518 yards to 377 and Bryant pulled out every trick he could, including both the tackle eligible (which would soon be outlawed) and more than one onsides kick, in completing a masterful 39-28 victory. Although it had not been picturesque, Bryant joined Minnesota's Bernie Bierman (1940–1941), Army's Red Blaik (1944–1945), Notre Dame's Frank Leahy (1946–1947), and Oklahoma's Bud Wilkinson (1955–1956) as the only coaches to win back-to-back national titles.

Incidentally, Notre Dame was able to leapfrog three teams in somewhat similar style in 1977, thanks to a 38-10 victory against No. 1 Texas and three other outcomes: Despite the suspensions of three key players Arkansas shocked No. 2 Oklahoma in the Orange Bowl, No. 3 Alabama won at the Sugar Bowl against low-ranked Ohio State, 35-6, and No. 4 Michigan lost to Washington in the Rose Bowl, 27-20. There may have been something to the luck of the Irish that season, especially after Dan Devine pulled out the green jerseys against No. 5 Southern California and Notre Dame defeated its rival for the first time in four years, 49-19.

Due to pressure, the Associated Press reverted to holding its final poll at the end of the regular season, but switched back for good in 1969. The coaches' poll by United Press International held firm until 1973. The Cotton Bowl at the end of the 1970 season, when No. 6 Notre Dame defeated No. 1 Texas, 24-11, giving Nebraska a split title, brought it to the threshold. What crossed it was the Sugar Bowl concluding the 1973 season, when No. 3 Notre Dame beat No. 1 Alabama, and Bryant, 24-23, in a game featuring six lead changes and a late field goal. Although the Irish were the clear consensus national champions, the Crimson Tide still claims 1973 as one of its 12 national titles.

Meanwhile, there was another controversy regarding the 1973 season, stemming from the Big Ten. With their 10-10 season-ending game, Michigan and Ohio State tied for the conference title and both had yet to lose. Beforehand, Ohio State was No. 1, and Michigan No. 4, but voters dropped them both behind Alabama (11-0), Oklahoma (10-0-1), and Notre Dame (10-0).

According to Big Ten rules (which have since been changed), league athletic directors had to vote on which team would represent the conference at the Rose Bowl. By chance, the deciding vote came down to Michigan State, which cast it for Ohio State.

While the decision infuriated Michigan's Bo Schembechler, Ohio State went on to defeat Southern California, 42-21. Combined with Alabama's loss, that's how the Irish leapfrogged into the No. 1 spot ahead of: 2. Ohio State (10-0-1); 3. Oklahoma (10-0-1); 4. Alabama (11-1); 5. Penn State (12-0); and finally, 6. Michigan (10-0-1).

7. Who's No. 2? (2000)

The biggest problem the Bowl Championship Series, and its previous incantations, has regularly experienced in determining which two teams should play for the national title hasn't been "Who's #1?" but which team should be No. 2.

The 2006 season was a perfect example. When Ohio State and Michigan closed their regular seasons against one another, both were undefeated and for the first time they met ranked 1-2 in the polls. After the Buckeyes won 42-39, the Wolverines remained at No. 2, but not for long.

Lurking at No. 3 was Southern California, which subsequently won its ballyhooed matchup with No. 6 Notre Dame, 44-24. After moving up in the following week's poll, all the Trojans had to do was defeat UCLA in their season finale to secure a spot in the championship game against Ohio State.

Only the Bruins pulled off a 13-9 upset.

Meanwhile, at the SEC Championship, No. 4 Florida began lobbying for a chance immediately after finishing off Arkansas, 38-28.

"We're going to tell a group of young men who just went 12-1 with the most difficult schedule against six ranked opponents that they don't have a chance to go play for a national championship?" Florida coach Urban Meyer said. "I'm going to need help with that one."

"Michigan already had its chance," game MVP Percy Harvin said. "I think we deserve a chance."

Florida got it, but barely, and took advantage of the opportunity by crushing, or this case chomping, on the Buckeyes 41-14 to win the title.

Of course, it wasn't anything new for the BCS. Even in its first year, 1998, there was a similar dispute with nearly everyone in agreement that 12-0 Tennessee was No. 1, but Ohio State fans felt the Buckeyes were more deserving to play for the championship than Florida State (11-1). The following year, the Seminoles were the undisputed top choice, but Virginia Tech (11-0), and Nebraska (11-1), both thought they deserved a shot at the title.

So how often does the No. 2 team win the championship game? Well, Florida was the third team to do it in five years. Here are all the Bowl Coalition (1992-04), Bowl Alliance (1995-97) and Bowl Championship Series title game results since 1992 (FYI, in 1997, No. 1 Michigan played No. 8 Washington State in the Rose Bowl, and won 21-16).

Bowl Coalition/Alliance/BCS Championship Games

Season	Bowl	Result (rankings are BCS standings)
1992	Sugar	No. 2 Alabama 34, No. 1 Miami 13
1993	Orange	No. 1 Florida State 18, No. 2 Nebraska 16
1994	Orange	No. 1 Nebraska 24, No. 3 Miami 17
1995	Fiesta	No.1 Nebraska 62, No. 2 Florida 24
1996	Sugar	No. 3 Florida 52, No. 1 Florida State 20
1997-x	Orange	No. 2 Nebraska 42, No. 3 Tennessee 17
1998	Fiesta	No. 1 Tennessee 23, No. 2 Florida State 16
1999	Sugar	No. 1 Florida State 46, No. 2 Virginia Tech 29
2000	Orange	No. 1 Oklahoma 13, No. 2 Florida State 2
2001	Rose	No. 1 Miami 37, No. 2 Nebraska 14
2002	Fiesta	No. 2 Ohio State 31, No. 1 Miami 24 (2OT)
2003	Sugar	No. 2 LSU 21, No. 1 Oklahoma 14
2004	Orange	No. 1 Southern California 55, No.2 Oklahoma 19
2005	Rose	No. 2 Texas 41, No. 1 Southern California 38
2006	Championship	No. 2 Florida 41, No. 1 Ohio State 14

Of course, few teams have been able to defy the odds, get into the championship and then win like Florida. Even before its first decade was complete, the Bowl Championship Series had eight No. 1- or 2-ranked teams lose in the season finale, all but eliminating it from consideration for the national championship.

Strangely, it happened more than once during the same season three times:

1998:	Miami 49, No. 2 UCLA 45
2001:	No. 15 Colorado, 62, No. 2 Nebraska 36
2001:	No. 6 Tennessee, 34, No. 2 Florida 32
2001:	No. 21 LSU 31, No. 2 Tennessee 20 (SEC Championship)
2003:	No. 9 Michigan 35, No. 2 Ohio State 21
2003:	No. 15 Kansas State 35, No. 1 Oklahoma 7 (Big 12 Championship)
2006:	No. 1 Ohio State 42, No. 2 Michigan 39
2006:	UCLA 13, No. 2 Southern California 9

Kansas State also missed out on a golden opportunity in 1998 when it was 11-0 heading into the Big 12 Championship game, especially with No. 3 UCLA losing to Miami in its regular-season finale, 49-45. But with No. 10 Texas A&M playing spoiler and pulling off the 36-33 upset in the Big 12 Championship game, Florida State went to the Fiesta Bowl instead (where it lost to Tennessee, 23-16).

At the end of the 2001 regular season, Oregon was 10-1 and ranked second in both the Associated Press and coaches' polls. However, four of the eight computers had Oregon much lower, which dropped the Ducks down to No. 4 in the BCS rankings behind No. 2 Nebraska, and No. 3 Colorado, even though the Buffalos had failed to qualify for the Big 12 title game.

Instead, Nebraska went to the national championship, and was promptly crushed by Miami, 37-14. Oregon defeated Colorado, 38-16, to finish No. 2.

That came on the heels of an arguably even bigger controversy in the BCS selection/rankings process, which decided the opponent for No. 1 Oklahoma (12-0) in the Orange Bowl and the 2000 national championship. There were three worthy candidates:

Miami: The Hurricanes were 10-1, second in both major polls and had defeated Florida State, 27-24 during the regular season.

Florida State: The Seminoles were 11-1, but ranked No. 3, in both the Associated Press and coaches' polls.

Washington: The Pac-10 champions ranked fourth, but early in the season defeated Miami, 34-29. The Huskies' lone loss came two weeks later, 23-16, to Oregon.

The complicated mathematical formula scored the Sooners with 3.30 points (the fewer points, the better). In second were the Seminoles at 5.37, and Miami third with 5.69. It basically meant that the computers overruled the humans, giving a 1.28-point edge to Florida State, which was enough to put it in the championship game.

However, it also meant that there was a real possibility for a split championship, the one thing the BCS was created to avoid, if Florida State could pull off the upset. While the winner of the BCS title game was automatically named No. 1 in the coaches' poll, the Associated Press poll was not bound to do so.

Even though Oklahoma was a 10-point favorite, the Sooners had only squeaked by Kansas State in the Big Eight Championship game, 27-24, causing the potential controversy to loom larger as the game approached.

"Everything was run through the computer," Florida State coach Bobby Bowden said. "We had nothing to do with it. The facts were fed in during the season and it came out ranking us second. We will accept that.

"It's number one vs. number two in the BCS, and if we were to beat Oklahoma, then I think we should be number one in the nation in the BCS. But that probably won't happen in the AP unless Florida beats Miami."

Washington went to the Rose Bowl and defeated Purdue, 34-24.

In the Sugar Bowl, quarterback Ken Dorsey completed 22 of 40 passes for 270 yards and three touchdowns, as Miami defeated No. 7 Florida, 37-20. The Hurricanes then had to sit and wait.

"I hope the people recognize the fact that we won ten straight," Miami coach Butch Davis said. "I think we got a shot. I think we ought to be national champions."

It didn't happen. Oklahoma's defense shut down Heisman Trophy winner Chris Weinke for a 13-2 victory, and an undefeated season.

While the results on the field may not have been in dispute, the process made it one of the most controversial championships in history.

6. Splitsville (1997)

In 1954, the Associated Press voters favored Ohio State, while the coaches preferred UCLA. The only thing they could agree on was that Oklahoma was No. 3, even though all three teams were undefeated.

However, instead of a No. 1 vs. No. 2 meeting in the Rose Bowl, out of the three only Ohio State played in a postseason game and was paired against Southern California (8-3) because both the Big Ten and Pac-10 had rules prohibiting teams from playing in the Rose Bowl in consecutive years. UCLA had lost to Michigan State the year before, 28-20, and returned after the 1955 season only to lose again to the Spartans, 17-14.

Despite playing in the rain, Woody Hayes' first bowl trip to Pasadena proved to be successful. USC's lone touchdown came on a punt return and Ohio State left victorious, 20-7.

With the mathematical rankings declaring their champions after the Rose Bowl, Ohio State was considered the consensus national champion. The Associated Press poll held its final voting after the bowl in 1965, and permanently in 1969. The coaches' poll didn't do so until 1973.

The toughest choice may have been in 1991, the last season before the bowl alliance was created. Both Miami and Washington were 12-0, with impressive credentials. Miami edged preseason No. 1 Florida State (on a missed last-minute field goal, in typical fashion for that rivalry) and crushed Nebraska in the Orange Bowl, 22-0. Washington also defeated the Cornhuskers (36-21 at No. 9 Nebraska in September) and handily beat Michigan in the Rose Bowl, 34-14.

The most controversial, though, was 1997, when the Bowl Alliance was in place, but didn't include the Rose Bowl.

Split National Champions since 1950

Year	Writers' Champion (AP)	Coaches' Champion (UPI/*USA Today*)
1954	Ohio State	UCLA
1957	Auburn	Ohio State
1965	Alabama	Michigan State
1970	Nebraska	Texas
1973	Notre Dame	Alabama
1974	Oklahoma	Southern California
1978	Alabama	Southern California
1990	Colorado	Georgia Tech
1991	Miami	Washington
1997	Michigan	Nebraska
2003	Southern California	LSU

No. 1 Michigan (11-0), with Heisman Trophy winner Charles Woodson, was heavily favored against Washington State, but didn't live up to lofty expectations. Quarterback Brian Griese, son of former Purdue star Bob Griese, completed 18 of 30 passes for 251 yards and three touchdowns. Wide receiver Tai Streets had touchdown receptions of 58 and 53 yards, and tight end Jerame Tuman the other score (23 yards).

Even though Washington State quarterback Ryan Leaf had a pass intercepted in the end zone by Woodson, he pulled the Cougars to within 23-16, only to run out of time while trying to stop the clock by spiking the ball at the Michigan 26 with two seconds to play.

So the Wolverines were No. 1, correct?

Well, not exactly. At the Orange Bowl, undefeated Nebraska had a much better showing against No. 3 Tennessee, handily winning 42-17.

No major college football team had gone 13-0 and not been declared the national champion, but no No. 1 team had ever won its bowl game and been dropped by voters either.

The writers' poll wasn't close, Michigan was the clear choice. Nebraska's Tom Osborne, who had just coached his last game, didn't hear about the coaches' poll until he was in his pajamas and packing for home. The Cornhuskers won the coaches' poll by a mere two points to split the title.

"Being a coach, I know a little bit how they think," Osborne said the next morning. "They probably looked at the fact we were 13-0, and to be unrewarded in some way would be ... I don't mean to say an injustice. But it wouldn't be a good thing."

5. The Fifth Down (1990)

Undefeated Colorado was trailing at Missouri, 31-27, on October 6, 1990, when it had first down at the Tigers' 3-yard line with 30 seconds remaining in the game.

On the first play, quarterback Charles Johnson spiked the ball to stop the clock.

Following a 2-yard carry by running back Eric Bieniemy on second down, Colorado called time out, which is when officials failed to realize that it was, in fact, third down.

After Bieniemy was stopped for no gain, on what should have been fourth down quarterback Johnson downed the ball to stop the clock. With the extra down, Johnson ran off the right tackle, a quarterback sneak for a touchdown and 33-31 victory, though Missouri also maintains that he was down before reaching the end zone.

"If we screwed this up, nobody's going away from here feeling any worse than we are," umpire Frank Gaines said after referee J.C. Louderback's crew conferred for nearly 20 minutes on the matter before upholding the score.

Missouri coach Bob Stull was livid, saying it made him feel ill. From there, things only escalated.

Colorado coach Bill McCartney ripped Missouri's artificial turf, comparing it to a playing on an "ice rink," and Missouri athletic director Dick Tamburo responded, "If he's complaining about slipping on the turf, then I'm complaining about the seven officials who can't count."

Missouri's chancellor, Haskell Monroe Jr., appealed to the Big Eight, asking that the Tigers be declared the winner.

"It has been determined that, in accordance with the football playing rules, the allowance of the fifth down to Colorado is not a post-game correctable error," Big Eight commissioner Carl James said in a statement. "The final score in the Colorado-Missouri football game will remain as posted."

The Big Eight conference suspended the officials for two weeks, and then broke up the crew. Meanwhile, Colorado continued its march toward the national title. Unlike the previous year, when the No. 1 Buffaloes blew "the opportunity of a lifetime" according to McCartney, with the 21-6 loss to Notre Dame in the Orange Bowl, Colorado narrowly won the rematch, 10-9.

However, the coaches still didn't vote Colorado No. 1. Instead, Georgia Tech (11-0-1), suddenly found itself moving up despite not playing in one of the major bowl games (it defeated No. 19 Nebraska in the Florida Citrus Bowl, 45-21), resulting in a split championship.

That wasn't the only high-profile fifth-down game in history. The other occurred in 1940, when No. 2 Cornell (6-0) visited Dartmouth (3-4), and hadn't lost a game since 1938. In the final minute, Dartmouth, which was led by future Army coach Earl "Red" Blaik, had a 3-0 lead, but Cornell had first down with the ball just 6 yards away from the end zone.

Fullback Mort Landsberg took the first handoff for a 3-yard gain, followed by halfback Walt Scholl reaching the 1. On third down, Landsberg dove over the middle, but failed to score. Cornell was called for delay of game prior to fourth down, when with 9 seconds remaining Scholl lined up at quarterback only to see his pass into the end zone fall incomplete.

However, linesman Joe McKenny signaled that it was fourth down again, and referee Red Friesell, who had also lost count of the downs, didn't overrule. With the extra snap, Scholl threw a touchdown pass and Cornell won, 7-3.

Friesell watched the game film and after seeing the error contacted Asa Bushnell, commissioner of the Central Office for Eastern Intercollegiate Athletics.

"On the basis of numerous charts kept by the press and motion pictures taken by both of the competing colleges, I am now convinced beyond shadow of doubt that I was in error in allowing Cornell possession of the ball for the play on which they scored," Friesell wrote. "This mistake was entirely mine as the game's referee, and not shaped in or contributed to by any of the three other officials. I realize, of course, that my jurisdiction ceased at the close of the game and that the football rules give me no authority to change even an incorrect decision such as the one described, but I do want to acknowledge my mistake to you as commissioner of the Eastern Intercollegiate Football Association and, if you see fit, to the football public as well."

Bushnell's ruling was that the final score would stand.

When Cornell knew that a mistake had indeed definitely been made, coach Carl Snavely, after consulting with school president Edmund E. Day and athletic director Jim Lynah, sent the following telegram: "I accept the final conclusion of the officials and without reservations concede the victory to Dartmouth, with hearty congratulations to you and the gallant Dartmouth team."

Dartmouth athletic director W.H. McCarter quickly responded: "Thank you for your wire. Dartmouth accepts the victory and your congratulations and salutes the Cornell team, the honorable and honored opponent of her longest football rivalry."

Had Cornell—which lost the following week to Penn, 22-20—not forfeited the game, it probably wouldn't have finished No. 1 anyway. Minnesota, which surpassed Cornell in the Associated Press poll after it defeated No. 3 Michigan, 7-6, finished the season 8-0. No. 2 Stanford, which defeated No.7 Nebraska in the Rose Bowl, 21-13, was also unbeaten at 9-0.

Afterward, Friesell, who two weeks after the gaffe quit college refereeing to work pro games exclusively, actually received letters addressed: "Fifth Downer, U.S.A."

4. Auburn (1957)

Auburn University is able to claim one national championship, 1957, when Ralph "Shug" Jordan's team yielded only 28 points, seven of which to a Southeastern Conference opponent. It shut out six of the 10 teams it played that season, including Alabama (40-0), and Georgia (6-0), with the win against the Bulldogs highlighted by two goal-line stands.

The problem was the Tigers were banned from playing in a bowl game due to recruiting violations and on National Collegiate Athletic Association probation—though both polls would still rank sanctioned teams, and thus still consider them for the national championship. Still, it was a split championship. Had the Associated Press not considered Auburn, Ohio State, No. 1 in the United Press International rankings, would likely have been its national champion (although No. 4 Oklahoma could have made a strong case after its 48-21 victory against No. 16 Duke in the Orange Bowl, while the Buckeyes barely edged Oregon at the Rose Bowl, 10-7).

The rule was partially changed in 1974, when an agreement with the American Football Coaches Association made teams on probation ineligible for ranking and national championship consideration. The team directly affected that season was Oklahoma, which was serving a two-year penalty, and had finished second or third in each of the three previous years. The undefeated Sooners averaged 508 yards of total offense and defeated its opponents by an average final score of 43-8, but United Press International's champion was Southern California, the Associated Press runner-up.

Auburn had a similar situation arise in 1993, when first-year coach Terry Bowden led the Tigers to an 11-0 finish, including wins against No. 4 Florida and defending national champion Alabama. But the Tigers were again under probation from the NCAA, keeping them off television and out of any potential bowl. Auburn was ranked No. 4 by the Associated Press, with 12-1 Florida State winning the national championship.

What really gets Auburn fans, though, was 2004.

The Tigers were coming off an unimpressive 8-5 season when they were supposed to contend for the national championship, and had endured a tumultuous offseason with school officials visiting Louisville coach Bobby Petrino and offering him the head coaching job even though Tommy Tuberville was still under contract.

"I had already filled out my application at Wal-Mart to be a greeter," Tuberville joked much, much later. "I was done."

Due to the scandal, Tuberville was set for at least one more season, with Auburn ranked No. 17 in the preseason poll. Only the Tigers didn't lose. With four players—quarterback Jason Campbell, running backs Carnell Williams and Ronnie Brown, and cornerback Carlos Rogers—who would be selected in the first round of the following National Football League draft, and the nation's top defense, Auburn defeated No. 4 LSU (10-9), No. 11 Tennessee (34-10), and No. 8 Georgia (24-6), en route to an 11-0 regular season.

But even after defeating Tennessee again in the SEC Championship game, 38-28, the 12-0 Tigers were still only third in both major polls and the Bowl Championship Series standings. Instead, No. 1 Southern California (12-0), and No. 2 Oklahoma (12-0), which had maintained their rankings through the whole season, would meet for the title in the Orange Bowl.

"You always have hope," said Auburn athletic director David Housel, who resigned along with Auburn president William Walker after the coaching scandal. "Winston Churchill was right. Never, never, never, never, never give up."

Auburn defeated Virginia Tech in the Sugar Bowl, 16-13.

"Neither team is better than us," Tuberville said. "We'll play them anytime, anywhere."

"People just don't understand how hard it is to go 13-0," Campbell said. "I'm not going to sit here and say we're No. 2 behind anybody."

Southern California, which had been the odd-team out of the previous championship game, crushed Oklahoma, 55-19.

3. Wait, I Want to Vote Again (1947)

After the Associated Press poll was created in 1936, it took only two years for the bowls to cast doubt on teams already selected the national champion. Led by Davey O'Brien,

Texas Christian went 10-0 during the 1938 regular season, with the quarterback inspiring a second-half comeback in the Sugar Bowl to defeat No. 6 Carnegie Tech by the unimpressive score of 15-7. Meanwhile, No. 2 Tennessee and No. 4 Oklahoma, both 11-0, played in what's become known as the "Orange Brawl," a brutal 17-0 victory for the Volunteers, while No. 3 Duke lost to Southern California at the Rose Bowl, 7-3.

Had the Associated Press poll been recast, there's a decent chance that the Volunteers, instead of the Horned Frogs, would have been No. 1.

Incidentally, the following year No. 2 Tennessee was 10-0 when it faced No. 3 Southern California in the Rose Bowl, only to be shut out 14-0 to snap a 23-game winning streak. Texas A&M was the clear national champion, although No. 4 Colgate also finished undefeated at 8-0.

As previously mentioned, what sparked the debate about when the final polls should be held was a four-year period in the early 1950s in which the national champion subsequently lost (Michigan State didn't play in a bowl in 1952), including Maryland in 1953. The Terrapins were the only unbeaten and untied major college football team in the country before falling to No. 4 Oklahoma in the Orange Bowl, 7-0. Notre Dame had been No. 1 until it tied Iowa, 14-14, thanks to snapping Georgia Tech's 31-game unbeaten streak, only to see coach Frank Leahy (107-13-9) collapse at halftime and retire at the end of the season.

National Champions Who Subsequently Lost in the Postseason

Season	Bowl	Teams (AP rank)
1950	Sugar	No. 7 Kentucky beat No. 1 Oklahoma 13-7
1951	Sugar	No. 3 Maryland beat No. 1 Tennessee 28-13
1953	Orange	No. 4 Oklahoma beat No. 1 Maryland 7-0
1960	Rose	No. 6 Washington beat No. 1 Minnesota 17-7
1964	Orange	No. 5 Texas beat No. 1 Alabama 21-17

In 1947, Michigan and Notre Dame had taken turns atop the Associated Press poll, and wouldn't meet on the field. The Irish were at No. 1 in the initial rankings that season, released October 6, only to see the Wolverines replace them a week later, with Notre Dame back on top by the end of the month, and so forth. They switched places four times even though neither sustained a loss or tie. At the conclusion of the regular season, both teams were 9-0.

The Irish and Wolverines had two common opponents, Pittsburgh and Northwestern. Notre Dame won 40-6 and 26-19, respectively, while Michigan did likewise in the same order, 69-0 and 49-21.

In the final poll, released December 8, Notre Dame was listed first, and its season was complete. The Irish were in the midst of a 44-year stretch (1925-69) in which they rejected all bowl invitations, primarily citing academic reasons and that the games would interfere with final exams.

Michigan, however, had no such policy, and Fritz Crisler's team accepted the invitation to play No. 8 Southern California (7-1-1) in the Rose Bowl. The game was a slaughter, with the Wolverines celebrating a crushing 49-0 victory, at that point the worst loss in USC history. Jack Weisenburger scored three touchdowns and despite an injured hamstring Robert Chappuis passed for 188 yards while setting Rose Bowl records for total offense (279 yards) and pass completions (14).

Following the game, every mathematical ranking opted for Michigan as the national champion except the Williamson System, which like the Associated Press issued its final report prior to the postseason.

Due to the outcry, on January 6, 1948, the Associated Press held a special nonbinding postseason poll that had 1. Michigan, 2. Notre Dame, by vote total of 226-119, only it didn't supersede the final regular season poll. Thus, Notre Dame (which defeated Southern California earlier in the season, 38-7) was considered the "official" national champion, with Michigan the consensus national champion except the Williamson System.

Due to a strange twist, the Heisman Trophy also came down to between Michigan and Notre Dame. Again, the Fighting Irish came out on top as quarterback Johnny Lujack beat out halfback Bob Chappuis, 742-555. Rounding out the top eight were Doak Walker (Southern Methodist), Charlie Conerly (Ole Miss), Harry Gilmer (Alabama), Bobby Layne (Texas), Chuck Bednarik (Penn), and Bill Swiacki (Columbia).

2. The Most Famous Tie in Football (1946)

College football had never seen a lineup like the one Army boasted beginning with the 1944 season. Under the direction of Earl "Red" Blaik, the Cadets destroyed the competition by an average score of 56-4.

Leading the team was the Mr. Inside and Mr. Outside backfield of fullback Doc Blanchard and halfback Glenn Davis. They finished second and third in Heisman Trophy voting behind Ohio State's Les Horvath in 1944 (Davis was second), Blanchard won the award in 1945 with Davis second, and Davis finally took home the trophy in 1946 with Blanchard finishing fourth.

In 1946, Army appeared poised to become the first team in the modern era to secure three straight national titles when it arrived at Yankee Stadium for another showdown with Notre Dame, with both teams again undefeated. The two previous years, the Fighting Irish lost 59-0 (the worst defeat in program history) and 48-0 and had been ranked fifth and second, respectively, in the Associated Press poll. However, after two years serving in the Navy, Frank Leahy was back coaching Notre Dame.

This time it was different, and the media buildup could only be described as intense. "It was almost eerie along the sideline," Notre Dame's George Connor was quoted as saying years later. "I've never felt like I did that day on a football field. Everybody was very tense, everything was electric."

Six times Army had the ball inside the Notre Dame 30-yard line, only to be rebuffed, with the Fighting Irish crossing midfield three times, yet for the same result.

With both coaches playing more not to lose rather than to win, the pivotal moment came in the second quarter, after Notre Dame drove all the way to the Army 4 in the second quarter, when Leahy supposedly turned to kicker Fred Earley and asked, "Can you make it?"

"Sir, it's like an extra point to me," was the reply regarding the 21-yard attempt.

"No, we need six, not three. Three points will never win this game," and Leahy went for the first down, only to be unsuccessful.

Army's best chance to score may have been when Blanchard broke into the open field, only to be stopped by a sensational open-field tackle by Johnny Lujack.

"I guess I should be elated over the tie," Leahy said after the game. "After all, we didn't lose. But I'm not."

"There is no jubilation in this dressing room," Blaik said.

Army remained at No. 1, but Notre Dame, after dominating Northwestern (27-0), Tulane (41-0), and No. 16 Southern California (26-6), narrowly surpassed it in the final Associated Press poll. Although the Fighting Irish won the national championship, the 0-0 tie haunted Leahy for years.

After Notre Dame won the rematch a year later, 27-7, and went on to win the controversial 1947 national championship (see #3 for the dispute with Michigan), the Army series was discontinued and they've sporadically played since.

1. "Tie One for the Gipper" (1966)

It was dubbed the "Game of the Century," if not more, long before the teams even took the field. No. 1 Notre Dame vs. No. 2 Michigan State on November 19, 1966, had been building up for two years due to the circumstances regarding those seasons. In 1964, No. 1 Notre Dame lost in the final moments of its season finale against Southern California, 20-17, costing it the national championship. In 1965, Michigan State made it through the regular season with a 10-0 record, only to be upset by No. 5 UCLA in the Rose Bowl, 14-12, nullifying the title when for the first time the Associated Press held its final voting after the postseason.

The expectation was for a rare winner-takes-all type of showdown.

Originally slated for a regional broadcast, ABC received a legal suit and 50,000 letters requesting it be shown nationally. The National Collegiate Athletic Association finally agreed, but only if the telecast was delayed in some areas. Still, 80,011 fans, approximately 4,000 over capacity, crammed into Spartans Stadium on a cold, overcast morning, with a then-record 745 media credentials distributed.

Things looked bleak for the visiting team after Michigan State jumped out a 10-0 lead. Notre Dame was already without leading rusher Nick Eddy, who slipped on ice getting off the train in East Lansing and aggravated his shoulder injury, and quarterback Terry Hanratty had to leave the game with a separated shoulder injury following a hit from massive defensive lineman Bubba Smith (with Charley Thornhill helping out) midway through the first quarter. He was replaced by Coley O'Brien, a diabetic who required two insulin shots a day, who connected with backup sophomore receiver Bob Gladieux for a 34-yard touchdown.

The score stood at 10-7 until Joe Azzaro made a 28-yard field goal on the first play of the fourth quarter to tie it at 10. However, he missed a 41-yard attempt with 4:39 remaining that could have been the difference.

With just 1:24 left, Notre Dame got the ball back at its own 30 with plenty of time to at least try and reach field-goal range, when Ara Parseghian told his players to run out the clock for the 10-10 final score.

"We'd fought hard to come back and tie it up," he later said. "After all that, I didn't want to risk giving it to them cheap. They get reckless and it could cost them the game. I wasn't going to do a jackass thing like that at this point."

Notre Dame football player Rocky Bleier wrote in the book *Fighting Back* that Parseghian told them in the locker room: "Men, I'm proud of you. God knows I've never been more proud of any group of young men in my life. Get one thing straight, though. We did not lose. We were number one when we came, we fell behind, had some tough things happen, but you overcame them. No one could have wanted to win this one more than I. We didn't win, but, by God, we did not lose. They're crying about a tie, trying to detract from your efforts. They're trying to make it come out a win. Well, don't you believe it. Their season is over. They can't go anywhere. It's all over and we're still number one. Time will prove everything that has happened here today. And you'll see that after the rabble-rousers have had their say, cooler minds who understand the true odds will know that Notre Dame is a team of champions."

Despite the widespread criticism that Parseghian accurately foresaw, including Dan Jenkins of *Sports Illustrated* writing that the Irish "tied one for the Gipper," there was no change in the Associated Press rankings, with Notre Dame still No.1 and Michigan State at No. 2.

Because Notre Dame still had a policy of rejecting all postseason invitations, its season concluded with the annual rivalry game at Southern Cal, which was 7-2 and coming off a 14-7 loss to UCLA. Any suspense was quickly dismissed as the Fighting Irish easily won, 51-0. Meanwhile, Purdue represented the Big Ten in the Rose Bowl, with Michigan State's season complete.

As if the tie wasn't controversial enough, there's also the matter of No. 3 Alabama, which some believe had its best team ever under Paul W. "Bear" Bryant. The Crimson Tide was coming off national championships in 1964 and 1965, was the preseason No. 1 selection, and finished the regular season as the only team with an unblemished record, 10-0.

Alabama was paired against No. 6 Nebraska in the Sugar Bowl—a rematch of the previous year's Orange Bowl, where Alabama won 39-28 to vault from No. 4 to No. 1 in the final polls. This time it wouldn't be anywhere near as close. Led by quarterback Kenny Stabler, the Crimson Tide jumped out a 17-0 lead and won convincingly, 34-7.

But still the Tide didn't rise in the polls, and felt it was robbed of its place in history as the first program to win three consecutive national titles.

What can't be measured was the impact civil rights might have had on the voting. At the time, Alabama, the state, was the focal point of the national debate, and tensions were at an all-time high.

Already, Rosa Parks had refused to sit in the back of a bus, and Martin Luther King, Jr. wrote his famous "Letter from a Birmingham Jail." Televisions across the country had showed images of police commissioner Eugene "Bull" Connor ordering the use of fire hoses and dogs to drive back the unarmed demonstrators, many of them kids.

The U.S. Supreme Court ruled racial segregation in public schools unconstitutional in 1954, but Alabama avoided implementing the decision until 1963. That same year, one of numerous bombings in the state claimed the lives of four young girls—Addie Mae

Collins, Denise McNair, Carole Robertson, and Cynthia Wesley—at the Sixteenth Street Baptist Church. Widespread outrage helped lead to the Civil Rights Act of 1964, which outlawed segregation.

On June 11, 1963, Governor George Wallace kept a campaign pledge to stand in the schoolhouse door to block integration of Alabama public schools, and did so on the University of Alabama campus to try and stop its first two black students, Vivian Malone and James Hood. The admission of the first black student to nearby Ole Miss had led to riots in 1962, with two people killed and at least 75 injured. Consequently, President John F. Kennedy federalized the Alabama National Guard and ordered its units to the university campus, where Wallace stepped aside.

In March 1965, more than 500 marched from Selma to Montgomery to protest discrimination in voter registration, and commemorate the death of Jimmie Lee Jackson, shot three weeks earlier by a state trooper while trying to protect his mother at a demonstration. After crossing the Edmund Pettus Bridge they were brutally assaulted in front of journalists and photographers by heavily armed state troopers and deputies. Congress responded with the Voting Rights Act of 1965, which helped blacks get into the voting booths in Alabama.

Meanwhile, the Alabama football team had yet to integrate, with Bryant publicly saying the time wasn't right yet while helping some standout black athletes land at other top programs, including, ironically, Michigan State and his friend Duffy Daugherty.

Daugherty is believed to have coined the phrase, "A tie is like kissing your sister," a line Bryant frequently used.

Alabama had yielded only 37 points the entire season and five opponents failed to score, including LSU (21-0), and Auburn (34-0).

As for his reaction to the Notre Dame-Michigan State tie, Bryant said: "At Alabama, we teach our men to win."

PART IV

"Who Has the Best Football Program?"

S O YOU'RE standing with a friend at the water cooler, maybe tailgating before a game, or just hanging out Friday night at the local watering hole, when he (or she) reaches deep into his (or her) brain looking for a conversation topic that will take up the rest of the night's discussion and provide an opportunity to look impressively hip and knowledgeable, and comes up with the whopper of all college football questions.

"So who do you think has the best football program?"

It's sort of like what Douglas Adams wrote in the *Hitchhiker's Guide to the Galaxy* about the ultimate question of life, universe and everything, it's a lot easier to figure out the answer once you know what the actual question is. And similar to religion, there are numerous ways to try and formulate any sort of explanation.

Without putting it in some sort of context, "who's #1?" in college football is about as open-ended a question as what's the meaning of life. Are you talking the most recent season or all-time? Does the pre-modern era count? How do you consider individual and coaching accomplishments compared to teams?

Just coming up with the criteria could take hours, especially if one of the persons involved is a rabid fan of one particular team, making it extremely difficult to be objective (if that's the intent, often it isn't).

Let's start with all-time statistics, and the obvious one of wins. Here are the numbers heading into the 2006 season (and thus half the decade):

Team	Years	Won	Lost	Tied	Pct.	Games
Michigan	126	849	280	36	.744	1,165
Notre Dame	117	811	266	42	.744	1,119
Texas	113	800	310	33	.714	1,143
Nebraska	116	794	321	40	.705	1,155
Alabama	111	774	301	43	.712	1,118
Ohio State	116	774	300	53	.710	1,127
Penn State	119	771	339	41	.688	1,151
Oklahoma	111	757	289	53	.713	1,099
Tennessee	109	752	312	53	.697	1,117
Southern California	113	732	298	54	.700	1,084

But wait, doesn't Michigan have an unfair advantage because it's been playing football longer then the other teams at the top of the list?

Actually, if you go by winning percentages, no.

Team	Years	Won	Lost	Tied	Pct.	Games
Michigan	126	849	280	36	.7442	1,165
Notre Dame	117	811	266	42	.7435	1,119
Texas	113	800	310	33	.714	1,143
Oklahoma	111	757	289	53	.713	1,099
Alabama	111	774	301	43	.712	1,118
Ohio State	116	774	300	53	.710	1,127
Nebraska	116	794	321	40	.705	1,155
Southern California	113	732	298	54	.700	1,084
Tennessee	109	752	312	53	.697	1,117
Penn State	119	771	339	41	.688	1,151

FYI, the next two schools on the list were Florida State and Boise State, which in the grand scheme of college football are about as much of a blip as the United States is to world history. The Seminoles made their mark in the 1990s, and the Broncos are a recent addition to Division I-A (Football Bowl Subdivision) football. However, Michigan's high placement is especially interesting due to the fact that the Wolverines had not been the dominant team in any decade since 1950 (bowls and playoffs not included prior to 1970):

2000–2005

Team	W	L	Pct.
1. Miami (Fla.)	64	10	.865
2. Oklahoma	68	11	.861
3. Texas	65	11	.855
4. Boise St.	63	13	.829
5. Georgia	60	17	.779
6. Southern California	59	17	.776
7. Ohio State	58	17	.773
8. LSU	59	18	.766
9. Virginia Tech	58	18	.763
10. Louisville	56	19	.747

1990–1999

Rank	Team	W	L	T	Pct.
1.	Florida State	109	13	1	.890
2.	Nebraska	108	16	1	.868
3.	Marshall	114	25	0	.820
4.	Florida	102	22	1	.820
5.	Tennessee	99	22	2	.813
6.	Penn State	97	26	0	.789
7.	Michigan	93	26	3	.775
8.	Miami (Fla.)	92	27	0	.773
9.	Texas A&M	94	28	2	.766
10.	Ohio State	91	29	3	.752

1980–1989

Rank	Team	W	L	T	Pct.
1.	Nebraska	103	20	0	.837
2.	Miami (Fla.)	98	20	0	.831
3.	Brigham Young	102	26	0	.797
4.	Oklahoma	91	25	2	.780
5.	Clemson	86	25	4	.765
6.	Penn State	89	27	2	.763
7.	Georgia	88	27	4	.756
8.	Florida State	87	28	3	.750
9.	Michigan	89	29	2	.750
10.	Auburn	86	31	1	.733

1970–1979

Rank	Team	W	L	T	Pct.
1.	Oklahoma	102	13	3	.877
2.	Alabama	103	16	1	.863
3.	Michigan	96	16	3	.848
4.	Tennessee St.	85	17	2	.827
5.	Nebraska	98	20	4	.820
6.	Penn State	96	22	0	.814
7.	Ohio State	91	20	3	.811
8.	Notre Dame	91	22	0	.805
9.	Southern California	93	21	5	.803
10.	Texas	88	26	1	.770

1960–1969

Rank	Team	W	L	T	Pct.
1.	Alabama	85	12	3	.865
2.	Texas	80	18	2	.810
3.	Arkansas	80	19	1	.805
4.	Mississippi	72	20	6	.765
5.	Southern California	73	23	4	.750
6.	Bowling Green	71	22	2	.758
7.	Dartmouth	68	22	0	.756
8.	Ohio State	67	21	2	.756
9.	Missouri	72	22	6	.750
10.	Penn State	73	26	0	.737

1950–1959

Rank	Team	W	L	T	Pct.
1.	Oklahoma	93	10	2	.895
2.	Mississippi	80	21	5	.778
3.	Michigan St.	70	21	1	.766
4.	Princeton	67	22	1	.750
5.	Georgia Tech	79	26	6	.739
6.	UCLA	68	26	3	.716
7.	Ohio State	63	24	5	.712
8.	Tennessee	71	31	4	.692
9.	Penn State	62	28	4	.681
10.	Maryland	67	31	3	.678

So wins and losses don't tell the whole story. What about polls?

Although there are obviously numerous rankings services, the clear standard is the Associated Press poll, which was been around since 1936 and for the most part has been the least controversial.

Former Southeastern Conference assistant director of media relations Charles Woodroof came up with the idea of creating a compiled ranking for the AP poll, based on the same methodology as the weekly rankings. Specifically, points are awarded based on a team's finish each year. Points were awarded on a 20-19-18 ... 3-2-1 basis from 1936-88, and 25-24-23 ... 3-2-1 basis from 1989–2006.

All-Time Associated Press Poll

Rank	Team	Points	Top 20	Top 10	Top 5	1st	2nd
1.	Michigan	733	52	37	15	2	2
2.	Notre Dame	710.5	48	35	22	8	5
3.	Oklahoma	704.5	45	32	27	6	4
4.	Ohio State	654	45	27	18	4	7
5.	Alabama	637	44	32	18	6	2
6.	Nebraska	617	41	30	13	4	2
7.	Texas	557.5	38	23	8	3	1
8.	Southern California	552	40	23	16	5	5
9.	Tennessee	534	39	23	13	2	4
10.	Penn State	486	37	22	14	2	3
11.	Miami	439	27	15	10	5	4
12.	Florida State	413	23	15	15	2	2
13.	LSU	387	30	18	7	1	2
14.	Auburn	385	31	16	7	1	1
15.	Georgia	376	27	17	8	1	1
16.	Florida	357.5	23	14	9	2	1
17.	UCLA	352	30	16	9	0	1
18.	Arkansas	293	26	13	3	0	1
19.	Michigan State	266	20	13	7	1	4
20.	Texas A&M	264	22	11	2	1	0
21.	Washington	260	20	10	5	0	2
22.	Georgia Tech	227.5	20	10	5	0	2
23.	Ole Miss	223.5	18	10	4	0	2
24.	Colorado	218	18	8	5	1	0
25.	Iowa	217	18	11	3	0	1

So Notre Dame's been voted No. 1 more than any other team (eight times). Ohio State has finished second the most (seven), Oklahoma has the most top five finishes (27), and Michigan has been ranked more years than any other team (37).

But there are two other things to note about the rankings.

First, the methodology is slightly flawed. From 1936 to 1961, the wire service ranked 20 teams. From 1962 to 1967, only 10 teams were recognized. From 1968 to 1988, it went back to 20 teams before expanding to 25 in 1989.

So matter what, the results are far from absolute.

Second, it leaves little doubt about which conference has been the overall best over the past 70-plus years. While the Big Ten had three teams listed in the top 10 and five in the top 25, the Southeastern Conference had eight teams in the top 25 (for a complete listing, see Appendix C).

That's all and good, but what about championships?

Considering that there's so much debate about nearly each and every title, it should surprise no one that there are no quick and easy answers. For example, Princeton can claim 28 national championships, and Yale 27, of which all but one were before the Associated Press poll was created. Of course, neither has been a factor in the national-title picture for 50-plus years, and both Ivy League schools now play in Division I-AA (Football Championship Subdivision).

Some programs probably claim more championships than they should, and others don't claim titles that they could. Alabama professes 12 championships (some obviously more legitimate that others), while Michigan and Notre Dame both tout 11 and Oklahoma seven.

Again, we'll consider the Associated Press final ranking, again since 1936, even though the top team has already been revealed (through 2006):

Most Associated Press Championships

1.	Notre Dame	8
2.	Oklahoma	7
3.	Alabama	6
4.	Miami	5
	Southern California	5
6.	Minnesota	4
	Nebraska	4
	Ohio State	4
9.	Texas	3
10.	Army	2
	Florida	2
	Florida State	2
	Michigan	2
	Penn State	2
	Pittsburgh	2
	Tennessee	2

However, the coaches' poll, dating back to 1950, paints a very different picture:

Most Coaches' Poll Championships

1. Oklahoma	6
Southern California	6
3. Alabama	5
4. Miami	4
Nebraska	4
Texas	4
7. Notre Dame	3
Ohio State	3
9. Florida	2
Florida State	2
Penn State	2
LSU	2
Tennessee	2

Yes, they were watching the same games and the same teams, but it's a good, simple measure of how controversial the championships have been. It also helps dispel popular notions that simply are not true. For example, if Notre Dame has received so much national championship consideration it would only make sense that the Fighting Irish would have enjoyed tremendous success in bowl games.

Actually the Fighting Irish haven't, partially due to rejecting all invitations from 1925–1969. The policy changed under Ara Parseghian, and it didn't take long for Notre Dame to quickly develop another reputation, as being opportunistic and only accepting bowl bids against higher-ranked teams in order to improve its own standing. After returning to the postseason, the first five times Notre Dame played in a bowl it was the lower-ranked team, and six of the first nine appearances were against the No. 1 team. Its record was 6-3 (4-2 against No. 1 teams).

Notre Dame Bowl Results (1969–1980)

Season	Bowl	Result (AP Rankings)	ND Final Ranking
1969	Cotton	No. 1 Texas 21, No. 9 Notre Dame 17	5
1970	Cotton	No. 5 Notre Dame 24, No. 1 Texas 11	2
1972	Orange	No. 9 Nebraska 40, No. 12 Notre Dame 6	14
1973	Sugar	No. 3 Notre Dame 24, No. 1 Alabama 23	1
1974	Orange	No. 9 Notre Dame 13, No. 2-x Alabama 11	6
1976	Gator	No. 15 Notre Dame 20, No. 20 Penn State 9	12
1977	Cotton	No. 5 Notre Dame 38, No. 1 Texas 10	1
1978	Cotton	No. 10 Notre Dame 35, No. 9 Houston 34	7
1980	Sugar	No. 1 Georgia 17, No. 7 Notre Dame 10	9

x=Ranked no. 1 by coaches.

The only time Notre Dame went into a bowl game ranked No. 1 was the 1989 Fiesta Bowl, when it defeated West Virginia, 34-21, to secure the national championship. Overall, the Irish are 13-15 in bowl games, thanks to a nine-game losing streak that was still ongoing in 2006.

Instead, another football power is the clear leader in postseason play:

Bowl Appearances (through 2006)

1.	Alabama	54
2.	Tennessee	46
	Texas	46
4.	Southern California	45
5.	Nebraska	44
6.	Georgia	42
7.	Oklahoma	40
8.	Penn State	39
9.	LSU	38
	Ohio State	38
	Michigan	38
12.	Arkansas	35
	Florida State	35
	Georgia Tech	35
15.	Florida	34

Obviously, bowl appearances don't necessarily translate into bowl wins.

Bowl Victories (through 2006)

1.	Alabama	30
2.	Southern California	29
3.	Penn State	25
4.	Oklahoma	24
	Tennessee	24
6.	Georgia	23
	Texas	23
8.	Georgia Tech	22
	Nebraska	22
10.	Florida State	20
11.	Mississippi	19
	LSU	19
13.	Michigan	18
	Ohio State	18
	Auburn	18

Some coaches seem to have a gift for winning postseason games, like Penn State's Joe Paterno, who has both the most bowl appearances as a coach (33 through 2006) and victories (22). Right behind him on both lists is Bobby Bowden (30 and 20), along with Paul W. "Bear" Bryant (29 and 15), Tom Osborne (25 and 12), and Lou Holtz (22 and 12). No other coach in history has more than 10 bowl wins.

As for winning percentage in bowl games, Georgia Tech's Bobby Dodd set the mark with a 9-4 record (.692). Overall there have been nearly 1,000 major bowl games played, featuring more than 500 coaches.

It only makes sense that there's some sort of correlation between the best programs and the best coaches. However, just like there's no sure-fire definitive measure for ranking programs over a period of years, the same is true for evaluating coaches—in fact it's rarely been attempted.

The same measures can be explored, though because the National Collegiate Athletic Association doesn't crown a national championship it's therefore impossible to tell how many titles a particular coach may actually have.

Again, we'll start with all-time wins (through 2005):

All-Time Wins by Division I-A Coaches
(Minimum 10 Years as a Head Coach)

1. Bobby Bowden, Samford, West Virginia, Florida State, 359
2. Joe Paterno, Penn State, 354
3. Paul W. "Bear" Bryant, Maryland, Kentucky, Texas A&M, Alabama, 323
4. Glenn "Pop" Warner, Georgia, Cornell, Carlisle, Pitt, Stanford, Temple, 319
5. Amos Alonzo Stagg, Springfield, Chicago, Pacific, 314
6. LaVell Edwards, Utah State, Brigham Young, 257
7. Tom Osborne, Hastings, Nebraska, 255
8. Lou Holtz, Kent State, William & Mary, North Carolina State, Arkansas, Minnesota, Notre Dame, South Carolina, 249
9. Woody Hayes, Denison, Miami (Ohio), Ohio State, 238
10. Bo Schembechler, Miami (Ohio), Ohio State, 234

The list changes dramatically for winning percentage.

All-Time Winning Percentage by Division I-A Coaches
(Minimum 10 Years as a Head Coach)

1. Knute Rockne, Notre Dame, 105-12-5, .881
2. Frank Leahy, Boston College, Notre Dame, 107-13-9, .864
3. George Woodruff, Yale, Penn, Illinois, Carlisle, 142-25-2, .846
4. Barry Switzer, Arkansas, Oklahoma, 157-29-4, .837
5. Tom Osborne, Hastings, Nebraska, 255-149-3, .836

6. Percy Haughton, Cornell, Harvard, Columbia, 96-17-7, .832
7. Bob Neyland, Tennessee, 173-31-12, .829
8. Fielding Yost, Ohio Wesleyan, Nebraska, Kansas, Stanford, Michigan, 196-36-12, .828
9. Bud Wilkinson, Oklahoma, 145-29-4, .826
10. Jock Sutherland, Lafayette, Pittsburgh, 144-28-14, .812.

Only two on the winning-percentage list, Switzer and Osborne, have coached within the last 40 years.

So Paterno has coached at Penn State since 1966. He's second in all-time wins, has the most bowl victories and bowl appearances. His Nittany Lions have two consensus national titles, along with three other championships they could claim. Where would that put him among the all-time greats? How would he compare to, say, Knute Rockne? How does one factor in that he's been at his school so long and benefits from his team playing more games than his predecessors?

Bobby Bowden is neck-and-neck with Paterno for all-time wins and has two consensus titles to go with three non-consensus titles. How would either of them measure up to Bryant, who had six consensus titles at Alabama and could have claimed at least a share of three more?

In attempt to answer the impossible question, in 2004 CBS broadcasted the results of "Dell Presents College Football's Ten Greatest Coaches," which was determined by a mass survey including Heisman Trophy winners, members of the College Football Hall of Fame, more than 300 media, collegiate athletic directors, and fans.

The fan voting went as followed:

1. Tom Osborne
2. Bob Devaney
3. Barry Switzer
4. Joe Paterno
5. Bud Wilkinson
6. Paul W. "Bear" Bryant
7. Bobby Bowden
8. Woody Hayes
9. John Gagliardi
10. Duffy Daugherty

That the top two vote getters both came from Nebraska certainly makes one wonder if Conhuskers fans might have gone a little overboard stuffing the ballot box. It greatly differed from the final rankings, which obviously had a preference for modern coaches:

1. Paul W. "Bear" Bryant
2. Joe Paterno
3. Eddie Robinson
4. Bobby Bowden

5. Knute Rockne
6. Woody Hayes
7. Bud Wilkinson
8. Tom Osborne
9. Bo Schembechler
10. Amos Alonzo Stagg

Incidentally, it will probably surprise some to learn that the coach with college football's best overall winning percentage is not on either list, but the career leader is. Through 2006, when he won his ninth Division III championship in 14 years, Larry Kehres of Mount Union had a career record of 246-20-3, making him the only coach in college football history with a winning percentage above .900 (at .920).

Meanwhile, John Gagliardi completed his 58th year in college football, surpassing Amos Alonzo Stagg's mark of 57 years, and notched win No. 443. He's won two Division III national championships, 1976 and 2003, and twice won the NAIA title at St. John's University, in St. Joseph, Minnesota. Gagliardi's teams have won 28 conference titles, including 2005 and 2006, and have appeared in 54 postseason games.

Obviously, there's no way to make an accurate statistical comparison overlapping the different eras of the game. Every sport is the same way, thus one of the most important criteria baseball writers use in voting for the Hall of Fame every year isn't necessarily how someone's statistics measure up all-time, but against contemporaries. A person who dominated his era almost always gets enshrined.

So which school has the most players inducted into the College Football Hall of Fame? It shouldn't surprise anyone, making its permanent home in South Bend, Indiana, even more fitting.

Most Players Inducted into the CFHOF

1. Notre Dame 41
2. Michigan 27
3. Southern California 26
4. Yale 23
5. Army 22
6. Princeton 21
7. Navy 20
   Ohio State 20
9. Tennessee 18
   Pittsburgh 18

As for each specific year, there are other important gauges of a program's success in addition to the polls and conference standings.

One extremely important indicator of future potential is the annual team rankings in recruiting.

The column on the left is Rivals.com's rankings (FYI, Scout.com's ranking are also nationally well-known) after National Signing Day, held the first week of February. The column on the right is the final Associated Press rankings three years later.

Recruiting 2002

1. Texas
2. Tennessee
3. Georgia
4. Florida State
5. Ohio State

Final AP poll 2005

1. Texas
2. Southern California
3. Penn State
4. Ohio State
5. LSU

Recruiting 2003

1. LSU
2. Florida
3. Southern California
4. Oklahoma
5. Miami

Final AP poll 2006

1. Florida
2. Ohio State
3. LSU
4. Southern California
5. Wisconsin

The key word to remember with recruiting is "potential." For example, after having the No. 2-rated class in 2002, Tennessee finished a surprising 5-6 in 2005 and thus didn't secure the minimum number of victories, six, needed to be bowl eligible. Georgia went 10-3 and won the Southeastern Conference championship, while Florida State defeated Virginia Tech in the first Atlantic Coast Conference title game and finished 8-5.

Over time, this naturally affects the quality of players coming out of specific programs, which serve as the primary feeders of talent for the National Football League (and other professional outlets).

According to the NFL, rosters for the 2006 kickoff weekend were led by players from the following schools:

Most NFL Players, 2006 Kickoff Weekend

Rank	Team	NFL Players
1.	Miami	42
2.	Florida State	41
3.	Tennessee	40
4.	Georgia	39
	Ohio State	39
6.	Michigan	36
7.	Florida	35
8.	Nebraska	32
9.	LSU	31
10.	Penn State	29

Probably the most surprising thing about that list is the one obvious program not on it. Even though Southern California won three Heisman Trophies between 2002-6 and arguably came close to winning three consecutive national championships, the Trojans had just 26 players in the NFL, the same number as rival UCLA, Notre Dame and Wisconsin.

As mentioned elsewhere, what really makes the college football world go around nowadays is money, and there are three additional tangible ways of measuring it. The first is in attendance, which serves as an adequate indicator of a school's commitment to the program and fan interest. Just because a stadium might fit 100,000 doesn't mean that many people actually show up.

The final rankings from 2006 were as follows:

Total Attendance		Average Attendance	
1. Michigan	770,183	1. Michigan	110,026
2. Penn State	752,972	2. Penn State	107,567
3. Tennessee	740,521	3. Tennessee	105,789
4. LSU	737,696	4. Ohio State	105,096
5. Alabama	737,104	5. Georgia	92,746
6. Ohio State	735,674	6. LSU	92,212
7. Auburn	680,506	7. Alabama	92,138
8. Georgia	649,222	8. Southern California	91,480
9. Florida State	644,256	9. Florida	90,409
10. Florida	632,866	10. Texas	88,505

Note: The biggest reason for the discrepancy between the two columns is number of home games. Alabama and LSU had eight home games in 2006, while Southern California had only six.

By just charging, say, $50 a seat, it's easy to see why adding an extra 10,000 to a stadium's capacity is so appealing and being done on so many campuses across the country. However, the real money is in luxury box seats.

As of January 2007, Michigan was in the midst of a $226 million project to add 3,200 luxury seats and 83 suites, which would only increase capacity by about 750 to 108,251. Texas was spending $150 million to add 10,000 seats plus amenities to its stadium. Alabama, LSU and Tennessee had just completed projects, and so on ...

Second, is marketing and merchandise sales.

According to the Sporting Goods Manufacturers Association, college sports generated $2.9 billion in retail sales in 2005, up from $2.4 billion five years previous.

After winning the 2005 national championship in football, Texas made $8.2 million in licensing royalties the following year. With Florida holding national titles in men's basketball and football at the same time in 2006, some estimated the school would eclipse the $10 million mark for the first time in history.

According to The Collegiate Licensing Company, which represents more than 180 collegiate properties (including schools, bowl games, conferences, the Bowl Championship

Series, the Heisman Trophy and the NCAA), here were the rankings from the second quarter of the 2006–2007 fiscal year (October 1, 2006–December 31, 2006):

1. Texas
2. Notre Dame
3. Georgia
4. Michigan
5. Florida
6. Alabama
7. Penn State
8. Tennessee
9. North Carolina
10. Oklahoma

Next up for collegiate merchandise is the "College Vault" appeal line, which specializes in vintage apparel for more than 50 colleges and universities.

Another big moneymaker is video games. In 2006, EA Sports made more than $79 million from "NCAA Football 06." Many schools received more than $100,000 for being used in the game (it features uniform numbers and a player's physical attributes, but not names).

The third indicator is coaches' salaries, which have dramatically spiked of late, similar to what's occurred in the National Football League.

Alabama raised the stakes significantly when it lured Nick Saban away from the Miami Dolphins by offering a contract worth $4 million a year, making him the highest-paid coach in college football history by a wide margin. Critics immediately claimed that Alabama had gone overboard because it would take money away from students, education, and other athletics, when in fact it would do the opposite. Since Saban's contract would almost exclusively come out of television earnings and marketing, the resulting financial windfall expected from donations alone made the move a no-brainer.

Instead, critics started wondering a little louder why college football enjoyed tax-exempt status, when so many coaches were making 10 times more than the school presidents. Perhaps the real question that should have been asked is why Alabama was considered the trigger when it only followed the example set by other programs like Oklahoma, Notre Dame, and Southern California.

Although Charlie Weiss' contract had not been pinpointed (supposedly it was 10 years for between $30 to 40 million, but believed to be on the upper end), here, according to various reports, were the top 10 college football coaching contracts when Saban said yes to Alabama during the first week of January, 2007.

One immediate repercussion of the highly publicized coaching search by Alabama was that nearly every coach linked to it received a sizable raise, including South Carolina's Steve Spurrier, West Virginia's Rich Rodriguez, and even Rutgers' Greg Shiano. Petrino, who had a contract through 2010, also flirted with the Oakland Raiders (and

Top College Football Coaching Contracts (January 2007)

School	Coach	Average salary
1. Alabama	Nick Saban	$4 million
2. Oklahoma	Bob Stoops	$3.4 million
3. Notre Dame	Charlie Weis	$3.3 million
4. Southern California	Pete Carroll	$3 million
5. Iowa	Kirk Ferentz	$2.84 million
6. Texas	Mack Brown	$2.664 million
7. Louisville-x	Bobby Petrino	$2.5 million
8. Ohio State	Jim Tressel	$2.45 million
9. Auburn	Tommy Tuberville	$2.23 million
10. Tennessee	Philip Fulmer	$2.05 million

more than the one time it was widely reported). Less than a week after Saban was intro-duced in Tuscaloosa, Petrino accepted an offer to coach the Atlanta Falcons, five years for $24 million.

Finally, there's the all-important category that frequently gets overlooked, academics.

In 1990, the first Draddy Trophy was awarded, recognizing academic success, foot-ball performance, and exemplary community leadership. Known as the "academic Heis-man," it was named in honor of Vincent dePaul Draddy, who served as Chairman of the Board of the National Football Foundation and College Hall of Fame for 19 years.

Draddy Award Winners

1990	Chris Howard	Air Force
1991	John B. Culpepper	Florida
1992	Jim Hansen	Colorado
1993	Thomas D. Burns	Virginia
1994	Robert Zatchka	Nebraska
1995	Bobby Hoying	Ohio State
1996	Danny Wuerffel	Florida
1997	Peyton Manning	Tennessee
1998	Matt Stinchcomb	Georgia
1999	Chad Pennington	Marshall
2000	Kyle Vanden Bosch	Nebraska
2001	Joaquin Gonzalez	Miami
2002	Brandon Roberts	Washington University (St. Louis)
2003	Craig Krenzel	Ohio State
2004	Michael Munoz	Tennessee

2005	Rudy Niswanger	LSU
2006	Brian Leonard	Rutgers

Since 1952, the College Sports Information Directors of American (CoSIDA) has selected an All-American team including student-athletes in all divisions. To be eligible for consideration, students must have a minimum 3.2 grade-point average, on a 4.0 scale, during their careers.

Here are the top programs in Division I-A, with the number of times a student-athlete was selected first-team academic All-American:

Most CoSIDA Academic All-Americans

School	Academic A-A
1. Nebraska	62
2. Notre Dame	36
3. Ohio State	30
4. Penn State	26
5. Texas	23
6. Southern California	22
7. Stanford	20
8. Michigan	19
Northwestern	19
Oklahoma	19

Graduation rates used to be considered the benchmark for measuring a school's academic standing, but the lag between the time an athlete was under scholarship and performing, and the publication of the pertinent statistics, made it impossible to access progress and, in some cases, assign applicable and necessary penalties. For example, in order to gauge how well the 1980 incoming freshman class fared, one had to wait until after 1986, when all the athletes, and possibly the coaches as well, were long gone.

In 2004, the National Collegiate Athletic Association began using a new statistic, the Academic Progress Rate, which it considered an improvement compared to the Federal Graduation Rate. Every year, every sport and each athletic department as a whole is given a numerical score on how well each student-athlete is advancing toward graduation. Those not meeting the minimum requirements would be subject to penalties, possibly even the loss of scholarships, or worse.

In 2006, the NCAA disclosed the APR data for the 2003-04 and 2004-05 academic years, and issued its first penalties. A total of 99 programs from 66 schools lost scholarships, with the most, 23, in football—though very few at the Division I-A level.

The top scores that year were the following (a perfect score was 1,000):

School	APR score
1. Stanford	995
2. Navy	986
3. Boston College	982
4. Auburn	981
5. Duke	975
6. Connecticut	974
7. Rice	971
Southern Miss	971
9. Wake Forest	970
10. Air Force	967

Like just about everything else in college football, the program had its detractors, especially considering schools were computing their scores in different ways. Auburn in particular raised a few eyebrows especially later that summer when a *New York Times* investigation alleged that the interim chairman of the sociology department, Thomas Petee, was handing out high grades for courses that required little or no attendance, or work.

Specifically, Petee was accused of providing an inordinate number of independent study courses that athletes and non-athletes alike could use to improve their grade-point average and preserve their academic standing and athletic eligibility. Petee had assigned 272 students his directed-reading format, including 18 members of the undefeated 2004 football team. The football players had a grade-point average of 3.31 (out of 4.0) in Petee's classes, but 2.41 in all other courses.

Auburn immediately began an internal investigation in which university president Ed Richardson concluded that no wrongdoing was done by the athletic department (he termed Petee's number of students as "poor judgment"), and the players insisted they received no special treatment

However, the audit also found grades that had been changed without the professor's knowledge. In the case of one athlete, an incomplete went to an A, one of four A's received in the spring of 2003, with none of the four courses requiring classroom attendance. Fans also remembered in the 1990s when former Auburn running back James Brooks told a judge in a child-support case that he was illiterate.

Auburn's showing in the APR was the highest ranking of any Division I-A public university among the six major conferences. It was also higher than Southeastern Conference counterpart Vanderbilt, which graduated 88 percent of its students in 2004 compared to Auburn's 48 percent.

"It was a little surprising because the graduation rates are so much higher," Vanderbilt chancellor Gordon Gee told the *New York Times*. "I'm not quite certain I understood that."

Nevertheless, it all just adds to the daily debate at the water cooler, while tailgating, or just hanging out at the local watering hole.

"So who has the best football program?"

Texas finally won a national championship under Mack Brown in 2005, and the following year it was Florida's turn. Meanwhile ...

Ohio State added another Heisman Trophy to its collection, its seventh.

Michigan had the biggest stadium.

Miami had the most active players in the National Football League.

Overall, Notre Dame has won the most national championships according to the Associated Press; Oklahoma and Southern California have that honor according to the coaches.

Alabama has made the most bowl appearances and victories. ...

In 2006, the Tuscaloosa News took a stab at answering the question of which program was the best in college football by creating a formula that attempted to include every aspect of a college football program, while at the same time be as opinion-free as possible. Basically, it was taking everything previously mentioned in this chapter, shoving it all into a blender and turning it on.

The top 25 schools were ranked in each category, with points awarded similar to the weekly Associated Press poll, going from 25-24-23 ... down to 3-2-1.

That was the easy part. More difficult was selecting the categories.

Five were based on the 2005 season, while five were compiled on the overall history of the program.

The categories from the 2005 season were rankings (the final Associated Press poll), recruiting, attendance, pro potential, and academics (APR).

The all-time rankings were bowl appearances, Associated Press-awarded national championships, the all-time Associated Press poll, College Football Hall of Fame inductees (players only), and coaching legacy.

So "Who's #1?"

Southern California edged Ohio State by ½ point, 176½ compared to 176. Rounding out the top 10 were, in order, Penn State, Notre Dame, Michigan, Alabama, Oklahoma, Texas, Tennessee and Florida State.

A year later, the numbers would looked different, with USC barely holding off Michigan and Ohio State, and the Gators moving into the top 10. Another season after that ... well, you get the idea. No matter what, the debate goes on ...

Epilogue: What's Next?

DURING THE time surrounding the 2006 season, there were two important developments regarding the potential of college football eventually having some sort of a playoff to determine the national championship.

One dramatically increased the likelihood of another change, or "tweak," to the Bowl Championship Series format. The other all but eliminated any chance of a pure playoff similar to the other divisions, which utilize 16-team brackets.

The first change came well before the season started when the National Collegiate Athletic Association decided to switch to a permanent 12-game regular season. For the most part, coaches liked it because it added a game and made it easier to qualify for a bowl game. Presidents liked the extra money and players, of course, liked any opportunity to get out on a field.

So everyone was all for it, correct?

Well, then again . . .

"They add another game, but they don't give you any more scholarships," said Auburn coach Tommy Tuberville, who like many coaches had to scramble to fill his schedule. "The 12 game stinks basically, in the way we're doing it. I'm not against playing 12 games.

"I understand we need it to make more money. Give us another open date. Extend the season. I promise you, people across the country wouldn't complain about it. It's not going to affect the academics. We could have very easily had a lot better non-conference game. I saw a headline this morning, 'Cupcakes.' What do you expect when you have to force a game into a slot when you don't have very much to choose from.

"And for us, going 13-0, we didn't have a lot of people on the bandwagon trying to play us anyway. Then we had to pay an arm and a leg to get a team. If you're forced to do something, obviously you do it. I think there needs to be more communication with the coaches, athletic directors, and presidents on how we can generate more revenue.

"Obviously, I'm an advocate of a playoff system because for us in the SEC, it's almost going to be impossible for any of us to get to that championship game unless we just hit a run, which we did a few years ago. But, you know, we're going to play the 12 games. Again, we might play 13 in a few years, who knows. We just got to communicate on how we're doing it, take the load off these players because it is a tremendous load.

"One more game doesn't sound like a lot, but it's quite a bit. It's a lot of preparation time. I'm all for it because I love college football. You know, we could have organized this a little bit better than what we did."

In terms of the national title, adding the 12th game was essentially seen as a compromise, especially for those conferences that didn't have a championship game at the end of the regular season.

But playing a 12-game season in addition to a conference championship, and then possible playoff scenario on top of that, and the college football season would begin to resemble the National Football League with its 16-game season.

Tuberville's concern about a conference like the SEC, which top to bottom was almost certainly the toughest in the nation, and included four coaches who had already won a national title, would have a tougher time reaching Bowl Championship Series championship game, was echoed by other coaches.

"Well, I don't have to worry about that playoff any more," South Carolina's Steve Spurrier said. "I do think it is tougher for the top SEC teams to be one of the final two. It's tougher. It can be done. Heck, we've proven it can be done. I was reading something in the local paper here that in '92, of course, Alabama won it all going through the championship game. Of course, Tennessee did it one year. We did it one year.

"It can happen. But it is difficult. It is difficult with so many top SEC teams, whereas all the other sports, I mean, men's basketball, national champ, Florida Gators, South Carolina beat them twice, Tennessee beat them twice, but that's the regular season. End of the season, the Florida Gators were by far the best team in the country. That's sort of how sports is if you have a tournament and playoff system.

"Since we don't have that, a lot of it has to do with scheduling, voting instead of determining it on the field. But that's the way college football seems to want to do it. The presidents and athletic directors and commissioners, that's just the way they want to do it. I remember Commissioner [Roy] Kramer was here back in about '90. I said, 'Why do you want a playoff for the SEC championship but you don't want one for the national?' He just looked at me funny. He couldn't answer it either. He didn't have the answer for that one."

It should be noted that Spurrier was smiling when he made the last comment prior to the 2006 season. Six moths later, Florida proved it could still be done, this time under the direction of Urban Meyer. But the way the season unfolded only rekindled arguments that the Bowl Championship Series was simply too flawed of a system no matter how many tweaks it added, or the addition of the fifth game. Not surprisingly, the biggest outcry came from coaches like Tuberville, who, all things being considered, didn't believe his team would get a fair shot, especially after what happened in 2004.

"There is no reason on this earth why we can't have the best four and then play one more," he said. "That's the legitimate thing to do. We added a BCS game—for what in the world?—I understand we're avoiding lawsuits and making money. But let's take care of the players.

"The problem we have is you have 120 universities that are I-A and probably 25 would say they have a legitimate chance each year. And you have presidents that for some reason look at it more as for the money than having a national championship on the field. They keep coming up with lame excuses about academics. Football players miss fewer classes than anybody."

As previously noted, highlighting 2006 was the first-ever season-ending matchup between Ohio State and Michigan, with the rivals undefeated and ranked first and second in the polls. The game lived up to the hype with the Buckeyes pulling out a 42-39 victory. The subsequent poll had the teams still No. 1 and 2, but because the Big Ten didn't have a championship game they were done until their bowl appearances.

A week later Southern California manhandled No. 6 Notre Dame, 44-24, to surpass Michigan into the No. 2 slot. No. 4 Florida stayed in the picture with a 21-14 victory at rival Florida State.

Again, the non–Big Ten teams played. The Trojans lost to rival UCLA 13-9, while Florida handled No. 8 Arkansas in the SEC Championship game, 38-28. Everyone knew the final Bowl Championship standings would be extremely tight, and Meyer didn't back down from lobbying voters. In addition to the obvious gains for the program, some of the bonuses in his contract included $150,000 for reaching the BCS Championship game, another $100,000 for winning it, $75,000 for winning the SEC championship, $50,000 for a final Top 10 ranking, and the right to open a review of his contract after the 2007 season (in June he inked a six-year extension averaging $3.2 million per year).

Meyer suggested the entire BCS should be thrown out if the SEC was left out of the championship game again like Auburn in 2004, and called it an "imperfect system." Michigan coach Lloyd Carr also echoed statements previously made by Southern California's Pete Carroll and Joe Paterno of Penn State, advocating a system where everything was settled on the field.

Ohio State's Jim Tressel added to the controversy by abstaining for the first time that season from voting in the coaches' poll, calling it "somewhat of a conflict of interest."

Carr called the nonvote "real slick." Meyer said that was the very reason why he declined to vote in the poll at all. Tressel's vote wouldn't have determined who the Buckeyes played, but rival Michigan fans took it as an snub/insult.

The Ohio State vs. Florida final matchup wasn't the concluding controversy of the season. It came after the 41-14 victory by the Gators, because there was still a surprising undefeated team remaining. Boise State from the Western Athletic Conference was just the second team from outside the original six BCS conferences to play in the big-money bowl games, but proved it belonged. When the Broncos shocked Oklahoma in overtime at the Fiesta Bowl, 43-42, the call went out again to have everything settled on the field.

Following the 2006 season, one popular idea being floated was to add "plus-one" game, to which BCS commissioner Mike Slive said he was "very open-minded about."

"I think we need to take a very hard look at that," he told the Football Writers Association of America.

Such a change would be possible in two different models.

The first is to have the top four teams in the BCS standings paired into two of the marquee bowls, essentially creating national semifinals. The winners would play a week later for the national title.

In 2006, that would have resulted in Ohio State vs. LSU and Florida vs. Michigan. Southern California, which was ranked fourth by the computers but seventh by the Harris Poll and coaches' poll, would have been left out, along with No. 8 Boise State.

The other plus-one scenario would return the bowls to their traditional tie-ins and have the final BCS standings take place after all bowl games are played, with No. 1 vs. 2 for the championship.

Had that occurred in 2006, Ohio State would have faced Southern California in the Rose Bowl, with the winner almost certainly playing for the championship. Florida would have gone to the Sugar Bowl, possibly against Notre Dame or Louisville, while Michigan would have played LSU in the Capital One Bowl. In all likelihood, Boise State still wouldn't have had a shot at the national title, and there still would have been a controversy regarding which two teams should play for the title.

"The question is 'Is one and two enough?'" Slive said.

Either way, nothing can be changed until Fox's four-year $320 million broadcast deal ends with the 2010 bowls, while the Rose Bowl's contract with ABC runs through 2014. Additionally, the decision will still come down to the university presidents, who have never displayed any enthusiasm for a playoff.

"I think there's a willingness to talk about (the plus-one) more, but still I don't sense overwhelming support for it," Big East commissioner Mike Tranghese told the Associated Press. "I think that the Pac-10 and Big Ten in particular are pretty strong in their opposition for it.

"I think to get to the plus-one will be a struggle."

In addition to the relationship between the Rose Bowl and the Big Ten and Pac-10 conferences, with all sides reluctant to make any more concessions that could be seen as detrimental, other potential obstacles include concerns about whether fans would travel to more than one bowl game, especially after a conference championship, and that by advocating a plus-one system there would be no turning back even if other problems developed.

"There would be a clamor to increase it after that," Rose Bowl executive director Mitch Dorger said.

When Florida and Florida State played in November 2006, their presidents also met to discuss how a playoff system could be implemented, even if it potentially meant the end of the bowl system, which according to Scott Ramsey, chairman of the Football Bowl Association, distributed $210 million that season.

One idea Florida president Bernard Machen had was for the NCAA, or another national entity, to step in and create a playoff system.

"What you've got is system now that's run by people whose interest is the protection of their personal domain, that being the six (major) conferences," Machen said. "Any solution that they come up with is going to be based on how to protect themselves and their conference members. We need to have that go away."

After 100-plus years of controversies, don't count on it—at least not for a while.

National Champions

NATIONAL CHAMPIONS according to various services (+ = more than one champion named).

Sources: The National Collegiate Athletic Association, Associated Press (1936–present), Football Writers Association of America (1954–present); National Football Foundation and Hall of Fame (1959–1990, 1995–present); *USA Today*/CNN (*USA Today*/ESPN, 1997–present).

1869
Princeton: Billingsley, National Championship Foundation, Parke Davis+
Rutgers: Parke Davis+

1870
Princeton: Billingsley, National Championship Foundation, Parke Davis

1871
No national champions selected.

1872
Princeton: Billingsley, National Championship Foundation, Parke Davis+
Yale: Parke Davis+

1873
Princeton: Billingsley, National Championship Foundation, Parke Davis

1874
Harvard: Parke Davis+
Princeton: Billingsley, Parke Davis+
Yale: National Championship Foundation, Parke Davis+

1875
Colgate: Parke Davis+
Harvard: National Championship Foundation, Parke Davis+
Princeton: Billingsley, Parke Davis+

1876
Yale: Billingsley, National Championship Foundation, Parke Davis

1877
Princeton: Billingsley, Parke Davis+
Yale: National Championship Foundation, Parke Davis+

1878
Princeton: Billingsley, National Championship Foundation, Parke Davis

1879
Princeton: Billingsley, National Championship Foundation, Parke Davis+
Yale: Parke Davis+

1880
Princeton: National Championship Foundation+, Parke Davis+
Yale: Billingsley, National Championship Foundation+, Parke Davis+

1881
Princeton: Billingsley, Parke Davis+
Yale: National Championship Foundation, Parke Davis+

1882
Yale: Billingsley, National Championship Foundation, Parke Davis

1883
Yale: Billingsley, Helms, National Championship Foundation, Parke Davis

1884
Princeton: Billingsley, Parke Davis+
Yale: Helms, National Championship Foundation, Parke Davis+

1885
Princeton: Billingsley, Helms, Houlgate, National Championship Foundation, Parke Davis

1886
Princeton: Billingsley, Parke Davis+
Yale: Helms, National Championship Foundation, Parke Davis+

1887
Yale: Billingsley, Helms, Houlgate, National Championship Foundation, Parke Davis

1888
Yale: Billingsley, Helms, Houlgate, National Championship Foundation, Parke Davis

1889
Princeton: Billingsley, Helms, Houlgate, National Championship Foundation, Parke Davis

1890
Harvard: Billingsley, Helms, Houlgate, National Championship Foundation, Parke Davis

1891
Yale: Billingsley, Helms, Houlgate, National Championship Foundation, Parke Davis

1892
Yale: Billingsley, Helms, Houlgate, National Championship Foundation, Parke Davis

1893
Princeton: Billingsley, Helms, Houlgate, National Championship Foundation
Yale: Parke Davis

1894
Penn: Parke Davis+
Princeton: Houlgate
Yale: Billingsley, Helms, National Championship Foundation, Parke Davis+

1895
Penn: Billingsley, Helms, Houlgate, National Championship Foundation, Parke Davis+
Yale: Parke Davis+

1896
Lafayette: National Championship Foundation+, Parke Davis+
Princeton: Billingsley, Helms, Houlgate, National Championship Foundation+, Parke Davis+

1897
Penn: Billingsley, Helms, Houlgate, National Championship Foundation, Parke Davis+
Yale: Parke Davis+

1898
Harvard: Billingsley, Helms, Houlgate, National Championship Foundation
Princeton: Parke Davis

1899
Harvard: Helms, Houlgate, National Championship Foundation
Princeton: Billingsley, Parke Davis

1900
Yale: Billingsley, Helms, Houlgate, National Championship Foundation, Parke Davis

1901
Harvard: Billingsley
Michigan: Helms, Houlgate, National Championship Foundation
Yale: Parke Davis

1902
Michigan: Billingsley, Helms, Houlgate, National Championship Foundation, Parke Davis+
Yale: Parke Davis+

1903
Michigan: National Championship Foundation+
Princeton: Billingsley, Helms, Houlgate, National Championship Foundation+, Parke Davis

1904
Michigan: National Championship Foundation+
Minnesota: Billingsley
Penn: Helms, Houlgate, National Championship Foundation+, Parke Davis

1905
Chicago: Billingsley, Helms, Houlgate, National Championship Foundation
Yale: Parke Davis, Whitney

1906
Princeton: Helms, National Championship Foundation
Yale: Billingsley, Parke Davis, Whitney

1907
Yale: Billingsley, Helms, Houlgate, National Championship Foundation, Parke Davis, Whitney

1908
Harvard: Billingsley
Louisiana State: National Championship Foundation+
Penn: Helms, Houlgate, National Championship Foundation+, Parke Davis

1909
Yale: Billingsley, Helms, Houlgate, National Championship Foundation, Parke Davis

1910
Harvard: Billingsley, Helms, Houlgate, National Championship Foundation+
Pittsburgh: National Championship Foundation+

1911
Penn State: National Championship Foundation+
Princeton: Billingsley, Helms, Houlgate, National Championship Foundation+, Parke Davis

1912
Harvard: Billingsley, Helms, Houlgate, National Championship Foundation+, Parke Davis
Penn State: National Championship Foundation+

1913
Auburn: Billingsley
Chicago: Parke Davis+
Harvard: Helms, Houlgate, National Championship Foundation, Parke Davis+

1914
Army: Helms, Houlgate, National Championship Foundation, Parke Davis+
Illinois: Parke Davis+
Texas: Billingsley

1915
Cornell: Helms, Houlgate, National Championship Foundation, Parke Davis+
Oklahoma: Billingsley
Pittsburgh: Parke Davis+

1916
Army: Parke Davis+
Pittsburgh: Billingsley, Helms, Houlgate, National Championship Foundation, Parke Davis+

1917
Georgia Tech: Billingsley, Helms, Houlgate, National Championship Foundation

1918
Michigan: Billingsley, National Championship Foundation+
Pittsburgh: Helms, Houlgate, National Championship Foundation+

1919
Harvard: Football Research+, Helms, Houlgate, National Championship Foundation+, Parke Davis+
Illinois: Boand, Football Research+, Parke Davis+, Sagarin (ELO-Chess)+
Notre Dame: National Championship Foundation+, Parke Davis+
Texas A&M: Billingsley, National Championship Foundation+
Centre (Ky.): Sagarin+

1920
California: Football Research, Helms, Houlgate, National Championship Foundation, Sagarin, Sagarin (ELOChess)
Harvard: Boand+
Notre Dame: Billingsley, Parke Davis+
Princeton: Boand+, Parke Davis+

1921
California: Billingsley, Boand+, Football Research, Sagarin, Sagarin (ELO-Chess)
Cornell: Helms, Houlgate, National Championship Foundation, Parke Davis+
Iowa: Parke Davis+
Lafayette: Boand+, Parke Davis+
Washington & Jefferson: Boand+

1922
California: Billingsley, Houlgate, National Championship Foundation+, Sagarin+
Cornell: Helms, Parke Davis+
Princeton: Boand, Football Research, National Championship Foundation+, Parke Davis+, Sagarin (ELO-Chess)+

1923
California: Houlgate
Cornell: Sagarin+
Illinois: Boand, Football Research, Helms, National Championship Foundation+, Parke Davis, Sagarin (ELOChess)+
Michigan: Billingsley, National Championship Foundation+

1924
Notre Dame: Billingsley, Boand, Dickinson, Football Research, Helms, Houlgate, National Championship Foundation, Poling, Sagarin, Sagarin (ELO-Chess)
Penn: Parke Davis

1925
Alabama: Billingsley, Boand, Football Research, Helms, Houlgate, National Championship Foundation, Poling, Sagarin (ELO-Chess)+

Dartmouth: Dickinson, Parke Davis
Michigan: Sagarin+

1926
Alabama: Billingsley, Football Research, Helms+, National Championship Foundation+, Poling
Lafayette: Parke Davis
Michigan: Sagarin+
Navy: Boand, Houlgate
Stanford: Dickinson, Helms+, National Championship Foundation+, Sagarin (ELO-Chess)+

1927
Georgia: Boand, Poling
Illinois: Billingsley, Dickinson, Helms, National Championship Foundation, Parke Davis
Notre Dame: Houlgate
Texas A&M: Sagarin, Sagarin (ELO-Chess)
Yale: Football Research

1928
Detroit: Parke Davis+
Georgia Tech: Billingsley, Boand, Football Research, Helms, Houlgate, National Championship Foundation, Parke Davis+, Poling, Sagarin (ELO-Chess)+
Southern California: Dickinson, Sagarin+

1929
Notre Dame: Billingsley, Boand, Dickinson, Dunkel, Football Research, Helms, National Championship Foundation, Poling, Sagarin (ELO-Chess)+
Pittsburgh: Parke Davis
Southern California: Houlgate, Sagarin+

1930
Alabama: Football Research, Parke Davis+, Sagarin, Sagarin (ELO-Chess)
Notre Dame: Billingsley, Boand, Dickinson, Dunkel, Helms, Houlgate, National Championship Foundation, Parke Davis+, Poling

1931
Pittsburgh: Parke Davis+
Purdue: Parke Davis+
Southern California: Billingsley, Boand, Dickinson, Dunkel, Helms, Houlgate, Football Research, National Championship Foundation, Poling, Sagarin, Sagarin (ELO-Chess), Williamson

1932
Colgate: Parke Davis+
Michigan: Dickinson, Parke Davis+, Sagarin (ELOChess)+
Southern California: Billingsley, Board, Dunkel, Football Research, Helms, Houlgate, National Championship Foundation, Parke Davis+, Poling, Sagarin+, Williamson

1933
Michigan: Billingsley, Board, Dickinson, Helms, Houlgate, Football Research, National Championship Foundation, Parke Davis+, Poling, Sagarin, Sagarin (ELOChess)
Ohio State: Dunkel
Princeton: Parke Davis+
Southern California: Williamson

1934
Alabama: Dunkel, Houlgate, Poling, Williamson
Minnesota: Billingsley, Board, Dickinson, Football Research, Helms, Litkenhous, National Championship Foundation, Sagarin, Sagarin (ELO-Chess)

1935
Louisiana State: Williamson+
Minnesota: Billingsley, Board, Football Research, Helms, Litkenhous, National Championship Foundation, Poling
Princeton: Dunkel
Southern Methodist: Dickinson, Houlgate, Sagarin, Sagarin (ELO-Chess)
Texas Christian: Williamson+

1936
Louisiana State: Sagarin, Sagarin (ELO-Chess), Williamson
Minnesota: Associated Press, Billingsley, Dickinson, Dunkel, Helms, Litkenhous, National Championship Foundation, Poling
Pittsburgh: Board, Football Research, Houlgate

1937
California: Dunkel, Helms
Pittsburgh: Associated Press, Billingsley, Board, Dickinson, Football Research, Houlgate, Litkenhous, National Championship Foundation, Poling, Sagarin, Sagarin (ELO-Chess), Williamson

1938
Notre Dame: Dickinson
Tennessee: Billingsley, Board, Dunkel, Football Research, Houlgate, Litkenhous, Poling, Sagarin, Sagarin (ELO-Chess)

Six SEC football coaches participate in a televised roundtable discussion circa 1965. From left, Paul Davis of Mississippi State, Charlie McClendon of LSU, and Paul "Bear" Bryant of Alabama. From right, Doug Dickey of Tennessee, Vince Dooley of Georgia, and Ray Graves of Florida. Courtesy of the Paul W. Bryant Museum.

Nebraska quarterback Jerry Tagge lunges over the goal-line for the winning touchdown in the 17-12 victory against No. 5 LSU in the 1971 Orange Bowl. With No. 1 Texas losing to No. 5 Notre Dame in the Cotton Bowl, and No. 12 Stanford beating No. 2 Ohio State in the Rose Bowl, the Cornhuskers won the national championship. Courtesy of the Orange Bowl Committee.

Nebraska quarterback Jerry Tagge fires a pass to help lead the Cornhuskers to a 38-6 victory against Alabama in the 1972 Orange Bowl, and their second-straight national championship. Courtesy of the Orange Bowl Committee.

Coach Frank Broyles led the Razorbacks from 1958 to 1976 before concentrating on being Arkansas' athletic director. Courtesy of the SEC.

Pete Johnson scores a touchdown for Ohio State, which won 42-21 in second of three straight Rose Bowl meetings against Southern California. The Buckeyes (10-0-1) finished second in the final 1973 Associated Press poll. Courtesy of the Tournament of Roses archives.

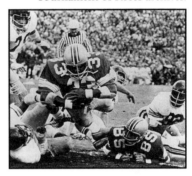

Notre Dame's defense, here shutting down Northwestern in the 1973 season opener yielded an average of 6.6 points per game during the regular season. The Fighting Irish went on to defeat No. 1 Alabama in the Sugar Bowl, 24-23, to win the national championship. Courtesy of the University of Notre Dame.

Steve Davis helps lead a 14-6 victory against Michigan in the 1976 Orange Bowl as the Oklahoma Sooners finished 11-1 to be named the consensus national champions. Courtesy of the Orange Bowl Committee.

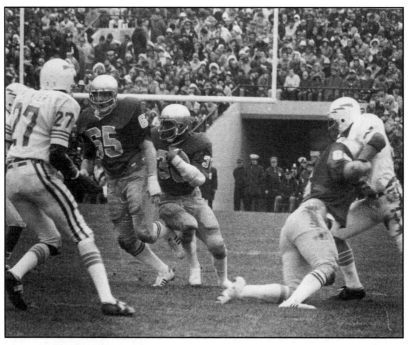

The Fighting Irish, here defeating Air Force 49-0, had an early loss to Ole Miss, 30-13, but then won 10 straight games including a 38-10 victory against Texas in the Cotton Bowl, to be the 1977 consensus national champion. Courtesy of the University of Notre Dame.

Georgia Coach Vince Dooley is carried off the field after the victory against Georgia Tech to put the Bulldogs in position to win the 1980 national championship. Courtesy of the SEC.

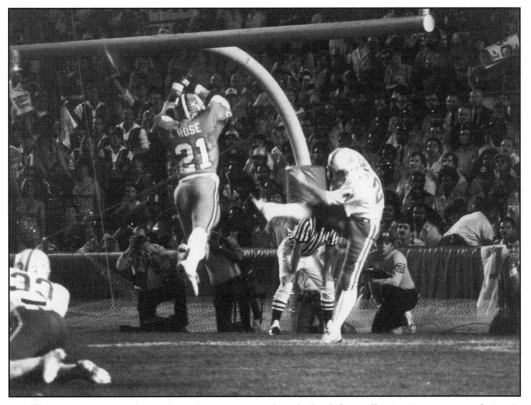

Clemson swarmed Nebraska in the 1982 Orange Bowl, with the defense allowing just one completion in the second half to secure a 22-15 victory and the Tigers' first national championship. Courtesy of the Orange Bowl Committee

After a couple of near-misses, including the 1979 Sugar Bowl where Joe Paterno is pictured, Penn State finally won its first national championship after it defeated Georgia in the 1963 Sugar Bowl, 27-23. Courtesy of the Paul W. Bryant Museum.

Howard Schnellenberger is carried off the field at the 1984 Orange Bowl after the 31-30 victory against Nebraska clinched Miami's first national championship. He called in the best game he had ever been involved with, and four months later left for the USFL. Courtesy of the Orange Bowl Committee.

Bo Jackson had an immediate impact with Auburn, and went on to record a school-record 1,786 rushing yards and 17 touchdowns as a senior in 1985 to win the Heisman Trophy. Courtesy of the Paul W. Bryant Museum.

Although Bo Schembechler coached in the most Rose Bowls, 10, and won 13 Big Ten titles, he never won a national championship—even when former Michigan player President Gerald Ford visited practice. The 1985 Wolverines (10-1-1) defeated Nebraska in the Fiesta Bowl, 27-23, but finished No. 2 to Oklahoma. Courtesy of the Bentley Historical Library (BL003031), the University of Michigan.

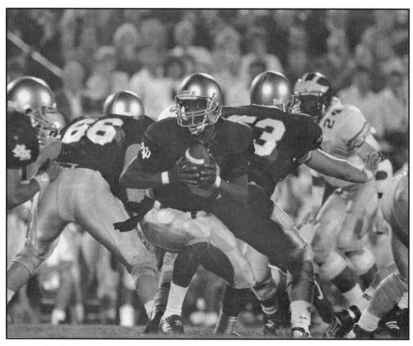

Quarterback Tony Rice, here leading the season-opening 19-17 victory against Michigan, ran for 75 yards and passed for 213 more in the Fiesta Bowl, where Notre Dame defeated West Virginia, 34-21, to win the 1988 national championship. Courtesy of the University of Notre Dame.

When Lou Holtz, pictured here running a practice at South Carolina, won the 1988 national championship with Notre Dame, he proclaimed: "This team will go down as a great football team because nobody proved otherwise." Courtesy of the Southeastern Conference.

Although Colorado's split national championship with Georgia Tech in 1990 was controversial due to the fifth-down call at Missouri, the Buffaloes played the toughest schedule in the country including Tennessee, Stanford, Illinois, Texas, and Washington in addition to its conference rivals. Courtesy of the University of Colorado.

Coach Gene Stallings is carried off the field at the 1993 Sugar Bowl after Alabama (13-0) became the first team to win the national championship under the new Bowl Coalition. Courtesy of the Paul W. Bryant Museum.

Desmond Howard won the Heisman Trophy, but only had one reception in the 1992 Rose Bowl, as Washington defeated No. 4 Michigan, 34-14, to gain a share of the national championship with Miami. Courtesy of the Bentley Historical Library (photo BL001380), the University of Michigan.

Crimson Tide players celebrate in the end zone during the convincing 34-13 victory against Miami in the 1993 Sugar Bowl to win the national championship. Courtesy of the Paul W. Bryant Museum.

With Arizona State losing in the Rose Bowl, the 1996 national championship came down to No. 1 Florida State vs. No. 3 Florida, which had closed the regular season with a No. 1 vs. No. 2 meeting won by the Seminoles. This time Steve Spurrier's Gators dominated, 52-20, to win Florida's first national title. Courtesy of the Southeastern Conference.

Florida Quarterback Danny Wuerffel won the Heisman Trophy in 1996. Courtesy of University of Florida Sports Information.

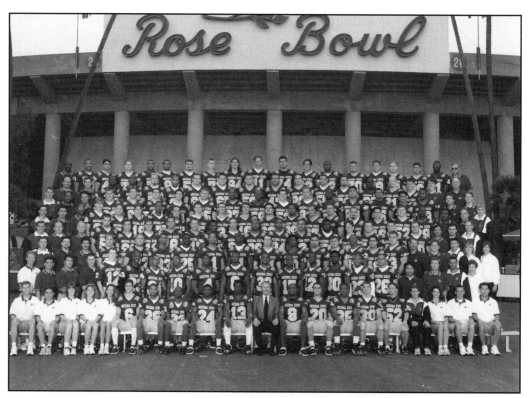

After pulling off a shocking 19-0 victory against No. 1 Nebraska (a year after losing 77-28), Bruce Snyder's Sun Devils came within 19 seconds of winning the 1996 national championship. Quarterback Jake Plummer is in the middle of the fifth row wearing No. 16, with Pat Tillman, who gave up a high-paying career in the NFL to serve in the military and was killed by friendly-fire in Afghanistan, three places to his right. Courtesy of Arizona State University.

Quarterback James Brown hands off to sophomore Ricky Williams in the first Big 12 Championship game in 1996. Two years later, Williams won the Heisman Trophy. Courtesy of the Big 12 Conference.

Texas begins to celebrate after upsetting No. 3 Nebraska in the first Big 12 Championship game in 1996, 37-27. The outcome propelled Florida into the national championship game, a rematch with Florida State at the Sugar Bowl. Courtesy of the Big 12 Conference.

Longhorns quarterback Major Applewhite sets to pass against Nebraska in the 1999 Big 12 Championship game. The No. 3 Cornhuskers won, 22-6, but couldn't move up in the polls. Courtesy of the Big 12 Conference.

Nick Saban holds up the national championship trophy after LSU defeated Oklahoma in the 2004 Sugar Bowl, 21-14. Even though the Tigers wound up the BCS champion, it was still a split title with the Associated Press voters opting for Southern California. Photo by Steve Franz. Courtesy of Louisiana State University.

Although the 1998 Tennessee Volunteers were ranked No. 10 in the preseason, Phillip Fulmer's team survived both the SEC regular season and SEC Championship game unscathed, and defeated Florida State in the Fiesta Bowl, 23-16, for the national championship. Courtesy of the Southeastern Conference.

Despite a 12-0 regular season, Auburn was only able to celebrate the 2004 SEC championship after the BCS rankings paired Oklahoma and Southern California in the national championship. Auburn defeated Virginia Tech in the Sugar Bowl, 16-13, to finish No. 2. Courtesy of the Southeastern Conference.

Quarterback Chris Leak, pictured here wearing a retro uniform against Alabama, helped the Gators squeeze into the 2006 national championship game, where Florida crushed No. 1 Ohio State, 41-14. Photo by Michelle Williams. Courtesy of the Tuscaloosa News.

Receiver Dallas Baker catches a key late 21-yard touchdown pass to help secure a 28-13 home victory against Alabama. Florida went on to win the 2006 national championship. Photo by Michelle Williams. Courtesy of the Tuscaloosa News.

Texas Christian: Associated Press, Helms, National Championship Foundation, Williamson

1939
Cornell: Litkenhous, Sagarin+
Southern California: Dickinson
Texas A&M: Associated Press, Billingsley, Boand, DeVold, Dunkel, Football Research, Helms, Houlgate, National Championship Foundation, Poling, Sagarin (ELO-Chess)+, Williamson

1940
Minnesota: Associated Press, Berryman, Boand, DeVold, Dickinson, Football Research, Houlgate, Litkenhous, National Championship Foundation, Sagarin, Sagarin (ELO-Chess)
Stanford: Billingsley, Helms, Poling
Tennessee: Dunkel, Williamson

1941
Alabama: Houlgate
Minnesota: Associated Press, Billingsley, Boand, DeVold, Dunkel, Football Research, Helms, Litkenhous, National Championship Foundation, Poling, Sagarin, Sagarin (ELO-Chess)
Texas: Berryman, Williamson

1942
Georgia: Berryman, Billingsley, DeVold, Houlgate, Litkenhous, Poling, Sagarin, Sagarin (ELO-Chess), Williamson
Ohio State: Associated Press, Boand, Dunkel, Football Research, National Championship Foundation
Wisconsin: Helms

1943
Notre Dame: Associated Press, Berryman, Billingsley, Boand, DeVold, Dunkel, Football Research, Helms, Houlgate, Litkenhous, National Championship Foundation, Poling, Sagarin, Sagarin (ELO-Chess), Williamson

1944
Army: Associated Press, Berryman, Billingsley, Boand, DeVold, Dunkel, Football Research, Helms, Houlgate, Litkenhous, National Championship Foundation+, Poling, Sagarin+, Williamson
Ohio State: National Championship Foundation+, Sagarin (ELO-Chess)+

1945
Alabama: National Championship Foundation+
Army: Associated Press, Berryman, Billingsley, Boand, DeVold, Dunkel, Football Research, Helms, Houlgate, Litkenhous, National Championship Foundation+, Poling, Sagarin, Sagarin (ELO-Chess), Williamson

1946
Army: Billingsley, Boand+, Football Research, Helms+, Houlgate, Poling+
Georgia: Williamson
Notre Dame: Associated Press, Berryman, Boand+, DeVold, Dunkel, Helms+, Litkenhous, National Championship Foundation, Poling+, Sagarin, Sagarin (ELO-Chess)

1947
Michigan: Berryman, Billingsley, Boand, DeVold, Dunkel, Football Research, Helms+, Houlgate, Litkenhous, National Championship Foundation, Poling, Sagarin, Sagarin (ELO-Chess)
Notre Dame: Associated Press, Helms+, Williamson

1948
Michigan: Associated Press, Berryman, Billingsley, Boand, DeVold, Dunkel, Football Research, Helms, Houlgate, Litkenhous, National Championship Foundation, Poling, Sagarin, Sagarin (ELO-Chess), Williamson

1949
Notre Dame: Associated Press, Berryman, Billingsley, Boand, DeVold, Dunkel, Helms, Houlgate, Litkenhous, National Championship Foundation, Poling, Sagarin, Sagarin (ELO-Chess), Williamson
Oklahoma: Football Research

1950
Kentucky: Sagarin+
Oklahoma: Associated Press, Berryman, Helms, Litkenhous, United Press, Williamson
Princeton: Boand, Poling
Tennessee: Billingsley, DeVold, Dunkel, Football Research, National Championship Foundation, Sagarin (ELO-Chess)+

1951
Georgia Tech: Berryman, Boand+
Illinois: Boand+
Maryland: DeVold, Dunkel, Football Research, National Championship Foundation, Sagarin, Sagarin (ELO-Chess)
Michigan State: Billingsley, Helms, Poling
Tennessee: Associated Press, Litkenhous, United Press, Williamson

1952

Georgia Tech: Berryman, Billingsley, International News Service, Poling, Sagarin (ELO-Chess)+

Michigan State: Associated Press, Boand, DeVold, Dunkel, Football Research, Helms, Litkenhous, National Championship Foundation, Sagarin+, United Press, Williamson

1953

Maryland: Associated Press, International News Service, United Press

Notre Dame: Billingsley, Boand, DeVold, Dunkel, Helms, Litkenhous, National Championship Foundation, Poling, Sagarin, Sagarin (ELO-Chess), Williamson

Oklahoma: Berryman, Football Research

1954

Ohio State: Associated Press, Berryman, Billingsley, Boand, DeVold, Football Research+, Helms+, International News Service, National Championship Foundation+, Poling, Sagarin, Sagarin (ELO-Chess), Williamson

UCLA: Dunkel, Football Research+, Football Writers Association of America, Helms+, Litkenhous, National Championship Foundation+, United Press

1955

Michigan State: Boand

Oklahoma: Associated Press, Berryman, Billingsley, DeVold, Dunkel, Football Research, Football Writers Association of America, Helms, International News Service, Litkenhous, National Championship Foundation, Poling, Sagarin, Sagarin (ELO-Chess), United Press, Williamson

1956

Georgia Tech: Berryman, Sagarin+

Iowa: Football Research

Oklahoma: Associated Press, Billingsley, Boand, DeVold, Dunkel, Football Writers Association of America, Helms, International News Service, Litkenhous, National Championship Foundation, Sagarin, United Press, Williamson

Tennessee: Sagarin (ELO-Chess)+

1957

Auburn: Associated Press, Billingsley, Football Research, Helms, National Championship Foundation, Poling, Sagarin, Sagarin (ELO-Chess), Williamson

Michigan State: Dunkel

Ohio State: Boand, DeVold, Football Writers Association of America, International News Service, Litkenhous, United Press

Oklahoma: Berryman

1958

Iowa: Football Writers Association of America

Louisiana State: Associated Press, Berryman, Billingsley, Board, DeVold, Dunkel, *Football News*, Football Research, Helms, Litkenhous, National Championship Foundation, Poling, Sagarin, Sagarin (ELO-Chess), United Press International, Williamson

1959

Ole Miss: Berryman, Dunkel, Sagarin+

Syracuse: Associated Press, Billingsley, Board, DeVold, *Football News*, Football Research, Football Writers Association of America, Helms, Litkenhous, National Championship Foundation, National Football Foundation, Poling, Sagarin (ELOChess)+, United Press International, Williamson

1960

Iowa: Berryman, Board, Litkenhous, Sagarin, Sagarin (ELO-Chess)

Minnesota: Associated Press, *Football News*, National Football Foundation, United Press International

Ole Miss: Billingsley, DeVold, Dunkel, Football Research, Football Writers Association of America, National Championship Foundation, Williamson

Missouri: Poling

Washington: Helms

1961

Alabama: Associated Press, Berryman, Billingsley, DeVold, Dunkel, *Football News*, Football Research, Helms, Litkenhous, National Championship Foundation, National Football Foundation, Sagarin, Sagarin (ELOChess), United Press International, Williamson

Ohio State: Football Writers Association of America, Poling

1962

Louisiana State: Berryman+

Ole Miss: Billingsley, Litkenhous, Sagarin, Sagarin (ELO-Chess)

Southern California: Associated Press, Berryman+, DeVold, Dunkel, *Football News*, Football Research, Football Writers Association of America, Helms, National Championship Foundation, National Football Foundation, Poling, United Press International, Williamson

1963

Texas: Associated Press, Berryman, Billingsley, DeVold, Dunkel, *Football News*, Football Research, Football Writers Association of America, Helms, Litkenhous, National Championship Foundation, National Football Foundation, Poling, Sagarin, Sagarin (ELO-Chess), United Press International, Williamson

1964

Alabama: Associated Press, Berryman, Litkenhous, United Press International
Arkansas: Billingsley, Football Research, Football Writers Association of America, Helms, National Championship Foundation, Poling, Sagarin, Sagarin (ELO-Chess)
Michigan: Dunkel
Notre Dame: DeVold, *Football News*, National Football Foundation

1965

Alabama: Associated Press, Football Research, Football Writers Association of America +, National Championship Foundation
Michigan State: Berryman, Billingsley, DeVold, Dunkel, *Football News*, Football Writers Association of America+, Helms, Litkenhous, National Football Foundation, Poling, Sagarin, Sagarin (ELO-Chess), United Press International

1966

Alabama: Berryman, Sagarin (ELO-Chess)+
Michigan State: Football Research, Helms+, National Football Foundation+, Poling+
Notre Dame: Associated Press, Billingsley, DeVold, Dunkel, *Football News*, Football Writers Association of America, Helms+, Litkenhous, Matthews, National Championship Foundation, National Football Foundation +, Poling+, Sagarin+, United Press International

1967

Notre Dame: Dunkel
Oklahoma: Poling
Southern California: Associated Press, Berryman, Billingsley, DeVold, *Football News*, Football Research, Football Writers Association of America, Helms, Matthews, National Championship Foundation, National Football Foundation, Sagarin, Sagarin (ELO-Chess), United Press International
Tennessee: Litkenhous

1968

Georgia: Litkenhous
Ohio State: Associated Press, Berryman, Billingsley, Dunkel, FACT, *Football News*, Football Research, Football Writers Association of America, Helms, National Championship Foundation, National Football Foundation, Poling, Sagarin (ELO-Chess)+, United Press International
Texas: DeVold, Matthews, Sagarin+

1969

Ohio State: Matthews
Penn State: FACT+, Sagarin (ELO-Chess)+
Texas: Associated Press, Berryman, Billingsley, DeVold, Dunkel, FACT+, *Football News*, Football Research, Football Writers Association of America, Helms, Litkenhous,

National Championship Foundation, National Football Foundation, Poling, Sagarin+, United Press International

1970

Arizona State: Poling
Nebraska: Associated Press, Billingsley, DeVold, Dunkel, FACT+, *Football News*, Football Research, Football Writers Association of America, Helms, National Championship Foundation, Sagarin (ELO-Chess)+
Notre Dame: FACT+, Matthews, Sagarin+
Ohio State: National Football Foundation +
Texas: Berryman, FACT+, Litkenhous, National Football Foundation +, United Press International

1971

Nebraska: Associated Press, Berryman, Billingsley, DeVold, Dunkel, FACT, *Football News*, Football Research, Football Writers Association of America, Helms, Litkenhous, Matthews, National Championship Foundation, National Football Foundation, Poling, Sagarin, Sagarin (ELO-Chess), United Press International

1972

Southern California: Associated Press, Berryman, Billingsley, DeVold, Dunkel, FACT, *Football News*, Football Research, Football Writers Association of America, Helms, Litkenhous, Matthews, National Championship Foundation, National Football Foundation, Poling, Sagarin, Sagarin (ELO-Chess), United Press International

1973

Alabama: Berryman, United Press International
Michigan: National Championship Foundation+, Poling+
Notre Dame: Associated Press, Billingsley, *Football News*, Football Writers Association of America, Helms, National Championship Foundation+, National Football Foundation
Ohio State: FACT, National Championship Foundation+, Poling+, Sagarin (ELO-Chess)+
Oklahoma: DeVold, Dunkel, Football Research, Sagarin+

1974

Ohio State: Matthews
Oklahoma: Associated Press, Berryman, Billingsley, DeVold, Dunkel, FACT, *Football News*, Football Research, Helms+, Litkenhous, National Championship Foundation+, Poling, Sagarin, Sagarin (ELO-Chess)
Southern California: Football Writers Association of America, Helms+, National Championship Foundation+, National Football Foundation, United Press International

1975

Alabama: Matthews+
Arizona State: National Championship Foundation+, *Sporting News*

Ohio State: Berryman, FACT+, Helms+, Matthews+, Poling

Oklahoma: Associated Press, Billingsley, DeVold, Dunkel, FACT+, *Football News*, Football Research, Football Writers Association of America, Helms+, National Championship Foundation+, National Football Foundation, Sagarin, Sagarin (ELO-Chess), United Press International

1976

Pittsburgh: Associated Press, FACT, *Football News*, Football Writers Association of America, Helms, National Championship Foundation, National Football Foundation, Poling, Sagarin, Sagarin (ELO-Chess), *Sporting News*, United Press International

Southern California: Berryman, Billingsley, DeVold, Dunkel, Football Research, Matthews

1977

Alabama: Football Research+

Arkansas: FACT+

Notre Dame: Associated Press, Billingsley, DeVold, Dunkel, FACT+, *Football News*, Football Research+, Football Writers Association of America, Helms, Matthews, National Championship Foundation, National Football Foundation, Poling, Sagarin+, *Sporting News*, United Press International

Texas: Berryman, FACT+, Sagarin (ELO-Chess)+

1978

Alabama: Associated Press, FACT+, Football Research, Football Writers Association of America, Helms+, National Championship Foundation+, National Football Foundation

Oklahoma: DeVold, Dunkel, FACT+, Helms+, Litkenhous, Matthews, Poling, Sagarin+

Southern California: Berryman, Billingsley, FACT+, *Football News*, Helms+, National Championship Foundation+, Sagarin (ELO-Chess)+, *Sporting News*, United Press International

1979

Alabama: Associated Press, Berryman, Billingsley, DeVold, Dunkel, FACT, *Football News*, Football Writers Association of America, Helms, Matthews, National Championship Foundation, National Football Foundation, *New York Times*, Poling, Sagarin, Sagarin (ELO-Chess), *Sporting News*, United Press International

Southern California: Football Research

1980

Florida State: FACT+

Georgia: Associated Press, Berryman, Billingsley, FACT+, *Football News*, Football Writers Association of America, Helms, National Championship Foundation, National Football Foundation, Poling, Sagarin (ELO-Chess)+, *Sporting News*, United Press International

Nebraska: FACT+
Oklahoma: Dunkel, Matthews
Pittsburgh: DeVold, FACT+, Football Research, New York Times, Sagarin+

1981

Clemson: Associated Press, Berryman, Billingsley, DeVold, FACT, *Football News*, Football Research, Football Writers Association of America, Helms, Litkenhous, Matthews, National Championship Foundation+, National Football Foundation, *New York Times*, Poling, Sagarin, Sagarin (ELO-Chess), *Sporting News*, United Press International
Nebraska: National Championship Foundation+
Penn State: Dunkel
Pittsburgh: National Championship Foundation+
Southern Methodist: National Championship Foundation+
Texas: National Championship Foundation+

1982

Nebraska: Berryman
Penn State: Associated Press, Billingsley, DeVold, Dunkel, FACT, *Football News*, Football Research, Football Writers Association of America, Helms+, Litkenhous, Matthews, National Championship Foundation, National Football Foundation, *New York Times*, Poling, Sagarin, Sagarin (ELO-Chess), *Sporting News*, United Press International, *USA Today*/CNN
Southern Methodist: Helms+

1983

Auburn: Billingsley, FACT+, Football Research, *New York Times*, Sagarin (ELO-Chess)+
Miami (Fla.): Associated Press, Dunkel, *Football News*, Football Writers Association of America, National Championship Foundation, National Football Foundation, *Sporting News*, United Press International, *USA Today*/CNN
Nebraska: Berryman, DeVold, FACT+, Litkenhous, Matthews, Poling, Sagarin+

1984

Brigham Young: Associated Press, Billingsley, Football Research, Football Writers Association of America, National Championship Foundation+, National Football Foundation, Poling, Sagarin (ELO-Chess)+, United Press International, *USA Today*/CNN
Florida: DeVold, Dunkel, FACT, Matthews, *New York Times*, Sagarin+, *Sporting News*
Nebraska: Litkenhous
Washington: Berryman, *Football News*, National Championship Foundation+

1985

Florida: Sagarin (ELO-Chess)+
Michigan: Matthews

Oklahoma: Associated Press, Berryman, Billingsley, DeVold, Dunkel, FACT, *Football News*, Football Research, Football Writers Association of America, National Championship Foundation, National Football Foundation, *New York Times*, Sagarin+, *Sporting News*, United Press International , *USA Today*/CNN

1986

Miami (Fla.): FACT+

Oklahoma: Berryman, DeVold, Dunkel, Football Research, *New York Times*, Sagarin+

Penn State: Associated Press, Billingsley, FACT+, *Football News*, Football Writers Association of America, Matthews, National Championship Foundation, National Football Foundation, Sagarin (ELO-Chess)+, *Sporting News*, United Press International, *USA Today*/CNN

1987

Florida State: Berryman

Miami (Fla.): Associated Press, Billingsley, DeVold, Dunkel, Eck, FACT, *Football News*, Football Research, Football Writers Association of America, Matthews, National Championship Foundation, National Football Foundation, *New York Times*, Sagarin, Sagarin (ELO-Chess), *Sporting News*, United Press International, *USA Today*/CNN

1988

Miami (Fla.): Berryman, Sagarin+

Notre Dame: Associated Press, Billingsley, DeVold, Dunkel, Eck, FACT, *Football News*, Football Research, Football Writers Association of America, Matthews, National Championship Foundation, National Football Foundation, *New York Times*, Sagarin, (ELO-Chess)+, *Sporting News*, United Press International, *USA Today*/CNN

1989

Miami (Fla.): Associated Press, Billingsley, DeVold, Dunkel, FACT+, *Football News*, Football Research, Football Writers Association of America, Matthews, National Championship Foundation, National Football Foundation, *New York Times*, *Sporting News*, United Press International, *USA Today*/CNN

Notre Dame: Berryman, Eck, FACT+, Sagarin, Sagarin (ELO-Chess)

1990

Colorado: Associated Press, Berryman, Billingsley, DeVold, FACT+, *Football News*, Football Research, Football Writers Association of America, Matthews, National Championship Foundation+, National Football Foundation, *Sporting News*, *USA Today*/CNN

Georgia Tech: Dunkel, FACT+, National Championship Foundation+, Sagarin (ELO-Chess)+, United Press International

Miami (Fla.): Eck, FACT+, *New York Times*, Sagarin+

Washington: FACT+

1991

Miami (Fla.): Associated Press, Billingsley, Eck, Football Research, National Championship Foundation+, *New York Times*, Sagarin (ELO-Chess)+, *Sporting News*

Washington: Berryman, DeVold, Dunkel, FACT, *Football News*, Football Writers Association of America, Matthews, National Championship Foundation+, Sagarin+, United Press International/National Football Foundation, *USA Today*/CNN

1992

Alabama: Associated Press, Berryman, Billingsley, DeVold, Dunkel, Eck, FACT, *Football News*, Football Research, Football Writers Association of America, Matthews, National Championship Foundation, *New York Times*, Sagarin (ELO-Chess)+, *Sporting News*, United Press International/National Football Foundation, *USA Today*/CNN

Florida State: Sagarin+

1993

Auburn: National Championship Foundation+

Florida State: Associated Press, Berryman, Billingsley, DeVold, Dunkel, Eck, FACT, *Football News*, Football Writers Association of America, National Championship Foundation+, *New York Times*, Sagarin, Sagarin (ELO-Chess), *Sporting News*, United Press International, *USA Today*/CNN, *USA Today*/National Football Foundation

Nebraska: National Championship Foundation+

Notre Dame: Matthews, National Championship Foundation+

1994

Florida State: Dunkel

Nebraska: Alderson, Associated Press, Berryman, Billingsley, FACT+, *Football News*, Football Writers Association of America, National Championship Foundation+, Sagarin (ELO-Chess)+, *Sporting News*, United Press International, *USA Today*/CNN, *USA Today*/National Football Foundation

Penn State: DeVold, Eck, FACT+, Matthews, National Championship Foundation+, *New York Times*, Sagarin+

1995

Nebraska: Alderson, Associated Press, Berryman, Billingsley, DeVold, Dunkel, Eck, FACT, *Football News*, Football Writers Association of America, Matthews, National Championship Foundation, National Football Foundation, *New York Times*, Sagarin, Sagarin (ELO-Chess), *Sporting News*, United Press International, *USA Today*/CNN

1996

Florida: Associated Press, Berryman, Billingsley, Eck, FACT, *Football News*, Football Writers Association of America, National Football Foundation, Sagarin, Sagarin (ELO-Chess), *Sporting News*, *USA Today*/CNN, *New York Times*, National Championship Foundation, Dunkel, Matthews, DeVold

Florida State: Alderson

1997

Michigan: Associated Press, *Football News*, Football Writers Association of America, National Championship Foundation+, National Football Foundation, *Sporting News*
Nebraska: Alderson, Berryman, Billingsley, DeVold, Dunkel, Eck, FACT, Matthews, National Championship Foundation+, *New York Times*, Sagarin, Sagarin (ELO-Chess), *Seattle Times*, *USA Today*/ESPN

1998

Tennessee: Alderson, Associated Press, Berryman, Billingsley, DeVold, Dunkel, Eck, FACT, *Football News*, Football Writers Association of America, Matthews, National Championship Foundation, National Football Foundation, *New York Times*, Sagarin, Sagarin (ELO-Chess), *Seattle Times*, *Sporting News*, *USA Today*/ESPN

1999

Florida State: Associated Press, Berryman, Billingsley, DeVold, Dunkel, Eck, FACT, *Football News*, Football Writers Association of America, Massey, Matthews, National Championship Foundation, National Football Foundation, *New York Times*, Sagarin, Sagarin (ELO-Chess), *Seattle Times*, *Sporting News*, *USA Today*/ESPN

2000

Miami (Fla.): *New York Times*
Oklahoma: Associated Press, Berryman, Billingsley, DeVold, Dunkel, Eck, FACT, *Football News*, Football Writers Association of America, Massey, Matthews, National Championship Foundation, National Football Foundation, Sagarin, Sagarin (ELO-Chess), *Seattle Times*, *Sporting News*, *USA Today*/ESPN

2001

Miami (Fla.): Associated Press, Berryman, Billingsley, Colley Matrix, DeVold, Dunkel, Eck, FACT, *Football News*, Football Writers Association of America, Massey, Matthews, National Football Foundation, *New York Times*, Sagarin, Sagarin (ELO-Chess), *Seattle Times*, *Sporting News*, *USA Today*/ESPN, Wolfe

2002

Ohio State: Associated Press, Berryman, Billingsley, Colley Matrix, DeVold, Eck, FACT, *Football News*, Football Writers Association of America, Massey, National Football Foundation, *New York Times*, Sagarin (ELO-Chess)+, *Seattle Times*, *Sporting News*, *USA Today*/ESPN, Wolfe
Southern California: Dunkel, Matthews, Sagarin+

2003

Louisiana State: Billingsley, Colley Matrix, DeVold, Dunkel, FACT, Massey, National Football Foundation, Sagarin, Sagarin (ELO-Chess), *Seattle Times*, *USA Today*/ESPN, Wolfe

Oklahoma: Berryman

Southern California: Associated Press, Eck, Football Writers Association of America, Matthews, *New York Times*, *Sporting News*

2004

Southern California: Associated Press, Berryman, Billingsley, Colley Matrix, DeVold, Dunkel, Eck, FACT, Football Writers Association of America, Massey, Matthews, *New York Times*, National Football Foundation, Sagarin, Sagarin (ELO-Chess), *Seattle Times*, *Sporting News*, *USA Today*/ESPN, Wolfe

2005

Texas: Associated Press, Berryman, Billingsley, Colley Matrix, DeVold, Dunkel, Eck, FACT, Football Writers Association of America, Massey, Matthews, National Football Foundation, Sagarin, Sagarin (ELO-Chess), *Seattle Times*, *Sporting News*, *USA Today*/ESPN, Wolfe

2006
Florida

The Associated Press Poll

THE FINAL Associated Press poll each season since its inception in 1936. Note: From 1962–1967 the poll only ranked 10 teams. The final poll was held at the end of the regular season through 1964, and from 1966–1969. In 1965 and from 1970 on the final ranking was after all bowl games.

1936
1. Minnesota
2. Louisiana State
3. Pittsburgh
4. Alabama
5. Washington
6. Santa Clara
7. Northwestern
8. Notre Dame
9. Nebraska
10. Pennsylvania
11. Duke
12. Yale
13. Dartmouth
14. Duquesne
15. Fordham
16. Texas Christian
17. Tennessee
18. Arkansas
    Navy (tie)
20. Marquette

1937
1. Pittsburgh
2. California
3. Fordham
4. Alabama
5. Minnesota
6. Villanova
7. Dartmouth
8. Louisiana State
9. Notre Dame
   Santa Clara
11. Nebraska
12. Yale
13. Ohio State
14. Holy Cross
    Arkansas (tie)
16. Texas Christian
17. Colorado
18. Rice
19. North Carolina
20. Duke

1938
1. Texas Christian
2. Tennessee
3. Duke
4. Oklahoma
5. Notre Dame
6. Carnegie Tech
7. Southern California
8. Pittsburgh
9. Holy Cross
10. Minnesota
11. Texas Tech
12. Cornell
13. Alabama
14. California
15. Fordham
16. Michigan
17. Northwestern
18. Villanova
19. Tulane
20. Dartmouth

1939

1. Texas A&M
2. Tennessee
3. Southern California
4. Cornell
5. Tulane
6. Missouri
7. UCLA
8. Duke
9. Iowa
10. Duquesne
11. Boston College
12. Clemson
13. Notre Dame
14. Santa Clara
15. Ohio State
16. Georgia Tech
17. Fordham
18. Nebraska
19. Oklahoma
20. Michigan

1940

1. Minnesota
2. Stanford
3. Michigan
4. Tennessee
5. Boston College
6. Texas A&M
7. Nebraska
8. Northwestern
9. Mississippi State
10. Washington
11. Santa Clara
12. Fordham
13. Georgetown
14. Pennsylvania
15. Cornell
16. Southern Methodist
17. Hardin-Simmons
18. Duke
19. Lafayette
(Only 19 teams ranked)

1941

1. Minnesota
2. Duke
3. Notre Dame
4. Texas
5. Michigan
6. Fordham
7. Missouri
8. Duquesne
9. Texas A&M
10. Navy
11. Northwestern
12. Oregon State
13. Ohio State
14. Georgia
15. Pennsylvania
16. Mississippi State
17. Mississippi
18. Tennessee
19. Washington State
20. Alabama

1942

1. Ohio State
2. Georgia
3. Wisconsin
4. Tulsa
5. Georgia Tech
6. Notre Dame
7. Tennessee
8. Boston College
9. Michigan
10. Alabama
11. Texas
12. Stanford
13. UCLA
14. William & Mary
15. Santa Clara
16. Auburn
17. Washington State
18. Mississippi State
19. Minnesota
    Holy Cross (tie)
    Penn State (tie)

1943

1. Notre Dame
2. Iowa Pre-Flight
3. Michigan
4. Navy
5. Purdue
6. Great Lakes
7. Duke
8. Del Monte P-F
9. Northwestern
10. March Field
11. Army
12. Washington
13. Georgia Tech
14. Texas
15. Tulsa
16. Dartmouth
17. Bainbridge NTS
18. Colorado College
19. Pacific
20. Pennsylvania

1944

1. Army
2. Ohio State
3. Randolph Field
4. Navy
5. Bainbridge NTS
6. Iowa Pre-Flight
7. Southern California
8. Michigan
9. Notre Dame
10. March Field
11. Duke
12. Tennessee
13. Georgia Tech
    Norman Pre-Flight (tie)
15. Illinois
16. El Toro Marines
17. Great Lakes
18. Fort Pierce
19. State Mary's P-F
20. Sec. Air Force

1945

1. Army
2. Alabama
3. Navy
4. Indiana
5. Oklahoma State
6. Michigan
7. State Mary's (Calif.)
8. Pennsylvania
9. Notre Dame
10. Texas
11. Southern California
12. Ohio State
13. Duke
14. Tennessee
15. Louisiana State
16. Holy Cross
17. Tulsa
18. Georgia
19. Wake Forest
20. Columbia

1946

1. Notre Dame
2. Army
3. Georgia
4. UCLA
5. Illinois
6. Michigan
7. Tennessee
8. Louisiana State
9. North Carolina
10. Rice
11. Georgia Tech
12. Yale
13. Pennsylvania
14. Oklahoma
15. Texas
16. Arkansas
17. Tulsa
18. North Carolina State
19. Delaware
20. Indiana

1947

1. Notre Dame
2. Michigan
3. Southern Methodist
4. Penn State
5. Texas
6. Alabama
7. Pennsylvania
8. Southern California
9. North Carolina
10. Georgia Tech
11. Army
12. Kansas
13. Mississippi
14. William & Mary
15. California
16. Oklahoma
17. North Carolina State
18. Rice
19. Duke
20. Columbia

1948

1. Michigan
2. Notre Dame
3. North Carolina
4. California
5. Oklahoma
6. Army
7. Northwestern
8. Georgia
9. Oregon
10. Southern Methodist
11. Clemson
12. Vanderbilt
13. Tulane
14. Michigan State
15. Mississippi
16. Minnesota
17. William & Mary
18. Penn State
19. Cornell
20. Wake Forest

1949

1. Notre Dame
2. Oklahoma
3. California
4. Army
5. Rice
6. Ohio State
7. Michigan
8. Minnesota
9. Louisiana State
10. Pacific
11. Kentucky
12. Cornell
13. Villanova
14. Maryland
15. Santa Clara
16. North Carolina
17. Tennessee
18. Princeton
19. Michigan State
20. Missouri
    Baylor (tie)

1950

1. Oklahoma
2. Army
3. Texas
4. Tennessee
5. California
6. Princeton
7. Kentucky
8. Michigan State
9. Michigan
10. Clemson
11. Washington
12. Wyoming
13. Illinois
14. Ohio State
15. Miami (Fla.)
16. Alabama
17. Nebraska
18. Washington & Lee
19. Tulsa
20. Tulane

1951
1. Tennessee
2. Michigan State
3. Maryland
4. Illinois
5. Georgia Tech
6. Princeton
7. Stanford
8. Wisconsin
9. Baylor
10. Oklahoma
11. Texas Christian
12. California
13. Virginia
14. San Francisco
15. Kentucky
16. Boston University
17. UCLA
18. Washington State
19. Holy Cross
20. Clemson

1952
1. Michigan State
2. Georgia Tech
3. Notre Dame
4. Oklahoma
5. Southern California
6. UCLA
7. Mississippi
8. Tennessee
9. Alabama
10. Texas
11. Wisconsin
12. Tulsa
13. Maryland
14. Syracuse
15. Florida
16. Duke
17. Ohio State
18. Purdue
19. Princeton
20. Kentucky

1953
1. Maryland
2. Notre Dame
3. Michigan State
4. Oklahoma
5. UCLA
6. Rice
7. Illinois
8. Georgia Tech
9. Iowa
10. West Virginia
11. Texas
12. Texas Tech
13. Alabama
14. Army
15. Wisconsin
16. Kentucky
17. Auburn
18. Duke
19. Stanford
20. Michigan

1954
1. Ohio State
2. UCLA
3. Oklahoma
4. Notre Dame
5. Navy
6. Mississippi
7. Army
8. Maryland
9. Wisconsin
10. Arkansas
11. Miami (Fla.)
12. West Virginia
13. Auburn
14. Duke
15. Michigan
16. Virginia Tech
17. Southern California
18. Baylor
19. Rice
20. Penn State

1955
1. Oklahoma
2. Michigan State
3. Maryland
4. UCLA
5. Ohio State
6. Texas Christian
7. Georgia Tech
8. Auburn
9. Notre Dame
10. Mississippi
11. Pittsburgh
12. Michigan
13. Southern California
14. Miami (Fla.)
15. Miami (Ohio)
16. Stanford
17. Texas A&M
18. Navy
19. West Virginia
20. Army

1956
1. Oklahoma
2. Tennessee
3. Iowa
4. Georgia Tech
5. Texas A&M
6. Miami (Fla.)
7. Michigan
8. Syracuse
9. Michigan State
10. Oregon State
11. Baylor
12. Minnesota
13. Pittsburgh
14. Texas Christian
15. Ohio State
16. Navy
17. George Washington
18. Southern California
19. Clemson
20. Colorado

1957

1. Auburn
2. Ohio State
3. Michigan State
4. Oklahoma
5. Navy
6. Iowa
7. Mississippi
8. Rice
9. Texas A&M
10. Notre Dame
11. Texas
12. Arizona State
13. Tennessee
14. Mississippi State
15. North Carolina State
16. Duke
17. Florida
18. Army
19. Wisconsin
20. Virginia Military

1958

1. Louisiana State
2. Iowa
3. Army
4. Auburn
5. Oklahoma
6. Air Force
7. Wisconsin
8. Ohio State
9. Syracuse
10. Texas Christian
11. Mississippi
12. Clemson
13. Purdue
14. Florida
15. South Carolina
16. California
17. Notre Dame
18. Southern Methodist
19. Oklahoma State
20. Rutgers

1959

1. Syracuse
2. Mississippi
3. Louisiana State
4. Texas
5. Georgia
6. Wisconsin
7. Texas Christian
8. Washington
9. Arkansas
10. Alabama
11. Clemson
12. Penn State
13. Illinois
14. Southern California
15. Oklahoma
16. Wyoming
17. Notre Dame
18. Missouri
19. Florida
20. Pittsburgh

1960

1. Minnesota
2. Mississippi
3. Iowa
4. Navy
5. Missouri
6. Washington
7. Arkansas
8. Ohio State
9. Alabama
10. Duke
11. Kansas
12. Baylor
13. Auburn
14. Yale
15. Michigan State
16. Penn State
17. New Mexico State
18. Florida
19. Syracuse
    Purdue (tie)

1961

1. Alabama
2. Ohio State
3. Texas
4. Louisiana State
5. Mississippi
6. Minnesota
7. Colorado
8. Michigan State
9. Arkansas
10. Utah State
11. Missouri
12. Purdue
13. Georgia Tech
14. Syracuse
15. Rutgers
16. UCLA
17. Rice
    Penn State (tie)
    Arizona (tie)
20. Duke

1962

1. Southern California
2. Wisconsin
3. Mississippi
4. Texas
5. Alabama
6. Arkansas
7. Louisiana State
8. Oklahoma
9. Penn State
10. Minnesota

1963
1. Texas
2. Navy
3. Illinois
4. Pittsburgh
5. Auburn
6. Nebraska
7. Mississippi
8. Alabama
9. Oklahoma
10. Michigan State

1964
1. Alabama
2. Arkansas
3. Notre Dame
4. Michigan
5. Texas
6. Nebraska
7. Louisiana State
8. Oregon State
9. Ohio State
10. Southern California

1965
1. Alabama
2. Michigan State
3. Arkansas
4. UCLA
5. Nebraska
6. Missouri
7. Tennessee
8. Louisiana State
9. Notre Dame
10. Southern California

1966
1. Notre Dame
2. Michigan State
3. Alabama
4. Georgia
5. UCLA
6. Nebraska
7. Purdue
8. Georgia Tech
9. Miami (Fla.)
10. Southern Methodist

1967
1. Southern California
2. Tennessee
3. Oklahoma
4. Indiana
5. Notre Dame
6. Wyoming
7. Oregon State
8. Alabama
9. Purdue
10. Penn State

1968
1. Ohio State
2. Penn State
3. Texas
4. Southern California
5. Notre Dame
6. Arkansas
7. Kansas
8. Georgia
9. Missouri
10. Purdue
11. Oklahoma
12. Michigan
13. Tennessee
14. Southern Methodist
15. Oregon State
16. Auburn
17. Alabama
18. Houston
19. Louisiana State
20. Ohio

1969

1. Texas
2. Penn State
3. Southern California
4. Ohio State
5. Notre Dame
6. Missouri
7. Arkansas
8. Mississippi
9. Michigan
10. Louisiana State
11. Nebraska
12. Houston
13. UCLA
14. Florida
15. Tennessee
16. Colorado
17. West Virginia
18. Purdue
19. Stanford
20. Auburn

1970

1. Nebraska
2. Notre Dame
3. Texas
4. Tennessee
5. Ohio State
6. Arizona State
7. Louisiana State
8. Stanford
9. Michigan
10. Auburn
11. Arkansas
12. Toledo
13. Georgia Tech
14. Dartmouth
15. Southern California
16. Air Force
17. Tulane
18. Penn State
19. Houston
20. Oklahoma
    Mississippi (tie)

1971

1. Nebraska
2. Oklahoma
3. Colorado
4. Alabama
5. Penn State
6. Michigan
7. Georgia
8. Arizona State
9. Tennessee
10. Stanford
11. Louisiana State
12. Auburn
13. Notre Dame
14. Toledo
15. Mississippi
16. Arkansas
17. Houston
18. Texas
19. Washington
20. Southern California

1972

1. Southern California
2. Oklahoma
3. Texas
4. Nebraska
5. Auburn
6. Michigan
7. Alabama
8. Tennessee
9. Ohio State
10. Penn State
11. Louisiana State
12. North Carolina
13. Arizona State
14. Notre Dame
15. UCLA
16. Colorado
17. North Carolina State
18. Louisville
19. Washington State
20. Georgia Tech

1973

1. Notre Dame
2. Ohio State
3. Oklahoma
4. Alabama
5. Penn State
6. Michigan
7. Nebraska
8. Southern California
9. Arizona State
   Houston (tie)
11. Texas Tech
12. UCLA
13. Louisiana State
14. Texas
15. Miami (Ohio)
16. North Carolina State
17. Missouri
18. Kansas
19. Tennessee
20. Maryland
    Tulane (tie)

1974

1. Oklahoma
2. Southern California
3. Michigan
4. Ohio State
5. Alabama
6. Notre Dame
7. Penn State
8. Auburn
9. Nebraska
10. Miami (Ohio)
11. North Carolina State
12. Michigan State
13. Maryland
14. Baylor
15. Florida
16. Texas A&M
17. Mississippi State
    Texas (tie)
19. Houston
20. Tennessee

1975
1. Oklahoma
2. Arizona State
3. Alabama
4. Ohio State
5. UCLA
6. Texas
7. Arkansas
8. Michigan
9. Nebraska
10. Penn State
11. Texas A&M
12. Miami (Ohio)
13. Maryland
14. California
15. Pittsburgh
16. Colorado
17. Southern California
18. Arizona
19. Georgia
20. West Virginia

1976
1. Pittsburgh
2. Southern California
3. Michigan
4. Houston
5. Oklahoma
6. Ohio State
7. Texas A&M
8. Maryland
9. Nebraska
10. Georgia
11. Alabama
12. Notre Dame
13. Texas Tech
14. Oklahoma State
15. UCLA
16. Colorado
17. Rutgers
18. Kentucky
19. Iowa State
20. Mississippi State

1977
1. Notre Dame
2. Alabama
3. Arkansas
4. Texas
5. Penn State
6. Kentucky
7. Oklahoma
8. Pittsburgh
9. Michigan
10. Washington
11. Ohio State
12. Nebraska
13. Southern California
14. Florida State
15. Stanford
16. San Diego State
17. North Carolina
18. Arizona State
19. Clemson
20. Brigham Young

1978
1. Alabama
2. Southern California
3. Oklahoma
4. Penn State
5. Michigan
6. Clemson
7. Notre Dame
8. Nebraska
9. Texas
10. Houston
11. Arkansas
12. Michigan State
13. Purdue
14. UCLA
15. Missouri
16. Georgia
17. Stanford
18. North Carolina State
19. Texas A&M
20. Maryland

1979
1. Alabama
2. Southern California
3. Oklahoma
4. Ohio State
5. Houston
6. Florida State
7. Pittsburgh
8. Arkansas
9. Nebraska
10. Purdue
11. Washington
12. Texas
13. Brigham Young
14. Baylor
15. North Carolina
16. Auburn
17. Temple
18. Michigan
19. Indiana
20. Penn State

1980
1. Georgia
2. Pittsburgh
3. Oklahoma
4. Michigan
5. Florida State
6. Alabama
7. Nebraska
8. Penn State
9. Notre Dame
10. North Carolina
11. Southern California
12. Brigham Young
13. UCLA
14. Baylor
15. Ohio State
16. Washington
17. Purdue
18. Miami (Fla.)
19. Mississippi State
20. Southern Methodist

1981
1. Clemson
2. Texas
3. Penn State
4. Pittsburgh
5. Southern Methodist
6. Georgia
7. Alabama
8. Miami (Fla.)
9. North Carolina
10. Washington
11. Nebraska
12. Michigan
13. Brigham Young
14. Southern California
15. Ohio State
16. Arizona State
17. West Virginia
18. Iowa
19. Missouri
20. Oklahoma

1982
1. Penn State
2. Southern Methodist
3. Nebraska
4. Georgia
5. UCLA
6. Arizona State
7. Washington
8. Clemson
9. Arkansas
10. Pittsburgh
11. Louisiana State
12. Ohio State
13. Florida State
14. Auburn
15. Southern California
16. Oklahoma
17. Texas
18. North Carolina
19. West Virginia
20. Maryland

1983
1. Miami (Fla.)
2. Nebraska
3. Auburn
4. Georgia
5. Texas
6. Florida
7. Brigham Young
8. Michigan
9. Ohio State
10. Illinois
11. Clemson
12. Southern Methodist
13. Air Force
14. Iowa
15. Alabama
16. West Virginia
17. UCLA
18. Pittsburgh
19. Boston College
20. East Carolina

1984
1. Brigham Young
2. Washington
3. Florida
4. Nebraska
5. Boston College
6. Oklahoma
7. Oklahoma State
8. Southern Methodist
9. UCLA
10. Southern California
11. South Carolina
12. Maryland
13. Ohio State
14. Auburn
15. Louisiana State
16. Iowa
17. Florida State
18. Miami (Fla.)
19. Kentucky
20. Virginia

1985
1. Oklahoma
2. Michigan
3. Penn State
4. Tennessee
5. Florida
6. Texas A&M
7. UCLA
8. Air Force
9. Miami (Fla.)
10. Iowa
11. Nebraska
12. Arkansas
13. Alabama
14. Ohio State
15. Florida State
16. Brigham Young
17. Baylor
18. Maryland
19. Georgia Tech
20. Louisiana State

1986
1. Penn State
2. Miami (Fla.)
3. Oklahoma
4. Arizona State
5. Nebraska
6. Auburn
7. Ohio State
8. Michigan
9. Alabama
10. Louisiana State
11. Arizona
12. Baylor
13. Texas A&M
14. UCLA
15. Arkansas
16. Iowa
17. Clemson
18. Washington
19. Boston College
20. Virginia Tech

1987
1. Miami (Fla.)
2. Florida State
3. Oklahoma
4. Syracuse
5. Louisiana State
6. Nebraska
7. Auburn
8. Michigan State
9. UCLA
10. Texas A&M
11. Oklahoma State
12. Clemson
13. Georgia
14. Tennessee
15. South Carolina
16. Iowa
17. Notre Dame
18. Southern California
19. Michigan
20. Arizona State

1988
1. Notre Dame
2. Miami (Fla.)
3. Florida State
4. Michigan
5. West Virginia
6. UCLA
7. Southern California
8. Auburn
9. Clemson
10. Nebraska
11. Oklahoma State
12. Arkansas
13. Syracuse
14. Oklahoma
15. Georgia
16. Washington State
17. Alabama
18. Houston
19. Louisiana State
20. Indiana

1989
1. Miami (Fla.)
2. Notre Dame
3. Florida State
4. Colorado
5. Tennessee
6. Auburn
7. Michigan
8. Southern California
9. Alabama
10. Illinois
11. Nebraska
12. Clemson
13. Arkansas
14. Houston
15. Penn State
16. Michigan State
17. Pittsburgh
18. Virginia
19. Texas Tech
20. Texas A&M
21. West Virginia
22. Brigham Young
23. Washington
24. Ohio State
25. Arizona

1990
1. Colorado
2. Georgia Tech
3. Miami (Fla.)
4. Florida State
5. Washington
6. Notre Dame
7. Michigan
8. Tennessee
9. Clemson
10. Houston
11. Penn State
12. Texas
13. Florida
14. Louisville
15. Texas A&M
16. Michigan State
17. Oklahoma
18. Iowa
19. Auburn
20. Southern California
21. Mississippi
22. Brigham Young
23. Virginia
24. Nebraska
25. Illinois

1991
1. Miami (Fla.)
2. Washington
3. Penn State
4. Florida State
5. Alabama
6. Michigan
7. Florida
8. California
9. East Carolina
10. Iowa
11. Syracuse
12. Texas A&M
13. Notre Dame
14. Tennessee
15. Nebraska
16. Oklahoma
17. Georgia
18. Clemson
19. UCLA
20. Colorado
21. Tulsa
22. Stanford
23. Brigham Young
24. North Carolina State
25. Air Force

1992
1. Alabama
2. Florida State
3. Miami (Fla.)
4. Notre Dame
5. Michigan
6. Syracuse
7. Texas A&M
8. Georgia
9. Stanford
10. Florida
11. Washington
12. Tennessee
13. Colorado
14. Nebraska
15. Washington State
16. Mississippi
17. North Carolina State
18. Ohio State
19. North Carolina
20. Hawaii
21. Boston College
22. Kansas
23. Mississippi State
24. Fresno State
25. Wake Forest

1993

1. Florida State
2. Notre Dame
3. Nebraska
4. Auburn
5. Florida
6. Wisconsin
7. West Virginia
8. Penn State
9. Texas A&M
10. Arizona
11. Ohio State
12. Tennessee
13. Boston College
14. Alabama
15. Miami (Fla.)
16. Colorado
17. Oklahoma
18. UCLA
19. North Carolina
20. Kansas State
21. Michigan
22. Virginia Tech
23. Clemson
24. Louisville
25. California

1994

1. Nebraska
2. Penn State
3. Colorado
4. Florida State
5. Alabama
6. Miami (Fla.)
7. Florida
8. Texas A&M
9. Auburn
10. Utah
11. Oregon
12. Michigan
13. Southern California
14. Ohio State
15. Virginia
16. Colorado State
17. North Carolina State
18. Brigham Young
19. Kansas State
20. Arizona
21. Washington State
22. Tennessee
23. Boston College
24. Mississippi State
25. Texas

1995

1. Nebraska
2. Florida
3. Tennessee
4. Florida State
5. Colorado
6. Ohio State
7. Kansas State
8. Northwestern
9. Kansas
10. Virginia Tech
11. Notre Dame
12. Southern California
13. Penn State
14. Texas
15. Texas A&M
16. Virginia
17. Michigan
18. Oregon
19. Syracuse
20. Miami (Fla.)
21. Alabama
22. Auburn
23. Texas Tech
24. Toledo
25. Iowa

1996

1. Florida
2. Ohio State
3. Florida State
4. Arizona State
5. Brigham Young
6. Nebraska
7. Penn State
8. Colorado
9. Tennessee
10. North Carolina
11. Alabama
12. Louisiana State
13. Virginia Tech
14. Miami (Fla.)
15. Northwestern
16. Washington
17. Kansas State
18. Iowa
19. Notre Dame
20. Michigan
21. Syracuse
22. Wyoming
23. Texas
24. Auburn
25. Army

1997

1. Michigan
2. Nebraska
3. Florida State
4. Florida
5. UCLA
6. North Carolina
7. Tennessee
8. Kansas State
9. Washington State
10. Georgia
11. Auburn
12. Ohio State
13. Louisiana State
14. Arizona State
15. Purdue
16. Penn State
17. Colorado State
18. Washington
19. Southern Miss
20. Texas A&M
21. Syracuse
22. Mississippi
23. Missouri
24. Oklahoma State
25. Georgia Tech

1998

1. Tennessee
2. Ohio State
3. Florida State
4. Arizona
5. Florida
6. Wisconsin
7. Tulane
8. UCLA
9. Georgia Tech
10. Kansas State
11. Texas A&M
12. Michigan
13. Air Force
14. Georgia
15. Texas
16. Arkansas
17. Penn State
18. Virginia
19. Nebraska
20. Miami (Fla.)
21. Missouri
22. Notre Dame
23. Virginia Tech
24. Purdue
25. Syracuse

1999

1. Florida State
2. Virginia Tech
3. Nebraska
4. Wisconsin
5. Michigan
6. Kansas State
7. Michigan State
8. Alabama
9. Tennessee
10. Marshall
11. Penn State
12. Florida
13. Mississippi State
14. Southern Miss
15. Miami (Fla.)
16. Georgia
17. Arkansas
18. Minnesota
19. Oregon
20. Georgia Tech
21. Texas
22. Mississippi
23. Texas A&M
24. Illinois
25. Purdue

2000

1. Oklahoma
2. Miami (Fla.)
3. Washington
4. Oregon State
5. Florida State
6. Virginia Tech
7. Oregon
8. Nebraska
9. Kansas State
10. Florida
11. Michigan
12. Texas
13. Purdue
14. Colorado State
15. Notre Dame
16. Clemson
17. Georgia Tech
18. Auburn
19. South Carolina
20. Georgia
21. Texas Christian
22. Louisiana State
23. Wisconsin
24. Mississippi State
25. Iowa State

2001

1. Miami (Fla.)
2. Oregon
3. Florida
4. Tennessee
5. Texas
6. Oklahoma
7. Louisiana State
8. Nebraska
9. Colorado
10. Washington State
11. Maryland
12. Illinois
13. South Carolina
14. Syracuse
15. Florida State
16. Stanford
17. Louisville
18. Virginia Tech
19. Washington
20. Michigan
21. Boston College
22. Georgia
23. Toledo
24. Georgia Tech
25. Brigham Young

2002

1. Ohio State
2. Miami (Fla.)
3. Georgia
4. Southern California
5. Oklahoma
6. Texas
7. Kansas State
8. Iowa
9. Michigan
10. Washington State
11. Alabama
12. North Carolina State
13. Maryland
14. Auburn
15. Boise State
16. Penn State
17. Notre Dame
18. Virginia Tech
19. Pittsburgh
20. Colorado
21. Florida State
22. Virginia
23. Texas Christian
24. Marshall
25. West Virginia

2003

1. Southern California
2. Louisiana State
3. Oklahoma
4. Ohio State
5. Miami (Fla.)
6. Michigan
7. Georgia
8. Iowa
9. Washington State
10. Miami (Ohio)
11. Florida State
12. Texas
13. Mississippi
14. Kansas State
15. Tennessee
16. Boise State
17. Maryland
18. Purdue
19. Nebraska
20. Minnesota
21. Utah
22. Clemson
23. Bowling Green
24. Florida
25. Texas Christian

2004

1. Southern California
2. Auburn
3. Oklahoma
4. Utah
5. Texas
6. Louisville
7. Georgia
8. Iowa
9. California
10. Virginia Tech
11. Miami (Fla.)
12. Boise State
13. Tennessee
14. Michigan
15. Florida State
16. Louisiana State
17. Wisconsin
18. Texas Tech
19. Arizona State
20. Ohio State
21. Boston College
22. Fresno State
23. Virginia
24. Navy
25. Pittsburgh

2005

1. Texas
2. Southern California
3. Penn State
4. Ohio State
5. West Virginia
6. Louisiana State
7. Virginia Tech
8. Alabama
9. Notre Dame
10. Georgia
11. Texas Christian
12. Florida
    Oregon (tie)
14. Auburn
15. Wisconsin
16. UCLA
17. Miami (Fla.)
18. Boston College
19. Louisville
20. Texas Tech
21. Clemson
22. Oklahoma
23. Florida State
24. Nebraska
25. California

2006

1. Florida
2. Ohio State
3. Louisiana State
4. Southern California
5. Boise State
6. Louisville
7. Wisconsin
8. Michigan
9. Auburn
10. West Virginia
11. Oklahoma
12. Rutgers
13. Texas
14. California
15. Arkansas
16. Brigham Young
17. Notre Dame
18. Wake Forest
19. Virginia Tech
20. Boston College
21. Oregon State
22. Texas Christian
23. Georgia
24. Penn State
25. Tennessee

All-Time Final Associated Press Poll

ORMER Southeastern Conference assistant director of media relations Charles Woodroof came up with the idea of creating a compiled ranking for the Associated Press Poll, which began in 1936. From 1936 to 1961, the wire service ranked 20 teams. From 1962 to 1967, only 10 teams were recognized. From 1968 to 1988, it went back to 20 teams before expanding to 25 in 1989. Points are awarded based on a team's finish in the final AP of each year. Points were awarded on a 20-19-18 ... 3-2-1 basis from 1936 to 1988, and 25-24-23 ... 3-2-1 basis from 1989 through 2006. Source: SEC.

Rank	Team	Points	Top 20	Top 10	Top 5	1st	2nd
1.	Michigan	733	52	37	15	2	2
2.	Notre Dame	710.5	48	35	22	8	5
3.	Oklahoma	704.5	45	32	27	6	4
4.	Ohio State	654	45	27	18	4	7
5.	Alabama	637	44	32	18	6	2
6.	Nebraska	617	41	30	13	4	2
7.	Texas	557.5	38	23	8	3	1
8.	Southern California	552	40	23	16	5	5
9.	Tennessee	534	39	23	13	2	4
10.	Penn State	486	37	22	14	2	3
11.	Miami	439	27	15	10	5	4
12.	Florida State	413	23	15	15	2	2
13.	LSU	387	30	18	7	1	2
14.	Auburn	385	31	16	7	1	1
15.	Georgia	376	27	17	8	1	1
16.	Florida	357.5	23	14	9	2	1
17.	UCLA	352	30	16	9	0	1

Rank	Team	Points	Top 20	Top 10	Top 5	1st	2nd
18.	Arkansas	293	26	13	3	0	1
19.	Michigan State	266	20	13	7	1	4
20.	Texas A&M	264	22	11	2	1	0
21.	Washington	260	20	10	5	0	2
22.	Georgia Tech	227.5	20	10	5	0	2
23.	Ole Miss	223.5	18	10	4	0	2
24.	Colorado	218	18	8	5	1	0
25.	Iowa	217	18	11	3	0	1
26.	Pittsburgh	207	17	10	6	2	1
27.	Wisconsin	203	15	10	3	0	1
28.	Clemson	198	20	6	1	1	0
29.	Minnesota	175	14	9	5	4	0
30.	Army	174	14	8	6	2	2
31.	Maryland	164.5	17	5	3	1	0
32.	Arizona State	157.5	14	7	3	0	1
33.	California	153	12	6	4	0	1
34.	Syracuse	150.5	12	5	2	1	0
35.	North Carolina	144	15	7	1	0	0
36.	Virginia Tech	144	10	5	2	0	1
37.	Navy	143.5	11	8	7	0	1
38.	Kansas State	143	8	6	0	0	0
39.	Purdue	135.5	15	5	1	0	0
40.	Illinois	131	10	6	3	0	0
41.	Duke	130	16	5	2	0	1
42.	Missouri	120.5	12	6	1	0	0
43.	Stanford	116	12	5	1	0	1
	Brigham Young	116	10	3	2	1	0
	West Virginia	116	12	5	2	0	0
46.	Texas Christian	115	9	4	1	1	0
47.	Southern Methodist	113	11	6	3	0	1
48.	Houston	106.5	12	5	2	0	0
49.	Boston College	104	9	3	2	0	0
	Washington State	98	9	4	0	0	0
51.	Northwestern	96	8	5	0	0	0
52.	Oregon	85	5	3	1	0	1
53.	Oregon State	80	5	3	1	0	0
54.	North Carolina State	69	10	0	0	0	0

Rank	Team	Points	Top 20	Top 10	Top 5	1st	2nd
55.	Baylor	68.5	10	1	0	0	0
56.	Louisville	68	5	2	0	0	0
57.	Rice	66	8	4	1	0	0
58.	Oklahoma State	61	6	2	1	0	0
	Texas Tech	61	7	0	0	0	0
60.	Pennsylvania	60	7	3	0	0	0
61.	Fordham	58	6	2	1	0	0
62.	Kansas	57	5	2	0	0	0
63.	Kentucky	56	8	2	0	0	0
	Virginia	56	6	0	0	0	0
	Boise State	56	4	1	1	0	0
66.	Santa Clara	55	6	2	0	0	0
	Air Force	55	5	2	0	0	0
68.	Mississippi State	53.5	8	1	0	0	0
69.	Utah	53	4	2	1	0	0
70.	Arizona	51	6	2	1	0	0
71.	Tulane	50.5	7	2	1	0	0
72.	Miami (Ohio)	48	5	2	0	0	0
73.	Tulsa	47	6	1	1	0	0
74.	Cornell	43	5	1	1	0	0
75.	South Carolina	42	5	0	0	0	0
76.	Indiana	38	5	2	2	0	0
77.	Dartmouth	35	5	1	0	0	0
	Princeton	35	4	2	0	0	0
79.	Yale	34	4	0	0	0	0
	Iowa Pre-Flight	34	2	2	1	0	1
81.	Wyoming	33	3	1	0	0	0
82.	Duquesne	31	3	2	0	0	0
	Colorado Springs	31	3	0	0	0	0
84.	Holy Cross	26.5	5	1	0	0	0
85.	Villanova	26	3	1	0	0	0
86.	Rutgers	25	3	0	0	0	0
87.	March Field	22	3	1	0	0	0
88.	Brainbridge NTS	20	2	1	1	0	0
89.	Southern Miss	19	2	0	0	0	0
	Great Lakes	19	2	1	0	0	0
	East Carolina	19	2	1	0	0	0

Rank	Team	Points	Top 20	Top 10	Top 5	1st	2nd
92.	Marshall	18	1	1	0	0	0
	William & Mary	18	1	1	1	0	0
	Toledo	18	2	0	0	0	0
	Randolph Field	18	1	1	1	0	0
96.	Carnegie Tech	15	1	1	0	0	0
97.	St. Mary's	14	1	1	0	0	0
98.	Pacific	13	2	1	0	0	0
	Del Monte P-F	13	1	1	0	0	0
100.	Wake Forest	12	3	0	0	0	0
101.	Utah State	11	1	1	0	0	0
102.	Vanderbilt	9	1	0	0	0	0
103.	Georgetown	8	1	0	0	0	0
104.	Norman P-F	7.5	1	0	0	0	0
105.	San Francisco	7	1	0	0	0	0
106.	Hawaii	6	1	0	0	0	0
	Fresno State	6	0	0	0	0	0
108.	Boston University	5	1	0	0	0	0
	San Diego State	5	1	0	0	0	0
	El Toro Maines	5	1	0	0	0	0
111.	George Washington	4	1	0	0	0	0
	New Mexico State	4	1	0	0	0	0
	Temple	4	1	0	0	0	0
	Hardin-Simmons	4	1	0	0	0	0
115.	Colorado College	3	1	0	0	0	0
	Iowa State	3	1	0	0	0	0
	Bowling Green	3	0	0	0	0	0
	Washington & Lee	3	1	0	0	0	0
	Fort Pierce	3	1	0	0	0	0
120.	Columbia	2	2	0	0	0	0
	Delaware	2	1	0	0	0	0
	Lafayette	2	1	0	0	0	0
	St. Mary's P-F	2	1	0	0	0	0
124.	Marquette	1	1	0	0	0	0
	Ohio University	1	1	0	0	0	0
	Virginia Military	1	1	0	0	0	0
	Second Air Force	1	1	0	0	0	0

Coaches' Polls

United Press International poll

United Press (UP), 1950–1957; United Press International (UPI) from 1958–1995 after merger with International News Service (INS). Served as the coaches' poll until 1991, when it was taken over by *USA Today*/Cable News Network (CNN)/ESPN poll. Note: On occasion not enough teams received votes, resulting in open spots at the bottom of the rankings.

1950
1. Oklahoma
2. Texas
3. Tennessee
4. California
5. Army
6. Michigan
7. Kentucky
8. Princeton
9. Michigan State
10. Ohio State
11. Illinois
12. Clemson
13. Miami (Fla.)
14. Wyoming
15. Washington
    Baylor (tie)
17. Alabama
18. Washington & Lee
19. Navy
20. Nebraska
    Wisconsin (tie)
    Cornell (tie)

1951
1. Tennessee
2. Michigan State
3. Illinois
4. Maryland
5. Georgia Tech
6. Princeton
7. Stanford
8. Wisconsin
9. Baylor
10. Texas Christian
11. Oklahoma
12. California
13. Notre Dame
14. San Francisco
    Purdue (tie)
    Washington State (tie)
17. Holy Cross
    UCLA (tie)
    Kentucky (tie)
20. Kansas

1952
1. Michigan State
2. Georgia Tech
3. Notre Dame
4. Oklahoma
    Southern California (tie)
6. UCLA
7. Mississippi
8. Tennessee
9. Alabama
10. Wisconsin
11. Texas
12. Purdue
13. Maryland
14. Princeton
15. Ohio State
    Pittsburgh (tie)
17. Navy
18. Duke
19. Houston
    Kentucky (tie)

1953

1. Maryland
2. Notre Dame
3. Michigan State
4. UCLA
5. Oklahoma
6. Rice
7. Illinois
8. Texas
9. Georgia Tech
10. Iowa
11. Alabama
12. Texas Tech
13. West Virginia
14. Wisconsin
15. Kentucky
16. Army
17. Stanford
18. Duke
19. Michigan
20. Ohio State

1954

1. UCLA
2. Ohio State
3. Oklahoma
4. Notre Dame
5. Navy
6. Mississippi
7. Army
8. Arkansas
9. Miami (Fla.)
10. Wisconsin
11. Southern California
    Maryland (tie)
    Georgia Tech (tie)
14. Duke
15. Michigan
16. Penn State
17. Southern Methodist
18. Denver
19. Rice
20. Minnesota

1955

1. Oklahoma
2. Michigan State
3. Maryland
4. UCLA
5. Ohio State
6. Texas Christian
7. Georgia Tech
8. Auburn
9. Mississippi
10. Notre Dame
11. Pittsburgh
12. Southern California
13. Michigan
14. Texas A&M
15. Army
16. Duke
17. West Virginia
18. Miami (Fla.)
19. Iowa
20. Navy
    Stanford (tie)
    Miami (Ohio) (tie)

1956

1. Oklahoma
2. Tennessee
3. Iowa
4. Georgia Tech
5. Texas A&M
6. Miami (Fla.)
7. Michigan
8. Syracuse
9. Minnesota
10. Michigan State
11. Baylor
12. Pittsburgh
13. Oregon State
14. Texas Christian
15. Southern California
16. Wyoming
17. Yale
18. Colorado
19. Navy
20. Duke

1957

1. Ohio State
2. Auburn
3. Michigan State
4. Oklahoma
5. Iowa
6. Navy
7. Rice
8. Mississippi
9. Notre Dame
10. Texas A&M
11. Texas
12. Arizona State
13. Army
14. Duke
    Wisconsin (tie)
16. Tennessee
17. Oregon
18. Clemson
    UCLA (tie)
20. North Carolina State

1958

1. Louisiana State
2. Iowa
3. Army
4. Auburn
5. Oklahoma
6. Wisconsin
7. Ohio State
8. Air Force
9. Texas Christian
10. Syracuse
11. Purdue
12. Mississippi
13. Clemson
14. Notre Dame
15. Florida
16. California
17. Northwestern
18. Southern Methodist

1959
1. Syracuse
2. Mississippi
3. Louisiana State
4. Texas
5. Georgia
6. Wisconsin
7. Washington
8. Texas Christian
9. Arkansas
10. Penn State
11. Clemson
12. Illinois
13. Alabama
    Southern California (tie)
15. Auburn
16. Michigan State
17. Oklahoma
18. Notre Dame
19. Pittsburgh
    Missouri (tie)
    Florida (tie)

1960
1. Minnesota
2. Iowa
3. Mississippi
4. Missouri
5. Wisconsin
6. Navy
7. Arkansas
8. Ohio State
9. Kansas
10. Alabama
11. Duke
    Baylor (tie)
    Michigan State (tie)
14. Auburn
15. Purdue
16. Florida
17. Texas
18. Yale
19. New Mexico State
    Tennessee (tie)

1961
1. Alabama
2. Ohio State
3. Louisiana State
4. Texas
5. Mississippi
6. Minnesota
7. Colorado
8. Arkansas
9. Michigan State
10. Utah State
11. Purdue
    Missouri (tie)
13. Georgia Tech
14. Duke
15. Kansas
16. Syracuse
17. Wyoming
18. Wisconsin
19. Miami (Fla.)
    Penn State (tie)

1962
1. Southern California
2. Wisconsin
3. Mississippi
4. Texas
5. Alabama
6. Arkansas
7. Oklahoma
8. Louisiana State
9. Penn State
10. Minnesota
11. Georgia Tech
12. Missouri
13. Ohio State
14. Duke
    Washington (tie)
16. Northwestern
    Oregon State (tie)
18. Arizona State
    Illinois (tie)
    Miami (Fla.) (tie)

1963
1. Texas
2. Navy
3. Pittsburgh
4. Illinois
5. Nebraska
6. Auburn
7. Mississippi
8. Oklahoma
9. Alabama
10. Michigan State
11. Mississippi State
12. Syracuse
13. Arizona State
14. Memphis
15. Washington
16. Penn State
    Southern California (tie)
    Missouri (tie)
19. North Carolina
20. Baylor

1964
1. Alabama
2. Arkansas
3. Notre Dame
4. Michigan
5. Texas
6. Nebraska
7. Louisiana State
8. Oregon State
9. Ohio State
10. Southern California
11. Florida State
12. Syracuse
13. Princeton
14. Penn State
    Utah (tie)
16. Illinois
    New Mexico (tie)
18. Tulsa
    Missouri (tie)
20. Mississippi
    Michigan State (tie)

1965
1. Michigan State
2. Arkansas
3. Nebraska
4. Alabama
5. UCLA
6. Missouri
7. Tennessee
8. Notre Dame
9. Southern California
10. Texas Tech
11. Ohio State
12. Florida
13. Purdue
14. Louisiana State
15. Georgia
16. Tulsa
17. Mississippi
18. Kentucky
19. Syracuse
20. Colorado

1966
1. Notre Dame
2. Michigan State
3. Alabama
4. Georgia
5. UCLA
6. Purdue
7. Nebraska
8. Georgia Tech
9. Southern Methodist
10. Miami (Fla.)
11. Florida
12. Mississippi
13. Arkansas
14. Tennessee
15. Wyoming
16. Syracuse
17. Houston
18. Southern California
19. Oregon State
20. Virginia Tech

1967
1. Southern California
2. Tennessee
3. Oklahoma
4. Notre Dame
5. Wyoming
6. Indiana
7. Alabama
8. Oregon State
9. Purdue
10. UCLA
11. Penn State
12. Syracuse
13. Colorado
14. Minnesota
15. Florida State
16. Miami (Fla.)
17. North Carolina State
18. Georgia
19. Houston
20. Arizona State

1968
1. Ohio State
2. Southern California
3. Penn State
4. Georgia
5. Texas
6. Kansas
7. Tennessee
8. Notre Dame
9. Arkansas
10. Oklahoma
11. Purdue
12. Alabama
13. Oregon State
14. Florida State
15. Michigan
16. Southern Methodist
17. Missouri
18. Ohio
    Minnesota (tie)
20. Houston
    Stanford (tie)

1969
1. Texas
2. Penn State
3. Arkansas
4. Southern California
5. Ohio State
6. Missouri
7. Louisiana State
8. Michigan
9. Notre Dame
10. UCLA
11. Tennessee
12. Nebraska
13. Mississippi
14. Stanford
15. Auburn
16. Houston
17. Florida
18. Purdue
    San Diego State (tie)
    West Virginia (tie)

1970
1. Texas
2. Ohio State
3. Nebraska
4. Tennessee
5. Notre Dame
6. Louisiana State
7. Michigan
8. Arizona State
9. Auburn
10. Stanford
11. Air Force
12. Arkansas
13. Houston
    Dartmouth (tie)
15. Oklahoma
16. Colorado
17. Georgia Tech
    Toledo (tie)
19. Penn State
    Southern California
    (tie)

1971

1. Nebraska
2. Alabama
3. Oklahoma
4. Michigan
5. Auburn
6. Arizona State
7. Colorado
8. Georgia
9. Tennessee
10. Louisiana State
11. Penn State
12. Texas
13. Toledo
14. Houston
15. Notre Dame
16. Stanford
17. Iowa State
18. North Carolina
19. Florida State
20. Arkansas
    Mississippi (tie)

1972

1. Southern California
2. Oklahoma
3. Ohio State
4. Alabama
5. Texas
6. Michigan
7. Auburn
8. Penn State
9. Nebraska
10. Louisiana State
11. Tennessee
12. Notre Dame
13. Arizona State
14. Colorado
    North Carolina (tie)
16. Louisville
17. UCLA
    Washington State (tie)
19. Utah State
20. San Diego State

1973

1. Alabama
2. Oklahoma
3. Ohio State
4. Notre Dame
5. Penn State
6. Michigan
7. Southern California
8. Texas
9. UCLA
10. Arizona State
11. Nebraska
    Texas Tech (tie)
13. Houston
14. Louisiana State
15. Kansas
    Tulane (tie)
17. Miami (Ohio)
18. Maryland
19. San Diego State
    Florida (tie)

1974

1. Southern California
2. Alabama
3. Ohio State
4. Notre Dame
5. Michigan
6. Auburn
7. Penn State
8. Nebraska
9. North Carolina State
10. Miami (Ohio)
11. Houston
12. Florida
13. Maryland
14. Baylor
15. Texas A&M
    Tennessee (tie)
17. Mississippi State
18. Michigan State
19. Tulsa

1975

1. Oklahoma
2. Arizona State
3. Alabama
4. Ohio State
5. UCLA
6. Arkansas
7. Texas
8. Michigan
9. Nebraska
10. Penn State
11. Maryland
12. Texas A&M
13. Arizona
    Pittsburgh (tie)
15. California
16. Miami (Ohio)
17. Notre Dame
    West Virginia (tie)
19. Georgia
    Southern California (tie)

1976

1. Pittsburgh
2. Southern California
3. Michigan
4. Houston
5. Ohio State
6. Oklahoma
7. Nebraska
8. Texas A&M
9. Alabama
10. Georgia
11. Maryland
12. Notre Dame
13. Texas Tech
14. Oklahoma State
15. UCLA
16. Colorado
17. Rutgers
18. Iowa State
19. Baylor
    Kentucky (tie)

1977

1. Notre Dame
2. Alabama
3. Arkansas
4. Penn State
5. Texas
6. Oklahoma
7. Pittsburgh
8. Michigan
9. Washington
10. Nebraska
11. Florida State
12. Ohio State
    Southern California (tie)
14. North Carolina
15. Stanford
16. North Texas
    Brigham Young (tie)
18. Arizona State
19. San Diego State
    North Carolina State
    (tie)

1978

1. Southern California
2. Alabama
3. Oklahoma
4. Penn State
5. Michigan
6. Notre Dame
7. Clemson
8. Nebraska
9. Texas
10. Arkansas
11. Houston
12. UCLA
13. Purdue
14. Missouri
15. Georgia
16. Stanford
17. Navy
18. Texas A&M
19. Arizona State
    North Carolina State
    (tie)

1979

1. Alabama
2. Southern California
3. Oklahoma
4. Ohio State
5. Houston
6. Pittsburgh
7. Nebraska
8. Florida State
9. Arkansas
10. Purdue
11. Washington
12. Brigham Young
13. Texas
14. North Carolina
15. Baylor
16. Indiana
17. Temple
18. Penn State
19. Michigan
20. Missouri

1980

1. Georgia
2. Pittsburgh
3. Oklahoma
4. Michigan
5. Florida State
6. Alabama
7. Nebraska
8. Penn State
9. North Carolina
10. Notre Dame
11. Brigham Young
12. Southern California
13. Baylor
14. UCLA
15. Ohio State
16. Purdue
17. Washington
18. Miami (Fla.)
19. Florida
20. Southern Methodist

1981

1. Clemson
2. Pittsburgh
3. Penn State
4. Texas
5. Georgia
6. Alabama
7. Washington
8. North Carolina
9. Nebraska
10. Michigan
11. Brigham Young
12. Ohio State
13. Southern California
14. Oklahoma
15. Iowa
16. Arkansas
17. Mississippi State
18. West Virginia
19. Southern Miss
20. Missouri

1982

1. Penn State
2. Southern Methodist
3. Nebraska
4. Georgia
5. UCLA
6. Arizona State
7. Washington
8. Arkansas
9. Pittsburgh
10. Florida State
11. Louisiana State
12. Ohio State
13. North Carolina
14. Auburn
15. Michigan
16. Oklahoma
17. Alabama
18. Texas
19. West Virginia
20. Maryland

1983

1. Miami (Fla.)
2. Nebraska
3. Auburn
4. Georgia
5. Texas
6. Florida
7. Brigham Young
8. Ohio State
9. Michigan
10. Illinois
11. Southern Methodist
12. Alabama
13. UCLA
14. Iowa
15. Air Force
16. West Virginia
17. Penn State
18. Oklahoma State
19. Pittsburgh
20. Boston College

1984

1. Brigham Young
2. Washington
3. Nebraska
4. Boston College
5. Oklahoma State
6. Oklahoma
7. Florida
8. Southern Methodist
9. Southern California
10. UCLA
11. Maryland
12. Ohio State
13. South Carolina
14. Auburn
15. Iowa
16. Louisiana State
17. Virginia
18. West Virginia
19. Kentucky
    Florida State (tie)

1985

1. Oklahoma
2. Michigan
3. Penn State
4. Tennessee
5. Air Force
6. UCLA
7. Texas A&M
8. Miami (Fla.)
9. Iowa
10. Nebraska
11. Ohio State
12. Arkansas
13. Florida State
14. Alabama
15. Baylor
16. Fresno State
17. Brigham Young
18. Georgia Tech
19. Maryland
20. Louisiana State

1986

1. Penn State
2. Miami (Fla.)
3. Oklahoma
4. Nebraska
5. Arizona State
6. Ohio State
7. Michigan
8. Auburn
9. Alabama
10. Arizona
11. Louisiana State
12. Texas A&M
13. Baylor
14. UCLA
15. Iowa
16. Arkansas
17. Washington
18. Boston College
19. Clemson
20. Florida State

1987

1. Miami (Fla.)
2. Florida State
3. Oklahoma
4. Syracuse
5. Louisiana State
6. Nebraska
7. Auburn
8. Michigan State
9. Texas A&M
10. Clemson
11. UCLA
12. Oklahoma State
13. Tennessee
14. Georgia
15. South Carolina
16. Iowa
17. Southern California
18. Michigan
19. Texas
20. Indiana

1988

1. Notre Dame
2. Miami (Fla.)
3. Florida State
4. Michigan
5. West Virginia
6. UCLA
7. Auburn
8. Clemson
9. Southern California
10. Nebraska
11. Oklahoma State
12. Syracuse
13. Arkansas
14. Oklahoma
15. Georgia
16. Washington State
17. North Carolina State
    Alabama (tie)
19. Indiana
20. Wyoming

1989
1. Miami (Fla.)
2. Florida State
3. Notre Dame
4. Colorado
5. Tennessee
6. Auburn
7. Alabama
8. Michigan
9. Southern California
10. Illinois
11. Clemson
12. Nebraska
13. Arkansas
14. Penn State
15. Virginia
16. Texas Tech
    Michigan State (tie)
18. Brigham Young
19. Pittsburgh
20. Washington

1990
1. Georgia Tech
2. Colorado
3. Miami (Fla.)
4. Florida State
5. Washington
6. Notre Dame
7. Tennessee
8. Michigan
9. Clemson
10. Penn State
11. Texas
12. Louisville
13. Texas A&M
14. Michigan State
15. Virginia
16. Iowa
17. Brigham Young
    Nebraska (tie)
19. Auburn
20. San Jose State
21. Syracuse
22. Southern California
23. Mississippi
24. Illinois
25. Virginia Tech

1991
1. Washington
2. Miami (Fla.)
3. Penn State
4. Florida State
5. Alabama
6. Michigan
7. Florida
8. California
9. East Carolina
10. Iowa
11. Syracuse
12. Notre Dame
13. Texas A&M
14. Tennessee
15. Nebraska
16. Oklahoma
17. Clemson
18. Colorado
19. UCLA
20. Georgia
21. Tulsa
22. Stanford
23. North Carolina State
24. Brigham Young
25. Ohio State

1992

1. Alabama
2. Florida State
3. Miami (Fla.)
4. Notre Dame
5. Michigan
6. Syracuse
7. Texas A&M
8. Georgia
9. Stanford
10. Florida
11. Washington
12. Tennessee
13. Colorado
14. Nebraska
15. Washington State
16. Mississippi
17. North Carolina State
18. North Carolina
19. Ohio State
20. Hawaii
21. Boston College
22. Kansas
23. Fresno State
24. Penn State
25. Mississippi State

1993

1. Florida State
2. Notre Dame
3. Nebraska
4. Florida
5. Wisconsin
6. Texas A&M
7. Penn State
8. West Virginia
9. Ohio State
10. Arizona
11. Boston College
12. Tennessee
13. Alabama
14. Miami (Fla.)
15. Oklahoma
16. Colorado
17. UCLA
18. Kansas State
19. Michigan
20. North Carolina
21. Virginia Tech
22. Louisville
23. Clemson
24. California
25. Southern California

1994

1. Nebraska
2. Penn State
3. Colorado
4. Florida State
5. Alabama
6. Miami (Fla.)
7. Florida
8. Utah
9. Michigan
10. Ohio State
11. Oregon
12. Brigham Young
13. Southern California
14. Colorado State
15. Virginia
16. Kansas State
17. North Carolina State
18. Tennessee
19. Washington State
20. Arizona
21. North Carolina
22. Boston College
23. Texas
24. Virginia Tech
25. Mississippi State

1995

1. Nebraska
2. Florida
3. Tennessee
4. Colorado
5. Florida State
6. Ohio State
7. Kansas State
8. Northwestern
9. Virginia Tech
10. Kansas
11. Southern California
12. Penn State
13. Notre Dame
14. Texas A&M
15. Texas
16. Virginia
17. Syracuse
18. Oregon
19. Michigan
20. Texas Tech
21. Auburn
22. Toledo
23. Iowa
24. East Carolina
25. Louisiana State

USA Today/ESPN polls

Replaced UPI as coaches poll in 1991 (Cable News Network, 1982-96; ESPN 1997-present).

1982

1. Penn State
2. Southern Methodist
3. Nebraska
4. Georgia
5. UCLA
6. Arizona State
7. Pittsburgh
8. Arkansas
9. Clemson
10. Washington
11. Louisiana State
12. Florida State
13. Ohio State
14. Southern California
15. Oklahoma
16. Auburn
17. West Virginia
18. Maryland
19. North Carolina
20. Texas
21. Michigan
22. Alabama
23. Tulsa
24. Iowa
25. Florida

1983

1. Miami (Fla.)
2. Auburn
3. Nebraska
4. Georgia
5. Texas
6. Brigham Young
7. Michigan
8. Ohio State
9. Florida
10. Clemson
11. Illinois
12. Southern Methodist
13. Alabama
14. Air Force
15. West Virginia
16. Iowa
17. Tennessee
18. UCLA
19. Pittsburgh
20. Penn State
21. Oklahoma
22. Boston College
23. Oklahoma State
24. Maryland
25. East Carolina

1984

1. Brigham Young
2. Washington
3. Florida
4. Nebraska
5. Oklahoma
6. Boston College
7. Oklahoma State
8. Southern Methodist
9. Maryland
10. South Carolina
11. Southern California
12. UCLA
13. Louisiana State
14. Ohio State
15. Auburn
16. Miami (Fla.)
17. Florida State
18. Virginia
19. Kentucky
20. Iowa
21. West Virginia
22. Army
23. Georgia
24. Air Force
25. Notre Dame

1985

1. Oklahoma
2. Penn State
3. Michigan
4. Tennessee
5. Florida
6. Miami (Fla.)
7. Air Force
8. Texas A&M
9. UCLA
10. Iowa
11. Nebraska
12. Alabama
13. Ohio State
14. Florida State
15. Arkansas
16. Brigham Young
17. Maryland
18. Georgia Tech
19. Baylor
20. Auburn
21. Louisiana State
22. Army
23. Fresno State
24. Georgia
25. Oklahoma State

1986

1. Penn State
2. Miami (Fla.)
3. Oklahoma
4. Nebraska
5. Arizona State
6. Ohio State
7. Auburn
8. Michigan
9. Alabama
10. Louisiana State
11. Arizona
12. Texas A&M
13. UCLA
14. Baylor
15. Boston College
16. Iowa
17. Arkansas
18. Clemson
19. Washington
20. Virginia Tech
21. Florida State
22. Stanford
23. Georgia
24. North Carolina State
25. San Diego State

1987

1. Miami (Fla.)
2. Florida State
3. Oklahoma
4. Syracuse
5. Nebraska
6. Louisiana State
7. Auburn
8. Michigan State
9. Texas A&M
10. UCLA
11. Clemson
12. Oklahoma State
13. Georgia
14. Tennessee
15. Iowa
16. Notre Dame
17. Southern California
18. South Carolina
19. Michigan
20. Texas
21. Pittsburgh
22. Indiana
23. Penn State
24. Ohio State
25. Alabama

1988

1. Notre Dame
2. Miami (Fla.)
3. Florida State
4. UCLA
5. Michigan
6. West Virginia
7. Southern California
8. Nebraska
9. Auburn
10. Clemson
11. Oklahoma State
12. Syracuse
13. Oklahoma
14. Arkansas
15. Washington State
16. Georgia
17. Alabama
18. North Carolina State
19. Houston
20. Indiana
21. Wyoming
22. Louisiana State
23. Colorado
24. Southern Miss
25. Brigham Young

1989

1. Miami (Fla.)
2. Notre Dame
3. Florida State
4. Colorado
5. Tennessee
6. Auburn
7. Southern California
8. Michigan
9. Alabama
10. Illinois
11. Nebraska
12. Clemson
13. Arkansas
14. Houston
15. Penn State
16. Virginia
17. Michigan State
18. Texas Tech
19. Pittsburgh
20. Texas A&M
21. West Virginia
22. Brigham Young
23. Syracuse
24. Ohio State
25. Washington

1990

1. Colorado
2. Georgia Tech
3. Miami (Fla.)
4. Florida State
5. Washington
6. Notre Dame
7. Tennessee
8. Michigan
9. Clemson
10. Texas
11. Penn State
12. Houston
13. Florida
14. Louisville
15. Michigan State
16. Texas A&M
17. Oklahoma
18. Iowa
19. Auburn
20. Brigham Young
21. Mississippi
22. Southern California
23. Nebraska
24. Illinois
25. Virginia

1991

1. Washington
2. Miami (Fla.)
3. Penn State
4. Florida State
5. Alabama
6. Michigan
7. California
8. Florida
9. East Carolina
10. Iowa
11. Syracuse
12. Notre Dame
13. Texas A&M
14. Oklahoma
15. Tennessee
16. Nebraska
17. Clemson
18. UCLA
19. Georgia
20. Colorado
21. Tulsa
22. Stanford
23. Brigham Young
24. Air Force
25. North Carolina State

1992

1. Alabama
2. Florida State
3. Miami (Fla.)
4. Notre Dame
5. Michigan
6. Texas A&M
7. Syracuse
8. Georgia
9. Stanford
10. Washington
11. Florida
12. Tennessee
13. Colorado
14. Nebraska
15. North Carolina State
16. Mississippi
17. Washington State
18. North Carolina
19. Ohio State
20. Hawaii
21. Boston College
22. Fresno State
23. Kansas
24. Penn State
25. Wake Forest

1993

1. Florida State
2. Notre Dame
3. Nebraska
4. Florida
5. Wisconsin
6. West Virginia
7. Penn State
8. Texas A&M
9. Arizona
10. Ohio State
11. Tennessee
12. Boston College
13. Alabama
14. Oklahoma
15. Miami (Fla.)
16. Colorado
17. UCLA
18. Kansas State
19. Michigan
20. Virginia Tech
21. North Carolina
22. Clemson
23. Louisville
24. California
25. Southern California

1994
1. Nebraska
2. Penn State
3. Colorado
4. Alabama
5. Florida State
6. Miami (Fla.)
7. Florida
8. Utah
9. Ohio State
10. Brigham Young
11. Oregon
12. Michigan
13. Virginia
14. Colorado State
15. Southern California
16. Kansas State
17. North Carolina State
18. Tennessee
19. Washington State
20. Arizona
21. North Carolina
22. Boston College
23. Texas
24. Virginia Tech
25. Mississippi State

1995
1. Nebraska
2. Tennessee
3. Florida
4. Colorado
5. Florida State
6. Kansas State
7. Northwestern
8. Ohio State
9. Virginia Tech
10. Kansas
11. Southern California
12. Penn State
13. Notre Dame
14. Texas
15. Texas A&M
16. Syracuse
17. Virginia
18. Oregon
19. Michigan
20. Texas Tech
21. Auburn
22. Iowa
23. East Carolina
24. Toledo
25. Louisiana State

1996
1. Florida
2. Ohio State
3. Florida State
4. Arizona State
5. Brigham Young
6. Nebraska
7. Penn State
8. Colorado
9. Tennessee
10. North Carolina
11. Alabama
12. Virginia Tech
13. Louisiana State
14. Miami (Fla.)
15. Washington
16. Northwestern
17. Kansas State
18. Iowa
19. Syracuse
20. Michigan
21. Notre Dame
22. Wyoming
23. Texas
24. Army
25. Auburn

1997

1. Nebraska
2. Michigan
3. Florida State
4. North Carolina
5. UCLA
6. Florida
7. Kansas State
8. Tennessee
9. Washington State
10. Georgia
11. Auburn
12. Ohio State
13. Louisiana State
14. Arizona State
15. Purdue
16. Colorado State
17. Penn State
18. Washington
19. Southern Miss
20. Syracuse
21. Texas A&M
22. Mississippi
23. Missouri
24. Oklahoma State
25. Air Force

1998

1. Tennessee
2. Ohio State
3. Florida State
4. Arizona
5. Wisconsin
6. Florida
7. Tulane
8. UCLA
9. Kansas State
10. Air Force
11. Georgia Tech
12. Michigan
13. Texas A&M
14. Georgia
15. Penn State
16. Texas
17. Arkansas
18. Virginia
19. Virginia Tech
20. Nebraska
21. Miami (Fla.)
22. Notre Dame
23. Purdue
24. Syracuse
25. Missouri

1999

1. Florida State
2. Nebraska
3. Virginia Tech
4. Wisconsin
5. Michigan
6. Kansas State
7. Michigan State
8. Alabama
9. Tennessee
10. Marshall
11. Penn State
12. Mississippi State
13. Southern Miss
14. Florida
15. Miami (Fla.)
16. Georgia
17. Minnesota
18. Oregon
19. Arkansas
20. Texas A&M
21. Georgia Tech
22. Mississippi
23. Texas
24. Stanford
25. Illinois

2000

1. Oklahoma
2. Miami (Fla.)
3. Washington
4. Florida State
5. Oregon State
6. Virginia Tech
7. Nebraska
8. Kansas State
9. Oregon
10. Michigan
11. Florida
12. Texas
13. Purdue
14. Clemson
15. Colorado State
16. Notre Dame
17. Georgia
18. Texas Christian
19. Georgia Tech
20. Auburn
21. South Carolina
22. Mississippi State
23. Iowa State
24. Wisconsin
25. Tennessee

2001

1. Miami (Fla.)
2. Oregon
3. Florida
4. Tennessee
5. Texas
6. Oklahoma
7. Nebraska
8. Louisiana State
9. Colorado
10. Maryland
11. Washington State
12. Illinois
13. South Carolina
14. Syracuse
15. Florida State
16. Louisville
17. Stanford
18. Virginia Tech
19. Washington
20. Michigan
21. Marshall
22. Toledo
23. Boston College
24. Brigham Young
25. Georgia

2002

1. Ohio State
2. Miami (Fla.)
3. Georgia
4. Southern California
5. Oklahoma
6. Kansas State
7. Texas
8. Iowa
9. Michigan
10. Washington State
11. North Carolina State
12. Boise State
13. Maryland
14. Virginia Tech
15. Penn State
16. Auburn
17. Notre Dame
18. Pittsburgh
19. Marshall
20. West Virginia
21. Colorado
22. Texas Christian
23. Florida State
24. Florida
25. Virginia

2003
1. Louisiana State
2. Southern California
3. Oklahoma
4. Ohio State
5. Miami (Fla.)
6. Georgia
7. Michigan
8. Iowa
9. Washington State
10. Florida State
11. Texas
12. Miami (Ohio)
13. Kansas State
14. Mississippi
15. Boise State
16. Tennessee
17. Minnesota
18. Nebraska
19. Purdue
20. Maryland
21. Utah
22. Clemson
23. Bowling Green
24. Texas Christian
25. Florida

2004
1. Southern California
2. Auburn
3. Oklahoma
4. Texas
5. Utah
6. Georgia
7. Louisville
8. Iowa
9. California
10. Virginia Tech
11. Miami (Fla.)
12. Michigan
13. Boise State
14. Florida State
15. Tennessee
16. Louisiana State
17. Texas Tech
18. Wisconsin
19. Ohio State
20. Arizona State
21. Boston College
22. Fresno State
23. Virginia
24. Navy
25. Florida

2005
1. Texas
2. Southern California
3. Penn State
4. Ohio State
5. Louisiana State
6. West Virginia
7. Virginia Tech
8. Alabama
9. Texas Christian
10. Georgia
11. Notre Dame
12. Oregon
13. UCLA
14. Auburn
15. Wisconsin
16. Florida
17. Boston College
18. Miami (Fla.)
19. Texas Tech
20. Louisville
21. Clemson
22. Oklahoma
23. Florida State
24. Nebraska
25. California

2006

1. Florida
2. Ohio State
3. Louisiana State
4. Southern California
5. Wisconsin
6. Boise State
7. Louisville
8. Auburn
9. Michigan
10. West Virginia
11. Oklahoma
12. Rutgers
13. Texas
14. California
15. Brigham Young
16. Arkansas
17. Wake Forest
18. Virginia Tech
19. Notre Dame
20. Boston College
21. Texas Christian
22. Oregon State
23. Tennessee
24. Hawaii
25. Penn State

BCS Final Standings

Bowl Championship Series rankings, released at the end of the regular season.

No.	Team	Total score
1998		
1.	Tennessee	3.47
2.	Florida State	4.91
3.	Kansas State	9.96
4.	Ohio State	10.37
5.	UCLA	10.90
6.	Texas A&M	15.70
7.	Arizona	16.49
8.	Florida	19.95
9.	Wisconsin	21.61
10.	Tulane	26.67
11.	Nebraska	29.06
12.	Virginia	32.22
13.	Arkansas	32.28
14.	Georgia Tech	32.76
15.	Syracuse	34.80

No.	Team	Total score
1999		
1.	Florida State	2.24
2.	Virginia Tech	6.12
3.	Nebraska	7.42
4.	Alabama	12.11
5.	Tennessee	13.71
6.	Kansas State	15.23
7.	Wisconsin	16.71
8.	Michigan	18.08
9.	Michigan State	19.11
10.	Florida	23.06
11.	Penn State	28.75
12.	Marshall	31.15
13.	Minnesota	33.61
14.	Texas A&M	34.76
15.	Texas	34.81

2000

1.	Oklahoma	3.30
2.	Florida State	5.37
3.	Miami (Fla.)	5.69
4.	Washington	10.67
5.	Virginia Tech	12.20
6.	Oregon State	14.68
7.	Florida	14.75
8.	Nebraska	18.22
9.	Kansas State	24.30
10.	Oregon	24.32
11.	Notre Dame	25.07
12.	Texas	27.22
13.	Georgia Tech	29.62
14.	Texas Christian	33.01
15.	Clemson	33.17

2001

1.	Miami (Fla.)	2.62
2.	Nebraska	7.23
3.	Colorado	7.28
4.	Oregon	8.67
5.	Florida	13.09
6.	Tennessee	14.69
7.	Texas	17.79
8.	Illinois	19.31
9.	Stanford	20.41
10.	Maryland	21.29
11.	Oklahoma	21.54
12.	Washington State	26.91
13.	Louisiana State	27.73
14.	South Carolina	37.77
15.	Washington	38.17

2002

1.	Miami (Fla.)	2.93
2.	Ohio State	3.97
3.	Georgia	8.37
4.	Southern California	10.51
5.	Iowa	10.79
6.	Washington State	16.14
7.	Oklahoma	16.79
8.	Kansas State	20.13
9.	Notre Dame	20.93
10.	Texas	21.08
11.	Michigan	23.91
12.	Penn State	26.97
13.	Colorado	33.27
14.	Florida State	33.95
15.	West Virginia	35.97

2003

1.	Oklahoma	5.11
2.	Louisiana State	5.99
3.	Southern California	6.15
4.	Michigan	10.63
5.	Ohio State	14.28
6.	Texas	14.53
7.	Florida State	17.93
8.	Tennessee	19.64
9.	Miami (Fla.)	19.79
10.	Kansas State	22.73
11.	Miami (Ohio)	24.22
12.	Georgia	24.59
13.	Iowa	28.94
14.	Purdue	32.93
15.	Florida	36.80
16.	Washington State	39.09
17.	Boise State	39.53
18.	Texas Christian	40.47
19.	Mississippi	44.13
20.	Nebraska	44.20
21.	Oklahoma State	45.72
22.	Utah	46.53
23.	Maryland	49.57
24.	Bowling Green	53.11
25.	Minnesota	55.49

2004		Avg.		2005		
1.	Southern California	.9770		1.	Southern California	.9868
2.	Oklahoma	.9681		2.	Texas	.9732
3.	Auburn	.9331		3.	Penn State	.9187
4.	Texas	.8476		4.	Ohio State	.8559
5.	California	.8347		5.	Oregon	.7989
6.	Utah	.8181		6.	Notre Dame	.7329
7.	Georgia	.6966		7.	Georgia	.7182
8.	Virginia Tech	.6712		8.	Miami (Fla.)	.7037
9.	Boise State	.6564		9.	Auburn	.6747
10.	Louisville	.6490		10.	Virginia Tech	.6715
11.	Louisiana State	.6109		11.	West Virginia	.6403
12.	Iowa	.5553		12.	Louisiana State	.6293
13.	Michigan	.5058		13.	Alabama	.4538
14.	Miami (Fla.)	.4705		14.	Texas Christian	.4445
15.	Tennessee	.4057		15.	Texas Tech	.4288
16.	Florida State	.3466		16.	UCLA	.3693
17.	Wisconsin	.3439		17.	Florida	.3058
18.	Virginia	.2983		18.	Wisconsin	.3021
19.	Arizona State	.2700		19.	Louisville	.2624
20.	Texas A&M	.2225		20.	Michigan	.2579
21.	Pittsburgh	.1546		21.	Boston College	.2452
22.	Texas Tech	.1489		22.	Florida State	.1100
23.	Florida	.1375		23.	Oklahoma	.0999
24.	Oklahoma State	.0943		24.	Georgia Tech	.0945
25.	Ohio State	.0847		25.	Northwestern	.0887

2006

1.	Ohio State	.9999
2.	Florida	.9445
3.	Michigan	.9344
4.	Louisiana State	.8326
5.	Southern California	.7953
6.	Louisville	.7944
7.	Wisconsin	.7480
8.	Boise State	.7099
9.	Auburn	.6486
10.	Oklahoma	.6297
11.	Notre Dame	.6287
12.	Arkansas	.5166
13.	West Virginia	.5073
14.	Wake Forest	.4314
15.	Virginia Tech	.4282
16.	Rutgers	.4097
17.	Tennessee	.3851
18.	California	.3606
19.	Texas	.2875
20.	Brigham Young	.2082
21.	Texas A&M	.1468
22.	Oregon State	.1438
23.	Nebraska	.0936
24.	Boston College	.0885
25.	UCLA	.0645

First-Team All-Americans

Bold face signifies consensus, with * indicating the consensus year, # signifies unanimous selection.

Sources: National Collegiate Athletic Association; All-America Board; Associated Press; Walter Camp (published in *Harper's Weekly* 1897, *Collier's magazine*, 1898–1924); *Collier's* magazine (selections by Grantland Rice 1925–1947; it published American Football Coaches Association teams 1948–1956); ESPN College Football Encyclopedia; *Football World* magazine; Central Press; American Football Coaches Association (published by *Saturday Evening Post* magazine 1945–1947, *Collier's* 1948–1956); *Football News* Football Writers Association of America (published by *Look* magazine 1946–1970); International News Service (merged with United Press in 1958 to form UPI); *Look* magazine (published FWAA teams, 1946–1970, listed under FW); *Liberty* magazine; Frank Menke Syndicate; *Newsweek* magazine; North American Newspaper Alliance; Newspaper Enterprise Association; *Sporting News*; United Press (merged with INS in 1958 to form UPI); United Press International; Caspar Whitney (published in *The Week's Sport* in association with Walter Camp 1889–1890; *Harper's Weekly* 1891–1896; *Outing* magazine, 1898–1908. Walter Camp substituted for Whitney in 1897); Walter Camp Foundation.

AIR FORCE: Brock Strom, T, *1958; Ernie Jennings, E, *1970; Dave Lawson, PK-LB, 1974; Johnnie Jackson, DB, 1971; **Scott Thomas, DB, *1985;** Terry Maki, LB, 1976; **Chad Hennings, DT, #*1987; Carlton McDonald, DB, #*1992;** Chris MacInnis, P, 1993.

AKRON: Dwight Smith, DB, *2000.

ALABAMA: Hoyt Winslett, E, 1926; Tony Holm, FB, 1929; **Fred Sington, T, #*1930;** Johnny Cain, FB, 1931; **Don Hutson, E, *1934; Bill Lee, T, *1934; Dixie Howell, B, *1934; Riley Smith, B, *1935;** Arthur White, G, 1936; **Leroy Monsky, G, *1937;** Jim Ryba, T, 1937; Joe Kilgrow, HB, 1937; Carey Cox, G, 1939; **Holt Rast, E, *1941; Joe Domnanovich, C, *1942;** Don Whitmire, T, 1942; **Vaughn Mancha, C, *1945;** Harry Gilmer,

HB, 1945; Ed Salem, HB, 1950; **Billy Neighbors, T, *1961; Lee Roy Jordan, C, #*1962;** Dan Kearley, OT, 1964; Wayne Freeman, OG, 1964; **Paul Crane, C, *1965; Ray Perkins, SE, *1966; Cecil Dowdy, OT, #*1966; Dennis Homan, SE, 1967; Bobby Johns, DB,** 1966, ***1967;** Mike Hall, LB, 1968; **Johnny Musso, TB, *1971; John Hannah**, OT, 1971, **OG, #*1972;** Jim Krapf, C, 1972; John Mitchell, DE, 1972; Wayne Wheeler, SE, 1973; **Buddy Brown, OT, *1973; Woodrow Lowe, LB,** 1973, ***1974,** 1975; **Leroy Cook, DE, *1974, #*1975;** Sylvester Croom, C, 1974; **Ozzie Newsome, WR, *1977; Marty Lyons, DT, *1978; Jim Bunch, OT, *1979; E. J. Junior, DE, #*1980; Tommy Wilcox, DB, *1981; Mike Pitts, DE, *1982;** Jeremiah Castille, DB, 1982; **Cornelius Bennett, LB,** 1985, **#*1986;** Bobby Humphrey, RB, 1987; **Derrick Thomas, LB, #*1988; Keith McCants, LB, #*1989; Philip Doyle, PK, #*1990;** Robert Stewart, DL, 1991; **John Copeland, DL, *1992; Eric Curry, DL, *1992; Antonio Langham, DB, #*1993; David Palmer, KR, *1993;** Michael Proctor, PK, 1993, 1994; **Kevin Jackson, DB, #*1996;** Michael Myers, DL, 1996; Dwayne Rudd, LB, 1996; **Chris Samuels, OL, #*1999;** Shaun Alexander, RB, 1999; **DeMeco Ryans, LB, #*2005**.

AMHERST: John Hubbard, B, *1905.

ARIZONA: Ricky Hunley, LB, *1982, #*1983; Allan Durden, DB, 1985; **Chuck Cecil, DB, *1987; Darryl Lewis, DB, #*1990;** Josh Miller, P, 1992; **Rob Waldrop, DL, *1992, #*1993; Tony Bouie, DB, *1994; Steve McLaughlin, PK, *1994; Tedy Bruschi, DL, *1994, #*1995; Chris McAlister, DB, #*1998; Dennis Northcutt, AP, *1999**

ARIZONA STATE: Ron Pritchard, LB, 1968; **Woody Green, B, *1972, *1973;** Steve Holden, WR, 1972; Danny White, QB, 1973; Bob Breunig, LB, 1974; Mike Haynes, DB, 1975; **John Jefferson, WR, *1977; Al Harris, DE, #*1978; Mike Richardson, DB, *1981, *1982; Vernon Maxwell, LB, *1982; Luis Zendejas, PK, *1983; David Fulcher, DB, *1984, *1985; Danny Villa, OT, *1986; Randall McDaniel, OG,** 1986, ***1987;** Shante Carver, DL, 1993; Terry Battle, KR, 1996; Jake Plummer, QB, 1996; **Derrick Rodgers, DL, *1996; Juan Roque, OL, *1996;** Jeremy Staat, DL, 1997; Pat Tillman, LB, 1997; Grey Ruegamer, C, 1998; Marvel Smith, OL, 1999; **Terrell Suggs, DL,** 2001, **#*2002; Zach Miller, TE, *2006**.

ARKANSAS: Wear Schoonover, E, 1929; Jim Benton, E, 1937; **Clyde Scott, TB, *1948; Bud Brooks, T, *1954;** Jim Mooty, HB, 1959; Wayne Harris, G-LB, 1960; Lance Alworth, B, 1961; Bill Moore, QB, 1962; Ronnie Caveness, C, 1964; **Glen Ray Hines, OT, *1965; Loyd Phillips, DT, *1965, #*1966;** Bobby Crockett, E, 1965; Martine Bercher, DB, 1966; **Jim Barnes, OG, *1968; Rodney Brand, C, *1969;** Chuck Dicus, SE, 1969, 1970; Cliff Powell, LB, 1969; **Dick Bumpas, DT, *1970;** Bruce James, DT, 1970; Bill McClard, K, 1970; **Steve Little, PK,** 1976, ***1977; Leotis Harris, G, *1977;** Dan Hampton, DT, 1978; Jimmy Walker, DL, 1978; **Greg Kolenda, OT, #*1979; Billy Ray Smith, DL, #*1981, #*1982;** Bruce Lahay, PK, 1981; **Steve Korte, OG, #*1982;** Ron Faurot, DE, 1983; Greg Horne, P, 1986; Tony Cherico, MG, 1987; **Kendall Trainor, PK, *1988; Wayne Martin, DT, *1988;**

Jim Mabry, OT, *1989; Brandon Bulsworth, OL, 1998; Jermaine Petty, LB, 2001; **Shawn Andrews, OL, *2002, #*2003; Darren McFadden, RB, #*2006.**

ARKANSAS STATE: Ken Jones, OG, 1975; T. J. Humphreys, OG, 1976.

ARMY: Charles Romeyn, B, *1898; William Smith, E, *1900; Paul Bunker, T, *1901, T-HB, *1902; Charles Daly, QB (also Harvard), *1901; Robert Boyers, C, *1902; Arthur Tipton, C, *1904; Henry Torney, B, *1904, *1905; William Erwin, G, *1907; Leland Devore, T, *1911; Louis Merillat, E, *1913; John McEwan, C, *1914; Elmer Oliphant, HB, *1916, *1917; Edgar Garbisch, C, *1922, G 1924; Gus Farwick, G, 1924; Charles Born, E, 1925; Harry Wilson, HB, 1926; **Bud Sprague, T, *1926,** 1927; **Red Cagle, HB, *1927, #*1928, *1929;** Jack Price, T, 1930, 1931; **Milt Summerfelt, G, *1932;** Jack Buckler, B, 1933; Bill Shuler, E, 1935; Harry Stella, T, 1939; Robin Olds, T, 1942; Frank Merritt, T, 1942, 1943; **Casimir Myslinski, C, #*1943; Glenn Davis, HB*1944, #*1945, #*1946; Doc Blanchard, FB, *1944, #*1945, #*1946; Tex Coulter, T, *1945; John Green, G,** 1944, ***1945;** Barney Poole, E, 1944; Joe Stanowicz, G, 1944; Doug Kenna, QB, 1944; **Hank Foldberg, E,** 1945, ***1946;** Albert Nemetz, T, 1945; Arnold Tucker, QB, 1946; **Joe Steffy, G, *1947;** Joe Henry, G, 1948; Bobby Stuart, HB, 1948; **Arnold Galiffa, QB, *1949; Dan Foldberg, E,** 1949, **#*1950;** J. D. Kimmel, T, 1950; Charles Shira, T, 1950; Elmer Stout, C, 1950; Don Holleder, E, 1954; Ralph Chesnauskas, G, 1954; Tommy Bell, HB, 1954; **Bob Anderson, HB, *1957,** 1958; **Pete Dawkins, HB, #*1958;** Bob Novogratz, G, 1958; **Bill Carpenter, E, *1959;** Townsend Clarke, LB, 1966; Ken Johnson, LB, 1968; Don Smith, OG, 1985; Mike Mayweather, RB, 1990.

AUBURN: Jimmy Hitchcock, B, *1932; Roy Gafford, HB, 1942; Tex Warrington, C, 1944; Frank D'Agostino, T, 1955; Joe Childress, FB, 1955; **Jimmy Phillips, E, #*1957; Zeke Smith, G, *1958,** 1959; Jackie Burkett, C, 1958; **Ken Rice, T,** 1959, ***1960;** Ed Dyas, FB, 1960; Jimmy Sidle, QB, 1963; **Tucker Frederickson, B, *1964;** Jack Thornton, T, 1965; David Campbell, DT, 1968; **Buddy McClinton, DB, *1969; Larry Willingham, DB, *1970; Pat Sullivan, QB, #*1971; Terry Beasley, WR, #*1971; Ken Bernich, LB, *1974; Bo Jackson, TB, *1983, #*1985; Gregg Carr, LB, *1984;** Lewis Colbert, P, 1985; **Ben Tamburello, C, #*1986; Brent Fullwood, TB, #*1986; Tracy Rocker, DT, *1987, #*1988; Aundray Bruce, LB, *1987;** Stacy Searles, OT, 1987; Kurt Crain, LB, 1987; Ed King, OG, 1989, **#*1990; David Rocker, DL, *1990; Terry Daniel, P, *1993; Wayne Gandy, OL, *1993; Brian Robinson, DB, *1994;** Frank Sanders, WR, 1994; Chris Shelling, DB, 1994; Victor Riley, OL, 1997; Takeo Spikes, LB, 1997; **Damon Duval, PK, *2001;** Karlos Dansby, LB, 2003; Carnell Williams, RB, 2004; **Carlos Rogers, DB, *2004; Marcus McNeill, OL, *2005.**

BALL STATE: Brad Maynard, P, *1995, *1996.

BAYLOR: Barton Koch, G, *1930; Stan Williams, E, 1951; Larry Isbell, QB, 1951; Jim Ray Smith, T, 1953; **Bill Glass, G, #*1956;** Don Trull, QB, 1963; **Lawrence Elkins, E,**

*1963, B, *1964; Greg Pipes, DT, 1967; Roger Goree, DE, 1972; Aubrey Schulz, C, 1974; **Gary Green, DB, *1976; Mike Singletary, LB, *1979, #*1980;** Frank Ditta, OG, 1980; Gerald McNeil, WR, 1983; **Thomas Everett, DB,** 1985, #*1986; James Francis, LB, 1989; **Santana Dotson, DL, #*1991;** Adrian Robinson, DB, 1995; **Daniel Sepulveda, P, #*2006**.

BOSTON COLLEGE: Luke Urban, E, *1920; Charles Darling, B, 1924; Charles O'Rourke, HB, 1940; **Gene Goodreault, E, *1940;** Chet Gladchuck, C, 1940; **Mike Holovak, FB, *1942;** Fred Naumetz, C, 1942; Dan Currivan, E, 1942; Laurent Bouley, T, 1942; Al Krevis, OT, 1974; Steve Schindler, OG, 1976; **Doug Flutie, QB, #*1984; Tony Thurman, DB, *1984; Mike Ruth, MG, *1985;** Mark Chmura, TE, 1991; Stephen Boyd, LB, 1994; **Pete Mitchell, TE,** 1993, *1994; **Mike Cloud, RB, *1998;** Doug Brzezinski, OG, 1998; Chris Hovan, DL, 1999; Paul Zukauskas, OL, 2000; **William Green, RB, *2001;** Mathias Kiwanuka, DL, 2004; Josh Beekman, OL, 2006.

BOSTON UNIVERSITY: Harry Agganis, HB, 1951.

BOWLING GREEN: Chris Shale, P, 1990; Brian Leaver, PK, 1994.

BRIGHAM YOUNG: Eldon Forte, TB, 1962; Gifford Nielsen, QB, 1976; **Marc Wilson, QB, #*1979; Nick Eyre, OT, *1980; Jim McMahon, QB,** 1980, #*1982; **Gordon Hudson, TE, #*1982, #*1983; Steve Young, QB, #*1983;** Kyle Morrell, DB, 1984; **Jason Buck, DE, *1986;** Pat Thompson, P, 1988; **Mohammed Elewonibi, OG, *1989; Chris Smith, TE, #*1990; Ty Detmer, QB, *1990, *1991;** Itula Mili, TE, 1996; **Luke Staley, RB, *#2001;** Matt Payne, P, 2004; Johnny Harline, TE, 2006.

BROWN: Thomas Barry, HB, *1902; John Mayhew, HB, *1906; Adrian Regnier, E, *1909; Earl Sprackling, QB, *1910; George Crowther, QB, *1912; Fritz Pollard, HB, *1916; Hal Broda, E, 1926; Orland Smith, T, 1926; Roy Randall, QB, 1926.

BUCKNELL: John Dempsey, T, 1933.

CALIFORNIA: Brick Muller, E, *1921, *1922; Dan McMillan, T, *1921; Edwin Horrell, C, *1924; H. Dana Carey, G, 1925; **Irv Phillips, E, *1928;** Roy Riegles, C, 1929; Bert Schwarz, G, 1929; **Ted Beckett, G, *1930;** Rusty Gill, HB, 1931; Arleigh Williams, HB, 1934; **Larry Lutz, T, *1935;** Bob Herwig, C, 1936, 1937; **Sam Chapman, FB, *1937;** Vard Stockton, G, 1937; Perry Schwartz, E, 1937; **Vic Bottari, HB, *1938;** Bob Reinhard, T, 1940, 1941; Bill Hachten, G, 1944; **Jackie Jensen, FB, *1948; Rod Franz, G,** 1947, 1948, #*1949; Jim Turner, T, 1948, 1949; Forrest Klein, G, 1949; **Les Richter, G, *1950, *1951;** John Olszewski, HB, 1952; Matt Hazeltine, C, 1953, 1954; Paul Larson, QB, 1954; Joe Kapp, QB, 1958; Craig Morton, B, 1964; **Ed White, MG, *1968; Sherman White, DT, *1971; Steve Bartkowski, QB, *1974;** Chris Mackie, OG, 1974; **Chuck Muncie, RB, *1975; Steve Rivera, WR, *1975;** Ted Albrecht, OT, 1976; **Ron Rivera, LB, *1983;** Robbie Keen, P, 1989; Troy Auzenne, OL, 1991; **Russell White, RB, *1991; Sean Dawkins,**

WR, *1992; Todd Steussie, OL, 1993; Duane Clemons, LB, 1995; **Tony Gonzalez, TE, *1996;** Bobby Shaw, WR, 1997; **Deltha O'Neal, DB, *1999; Andre Carter, DL, #*2000; Nick Harris, P, *2000; J.J.Arrington, RB, *2004**; Ryan Riddle, DL, 2004; Marshawn Lynch, RB, 2006; **Daymeion Hughes, DB, *2006; DeSean Jackson, AP/KR, *2006**.

CARLISLE: Isaac Seneca, B, *1899; James Johnson, B, *1905; Albert Exendine, E, *1907; Peter Hauser, B, *1907; Jim Thorpe, HB, *1911, *1912.

CARNEGIE MELLON: Lloyd Yoder, T, 1926; Theodore Rosenzweig, E, 1928; **Howard Harpster, B, *1928.**

CENTENARY: Paul Geisler, E, *1933.

CENTRAL MICHIGAN: Brian Pruitt, AP, 1994.

CENTRE: James Weaver, C, *1919; Bo McMillin, QB, *1919, *1921; James Roberts, E, 1921.

CHICAGO: Clarence Herschberger, B, *1898; Fred Speik, E, *1904; Walter Eckersall, QB, *1904, *1905, *1906; Mark Catlin, E, *1905; Walter Steffen, B, *1908; Paul Des Jardien, C, *1913; C. G. Higgins, G, 1917; Charles McGuire, T, 1920, 1921; **John Thomas, B, *1922; Joe Pondelik, G, *1924;** Franklin Gowdy, T, 1924; Ellmore Patterson, C, 1934; **Jay Berwanger, HB,** 1934, ***1935.**

CINCINNATI: Mike Woods, LB, 1977; **Jonathan Ruffin, PK, *2000.**

CITADEL: John Small, LB, 1969; Brian Ruff, LB, 1976.

CLEMSON: Banks McFadden, HB, 1939; Joe Blaylock, E, 1941; Bobby Gage, DB, 1948; Jackie Calvert, DB, 1950; Wayne Mass, OT, 1966; **Harry Olszewski, OG, *1967; Bennie Cunningham, TE, *1974;** Joe Bostic, OG, 1977; Jerry Butler, SE, 1978; **Jim Stuckey, DT, *1979; Jeff Davis, LB, *1981; Terry Kinard, DB, *1981, #*1982; William Perry, MG, *1983**, 1984; John Phillips, OL, 1986; **Terrence Flagler, RB, *1986;** John Phillips, OG, 1986; **David Treadwell, PK, *1987;** Michael Dean Perry, DT, 1987; **Donnell Woolford, DB,** 1987, ***1988; Stacy Long, OL, *1990;** Rob Bodine, DL, 1991; **Jeb Flesch, OL, *1991; Levon Kirkland, LB, *1991; Tracy Seegars, OL, *1993; Anthony Simmons, LB,** 1996, ***1997; Keith Adams, LB,** 1999, ***2000; Tye Hill, DB, *2005; Gaines Adams, DL, #*2006.**

COLGATE: Ellery Huntington, QB, *1913; Earl Abell, T, 1915; **Clarence Horning, T, *1916; D. Belford West, T, *1916, *1919; Oscar Anderson, QB, *1916;** J. Edward Tryon, HB, 1925; **Leonard Macaluso, FB, *1930;** John Orsi, E, 1931; Robert Smith, G, 1932; Joe Bogdanski, E, 1934; Charles Wasicek, T, 1935; Macel Chesbro, T, 1936.

COLORADO: Byron "Whizzer" White, HB, *1937; Don Branby, E, 1952; Bob Stransky, HB, 1957; John Wooten, G, 1958; **Joe Romig, G, *1960, *1961;** Jerry Hillebrand, E, 1961; **Dick Anderson, DB, *1967; Mike Montler, OT, *1968; Bob Anderson, TB, *1969;** Bill Brundige, DE, 1969; **Don Popplewell, C, *1970;** Herb Orvis, DE, 1971; Bud Magrum, LB, 1972; **Cullen Bryant, DB, *1972;** Mark Koncar, OT, 1975; Matt Miller, OT, 1978; Mark Haynes, DB, 1979; **Barry Helton, P, *1985, *1986; Keith English, P, *1988; Alfred Williams, LB, *1989; Tom Rouen, P, *1989;** Kanavis McGhee, LB, 1989; **Eric Bieniemy, RB, #*1990; Joe Garten, OT, *1989, #*1990; Alfred Williams, LB, #*1990;** Jay Leeuwenburg, C, #*1991;** Joel Steed, DL, 1991; Mitch Berger, P, 1992; **Deon Figures, DB, *1992; Chris Hudson, DB, *1994; Rashaan Salaam, RB, #*1994; Michael Westbrook, WR, *1994;** Heath Irwin, OL, 1995; **Bryan Stoltenberg, C, *1995;** Rae Carruth, WR, 1996; **Chris Naeole, OL, *1996; Matt Russell, LB, *1996;** Brad Bedell, OG, 1999; Ben Kelly, DB, 1999; **Dan Graham, TE, *2001; Andre Gurode, OL, *2001;** Roman Hollowell, PR, 2001; Chris Brown, RB, 2002; Wayne Lucier, OL, 2002; **Mark Mariscal, P, *2002; Mason Crosby, PK, *2005,** 2006.

COLORADO COLLEGE: Earl Clark, QB, 1928.

COLORADO STATE: Thurman McGraw, T, 1948, 1949; Harvey Achziger, T, 1952; **Mike Bell, DL, *1978; Greg Myers, DB,** 1994, ***1995;** Anthony Cesario, OL, 1998.

COLUMBIA: Bill Morley, B, *1900, *1901; Harold Weekes, B, *1901; Richard Smith, B, *1903; Walter Koppisch, B, 1924; Tony Matal, E, 1933; Sid Luckman, QB, 1938; **Paul Governali, QB, *1942; Bill Swiacki, E, *1947.**

CORNELL: Clinton Wyckoff, B, *1895; Raymond Starbuck, B, *1900; William Warner, G, *1901, *1902; Sanford Hunt, G, *1901; Elmer Thompson, G, *1906; William Newman, C, *1906; Bernard O'Rourke, G, *1908; John O'Hearn, E, *1914; Charles Barrett, B, *1914, *1915; Murray Shelton, E, *1915; Edgar Kaw, B, *1921, *1922; George Pfann, B, *1923; Frank Sundstrom, T, 1923; Jose Martinez-Zorilla, E, 1932; **Brud Holland, E,** 1937, ***1938;** Sid Roth, G, 1938; William McKeever, T, 1938; **Nick Drahos, T, *1939, *1940; Ed Marinaro, RB,** 1970, **#*1971.**

DARTMOUTH: Henry Hooper, C, *1903; Myron Witham, QB, *1903; Joseph Gilman, G, *1904; Ralph Glaze, E, *1905; George Schildmiller, E, *1908; Clarke Tobin, G, *1908; Wesley Englehorn, T, *1912; Robert Hogsett, E, *1913; Clarence Spears, G, *1914, *1915; Milton Ghee, QB, 1914; **Eugene Neely, G, *1917; Adolph Youngstrom, G, *1919; Clark Diehl, G, *1924, *1925;** Henry Bjorkman, E, 1924; Edwin Dooley, B, 1924; Nathan Parker, T, 1925; **George Tully, E, *1925; Andy Oberlander, HB, #*1925;** Alton Marsters, HB, 1929; **Bob MacLeod, HB, *1938;** Dale Armstrong, E, 1948; Donald McKinnon, C, 1962; E. Winters Mabry, DB, 1966; Murry Bowden, DB, 1970; Reggie Williams, LB, 1975.

DAYTON: Fred Dugan, E, 1962.

DETROIT: Vince Banonis, C, 1941.

DRAKE: Ted Sloane, E, 1925; Johnny Bright, B, 1950

DUKE: Fred Crawford, T, *1933; Ace Parker, HB, *1936; Dan Hill, C, 1938; Eric Tipton, TB, 1938; Steve Lach, HB, 1941; Pat Preston, T, 1943; Bob Gantt, E, 1943; Ed Meadows, T, 1952, 1953; Tom Topping, T, 1957; Mike McGee, T, 1959; Claude Moorman, E, 1960; Jean Berry, G, 1962; Jay Wilkinson, HB, 1963; Bob Matheson, C, 1966; **Ernie Jackson, DB, *1971;** Billy Bryan, C, 1976; **Clarkston Hines, WR,** 1988, **#*1989;** Chris Port, OT 1989; Brian Morton, P, 2000; John Talley, DB, 2006.

DUQUESNE: Mike Basrak, C, *1936; John Rokisky, E, 1941.

EAST CAROLINA: Terry Long, OL, *1983; Carlester Crumpler, TE, 1993; **Robert Jones, LB, #*1991; Andrew Bayes, P, *1999.**

FLORIDA: Dale Vansickle, E, 1928; Charles LaPradd, T, 1952; John Barrow, G, 1956; Vel Heckman, T, 1958; Larry Dupree, FB, 1964; Chuck Casey, E, 1965; Lynn Matthews, E, 1965; Bruce Bennett, DB, 1965; **Steve Spurrier, QB,** 1965, **#*1966;** Guy Dennis, G, 1968; **Carlos Alvarez, FL, *1969;** Jack Youngblood, DE, 1970; **Sammy Green, LB, *1975;** Wes Chandler, SE, 1977; **David Little, LB, *1980;** David Galloway, DT, 1981; **Wilber Marshall, LB, *1982, *1983; Lomas Brown, OT, *1984;** Jeff Zimmerman, OT, 1985, 1986; Jarvis Williams, DB, 1987; **Louis Oliver, DB, *1988; Emmitt Smith, RB, #*1989;** Huey Richardson, DL, 1990; Will White, DB, 1990; **Brad Culpepper, DL, *1991;** Judd Davis, PK, 1993; Errict Rhett, RB, 1993; **Kevin Carter, DL, *1994; Jack Jackson, WR, *1994; Jason Odom, OL, #*1995; Reidel Anthony, WR, *1996; Ike Hilliard, WR, *1996; Danny Wuerffel, QB,** 1995, ***1996; Jacquez Green, WR, *1997; Fred Weary, DB, *1997;** Mike Peterson, LB, 1998; Jevon Kearse, LB, 1998; **Alex Brown, DL**, 1999, ***2001;** Lito Sheppard, DB, 2000; **Rex Grossman, QB, *2001; Jabar Gaffney, WR, *2001; Mike Pearson, OL, *2001;** Andra Davis, LB, 2001; Shannon Snell, OL, 2003; **Keiwan Ratliff, DB, *2003; Reggie Nelson, DB, *2006.**

FLORIDA STATE: Fred Biletnikoff, SE, *1964; Ron Sellers, FL, *1967, 1968; Dale McCullers, LB, 1968; Barry Smith, WR, 1972; Gary Huff, QB, 1972; **Ron Simmons, MG, *1979, *1980;** Rohn Stark, P, 1980, 1981; **Greg Allen, RB, *1983**, 1984; **Jamie Dukes, OG, *1985;** Paul McGowan, LB, 1987; Pat Tomberlin, OT, 1988; **Deion Sanders, DB, #*1987, #*1988; LeRoy Butler, DB, *1989;** Michael Tanks, C, 1989; Odell Haggins, MG, 1989; Lawrence Dawsey, WR, 1990; **Terrell Buckley, DB, #*1991; Marvin Jones, LB, *1991, #*1992;** Amp Lee, RB, 1991; Casey Weldon, QB, 1991; **Corey Sawyer, DB, *1993; Charlie Ward, QB, #*1993; Clifton Abraham, DB, *1994;** Derrick Alexander, DL, 1993,

1994; **Derrick Brooks, LB, #*1993, #*1994;** Kez McCorvey, WR, 1994; **Caly Shiver, OL,** 1994, ***1995; Peter Boulware, DL, *1996;** Warrick Dunn, RB, 1996; **Reinard Wilson, DL, *1996; Sam Cowart, LB, *1997;** Kevin Long, C, 1997; **Andre Wadsworth, DE, *1997; Peter Warrick, WR,** 1998, **#*1999; Sebastian Janikowski, PK,** 1998, **#*1999; Corey Simon, DL,** 1998, ***1999; Jason Whitaker, OL,** 1998, ***1999; Marvin Minnis, WR, *2000; Jamal Reynolds, DL, #*2000; Tay Cody, DB, *2000;** Chris Weinke, QB, 2000; Tarlos Thomas, OL, 2000; Brett Williams, OL, 2002; **Alex Barron, OL, *2003, #*2004;** Broderick Bunkley, DL, 2005; Buster Davis, LB, 2006.

FORDHAM: Henry Wisniewski, G, 1930; Jim Murphy, B, 1930; **Alex Wojciechowicz, C, *1936, *1937; Ed Franco, T, *1937;** Jim Lansing, E, 1941.

FRESNO STATE: Jackie Fellows, B, 1942; Steve Cordle, DB, 1981; Bernard Berrian, KR, 2001.

GEORGETOWN: Harry Connaughton, G, *1926; Augie Lio, G, 1940.

GEORGIA: Tom Nash, E, *1927; Ivey Shiver, E, 1927; Ralph Maddox, G, 1930; **Vernon Smith, E, *1931; Frank Sinkwich, HB, *1941, #*1942;** Mike Castonis, T, 1945; **Charley Trippi, HB, #*1946;** John Rauch, QB, 1948; John Carson, E, 1953; Pat Dye, G, 1959; Ray Rissmiller, E, 1964; Jim Wilson, T, 1964; George Patton, DT, 1965, 1966; **Ed Chandler, OG,** 1966, ***1967; Bill Stanfill, DT, *1968; Jake Scott, DB, *1968; Royce Smith, OG, #*1971;** Craig Hertwig, OT, 1974; **Randy Johnson, OG, *1975; Joel Parrish, OG, *1976;** Mike Wilson, OT, 1976; Rex Robinson, PK, 1980; Scott Woerner, DB, 1980; **Herschel Walker, TB, #*1980, #*1981, #*1982; Terry Hoage, DB, *1982, *1983;** Freddie Gilbert, DE, 1983; **Kevin Butler, PK, *1984; Jeff Sanchez, DB, *1984; Pete Anderson, C, *1985;** John Little, DB, 1986; Troy Sadowski, TE, 1988; **Tim Worley, RB, *1988; Garrison Hearst, RB, #*1992;** Bernard Williams, OL, 1993; Eric Zeier, QB, 1994; **Matt Stinchcomb, OL,** 1997, ***1998; Champ Bailey, DB, *1998;** Richard Seymour, DL, 2000; Jon Stinchcomb, OL, 2002; **David Pollack, DL, *2002,** 2003, ***2004;** Boss Bailey, LB, 2002; Sean Jones, DB, 2003; **Max Jean-Gilles, OL, *2005; Greg Blue, DB, *2005.**

GEORGIA TECH: Everett Strupper, B, *1917; Walker Carpenter, T, 1917; **Bill Fincher, E, *1918, *1920; Joe Guyon, T-HB, *1918; Ashel Day, C, *1918; Pete Pund, C, *1928;** Warner Mizell, B, 1928; Frank Speer, T, 1928; **Harvey Hardy, G, *1942;** John Steber, G, 1943; **Phil Tinsley, E, *1944; Paul Duke, C, *1946; Bob Davis, T, *1947;** George Brodnax, E, 1948; William Healy, DG, 1948; Lamar Wheat, T, 1951; Ray Beck, G, 1951; **Hal Miller, OT, *1952;** Buck Martin, E, 1952; Pete Brown, C, 1952; George Morris, LB, 1952; Bobby Moorhead, DB, 1952; Leon Hardeman, HB, 1952; **Larry Morris, C, *1953;** Don Stephenson, C, 1956, 1957; **Maxie Baughan, C, *1959;** Rufus Guthrie, G, 1962; Billy Lothridge, QB, 1963; Billy Martin, E, 1963; Gerry Bussell, DB, 1964; **Jim Breland, C, *1966;** Lenny Snow, TB, 1966; **Rock Perdoni, DT, *1970;** Smylie Gebhart, DE, 1971; **Randy Rhino, DB,**

1972, ***1973**, 1974; Lucius Sanford, LB, 1977; Pat Swilling, DE, 1985; **Ken Swilling, DB, #*1990;** Marco Coleman, LB, 1991; Coleman Rudolph, DL, 1992; Scott Sisson, PK, 1992; **Craig Page, C, *1998; Joe Hamilton, QB, *1999; Chris Brown, OL, *2001; Thomas Davis, DB, *2004; Calvin Johnson, WR,** 2005; **#*2006.**

GONZAGA: George Karamatic, TB, 1937.

GRAMBLING: Alphonse Dotson, E, 1964; Doug Williams, QB, 1977.

HARVARD: Arthur Cumnock, E, *1889; John Cranston, G, *1889; C, *1890; James Lee, HB, *1889; Frank Hallowell, E, *1890, *1892; Marshall Newell, T*1890, *1891, *1892, *1893; Dudley Dean, QB, *1890; John Corbett, HB, *1890; Everett Lake, HB, *1891; Bertram Waters, G, *1892, T, *1894; William Lewis, C, *1892, *1893; Charles Brewer, HB, *1892, *1893, *1895; Norman Cabot, E, *1895, *1896; Edgar Wrightington, HB, *1896; Alan Doucette, C, *1897; Benjamin Dibblee, B, *1897, *1898; John Hallowell, E, *1898, *1900; Walter Boal, G, *1898; Charles Daly, QB (also Army)*1898, *1899, *1900; David Campbell, E, *1899, *1900, *1901; Edward Bowditch, E, *1901, *1902; Oliver Cutts, T, *1901; Crawford Blagden, T, *1901; William Lee, G, *1901; Charles Barnard, G, *1901; Robert Kernan, HB, *1901; Thomas Graydon, FB, *1901, *1902; Daniel Knowlton, T, *1903; Andrew Marshall, G, *1903; Daniel Hurley, HB, *1904, *1905; Beaton Squires, T, *1905; Karl Brill, T, *1905; Francis Burr, G, *1905, *1906; Charles Osborne, T, *1906; Patrick Grant, C, *1907; John Wendell, HB, *1907; Hamilton Fish, T, *1908, *1909; Charles Nourse, C, *1908; Hamilton Corbett, HB, *1908; Wayland Minot, HB, *1909; Robert McKay, T, *1910; Robert Fisher, G, *1910, *1911; Percy Wendell, HB, *1910, *1911; Samuel Felton, E, *1912; Stanley Pennock, G, *1912, *1913, *1914; Charles Brickley, HB, *1912, *1913; Harvey Hitchcock, T, *1913; Edward Mahan, FB, *1913, *1914, *1915; Huntington Hardwick, E, *1914; Frederick Bradlee, HB, 1914; **Walter Trumbull, T, *1914; Joseph Gilman, T, *1915; Richard King, HB, *1915; Harrie Dadmun, G, *1916; Edward Casey, HB, *1919; Tom Woods, G, *1920;** James Tolbert, G, 1920; Arnold Horween, FB, 1920; **John Brown, G, *1921; Charles Hubbard, G, *1922, *1923; Ben Ticknor, C, *1929, *1930; Barry Wood, QB, *1931; Endicott Peabody, G, *1941;** Pat McInally, TE, 1974.

HASKELL: John Levi, HB, 1923.

HAWAII: Al Noga, DT, 1986; Jason Elam, PK, 1992.

HOLY CROSS: Hilary Mahaney, E, 1924; Chet Millett, G, 1951; **John Provost, DB-RB, *1974;** Gordon Lockbaum, DB-RB, 1986.

HOUSTON: J. D. Kimmel, DT, 1952; Hogan Wharton, T, 1958; **Rich Stotter, OG, *1967;** Ken Hebert, SE, 1967; Paul Gipson, FB, 1968; **Bill Bridges, OG, *1969; Elmo Wright,**

WR, *1970; Mack Mitchell, DE, 1974; Robert Giblin, DB, 1974; **Wilson Whitley, DT, *1976;** Melvin Jones, OT, 1979; David Hodge, LB, 1979; **Leonard Mitchell, DT, *1980;** Hosea Taylor, MG, 1980; **Jason Phillips, WR, *1988; Andre Ware, QB, *1989;** Emmanuel Hazard, WR, 1989; Ben Fricke, C, 1997.

IDAHO: John Yarno, C, 1976.

ILLINOIS: Perry Graves, E, *1914; Ralph Chapman, G, *1914; Bart Macomber, HB, *1915; John Depler, C, *1918; Charles Carney, E, *1920; James McMillen, G, *1923; Red Grange, HB, *1923, #*1924, *1925; Bernie Shively, G, *1926; Russ Crane, G, 1927; Robert Reitsch, C, 1927; Albert Nowack, T, 1928; Leroy Wietz, G, 1928; Lou Gordon, T, 1929; Jim Reeder, T, 1939; **Alex Agase, G,** 1942, *1946; Buddy Young, HB, 1944; Ralph Serpico, G, 1944; Bill Vohaska, C, 1950; Al Tate, T, 1950; **Johnny Karras, HB, *1951;** Al Brosky, DB, 1951; Charles Ulrich, T, 1951; Charles Boerio, LB, 1951; **J. C. Caroline, HB, *1953; Bill Burrell, G, *1959; Dick Butkus, C, #*1963, *1964;** George Donnelly, DB, 1964; **Jim Grabowski, FB,** 1964, #*1965; Don Thorpe, DT, 1983; **David Williams, WR, #*1984, #*1985; Moe Gardner, DT, #*1989, *1990;** Tim Simpson, OL, 1991; **Dana Howard, LB,** 1993, #*1994; Simeon Rice, LB, 1994, 1995; **Kevin Hardy, LB, *1995.**

INDIANA: Corby Davis, FB, 1937; **Billy Hillenbrand, HB, *1942;** Pete Pihos, E, 1943; **John Tavener, C, *1944; Bob Ravensberg, E, *1945;** George Taliaferro, HB, 1948; Tom Nowatzke, FB, 1964; Don Croftcheck, G, 1964; Garry Cassells, G, 1967; Ernie Jones, WR, 1987; **Anthony Thompson, RB, *1988, #*1989; Vaughn Dunbar, RB, #*1991**; Antwaan Randle El, QB, 2001; Marcus Thigpen, AP/KR, 2006.

IOWA: Lester Belding, E, *1919; Aubrey Devine, QB, *1921; Gordon Locke, FB, *1922; Dick Romney, E, 1925; Willis Glassgow, HB, 1929; Francis Schammel, G, 1933; Ozzie Simmons, HB, 1935; **Nile Kinnick, HB, *1939;** Mike Enich, T, 1940; Jerry Hilgenberg, C, 1953; **Calvin Jones, G, *1954, *1955; Alex Karras, T,** 1956, *1957; Jim Gibbons, E, 1957; Curt Merz, E, 1958; **Randy Duncan, QB, #*1958;** Don Norton, E, 1959; Mark Manders, G, 1960; Larry Ferguson, HB, 1960; Bill Van Buren, C, 1961; Mike Reilly, G, 1963; Karl Noonan, E, 1964; Craig Clemons, DB, 1971; **Andre Tippett, DE, *1981; Reggie Roby, P, *1981; Larry Station, LB, *1984, #*1985; Chuck Long, QB, #*1985;** Dave Croston, OT, 1986; Dave Haight, MG, 1988; **Marv Cook, TE, *1988; Leroy Smith, DL, *1991;** Mike Devlin, OL, 1992; **Tim Dwight, KR,** 1996, *1997; **Jared DeVries, DL, *1998; Dallas Clark, TE, *2002; Eric Steinbach, OL, *2002**; Brad Banks, QB, 2002; Bruce Nelson, OL, 2002; **Nate Kaeding, PK,** 2002, *2003; **Robert Gallery, OL, *2003**.

IOWA STATE: Ed Bock, G, *1938; Jim Doran, WR, 1950; Dwight Nichols, RB, 1959; Dave Hoppmann, TB, 1962; Tom Vaughn, FB, 1963; John Van Sicklen, OT, 1964; Matt Blair, LB, 1973; Luther Blue, SE, 1976; **Mike Busch, TE, *1989; Troy Davis, RB, *1995, *1996.**

KANSAS: Ray Evans, HB, 1947; George Mrkonic, DT, 1951; Oliver Spencer, T, 1952; Gil Reich, QB, 1952; John Hadl, HB, 1960, QB, 1961; **Gale Sayers, HB, *1963, *1964;** Bob Douglass, QB, 1968; **John Zook, DE, *1968; Dave Jaynes, QB, *1973;** Bruce Kallmeyer, PK, 1983; Ron Warner, LB, 1997.

KANSAS STATE: Henry Cronkite, E, 1931; George Maddox, T, 1934; Clarence Scott, DB, 1970; **Gary Spani, LB, *1977; Sean Snyder, P, *1992;** Jaime Mendez, DB, 1993; Tom Coleman, DL, 1995; **Chris Canty, DB, *1995, #*1996; Martin Gramatica, PK, *1997**, 1998; **Michael Bishop, QB, *1998; Jeff Kelly, LB, *1998; David Allen, KR, *1998,** RS 1999; **Mark Simoneau, LB, *1999;** Mario Fatafeni, DL, 2000; Quincy Morgan, WR, 2000; **Terence Newman, DB, #*2002;** Darren Sproles, RB, 2003; Josh Buhl, LB, 2003.

KENT STATE: Jim Corrigall, LB, 1969.

KENTUCKY: Clyde Johnson, T, 1942; **Bob Gain**, G, 1949, **T *1950; Babe Parilli, QB, *1950, *1951;** Doug Moseley, C, 1951; Steve Meilinger, E, 1952, 1953; Ray Correll, G, 1953; Howard Schnellenberger, E, 1955; **Lou Michaels, T, *1956, *1957;** Herschel Turner, T, 1963; **Sam Ball, OT, *1965;** Warren Bryant, OT, 1976; **Art Still, DE, #*1977; Tim Couch, QB, *1998; James Whalen, TE, *1999; Derek Abney, AP, *2002.**

LAFAYETTE: Walter Bachman, C, *1900, *1901; Frank Schwab, G, *1921, *1922; Charles Berry, E, 1924; George Wilson, HB, 1926.

LEHIGH: Bill Ciaravino, G, 1950.

LONG BEACH STATE: Leon Burns, FB, 1970.

LOUISIANA STATE: Gaynell Tinsley, E, *1935, #*1936; Ken Kavanaugh, E, *1939; George Tarasovic, C, 1951; **Sid Fournet, T, *1954;** Jimmy Taylor, FB, 1957; Max Fugler, C, 1958; **Billy Cannon, HB, #*1958, *1959; Roy Winston, G, #*1961; Jerry Stovall, HB, #*1962;** Fred Miller, T, 1962; Remi Prudhomme, T, 1964; John Garlington, E, 1967; George Bevan, LB, 1969; **Mike Anderson, LB, *1970; Tommy Casanova, DB, *1970, *1971;** Ronnie Estay, DT, 1971; **Bert Jones, QB, *1972;** Warren Capone, LB, 1972, 1973; Tyler Lafauci, OG, 1973; Mike Williams, DB, 1974; **Charles Alexander, RB, *1977, *1978;** Lance Smith, OT, 1984; Michael Brooks, LB, 1985; **Wendell Davis, SE,** 1986, ***1987; Nacho Albergamo, C, #*1987;** Kevin Faulk, AP, 1996; David LaFleur, TE, 1996; **Chad Kessler, P, *1997; Alan Faneca, OG, *1997;** Todd McClure, C, 1998; Anthony McFarland, DL, 1998; **Josh Reed, WR, *2001**; Bradie James, LB, 2002; Stephen Peterman, OL, 2003; **Chad Lavalais, DL, *2003**; Corey Webster, DB, 2003, 2004; **Ben Wilkerson, OL, *2004; Marcus Spears, DL, *2004**; Glenn Dorsey, DL, 2006; **LaRon Landry, DB, *2006.**

LOUISIANA TECH: Mike Barber, TE, 1975; **Willie Roaf, OL, *1992; Troy Edwards, WR, *1998.**

LOUISVILLE: Ken Kortas, E, 1963; Tom Jackson, LB, 1972; Jamie Asher, TE, 1994; Sam Madison, DB, 1996; Ibn Green, TE, 1999; Anthony Floyd, DB, 2000; **Elvis Dumervil, DL, #*2005.**

MARQUETTE: Arthur Krueger, C, 1932; **Ray Buivid, B, *1936.**

MARSHALL: Randy Moss, WR, #*1997; Jonathan Goddard, DL, 2004.

MARYLAND: Bob Ward, G, 1950, **#*1951;** Ed Modzelewski, FB, 1951; **Dick Modzelewski, DT, *1952; Jack Scarbath, QB, #*1952; Stan Jones, T, #*1953;** Bernie Faloney, QB, 1953; Mike Sandusky, T, 1955; **Bob Pellegrini, C, #*1955; Gary Collins, E, *1961;** Paul Vellano, DG, 1973; **Randy White, DT,** 1973, **#*1974; Joe Campbell, DT, *1976; Dale Castro, PK, *1979; J. D. Maarleveld, OT, *1985**; Bruce Perry, RB, 2001; Melvin Fowler, OL, 2001; **E.J. Henderson, LB, *2001, *2002;** Vernon Davis, TE, 2005; D'Qwell Jackson, LB, 2005.

MEMPHIS: Harry Schuh, T, 1963, 1964; Eric Harris, DB, 1976; **Joe Allison, PK, *1992**, DeAngelo Williams, RB, 2005.

MIAMI (FLORIDA): Al Carapella, T, 1950; Frank McDonald, E, 1954; Don Bosseler, FB, 1956; **Bill Miller, E,** 1960, ***1961;** George Mira, QB, 1962; Ed Weisacosky, E, 1965; **Tom Beier, DB, *1966; Ted Hendricks, DE, #*1967, #*1968; Tony Cristiani, MG, *1973; Rubin Carter, MG, *1974;** Eddie Edwards, DT, 1976; Don Smith, DT, 1978; Lester Williams, DT, 1981; **Fred Marion, DB, *1981; Eddie Brown, WR, *1984; Willie Smith, TE, *1985; Vinny Testaverde, QB, #*1986; Jerome Brown, DT, #*1986; Bennie Blades, DB, *1986, #*1987; Daniel Stubbs, DE, #*1987; Bill Hawkins, DE, *1988; Steve Walsh, QB, *1988; Greg Mark, DL, *1989; Maurice Crum, LB, *1990; Russell Maryland, DL, #*1990; Carlos Huerta, PK, *1991;** Leon Searcy, OL, 1991; **Darryl Williams, DB, *1991;** Kevin Williams, PR, 1991; Darrin Smith, LB, 1991, 1992; **Ryan McNeil, DB, *1992; Gino Torretta, QB, #*1992; Micheal Barrow, LB, *1992;** Kevin Patrick, DL, 1993; C. J. Richardson, DB, 1994; **Warren Sapp, DL, #*1994;** Ray Lewis, LB, 1995; K. C. Jones, C, 1996; Daniel Franks, TE, 1999; Richard Mercier, OG, 1999; Joaquin Gonzalez, OL, 2000; **Bryant McKinnie, OL,** 2000, ***#2001; Santana Moss, AP, *2000; Dan Morgan, LB, #*2000; Edward Reed, DB, *2000, #*2001**; Jeremy Shockey, TE, 2001; Joaquin Gonzalez, OL, 2001; Todd Sievers, PK, 2001; **Willis McGahee, RB, *2002; Brett Romberg, C, *2002**; Ken Dorsey, QB, 2002; Jerome McDougle, DL, 2002; **Kellen Winslow, TE, #*2003; Sean Taylor, DB, #*2003**; Jonathan Vilma, LB, 2003; Devin Hetser, KR, 2004; **Antrel Rolle, DB, #*2004**; Eric Winston, OL, 2005; Brandon Meriweather, DB, 2005.

MIAMI (OHIO): Bob Babich, LB, 1968; Brad Cousino, LB, 1974.

MICHIGAN: William Cunningham, C, *1898; Neil Snow, E, *1901; Willie Heston, HB, *1903, *1904; Adolph Schulz, C, *1907; Albert Benbrook, G, *1909, *1910; Stan-

field Wells, E, *1910; Miller Pontius, T, *1913; Jim Craig, HB, *1913; John Maulbetsch, HB, *1914; Frank Culver, G, 1917; Frank Steketee, FB, 1918; Henry Vick, C, 1921; **Harry Kipke, HB, *1922; Jack Blott, C, *1923;** Edliff Slaughter, G, 1924; Robert Brown, C, 1925; **Bennie Oosterbaan, E, *1925, *1926, #*1927; Benny Friedman, QB, *1925, *1926; Otto Pommerening, T, *1928;** Maynard Morrison, C, 1931; **Harry Newman, QB, #*1932;** Ted Petoskey, E, 1932, 1933; **Francis Wistert, T, *1933; Chuck Bernard, C,** 1932, **#*1933; Ralph Heikkinen, G, #*1938; Tom Harmon, HB, *1939, #*1940;** Ed Frutig, E, 1940; **Bob Westfall, FB, *1941; Albert Wistert, T, *1942; Julie Franks, G, *1942; Bill Daley, FB, #*1943;** Merv Pregulman, T, 1943; Elmer Madar, E, 1946; **Bob Chappuis, HB, #*1947;** Bump Elliott, HB, 1947; Pete Elliott, QB, 1948; **Dick Rifenburg, E, *1948; Alvin Wistert, T, *1948, *1949;** Allen Wahl, T, 1949, 1950; Lowell Perry, E, 1951; Art Walker, T, 1954; **Ron Kramer, E, *1955, #*1956;** Jim Pace, HB, 1957; Bob Timberlake, QB, 1964; **Bill Yearby, DT,** 1964, ***1965; Jack Clancy, E, #*1966;** Ron Johnson, HB, 1968; **Jim Mandich, TE, #*1969; Tom Curtis, DB, *1969;** Henry Hill, MG, 1970; Marty Huff, LB, 1970; **Dan Dierdorf, OT, *1970; Reggie McKenzie, OG, *1971; Mike Taylor, LB, #*1971;** Tom Darden, DB, 1971; **Paul Seymour, OT, *1972; Randy Logan, DB, *1972; Dave Gallagher, DT, *1973; Dave Brown, DB, *1973, #*1974;** Don Dufek, DB, 1975; Jim Smith, WR, 1976; Calvin O'Neal, LB, 1976; **Rob Lytle, RB, *1976; Mark Donahue, OG, *1976, #*1977;** Walt Downing, C, 1977; John Anderson, LB, 1977; Rick Leach, QB, 1978; **Ron Simpkins, LB, *1979;** Curtis Greer, DT, 1979; **Anthony Carter, WR,** 1980, **#*1981, #*1982; Ed Muransky, OT, *1981; Kurt Becker, OG, *1981;** Stefan Humphries, OG, 1983; Tom Dixon, C, 1983; **Mike Hammerstein, DT, *1985; Brad Cochran, DB, *1985; John Elliott, OT,** 1986, ***1987; Garland Rivers, DB, *1986; John Vitale, C, *1988; Mark Messner, DT, #*1988; Tripp Welborne, DB, #*1989, #*1990;** Dean Dingman, OL, 1990; **Greg Skrepanek, OL,** 1990, **#*1991;** Erick Anderson, LB, 1991; **Desmond Howard, WR, #*1991;** Chris Hutchinson, DL, 1992; Remy Hamilton, PK, 1994; Ty Law, DB, 1994; Jason Horn, DL, 1995; **Jarrett Irons, LB, *1996;** Rod Payne, C, 1996; **Charles Woodson, DB,** 1996, **#*1997;** Glen Steele, DL, 1997; Jerame Tuman, TE, 1997; Jon Jenson, OL, 1998; Rob Renes, DT, 1999; **Steve Hutchinson, OL, #*2000;** Marquise Walker, WR, 2001; Larry Foote, LB, 2001; **Chris Perry, RB, *2003; Braylon Edwards, WR, #*2004; David Baas, OL, *2004; Marlin Jackson, DB, *2004; Ernest Shazor, DB, *2004; Jake Long, OL,** 2006; **LaMarr Woodley, DL, #*2006; Leon Hall, DB, *2006**

MICHIGAN STATE: Neno Jerry DaPrato, HB, *1915; Sidney Wagner, G, *1935; Johnny Pingel, HB, 1938; Lynn Chandnois, HB, 1949; **Ed Bagdon, G, *1949;** Dorne Dibble, E, 1950; Sonny Grandelius, HB, 1950; Al Dorow, QB, 1951; **Bob Carey, E, *1951; Don Coleman, T, #*1951;** Frank Kush, G, 1952; Dick Tamburo, C, 1952; Don McAuliffe, HB, 1952; **Don Dohoney, E, *1953; Norman Masters, T, *1955; Earl Morrall, QB, *1955; Dan Currie, C, *1957; Walt Kowalczyk, HB, *1957; Sam Williams, E, *1958;** Dean Look, QB, 1959; Dave Behrman, G, 1961; **George Saimes, FB, *1962; Sherman Lewis, HB, *1963; Bubba Smith, DE, *1965, #*1966; George Webster, DB, #*1965, #*1966;** Gene Washington, E, 1965, 1966; Harold Lucas, MG, 1965; Ron Goovert, LB, 1965; Steve Juday, QB, 1965; **Clint Jones, HB,** 1965, ***1966;** Jerry West, T, 1966; Al Brenner, DB, 1968; Ron

Saul, OG, 1969; Eric Allen, RB, 1971; Ron Curl, DT, 1971; **Brad Van Pelt, DB,** 1971, **#*1972;** Kirk Gibson, FL, 1978; Mark Brammer, TE, 1978; Morten Andersen, PK, 1981; Carl Banks, LB, 1983; Greg Montgomery, P, 1986; **Lorenzo White, TB, #*1985, *1987; Tony Mandarich, OT, *1988; Bob Kula, OT, *1989; Percy Snow, LB, #*1989;** Flozell Adams, OL, 1997; Robaire Smith, DL, 1998; Julian Peterson, LB, 1999; Herb Haygood, KR, 2001; **Charles Rogers, WR, #*2002; Brandon Fields, P, *2004.**

MINNESOTA: Fred Schacht, T, ***1903; John McGovern, QB, *1909; James Walker, T, *1910; Bert Baston, E,** 1915, ***1916;** Claire Long, QB, 1916; **George Hauser, T,** 1916, ***1917; Ray Ecklund, E, *1923;** Earl Martineau, HB, 1923; **Herb Joesting, FB, *1926, *1927;** Harold Hanson, G, 1927; George Gibson, G, 1928; Kenneth Haycraft, E, 1928; **Bronko Nagurski, T, *1929;** Robert Tanner, E, 1929; **Biggie Munn, G, *1931; Frank Larson, E,** 1933, ***1934; Bill Bevan, G, *1934; Pug Lund, HB,** 1933, ***1934; Ed Widseth, T,** 1934, ***1935, #*1936;** Dick Smith, T, 1935; Sheldon Beise, FB, 1935; Andy Uram, FB, 1936; Ray King, E, 1937; Francis Twedell, G, 1938; Helge Pukema, G, 1940; **Urban Odson, T, *1940; George Franck, HB, *1940; Dick Wildung, T, *1941, *1942; Bruce Smith, HB, *1941; Leo Nomellini, T-G, *1948, *1949; Clayton Tonnemaker, C, #*1949; Paul Giel, HB,** 1952, **#*1953;** Bob McNamara, FB-HB, 1954; Bob Hobert, T, 1956; **Tom Brown, G, #*1960; Sandy Stephens, QB, *1961; Bobby Bell, T,** 1961, ***1962; Carl Eller, T, *1963; Aaron Brown, DE, *1965;** Bob Stein, E, 1967; Doug Kingsriter, TE, 1970; Lemanzer Williams, DL, 1997; **Tyrone Carter, DB,** 1998, ***1999; Ben Hamilton, C, OL, *1999, *2000;** Preston Gruening, P, 2000; **Greg Eslinger, OL,** 2004, **#*2005;** Matt Spaeth, TE, 2006.

OLE MISS: Frank Kinard, T, 1936, 1937; Parker Hall, HB, 1938; **Charley Conerly, TB, *1947;** Barney Poole, E, 1947, 1948; Kline Gilbert, T, 1952; **Crawford Mims, G, *1953;** Rex Boggan, T, 1954; Jack Simpson, G, 1957; **Charlie Flowers, FB, *1959;** Marvin Terrell, G, 1959; **Jake Gibbs, QB, #*1960;** Billy Ray Adams, FB, 1961; **Jim Dunaway, T, *1962;** Glynn Griffing, QB, 1962; Kenny Dill, C, 1963; Allen Brown, E, 1964; Glenn Cannon, DB, 1969; Harry Harrison, DB, 1973; **Jim Miller, P, *1979;** Fred Nunn, DE, 1984; Bill Smith, P, 1985, 1986; Wesley Walls, TE, 1988; **Everett Lindsay, OL, *1992; Rufus French, TE, #*1998; Terrence Metcalf, OL, *2001; Patrick Willis, LB, *2006.**

MISSISSIPPI STATE: Buddy Elrod, E, 1940; Jackie Parker, QB, 1953; Hal Easterwood, C, 1954; Scott Suber, G, 1955; Art Davis, HB, 1955; D.D. Lewis, LB, 1967; **Jimmy Webb, DT, *1974;** Glen Collins, DT, 1981; Johnnie Cooks, LB, 1981; Barrin Simpson, LB, 1999; **Fred Smoot, DB, *2000.**

MISSISSIPPI VALLEY: Jerry Rice, WR, 1984.

MISSOURI: Edgar Lindenmeyer, T, 1925; Paul Christman, TB, 1939; **Darold Jenkins, C, *1941;** Bob Steuber, HB, 1942; Harold Burnine, E, 1955; **Danny LaRose, E, #*1960;** Ed Blaine, T, 1961; Conrad Hitchler, E, 1962; **Johnny Roland, DB, *1965; Roger Wehrli,**

DB, *1968; Mike Carroll, OG, 1969; John Moseley, DB, 1973; Henry Marshall, SE, 1975; **Kellen Winslow, TE, *1978;** Jeff Gaylord, DT, 1981; Conrad Goode, OT, 1983; **John Clay, OL, *1986;** Devin West, RB, 1998; **Rob Riti, C, *1999;** Justin Smith, DL, 2000.

MONTANA STATE: Bill Kollar, DL, 1973.

NAVY: Bill Dague, E, *1907; Percy Northcroft, T, *1908; Ed Lange, QB, *1908; Jack Dalton, FB, *1911; John Brown, G, *1913; Ernest Von Heimberg, E, 1917; **Lyman Perry, G, *1918; Wolcott Roberts, HB, *1918; Wendell Taylor, E, *1922; Frank Wickhorst, T, #*1926;** Tom Hamilton, B, 1926; **Ed Burke, G, *1928;** Slade Cutter, T, 1934; **Fred Borries, HB, *1934; Don Whitmire, T, *1943, #*1944;** George Brown, G, 1943; **Ben Chase, G, *1944; Bob Jenkins, HB, *1944; Dick Duden, E, *1945;** Dick Scott, C, 1945, 1947; Steve Eisenhauer, G, 1952, 1953; **Ron Beagle, E, *1954, #*1955;** Bob Reifsnyder, T, 1957; Tom Forrestal, QB, 1957; **Joe Bellino, HB, #*1960;** Greg Mather, E, 1961; **Roger Staubach, QB, #*1963; Chet Moeller, DB, #*1975; Napoleon McCallum, TB, *1983, *1985.**

NEBRASKA: Vic Halligan, T, 1914; **Guy Chamberlin, E, *1915; Ed Weir, T, *1924, #*1925;** Lonnie Stiner, T, 1926; Dan McMullen, G, 1928; Ray Richards, T, 1929; Hugh Rhea, T, 1930; Lawrence Ely, C, 1932; **George Sauer, FB, *1933; Sam Francis, FB, *1936;** Fred Shirey, T, 1937; Charles Brock, C, 1937; Warren Alfson, G, 1940; Forrest Behm, T, 1940; Tom Novak, C, 1949; Bob Reynolds, HB, 1950; Jerry Minnick, T, 1952; **Bob Brown, G, #*1963; Larry Kramer, OT, #*1964; Freeman White, SE, *1965; Walt Barnes, DT, *1965;** Tony Jeter, TE, 1965; Larry Wachholtz, DB, 1966; **LaVerne Allers, OG, *1966; Wayne Meylan, MG, *1966, *1967;** Joe Armstrong, OG, 1968; Jerry Murtaugh, LB, 1970; **Bob Newton, OT, *1970; Johnny Rodgers, WB, *1971, #*1972; Willie Harper, DE, *1971, *1972; Rich Glover, MG,** 1971, #*1972; **Larry Jacobson, DT, *1971;** Daryl White, OT, 1972, 1973; **John Dutton, DT, #*1973; Marvin Crenshaw, OT, *1974; Rik Bonness, C,** 1974, *1975; David Humm, QB, 1974; Wonder Monds, DB, 1975; Mike Fultz, DT, 1976; **Dave Butterfield, DB, *1976;** Tom Davis, C, 1977; **Kelvin Clark, OT, *1978; Junior Miller, TE, #*1979; Randy Schleusener, OG, *1980; Jarvis Redwine, RB, *1980;** Derrie Nelson, DE, 1980; Jimmy Williams, DE, 1981; **Dave Rimington, C, #*1981, #*1982; Mike Rozier, RB, *1982, #*1983; Irving Fryar, WB, #*1983; Dean Steinkuhler, OG, *1983; Mark Traynowicz, C, #*1984;** Bret Clark, DB, 1984; Bill Lewis, C, 1985; Jim Skow, DT, 1985; **Danny Noonan, DL, *1986;** John McCormick, OL, 1987; **Jake Young, C, *1988, *1989; Broderick Thomas, DE,** 1987, #*1988; Doug Glaser, OT, 1989; Kenny Walker, DL, 1990; Travis Hill, DL, 1992; **Will Shields, OL, #*1992; Trev Alberts, LB, #*1993; Brenden Stai, OL, *1994; Ed Stewart, LB, *1994; Zach Wiegert, OL, #*1994; Tommie Frazier, QB, *1995;** Aaron Graham, OL, 1995; Jared Tomich, DL, 1995, 1996; **Aaron Taylor, C, *1996, #*1997; Grant Wistrom, DL, *1996, *1997; Jason Peter, DT, *1997; Ralph Brown, DB, *1999;** Mike Brown, DB, 1999; Carlos Polk, LB, 2000; Russ Hochstein, OL, 2000; **Dominic Raiola, C, *2000; Toniu Fonoti, OL, *2001;** Eric Crouch, QB, 2001; Keyou Craver, DB, 2001; DeJuan Groce, AP, 2002; Josh Bullocks, DB, 2003; Kyle Larson, P, 2003.

NEVADA: Stan Heath, QB, 1948; Marty Zendejas, PK, 1986, 1987; Nate Burleson, WR, 2002.

NEW MEXICO: Bob Berg, PK, 1975; **Terance Mathis, WR, *1989; Brian Urlacher, DB, *1999.**

NEW MEXICO STATE: Pervis Atkins, HB, 1960.

NEW YORK UNIVERSITY: Al Lassman, T, 1926; **Ken Strong, B, *1928.**

NORTH CAROLINA: George Barclay, G, 1934; **Andy Bershak, E, *1937;** Paul Severin, E, 1939, 1940; Art Weiner, E, 1948, 1949; **Charlie Justice, B, *1948,** 1949; Irvin Holdash, C, 1950; Al Goldstein, E, 1958; Bob Lacey, E, 1963; **Don McCauley, HB, *1970; Ron Rusnak, G, *1972; Ken Huff, G, *1974; Dee Hardison, DT, *1977; Lawrence Taylor, LB, #*1980;** David Drechsler, OG, 1981, 1982; Brian Blados, OT, 1983; **William Fuller, DT,** 1982, ***1983;** Harris Barton, OT, 1986; Bracey Walker, DB, 1993; **Marcus Jones, DL, *1995; Dre' Bly, DB, *1996, *1997,** 1998; **Greg Ellis, DE, *1997; Brian Simmons, LB, *1997;** Brian Schmitz, P, 1999; **Julius Peppers, DL, #*2001.**

NORTH CAROLINA STATE: Dick Christy, HB, 1957; Roman Gabriel, QB, 1960, 1961; **Dennis Byrd, DT,** 1966, ***1967;** Fred Combs, DB, 1967; Ron Carpenter, DT, 1968; **Bill Yoest, G, *1973;** Don Buckey, SE, 1975; **Jim Ritcher, C, *1978, #*1979; Ted Brown, RB, *1978; Marc Primanti, PK, *1996; Torry Holt, WR, *1998;** Levar Fisher, LB, 2000, 2001; Terrence Holt, DB, 2002.

NORTH TEXAS: Joe Greene, DT, *1968.

NORTHERN ILLINOIS: LeShon Johnson, RB, #*1993.

NORTHWESTERN: Tim Lowry, C, 1925; **Ralph Baker, HB, *1926;** Bob Johnson, T, 1926; Harry Anderson, G, 1929; **Frank Baker, E, *1930;** Fayette Russell, FB, 1930; Wade Woodworth, G, 1930; **Jack Riley, T, *1931; Dallas Marvil, T, *1931; Pug Rentner, HB, *1931;** Edgar Manske, E, 1933; Paul Tangora, G, 1935; **Steve Reid, G, *1936;** Bob Voigts, T, 1938; John Haman, C, 1939; **Alf Bauman, T, *1940,** 1941; Otto Graham, HB, 1943; Herb Hein, E, 1943; **Max Morris, E, *1945;** Alex Sarkisian, C, 1948; Art Murakowski, FB, 1948; Don Stonesifer, E, 1950; Joe Collier, E, 1952, 1953; Andy Cvercko, T, 1958; **Ron Burton, HB, *1959;** Jim Andreotti, C, 1959; **Jack Cvercko, G, *1962;** Tom Myers, QB, 1962; Eric Hutchinson, DB, 1971; Sam Valnzisi, PK, 1995; **Pat Fitzgerald, LB, *1995, *1996;** Darnell Autry, RB, 1996; **Damien Anderson, RB, *2000**; Zach Strief, OL, 2005.

NORTHWESTERN STATE: Marcus Spears, OL, 1993.

NOTRE DAME: Gus Dorais, QB, *1913; Stan Cofall, HB, 1916; **Frank Rydzewski, C, *1917;** Roger Kiley, E, 1920, 1921; **George Gipp, HB, *1920; Eddie Anderson, E, *1921;**

Hunk Anderson, G, 1921; Don Miller, HB, 1923; **Harry Stuhldreher, QB, *1924; Jimmy Crowley, HB, *1924; Elmer Layden, FB, *1924; Bud Boeringer, C, *1926; John Smith, G, *1927;** Christy Flanagan, HB, 1927; Fred Miller, T, 1928; **Jack Cannon, G, *1929; Frank Carideo, QB, #*1929, #*1930; Marchy Schwartz, HB, *1930, *1931;** Bert Metzger, G, 1930; Marty Brill, HB, 1930; **Tommy Yarr, C, *1931; Joe Kurth, T,** 1931, **#*1932;** Nordy Hoffman, G, 1931; **Jack Robinson, C, *1934; Wayne Millner, E, *1935;** Bill Shakespeare, HB, 1935; John Lautar, G, 1936; **Chuck Sweeney, E, *1937; Ed Beinor, T,** 1937, **#*1938;** Earl Brown, E, 1938; Bud Kerr, E, 1939; **Bob Dove, E, *1941, *1942;** Bernie Crimmins, G, 1941; **Angelo Bertelli, QB,** 1942, ***1943; John Yonakor, E, *1943; Jim White, T, *1943; Pat Filley, G, *1943; Creighton Miller, HB, *1943;** John Mastrangelo, G, 1945, 1946; George Strohmeyer, C, 1946; **George Connor, T, *1946, *1947; John Lujack, QB, #*1946, #*1947; Leon Hart, E,** 1947, ***1948, #*1949; Bill Fischer, G, *1947, *1948;** Ziggy Czarobski, T, 1947; Marty Wendell, G, 1948; **Emil Sitko, B, *1948, #*1949; Bob Williams, QB, *1949,** 1950; Jim Martin, T, 1949; **Jerry Groom, C, *1950;** Bob Toneff, T, 1951; **Johnny Lattner, HB, #*1952, #*1953; Art Hunter, T, *1953; Ralph Guglielmi, B, #*1954;** Frank Varrichione, T, 1954; Pat Bisceglia, G, 1955; Don Schaefer, FB, 1955; **Paul Hornung, HB, *1955,** QB, 1956; **Al Ecuyer, G, *1957,** 1958; Nick Pietrosante, FB, 1958; **Monty Stickles, E,** 1958, ***1959;** Jim Kelly, E, 1963; Jim Carroll, LB, 1964; **Jack Snow, E, *1964; John Huarte, QB, *1964; Dick Arrington, G, #*1965; Nick Rassas, DB, *1965; Tom Regner, G, *1966; Nick Eddy, HB, #*1966; Alan Page, DE, *1966; Jim Lynch, LB, #*1966;** Pete Duranko, DT, 1966; **Tom Schoen, DB, *1967;** Jim Seymour, E, 1967, 1968; Kevin Hardy, DE, 1967; **George Kunz, T, *1968; Terry Hanratty, QB, *1968; Mike McCoy, DT, #*1969;** Jim Reilly, OT, 1969; **Larry DiNardo, OG,** 1969, ***1970; Tom Gatewood, SE, *1970;** Joe Theismann, QB, 1970; **Clarence Ellis, DB,** 1970, ***1971; Walt Patulski, DE, #*1971; Greg Marx, DT, #*1972; Dave Casper, TE, *1973; Mike Townsend, DB, *1973; Pete Demmerle, SE, *1974; Gerry DiNardo, G, *1974;** Tom Clements, QB, 1974; Mike Fanning, DT, 1974; Greg Collins, LB, 1974; **Steve Niehaus, DT, #*1975; Ken MacAfee, TE,** 1975, ***1976, #*1977; Ross Browner, DE, #*1976, #*1977; Luther Bradley, DB, *1977; Dave Huffman, C, *1978; Bob Golic, LB, #*1978; Vagas Ferguson, RB, *1979;** Tim Foley, OT, 1979; Scott Zettek, DL, 1980; **John Scully, C, #*1980; Bob Crable, LB, *1980, *1981;** Dave Duerson, DB, 1982; Mark Bavaro, TE, 1984; **Tim Brown, FL,** 1986, **#*1987;** Andy Heck, OT, 1988; **Mike Stonebreaker, LB, *1988, #*1990; Frank Stams, DE, *1988; Chris Zorich, DT, *1989, DL, #*1990; Todd Lyght, DB, #*1989, *1990; Raghib Ismail, KR,** 1989, **#*1990;** Derek Brown, TE, 1991; **Mirko Jurkovic, OL, *1991; Aaron Taylor, OL, *1992, #*1993; Jeff Burris, DB, *1993;** Bryant Young, DL, 1993; **Bobby Taylor, DB,** 1993, ***1994;** Mike Rosenthal, OL, 1998; Jeff Faine, OL, 2002; **Shane Walton, DB, #*2002; Jeff Samardzija, WR, *2005,** 2006.

OHIO: Dave Zastudil, P, 2001; Dion Bynum, DB, 2005.

OHIO STATE: Robert Karch, T, 1916; **Charles Harley, B, *1916, *1917, *1919; Charles Bolen, E, *1917; Iolas Huffman, G, *1920, T, *1921; Gaylord Stinchcomb, B, *1920; Ed Hess, G, *1925;** Edwin Hayes, G, 1926; Marty Karow, B, 1926; Leo Raskowski, T, 1927;

Wes Fesler, E, *1928, *1929, #*1930; Joe Gailus, G, 1932; Regis Monahan, G, 1934; Merle Wendt, E, 1934, 1935; Gomer Jones, C, 1935; Inwood Smith, G, 1935; Gus Zarnas, G, 1937; **Esco Sarkkinen, E, *1939;** Donald Scott, B, 1939; Bob Shaw, E, 1942; Charles Csuri, T, 1942; Lindell Houston, G, 1942; **Jack Dugger, E, *1944; Bill Hackett, G, *1944; Les Horvath, QB, #*1944;** Bill Willis, T, 1944; **Warren Amling, G, #*1945, T, *1946; Vic Janowicz, HB, #*1950;** Bob Momsen, G, 1950; Bob McCullough, C, 1950; Mike Takacs, G, 1952; **Howard Cassady, HB, #*1954, #*1955;** Dean Dugger, E, 1954; **Jim Parker, G,** 1955, #***1956;** Aurelius Thomas, G, 1957; Jim Houston, E, 1958; Jim Marshall, T, 1958; **Bob White, B, *1958; Bob Ferguson, FB, #*1960, #*1961;** Dwight Kelley, LB, 1964, 1965; Arnold Chonko, DB, 1964; Jim Davidson, T, 1964; Doug Van Horn, OT, 1965; Ray Pryor, C, 1966; **Dave Foley, OT, #*1968; Jim Otis, FB, *1969; Jim Stillwagon, MG, *1969, #*1970; Jack Tatum, DB, *1969, #*1970;** Rex Kern, QB, 1969; John Brockington, FB, 1970; Mike Sensibaugh, DB, 1970; Jan White, TE, 1970; Tom DeLeone, C, 1971; **John Hicks, OT,** 1972, #***1973; Randy Gradishar, LB, *1972, #*1973;** Van DeCree, DE, 1973, 1974; **Archie Griffin, TB,** 1973, #***1974, #*1975; Kurt Schumacher, OT, *1974; Steve Myers, C, *1974;** Neal Colzie, DB, 1974; Tom Skladany, P, 1974, 1975; **Ted Smith, OG, *1975; Tim Fox, DB, *1975; Chris Ward, OT, *1976, #*1977; Bob Brudzinski, DE, *1976; Tom Cousineau, LB, *1977, *1978;** Aaron Brown, MG, 1977; **Ken Fritz, OG, *1979; Marcus Marek, LB, *1982; Jim Lachey, OG, *1984; Keith Byars, TB, #*1984;** Pepper Johnson, LB, 1985; **Cris Carter, SE, *1986; Chris Spielman, LB, *1986, #*1987; Tom Tupa, P (QB), #*1987;** Steve Tovar, LB, 1991, 1992; **Dan Wilkinson, DL, *1993; Korey Stringer, OL,** 1993, ***1994; Eddie George, RB, #*1995; Terry Glenn, WR, *1995; Orlando Pace, OL, #*1995, #*1996; Mike Vrabel, DL,** 1995, ***1996; Shawn Springs, DB, *1996; Andy Katzenmoyer, LB, *1997;** Rob Murphy, OL, 1997; Antoine Winfield, DB, 1997; **Rob Murphy, OL, *1998; Antoine Winfield, DB, #*1998;** David Boston, WR, 1998; Damon Moore, DB, 1998; Na'il Diggs, LB, 1999; Mike Doss, DB, 2000, 2001; **LeCharles Bentley, C, *2001; Mike Nugent, PK, *2002, #*2004; Matt Wilhelm, LB, *2002; Mike Doss, DB, #*2002**; Andy Groom, P, 2002; **Will Allen, DB, *2003;** Will Smith, DL, 2003; **A.J. Hawk, LB, *2004, #*2005; Troy Smith, QB, #*2006; Quinn Pitcock, DL, *2006; James Laurinaitis, LB, *2006.**

OKLAHOMA: Cash Gentry, T, 1934; Dub Wheeler, G, 1935; **Waddy Young, E, *1938;** Frank Ivy, E, 1939; **Buddy Burris, G, *1948;** Jim Owens, E, 1949; Wade Walker, T, 1949; Stan West, G, 1949; Darrell Royal, QB, 1949; George Thomas, HB, 1949; **Jim Weatherall, T, *1950, #*1951; Leon Heath, FB, *1950;** Frank Anderson, E, 1950; Buddy Jones, DB, 1950; **Billy Vessels, HB, *1952;** Tom Catlin, C, 1952; Buck McPhail, FB, 1952; **J. D. Roberts, G, *1953; Max Boydston, E, *1954; Kurt Burris, C, *1954; Bo Bolinger, G, *1955; Tommy McDonald, HB,** 1955, ***1956; Jerry Tubbs, C, #*1956;** Ed Gray, T, 1956; **Bill Krisher, G, *1957; Clendon Thomas, HB, *1957; Bob Harrison, C, *1958;** Leon Cross, G, 1962; **Jim Grisham, FB, *1963; Ralph Neely, T, *1964; Carl McAdams, LB,** 1964, ***1965; Granville Liggins, MG, #*1967;** Bob Kalsu, OT, 1967; **Steve Owens, TB, #*1969; Greg Pruitt, RB, #*1971, #*1972; Tom Brahaney, C, *1971, *1972;** Derland Moore, DT, 1972; Eddie Foster, OT, 1973; **Lucious Selmon, MG, #*1973; Ron Shoate,**

LB, *1973, #*1974; **John Roush, G, *1974; Joe Washington, RB, #*1974,** KR, 1975; Randy Hughes, DB, 1974; Terry Webb, OG, 1975; **Lee Roy Selmon, DT, #*1975; Dewey Selmon, MG, *1975; Jimbo Elrod, DE, *1975; Mike Vaughan, OT, #*1976; Zac Henderson, DB, #*1977;** Reggie Kinlaw, MG, 1977, 1978; **George Cumby, LB,** 1977, #*1979; **Greg Roberts, OG, #*1978; Billy Sims, RB, #*1978, #*1979; Louis Oubre, OT, *1980; Terry Crouch, OG, *1981; Rick Bryan, DT, *1982, #*1983; Tony Casillas, MG, *1984, *1985; Brian Bosworth, LB, #*1985, #*1986; Keith Jackson, TE, #*1986, #*1987; Mark Hutson, OG,** 1986, #*1987; **Dante Jones, LB, *1987; Rickey Dixon, DB, *1987;** Darrell Reed, DE, 1987; **Anthony Phillips, OG, #*1988;** Joe Bowden, LB, 1991; Cedric Jones, DL, 1995; **Josh Heupel, QB, *2000; Rocky Calmus, LB, *2000, *2001; J. T. Thatcher, DB, *2000**; Frank Romero, OL, 2001; **Roy Williams, DB, #*2001; Tommie Harris, DL, *2002, #*2003; Teddy Lehman, LB, *2002, #*2003**; Brandon Everage, DB, 2002; **Jason White, QB, #*2003; Antonio Perkins, AP, #*2003**; Mark Clayton, WR, 2003, 2004; **Jammal Brown, OL,** 2003, #*2004; **Derrick Strait, DB, #*2003; Adrian Peterson, RB, #*2004**; Vince Carter, OL, 2004; Dan Cody, DL, 2004; Rufus Alexander, LB, 2006.

OKLAHOMA STATE: Bob Fenimore, HB, 1944, *1945; Jim Wood, E, 1958; Harry Cheatwood, DB, 1967; **John Ward, OT, *1969;** Cleveland Vann, LB, 1973; **Terry Miller, RB,** 1976, #*1977; **Derrel Gofourth, C, *1976;** John Corker, LB, 1978; Gary Lewis, DL, 1982; **Leslie O'Neal, DT,** 1984, #*1985; **Rod Brown, DB, *1984;** Mark Moore, DB, 1985, 1986; **Thurman Thomas, RB, *1985**, 1987; **Hart Lee Dykes, WR, *1988; Barry Sanders, RB, #*1988; Alonzo Mayes, TE, *1997; Rashaun Woods, WR, *2002**, 2003; Sam Mayes, OL, 2004.

OREGON: Norm Van Brocklin, QB, 1948; Steve Barnett, T, 1962; **Mel Renfro, HB, *1962**, 1963; Bob Berry, QB, 1964; Jim Smith, DB, 1967; Bobby Moore, RB, 1971; Lew Barnes, WR, 1985; Chris Oldham, DB, 1989; Herman O'Berry, DB, 1994; Alex Molden, DB, 1995; **Haloti Ngata, DL, *2005**.

OREGON STATE: Gap Powell, FB, 1921; Norman Franklin, HB, 1933; Ade Schwammel, T, 1933; **John Witte, T,** 1955, *1956; **Ted Bates, T, *1958; Terry Baker, QB, #*1962; Vern Burke, E, *1963;** Jack O'Billovich, G, 1964; Jon Sandstrom, T, 1967; Jess Lewis, T, 1967; **John Didion, C, #*1968;** Bill Enyart, FB, 1968; Steve Brown, LB, 1972; Ken Simonton, RB, 2000; Mike Haas, WR, 2005, Alexis Serna, PK, 2005.

PACIFIC (CALIFORNIA): Art McCaffray, T, 1943; John Podesto, B, 1943; Eddie LeBaron, QB, 1949; Ken Buck, WR, 1953; Ryan Benjamin, AP, 1991.

PENNSYLVANIA: John Adams, C, *1891; Harry Thayer, B, *1892; Charles Gelbert, E, *1894, *1895, *1896; Arthur Knipe, B, *1894; George Brooke, B, *1894, *1895; Charles Wharton, G, *1895, *1896; Alfred Bull, C, *1895; Wylie Woodruff, G, *1896; John Outland, T, *1897, B, *1898; T. Truxton Hare, G, *1897, *1898, *1899, *1900; John Minds, B, *1897; Pete Overfield, C, *1898, *1899; Josiah McCracken, B, *1899; Frank Piekarski, G, *1904; Vincent Stevenson, B, *1904; Andrew Smith, B, *1904; Otis Lamson, T, *1905;

Robert Torrey, C, *1905; August Ziegler, G, *1906, *1907; William Hollenback, B, *1906, *1908; Dexter Draper, T, *1907; Hunter Scarlett, E, *1908; Ernest Cozens, C, *1910; E. LeRoy Mercer, B, *1910, *1912; J. Howard Berry, B, 1917; Henry Miller, E, *1917, *1919; Robert Hopper, E, 1918; John Thurman, T, *1922; Ed McGinley, T, *1924; Alton Papworth, G, 1924; George Thayer, E, 1925; John Butler, C, 1926; Charles Rodgers, B, 1926; Ed Hake, T, *1927; John Smith, T, 1927; Paul Scull, B, *1928; Harlan Gustafson, E, 1939; Francis Reagan, B, 1940; Ray Frick, C, 1940; Bernard Kuczynski, E, 1942; Bob Odell, HB, *1943; George Savitsky, T, 1944, *1945, 1946, 1947; Tony Minisi, B, 1947; Chuck Bednarik, C, *1947, *1948; John Schweder, G, 1949; Bernard Lemonick, G, 1950; Francis Bagnell, B, 1950; Ed Bell, E, 1951, 1952; Jack Shanefalt, T, 1953.

PENN STATE: William Dunn, C, *1906; Bob Higgins, E, 1915, *1919; Charles Way, HB, *1920; Glenn Killinger, HB, *1921; Harry Wilson, HB, *1923; Joe Bedenk, G, 1923; Leon Gajecki, C, 1940; Steve Suhey, G, 1947; Sam Tamburo, E, 1948; Sam Valentine, G, 1956; Richie Lucas, QB, *1959; Bob Mitinger, E, 1961; Roger Kochman, HB, 1962; Dave Robinson, E, 1962; Glenn Ressler, C-MG, *1964; Ted Kwalick, TE, 1967, #*1968; Dennis Onkotz, LB, *1968, *1969; Mike Reid, DT, #*1969; Charlie Pittman, HB, 1969; Neal Smith, DB, 1969; Jack Ham, LB, *1970; Dave Joyner, OT, *1971; Lydell Mitchell, HB, 1971; Charlie Zapiec, LB, 1971; John Hufnagel, QB, 1972; Bruce Bannon, DE, *1972; John Skorupan, LB, *1972; John Cappelletti, HB, #*1973; Ed O'Neil, LB, 1973; Randy Crowder, DT, 1973; John Nessel, OT, 1974; Mike Hartenstine, DE, *1974; Greg Buttle, LB, *1975; Tom Rafferty, OG, 1975; Chris Bahr, PK, 1975, 1978; Kurt Allerman, LB, 1976; Randy Sidler, MG, 1977; Matt Millen, DT, 1978; Pete Harris, DB, 1978; Keith Dorney, OT, 1977, #*1978; Chuck Fusina, QB, #*1978; Bruce Clark, DT, #*1978, *1979; Bill Dugan, OT, 1980; Curt Warner, TB, 1981; Sean Farrell, OG, #*1981; Kenny Jackson, FL, 1982; Mark Robinson, DB, 1982; Michael Zordich, DB, 1985; Chris Conlin, OT, 1986; Tim Johnson, DT, 1986; D. J. Dozier, HB, *1986; Shane Conlan, LB, *1986; Steve Wisniewaki, OG, 1988; Blair Thomas, RB, 1989; Andre Collins, LB, 1989; Darren Perry, DB, 1991; O. J. McDuffie, WR, *1992; Lou Benfatti, DL, 1993; Kyle Brady, TE, 1994; Bobby Engram, WR, 1994; Ki-Jana Carter, RB, #*1994; Kerry Collins, QB, *1994; Jeff Hartings, OL, 1994, *1995; Kim Herring, DB, 1996; Curtis Enis, RB, *1997; LaVar Arrington, LB, 1998, #*1999; Brandon Short, LB, *1999; Larry Johnson, RB, #*2002; Michael Haynes, DL, 2002; Jimmy Kennedy, DL, 2002; Tamba Hali, DL, #*2005; Paul Posluszny, LB, *2005, *2006; Dan Connor, LB, 2006.

PITTSBURGH: Robert Peck, C, 1914, *1915, *1916; James Herron, E, *1916; Claude Thornhill, G, 1916; Dale Seis, G, *1917; Jock Sutherland, G, *1917; George McLaren, B, 1917, *1918; Leonard Hilty, T, *1918; Tom Davies, B, *1918, 1920; Herb Stein, C, *1920, *1921; Ralph Chase, T, *1925; Bill Kern, T, 1927; Gibby Welch, B, #*1927; Mike Getto, T, *1928; Joe Donchess, E, #*1929; Ray Montgomery, G, *1929; Toby Uansa, B, 1929; Tom Parkinson, B, 1929; Jesse Quatse, T, *1931; Joe Skladany, E, *1932, *1933; Warren Heller, B, #*1932; Charles Hartwig, G, *1934; Ken Ormiston, G, 1934; George Shotwell, C, *1934; Art Detzel, T, 1935; Bill Glassford, G, 1936; Averell Daniell, T, *1936;

Art Souchak, E, 1937; **Tony Matisi, T, *1937; Marshall Goldberg, HB, *1937, #*1938;** Bill Daddio, E, 1937, 1938; Ralph Fife, G, 1941; Bernie Barkouskie, G, 1949; Eldred Kraemer, T, 1952; Joe Schmidt, LB, 1952; **Joe Walton, E, *1956; John Guzik, G, *1958; Mike Ditka, E, #*1960; Paul Martha, HB, *1963;** Ernie Borghetti, T, 1963; Gary Burley, MG, 1974; **Tony Dorsett, RB,** 1973, 1975, **#*1976; Al Romano, MG, *1976; Tom Brzoza, C, *1977; Randy Holloway, DT, *1977; Bob Jury, DB, *1977;** Matt Cavanaugh, QB, 1977; Gordon Jones, WR, 1978; **Hugh Green, DE, *1978, #*1979, #*1980; Mark May, OT, #*1980; Sal Sunseri, LB, *1981;** Julius Dawkins, SE, 1981; Dan Marino, QB, 1981; **Bill Fralic, OT,** 1982, **#*1983, #*1984; Jimbo Covert, OT, #*1983; Randy Dixon, OT, *1986; Tony Woods, DE, *1986;** Ezekial Gadson, LB, 1987; **Craig Heyward, RB, *1987;** Jerry Olsavky, LB, 1988; **Mark Stepnoski, OG, *1988; Brian Greenfield, P, *1990;** Rueben Brown, OL, 1994; **Antonio Bryant, WR, *2000; Larry Fitzgerald, WR, #*2003;** H.B. Blades, LB, 2006.

PRINCETON: Hector Cowan, T, *1889; William George, C, *1889; Edgar Allan Poe, B, *1889; Roscoe Channing, B, *1889; Knowlton Ames, B, *1889; Ralph Warren, E, *1890; Jesse Riggs, G, *1890, *1891; Sheppard Homans, B, *1890, *1891; Philip King, QB, *1891, *1892, *1893; Arthur Wheeler, G, *1892, *1893, *1894; Langdon Lea, T, *1893, *1894, *1895; Thomas Trenchard, E, *1893; Franklin Morse, B, *1893; Dudley Riggs, G, *1895; William Church, T, *1896; Robert Gailey, C, *1896; Addison Kelly, B, *1896, *1897; John Baird, B, *1896; Garrett Cochran, E, *1897; Lew Palmer, E, *1898; Arthur Hillebrand, T, *1898, *1899; Arthur Poe, E, *1899; Howard Reiter, B, *1899; Ralph Davis, E, *1901; John DeWitt, G, *1902, *1903; Howard Henry, E, *1903; J. Dana Kafer, B, *1903; James Cooney, T, *1904, *1906; James McCormick, FB, *1905, *1907; L. Casper Wister, E, *1906, *1907; Edward Dillon, B, *1906; Edwin Harlan, B, *1907; Frederick Tibbott, B, *1908; Talbot Pendleton, B, *1910; Sanford White, E, *1911; Edward Hart, T, *1911; Joseph Duff, G, *1911; John Logan, G, *1912; Harold Ballin, T, *1913, *1914; Frank Hogg, G, *1916; Frank Murrey, B, *1918; Stan Keck, T, *1920, G, *1921; Donold Lourie, B, *1920; Armant Legendre, E, 1920; **C. Herbert Treat, T, *1922;** Edmund Stout, E, 1924; Charles Beattie, T, 1924; **Ed McMillan, C, *1925;** Jacob Slagle, B, 1925; Mike Miles, T, 1927; Charles Howe, C, 1928; Charles Ceppi, T, 1933; **John Weller, G, *1935;** George Sella, B, 1949; **Dick Kazmaier, HB,** 1950, **#*1951;** Holland Donan, T, 1950; Redmond Finney, C, 1950; **Frank McPhee, E,** 1951, ***1952;** Cosmo Iacavazzi, B, 1964; **Stas Maliszewski,** G-LB, 1964, **OG, *1965.**

PURDUE: Elmer Sleight, T, *1929; Ralph Welch, HB, *1929; Charles Miller, C, 1931; Roy Horstmann, FB, 1932; **Paul Moss, E,** 1931, **#*1932; Duane Purvis, HB, *1933,** 1934; **Dave Rankin, E,** 1939, ***1940; Alex Agase, G, *1943;** Tony Butkovich, FB, 1943; Boris Dimancheff, HB, 1944; Tom Hughes, T, 1945; **Bernie Flowers, E, *1952;** Tom Bettis, G, 1954; Gene Selawski, T, 1958; Jerry Beabout, T, 1960; Don Brumm, T, 1962; Harold Wells, DE, 1964; **Bob Griese, QB, *1965,** 1966; Karl Singer, OT, 1965; Jerry Shay, DT, 1965; Jim Bierne, E, 1966; **Leroy Keyes, HB-DB, #*1967, #*1968; Chuck Kyle, MG, *1968; Mike Phipps, QB, #*1969; Otis Armstrong, HB, *1972; Dave Butz, DT, *1972;** Larry Burton,

WR, 1974; Ken Novak, DT, 1975; **Dave Young, TE, #*1980; Mark Herrmann, QB, #*1980; Rod Woodson, DB, *1986;** Brian Alford, WR, 1997; **Travis Dorsch, P, *2001; Taylor Stubblefield, WR, *2004.**

RICE: Bill Wallace, B, 1934; Hamilton Nichols, G, 1944; **Weldon Humble, G, *1946; James Williams, E, *1949;** Joe Watson, C, 1949; Bill Howton, E, 1951; John Hudson, T, 1953; Kosse Johnson, B, 1953; **Dicky Maegle, HB, *1954;** King Hill, QB, 1957; **Buddy Dial, E, *1958;** Malcolm Walker, C, 1964; **Tommy Kramer, QB, *1976; Trevor Cobb, RB, *1991.**

RICHMOND: Walker Gillette, WR, *1969; Jeff Nixon, DB, *1978.

RUTGERS: Paul Robeson, E, *1917, *1918; Homer Hazel, E, 1923, B, 1924; Billy Austin, RB, 1958; **Alex Kroll, C, *1961; Marco Battaglia, TE, #*1995**; Eric Foster, DL, 2006.

ST. MARY'S (CALIFORNIA): Larry Bettencourt, C, *1927; Ike Frankian, E, 1928; George Ackerman, T, 1929; Angel Brovelli, B, 1932; John Vezerski, T, 1933; **Herman Wedemeyer, HB, #*1945.**

SAN DIEGO STATE: Henry Allison, OG, 1970; Henry Williams, DB, 1978; **Marshall Faulk, RB,** 1991, **#*1992, #*1993;** Noel Prefontaine, P, 1996; **Kyle Turley, OT, *1997;** Mike Malano, C, 1999.

SAN FRANCISCO: Ollie Matson, B, 1951.

SAN JOSE STATE: Dave Chaney, LB, 1971; Dwight Lowery, DB, 2006.

SANTA CLARA: Nello Falaschi, B, 1936; **Alvord Wolff, T, *1938; John Schiechl, C, *1939;** Phil Daugherty, G, 1937.

SOUTH CAROLINA: Frank Mincevich, G, 1954; Warren Muir, FB, 1969; Jimmy Poston, DT, 1970; Dick Harris, DB, 1970; John LeHeup, DT, 1972; **George Rogers, RB,** 1979, **#*1980; Del Wilkes, OG, *1984;** James Seawright, LB, 1984; Sterling Sharpe, WB, 1987; Sheldon Brown, DB, 2000; Ko Simpson, DB, 2005.

SOUTHERN CALIFORNIA: Brice Taylor, G, 1925; **Mort Kaer, QB, *1926; Jesse Hibbs, T, *1927; Morley Drury, B, *1927;** Don Williams, B, 1928; Francis Tappaan, E, 1929; Garrett Arbelbide, E, 1930; **Erny Pinckert, B, *1930,** 1931; **John Baker, G, *1931; Gus Shaver, HB, *1931; Ernie Smith, T, #*1932; Aaron Rosenberg, G,** 1932, ***1933; Cotton Warburton, QB, #*1933;** Larry Stevens, G, 1933; **Harry Smith, G,** 1938, **#*1939; Ralph Heywood, E, *1943; John Ferraro, T, *1944,** 1947; **Paul Cleary, E, *1947;** Pat Cannamela, LB, 1951; Frank Gifford, HB, 1951; **Elmer Willhoite, G, *1952; Jim Sears, DB, *1952;** Jon Arnett, B, 1955; Marlin McKeever, E, 1959; Mike McKeever, G, 1959; **Hal Bledsole, E, *1962;** Damon Bame, LB, 1962, 1963; Bill Fisk, OG, 1964; **Mike Garrett, TB,** 1964,

#*1965; Ron Yary, OT, *1966, #*1967; Nate Shaw, DB, *1966; O. J. Simpson, TB, #*1967, #*1968; Tim Rossovich, DE, *1967; Adrian Young, LB, *1967; Mike Battle, B, 1968; Jim Gunn, DE, *1969; Al Cowlings, DT, 1969; Sid Smith, OT, 1969; Charlie Weaver, DE, *1970; John Vella, OT, 1971; Pete Adams, OT, 1972; Sam Cunningham, RB, 1972; John Grant, DT, 1972; Charles Young, TE, #*1972; Richard Wood, LB, 1972, *1973, *1974; Lynn Swann, WR, *1973; Booker Brown, OT, *1973; Artimus Parker, DB, *1973; Anthony Davis, RB, #*1974; Charles Phillips, DB, 1974; Marvin Powell, OT, 1975, 1976; Ricky Bell, TB, #*1975, #*1976; Gary Jeter, DT, *1976; Dennis Thurman, DB, *1976, #*1977; Pat Howell, G, #*1978; Charles White, TB, #*1978, #*1979; Brad Budde, OG, #*1979, Dennis Johnson, LB, 1979; Roy Foster, OG, 1980, *1981; Keith Van Horne, OT, *1980; Ronnie Lott, TB, #*1980; Marcus Allen, RB, #*1981; Chip Banks, LB, 1981; Don Mosebar, OT, #*1982; Bruce Matthews, OG, *1982; George Achica, MG, *1982; Tony Slaton, C, *1983; Jack Del Rio, LB, *1984; Duane Bickett, LB, 1984; Jeff Bregel, OG, *1985, *1986; Tim McDonald, DB, *1986; Dave Cadigan, OT, *1987; Erik Affholter, SE, 1988; Tim Ryan, DT, 1988, *1989; Rodney Peete, QB, 1988; Mark Carrier, DB, 1988, #*1989; Scott Ross, LB, 1990; Tony Boselli, OL, 1992, *1994; Curtis Conway, KR, 1992; Johnnie Morton, WR, *1993; Keyshawn Johnson, WR, #*1995; Chris Claiborne, LB, #*1998; Troy Polamalu, DB, 2001, *2002; Carson Palmer, QB, *2002; Mike Williams, WR, *2003; Jacob Rogers, OL, *2003; Kenechi Udeze, DL, *2003; Matt Leinart, QB, *2004, 2005; Reggie Bush, AP, *2004, #*2005; Shaun Cody, DL, *2004; Matt Grootegoed, LB, *2004; Mike Patterson, DL, 2004; Dwayne Jarrett, WR, #*2005, *2006; Taitusi Lutui, OL, *2005; Darnell Bing, DB, 2005; Sam Baker, OL, *2006.

SOUTHERN METHODIST: Marion Hammon, T, 1929; Clyde Carter, T, 1934; J. C. Wetsel, G, *1935; Bobby Wilson, HB, 1934, *1935; Truman Spain, T, 1935; Doak Walker, HB, *1947, #*1948, *1949; Kyle Rote, HB, *1950; Dick Hightower, C, *1951; Don Meredith, QB, 1958, 1959; John LaGrone, MG, *1966; Jerry LeVias, FL, *1968; Robert Popelka, DB, *1972; Louie Kelcher, MG, *1974; Emanuel Tolbert, WR, *1978; John Simmons, DB, *1980; Harvey Armstrong, DT, 1981; Eric Dickerson, TB, #*1982; Russell Carter, DB, #*1983; Reggie Dupard, TB, *1985; John Stewart, PK, 1993.

SOUTHERN MISS: Ray Guy, P, 1972; Adalius Thomas, LB, 1998; Michael Boley, LB, 2004.

SOUTHWESTERN (TEXAS): Harold Fischer, G, 1943.

STANFORD: Jim Lawson, E, *1924; Ernie Nevers, FB, *1925; Ted Shipkey, B, 1926; Seraphim Post, G, *1928; Don Robesky, G, *1928; Phil Moffatt, HB, 1930; Bill Corbus, G, *1932, *1933; Bob Reynolds, T, *1934; Bobby Grayson, B, *1934, #*1935; Monk Moscrip, E, 1934, *1935; Bones Hamilton, HB, 1934; Hugh Gallarneau, HB, 1940; Frank Albert, QB, *1940, *1941; Chuck Taylor, G, *1942; Ken Rose, E, 1949; Bill McColl, E, *1950, #*1951; Gary Kerkorian, QB, 1951; Sam Morley, E, 1953; Bob Garrett, QB, 1953; Paul Wiggin, T, 1955, 1956; John Brodie, B, *1956; Chris Burford, E, 1959; Don Parish,

LB, 1969; **Jim Plunkett, QB, *1970; Jeff Siemon, LB, *1971; Pat Donovan, DE,** 1973, ***1974;** Roger Stillwell, DL, 1973; Duncan McColl, DE, 1976; **Guy Benjamin, QB, *1977; Ken Margerum, FL, *1979, #*1980; John Elway, QB, #*1982; Brad Muster, RB, *1986;** Ed McCaffery, WR, 1990; **Bob Whitfield, OL, *1991;** Glyn Milburn, AP, 1992; Kailee Wong, DL, 1997; **Troy Walters, WR, *1999**; Eric Heitmann, OL, 2001; Luke Powell, KR, 2001; Tank Williams, DB, 2001.

SYRACUSE: Frank Horr, T, *1908; Harold White, G, *1915; Christopher Schlachter, G, 1915; **Alfred Cobb, T, *1917; Lou Usher, T, *1918; Joe Alexander, G, *1918, *1919,** C, 1920; Bertrand Gulick, T, 1920; **Pete McRae, E, *1923; Vic Hanson, E, *1926;** James Steen, T, 1934; Bob Fleck, G, 1952, 1953; **Jim Brown, HB, #*1956;** Ron Luciano, T, 1958; Robert Yates, T, 1959; **Roger Davis, G, #*1959;** Fred Mautino, E, 1959; **Ernie Davis, HB, *1960, #*1961;** Pat Killorin, C, 1964; Floyd Little, HB, 1964, 1965, 1966; Gary Bugenhagen, T, 1966; **Larry Csonka, FB,** 1966, **#*1967;** Joe Ehrmann, DT, 1970; Tom Myers, DB, 1971; Ray Preston, LB, 1975; Art Monk, WR, 1979; Gary Anderson, PK, 1981; Mike Charles, DT, 1982; **Tim Green, DT, #*1985; Don McPherson, QB, #*1987; Ted Gregory, MG, *1987;** Markus Paul, DB, 1988; **John Flannery, C, *1990;** Qadry Ismail, KR, 1991; **Chris Gedney, TE, #*1992;** Kevin Abrams, DB, 1995, 1996; Marvin Harrison, KR, 1995; Donovin Darius, DB, 1997; Kevin Johnson, RS, 1998; **Dwight Freeney, DL, #*2001**.

TEMPLE: Bill Singletary, OG, 1972; Steve Joachim, QB, 1974; **John Rienstra, OL, *1985; Paul Palmer, RB, #*1986.**

TENNESSEE: Gene McEver, B, *1929; Bobby Dodd, B, 1930; Herman Hickman, G, 1931; **Beattie Feathers, HB, *1933; Bowden Wyatt, E, *1938; Bob Suffridge, G,** 1938, 1939, **#*1940; Ed Molinski, G, *1939**, 1940; **George Cafego, HB,** 1938, ***1939; Dick Huffman, T, *1946;** Bud Sherrod, E, 1950; Ted Daffer, G, 1950, 1951; Bill Pearman, T, 1951; **Hank Lauricella, HB, #*1951; John Michels, G, *1952;** Doug Atkins, T, 1952; Darris McCord, T, 1954; **John Majors, HB, #*1956;** Buddy Cruze, E, 1956; Bill Johnson, G, 1957; Steve DeLong, G, 1963, 1964; **Frank Emmanuel, LB, *1965; Paul Naumoff, LB, *1966;** Austin Denney, E, 1966; Al Dorsey, B, 1967; **Bob Johnson, C, #*1967; Charles Rosenfelder, OG, #*1968; Steve Kiner, LB, *1968, #*1969;** Jim Weatherford, DB, 1968; **Chip Kell, OG, *1969, #*1970; Bobby Majors, DB, #*1971;** Jackie Walker, LB, 1970, 1971; Jamie Rotella, LB, 1972; Conrad Graham, DB, 1972; Ricky Townsend, PK, 1972, 1973; **Larry Seivers, WR, *1975, *1976; Roland James, DB, *1979;** Willie Gault, KR (WR), 1982; Jimmy Colquitt, P, 1983; **Reggie White, DT, #*1983; Bill Mayo, OG, *1984; Tim McGee, WR, *1985;** Keith DeLong, LB, 1988; **Eric Still, OG, #*1989; Antone Davis, OL, #*1990; Dale Carter, DB, *1991;** Carl Pickens, WR, 1991; John Becksvoort, PK, 1993; Leonard Little, LB, 1997; **Peyton Manning, QB, *1997; Al Wilson, LB, *1998; Cosey Coleman, OL, *1999; Deon Grant, DB, *1999;** Raynoch Thompson, LB, 1999; **John Henderson, DL, *2000, *2001**; Travis Stephens, RB, 2001; **Dustin Colquitt, P, *2003; Michael Munoz, OL, *2004;** Jesse Mahelona, DL, 2004; Kevin Burnett, LB, 2004; **Robert Meachem, WR, *2006; Aaron Sears, OL, *2006.**

TENNESSEE STATE: Ed Jones, DL, 1973.

TENNESSEE TECH: Jim Youngblood, LB, 1972.

TEXAS: Malcolm Kutner, E, 1941; Chal Daniel, G, 1941; Joe Parker, E, 1941; **Hubert Bechtol, E,** 1944, ***1945, *1946; Bobby Layne, QB, *1947;** Dick Harris, T, 1947; Randall Clay, B, 1949; **Bud McFadin, G,** 1949, **#*1950;** Don Menasco, E, 1950; Bobby Dillon, DB, 1951; Tom Stolhandske, E, 1952; Harley Sewell, G, 1952; **Carlton Massey, E, *1953;** Herb Gray, T, 1955; Maurice Doke, G, 1959; **Jimmy Saxton, HB, #*1961;** Don Talbert, T, 1961; **Johnny Treadwell, G, #*1962; Scott Appleton, T, #*1963;** Tommy Ford, B, 1963; **Tommy Nobis, OG-LB,** 1964, ***1965;** Corby Robertson, E, 1967; Loyd Wainscott, OT, 1968; **Chris Gilbert, HB, *1968; Bob McKay, OT, *1969;** Charles Speyrer, E, 1969; **Bobby Wuensch, OT,** 1969, ***1970;** Glen Halsell, LB, 1969; **Steve Worster, FB,** 1969, ***1970; Bill Atessis, DE, *1970;** Scott Henderson, LB, 1970; **Jerry Sisemore, OT, #*1971, #*1972; Bill Wyman, C, *1973; Roosevelt Leaks, FB, *1973; Bob Simmons, OT,** 1974, ***1975;** Doug English, DT, 1974; Marty Akins, QB, 1975; **Earl Campbell, RB,** 1975, **#*1977;** Russell Erxleben, PK-P 1976, 1977, 1978, **Brad Shearer, DT, #*1977; Johnnie Johnson, DB, #*1978, #*1979; Steve McMichael, DT, #*1979; Kenneth Sims, DT, *1980, #*1981; Terry Tausch, OT, *1981; Doug Dawson, OG, *1983; Jeff Leiding, LB, *1983; Jerry Gray, DB, *1983, #*1984;** Mossy Cade, DB, 1983; **Tony Degrate, DT, *1984;** Gene Chilton, C, 1985; Jeff Ward, PK, 1986; Britt Hager, LB, 1988; Stanley Richard, DB, 1990; Shane Dronett, DL, 1991; Lance Gunn, DB, 1992; Blake Brockermeyer, OL, 1994; **Tony Brackens, DL, *1995; Dan Neil, OL,** 1995, ***1996;** Pat Fitzgerald, TE, 1996; **Ricky Williams, RB, #*1997, #*1998;** Ben Adams, OL, 1998; Jay Humphrey, OT, 1998; **Casey Hampton, DL,** 1999, ***2000; Leonard Davis, OL, *2000; Mike Williams, OL, *2001; Derrick Dockery, OL, *2002,** Cory Redding, DL, 2002; **Derrick Johnson, LB, 2003, #2004;** Cedric Benson, RB, 2004; **Vince Young, QB, *2005; Jonathan Scott, OL, #*2005; Rodrique Wright, DL, *2005; Michael Huff, DB, #*2005; Justin Blalock, OL, #*2006; Aaron Ross, DB, *2006.**

TEXAS A&M: Joe Routt, G, 1936, ***1937; John Kimbrough, FB, *1939, #*1940;** Joe Boyd, T, 1939; **Marshall Robnett, G, *1940;** Bob Smith, FB, 1950; Jack Little, T, 1951; Charles Krueger, T, 1956, 1957; **John David Crow, HB, #*1957;** Jack Pardee, FB, 1956; Maurice Moorman, OT, 1966; Bill Hobbs, LB, 1967, 1968; **Dave Elmendorf, DB, *1970; Pat Thomas, DB, *1974, *1975; Ed Simonini, LB, *1975; Tony Franklin, PK, *1976,** 1978; **Robert Jackson, LB, #*1976;** Jacob Green, DE, 1979; Ray Childress, DE, 1984; **Johnny Holland, LB, *1985; John Roper, LB, *1987;** Darren Lewis, RB, 1988; Mike Arthur, C, 1990; **Darren Lewis, RB, *1990; Kevin Smith, DB, *1991;** Patrick Bates, DB, 1992; **Marcus Buckley, LB, #*1992; Sam Adams, DL, *1993; Aaron Glenn, DB, *1993;** Antonio Armstrong, LB, 1994; **Leeland McElroy, KR, *1994,** 1995; Ray Mickens, DB, 1995; Brandon Mitchell, DL, 1995; Keith Mitchell, LB, 1996; **Dat Nguyen, LB, #*1998;** Shane Lechler, P, 1998, 1999; **Quentin Jammer, DB, *2001.**

TEXAS A&M-KINGSVILLE: Johnny Bailey, RB, 1989.

TEXAS CHRISTIAN: Rags Matthews, E, 1927; John Vaught, G, 1932; **Darrell Lester, C, *1934, *1935**, 1936; **Sammy Baugh, QB,** 1935, ***1936;** J. B. Hale, T, 1937, 1938; **Ki Aldrich, C, *1938; Davey O'Brien, QB, #*1938;** Derrell Palmer, T, 1942; Clyde Flowers, T, 1944; Lindy Berry, QB, 1949; Doug Conaway, T, 1951; Keith Flowers, C, 1951; **Jim Swink, HB, #*1955**, 1956; Hugh Pitts, C, 1955; Norman Hamilton, T, 1956; **Don Floyd, T,** 1958, ***1959;** Jack Spikes, FB, 1959; **Bob Lilly, T, #*1960;** Tommy Crutcher, FB, 1963; Stanley Washington, SE, 1981; **Kenneth Davis, RB, #*1984; Kelly Blackwell, TE, *1991; Michael Reeder, PK, *1995; LaDainian Tomlinson, RB, #*2000; Nick Browne, PK, *2003.**

TEXAS TECH: E. J. Holub, C, 1959, ***1960;** David Parks, E, 1963; **Donny Anderson, B,** 1964, ***1965;** Phil Tucker, OG, 1967; Rick Campbell, DE, 1969; Denton Fox, DB, 1969; Andre Tillman, TE, 1973; Thomas Howard, LB, 1976; **Dan Irons, OT, *1977; Gabriel Rivera, MG-DT, *1982;** Tyrone Thurman, KR (WB), 1988; **Mark Bounds, P, #*1991;** Lloyd Hill, WR, 1992; **Zach Thomas, LB,** 1994, **#*1995;** Marcus Coleman, DB, 1995; **Byron Hanspard, RB, #*1996; Montae Reagor, DL, *1998;** Lawrence Flugence, LB, 2001.

TOLEDO: Tom Beutler, MG, 1967; Curtis Johnson, DB, 1969; **Mel Long, DT,** 1970, ***1971;** Gene Swick, QB, 1975.

TULANE: Charles Flourney, B, 1925; Willis Banker, B, 1929; **Jerry Dalrymple, E,** 1930, **#*1931; Don Zimmerman, B,** 1931, ***1932; Harley McCollum, T, *1939; Ernie Blandin, T, *1941;** Paul Lea, T, 1948; Eddie Price, FB, 1949; Jerome Helluin, G, 1950; Tony Sardisco, G, 1955; Charles Hall, DT, 1973; Marc Zeno, WR, 1987; Seth Marler, PK, 2001.

TULSA: Glenn Dobbs, HB, 1942; Felto Prewitt, C, 1944; Ellis Jones, G, 1944; Marv Matuszak, T, 1951, 1952; Jerry Rhome, QB, 1964; **Howard Twilley, SE, #*1965;** Drane Scrivener, DB, 1972; **Jerry Ostroski, OL, *1991.**

UCLA: Kenny Washington, HB, 1939; Al Sparlis, G, 1945; **Burr Baldwin, #*1946; Donn Moomaw, C,** 1950, ***1952; Paul Cameron, TB,** 1952, ***1953; Jack Ellena, T, *1954;** Jim Salisbury, G, 1954; Bob Davenport, FB, 1954, 1955; **Hardiman Cureton, G, *1955;** Rommie Loudd, E, 1955; James Brown, G, 1955; **Dick Wallen, E, *1957;** Bill Kilmer, HB, 1960; Ron Hull, C, 1961; John Richardson, G, 1966; **Mel Farr, HB, *1966; Gary Beban, QB, #*1967; Don Manning, LB, *1967;** Larry Slagle, DT, 1967; Floyd Reese, E, 1969; **Mike Ballou, LB, *1969;** Al Oliver, OT, 1973; Jimmy Allen, DB, 1973; **Kermit Johnson, RB, *1973; John Sciarra, QB, *1975;** Randy Cross, OG, 1975; Oscar Edwards, DB, 1976; **Jerry Robinson, LB, *1976, #*1977, #*1978; Kenny Easley, DB, *1978, #*1979, #*1980;** Freeman McNeil, TB, 1980; **Tim Wrightman, TE, #*1981; Don Rogers, DB, *1983; John Lee, PK,** 1984, **#*1985;** Gaston Green, TB, 1987; Ken Norton, LB, 1987; Carnell Lake, LB, 1988; **Darryl Henley, DB, *1988; Troy Aikman, QB, *1988;** Matt Darby, DB, 1991; **Carlton Gray, DB, *1992; Bjorn Merten, PK, *1993; Jamir Miller, LB, *1993; J. J. Stokes, WR, #*1993;** Kevin Jordan, WR, 1994; Karim Abdul-Jabbar, RB, 1995; **Jonathan Ogden, OL,**

#*1995; Skip Hicks, RB, 1997; **Chad Overhauser, OT, *1997;** Chris Sailer, P/PK, 1997; **Kris Farris, OL, *1998; Cade McNown, QB, *1998; Fred Mitchell, WR, *2000; Robert Thomas, LB, *2001**; Kenyon Coleman, DL, 2001; **Dave Ball, DL, #*2003; Mercedes Lewis, TE, *2005; Maurice Drew, AP/KR, #*2005; Justin Hickman, DL, *2006; Justin Medlock, K, *2006**

UNLV: Randall Cunningham, P (QB), 1983; **Joe Kristosik, P, *1998.**

UTAH: Earl Pomeroy, FB, 1929; Frank Christensen, FB, 1932; Lee Grosscup, QB, 1957; Roy Jefferson, SE, 1964; Marv Bateman, P, 1970; Steve Odom, KR (FL), 1973; Steve Clark, DT, 1981; Carlton Walker, OG, 1984; Erroll Tucker, KR (DB), 1985; **Luther Elliss, DL, *1994; Jordan Gross, OL, *2002**; Alex Smith, QB, 2004; Chris Kemoeatu, OL, 2004; **Eric Weddle, DB, *2006.**

UTAH STATE: Elmer Ward, C, 1934; Kent Ryan, B, 1936; **Merlin Olsen, T, 1960, *1961;** Bill Staley, T, 1967; **Phil Olsen, DE, *1969**; Kevin Curtis, WR, 2001.

UTEP: Fred Carr, B, 1967; Chris Jacke, PK, 1988; Ed Bunn, P, 1992; Barron Wortham, LB, 1993; **Brian Natkin, TE, #*2000**; Johnnie Lee Higgins, WR, 2006.

VANDERBILT: **Lynn Bomar, E, *1923; Henry Wakefield, E,** 1923, ***1924;** Bill Spears, QB, 1927; John Brown, G, 1929; **Pete Gracey, C, *1932;** Carl Hinkle, C, 1937; Bucky Curtis, E, 1950; **George Deiderich, G, *1958;** Chip Healy, LB, 1968; Bob Asher, OT, 1969; **Jim Arnold, P, #*1982; Ricky Anderson, P, #*1984;** Chris Gaines, LB, 1987; Bill Marinangel, P, 1996; Jamie Duncan, LB, 1997.

VILLANOVA: Ed Michaels, G, 1935; John Wysocki, E, 1937, 1938; Nick Liotta, G, 1951; Gene Filipski, HB, 1952; Al Atkinson, E, 1964.

VIRGINIA: **Eugene Mayer, HB, *1915; Bill Dudley, HB, *1941;** Joe Palumbo, MG, 1951; Tom Scott, DE, 1952; Jim Bakhtiar, FB, 1957; **Jim Dombrowski, OT, #*1985;** Ray Savage, DE, 1989; **Herman Moore, WR, *1990;** Shawn Moore, QB, 1990; Ray Roberts, OL, 1991; **Chris Slade, DL, *1992; Mark Dixon, OL, *1993;** Will Brice, P, 1995; Percy Ellsworth, DB, 1995; **Anthony Poindexter, DB,** 1997, ***1998;** Patrick Kerney, DL, 1998; **Thomas Jones, RB, *1999;** Noel LaMontagne, OG, 1999; **Heath Miller, TE, #*2004; Elton Brown, OL, *2004**; Ahmad Brooks, LB, 2004; D'Brickashaw Ferguson, OL, 2005.

VIRGINIA TECH: Carroll Dale, SE, 1959; Bob Schweickert, QB, 1964; **Frank Loria, DB,** 1966, ***1967;** Mike Widger, LB, 1968; **Bruce Smith, DT,** 1983, ***1984;** Eugene Chung, OL, 1991; **Jim Pyne, C, #*1993; Cornel Brown, DL, *1995**, 1996; Billy Conaty, C, 1996; **Corey Moore, DL,** 1998, **#*1999;** Michael Vick, QB, 1999; **Kevin Jones, RB, *2003; Jake Grove, C, #*2003; Jimmy Williams, DB, #*2005;** Darryl Tapp, DL, 2005.

WAKE FOREST: Bill Barnes, FB, 1956; Win Headley, DT, 1970; Chuck Ramsey, K, 1973; **Bill Armstrong, DB, #*1976;** Paul Kiser, OG, 1986; Ben Coleman, OL, 1992; Calvin Pace, DL, 2002; **Ryan Plackemeier, P, #*2005;** Steve Vallos, OL, 2006.

WASHINGTON: George Wilson, HB, *1925; Charles Carroll, HB, *1928; Merle Hufford, HB, 1929; Paul Schwegler, T, 1931; Dave Nisbet, E, 1932; Bill Smith, E, 1933; **Max Starcevich, G, *1936;** Jim Cain, HB, 1936; Vic Markov, T, 1937; **Rudy Mucha, C, *1940;** Jay MacDowell, E, 1940; **Ray Frankowski, G,** 1940, *1941; Don Heinrich, QB, 1950, 1952; Richard Sprague, DB, 1950; Hugh McElhenny, FB, 1951; Milt Bohart, G, 1953; Bob Schloredt, QB, 1959; Roy McKasson, C, 1960; **Rick Redman, G-LB, *1963, *1964; Tom Greenlee, DE, *1966; Al Worley, DB, *1968;** Calvin Jones, DB, 1972; Mark Stewart, LB, 1982; **Chuck Nelson, PK, #*1982; Ron Holmes, DT, *1984; Jeff Jaeger, PK, *1986; Reggie Rogers, DT, *1986;** Greg Lewis, RB, 1990; **Mario Bailey, WR, *1991; Steve Entman, DL, #*1991;** David Hoffman, LB, 1991, 1992; **Lincoln Kennedy, OL, #*1992; Lawyer Milloy, DB, #*1995;** Jason Chorak, LB, 1996; **Benji Olson, OL, *1996,** 1997; **Olin Kreutz, C, *1997;** Jerome Pathon, WR, 1997; Chad Ward, OL, 2000; **Reggie Williams, WR, 2002.**

WASHINGTON & JEFFERSON: John Spiegel, B, *1914; M. M. Witherspoon, T, 1915; **Wilbur Henry, T,** 1917, *1918, *1919; Russell Stein, T, 1921; Forrest Douds, G, 1928.

WASHINGTON STATE: A. G. Edwards, T, 1930; Mel Hein, C, 1930; Ed Goddard, QB, 1934, 1935, 1936; Bob Kennedy, B, 1942; Lauri Niemi, T, 1948; Bill Steiger, E, 1956; Clarence Williams, DB, 1964; Wayne Foster, T, 1965; Geoff Reece, C, 1974; Dan Lynch, OG, 1984; **Rueben Mayes, RB, *1984; Mark Utley, OL, *1988; Jason Hanson, PK, #*1989,** 1991; DeWayne Patterson, DL, 1994; Scott Sanderson, OL, 1996; Ryan Leaf, QB, 1997; Lamont Thompson, DB, 2001; Derrick Roche, OL, 2002; **Rien Long, DL, *2002;** Drew Dunning, PK, 2003; **Jerome Harrison, RB, *2005.**

WEST VIRGINIA: Russell Bailey, C, 1917; **Ira Rodgers, FB, *1919;** Bob Orders, C, 1953; Sam Huff, T, 1955; **Bruce Bosley, T, *1955;** Jim Braxton, TE, 1970; Danny Buggs, WR, 1973; **Darryl Talley, LB, #*1982;** Rob Bennett, TE, **1984; Brian Jozwiak, OT, *1985;** Major Harris, QB, 1989; **Mike Compton, C, *1992;** Rich Braham, OL, 1993; **Todd Sauerbrun, P, #*1994; Aaron Beasley, DB, *1995; Canute Curtis, LB, *1996;** Grant Wiley, LB, 2003; **Steve Slaton, RB, #*2006; Dan Mozes, OL, #*2006.**

WILLIAM & MARY: Gerrard Ramsey, G, 1942; Jack Cloud, HB, 1948.

WILLIAMS: Ben Boynton, B, *1917, *1919, 1920.

WISCONSIN: Robert Butler, T, *1912; Ray Keeler, G, *1913; Arlie Mucks, G, 1914; **Howard Buck, T, *1915; Charles Carpenter, C, *1919; Ralph Scott, T, *1920;** Frank Weston, E, 1920; **Marty Below, T, *1923; Milo Lubratovich, T, *1930;** Howard Weiss, FB, 1938; **Dave Schreiner, E,** 1941, #*1942; Pat Harder, FB, 1942; Earl Girard, QB, 1944; Ed Withers, DB, 1950; Pat O'Donahue, E, 1951; Hal Faverty, G-LB, 1951; Don Voss, E,

1952; David Suminski, OT, 1952; **Alan Ameche, FB,** 1953, **#*1954; Dan Lanphear, T, #*1959; Pat Richter, E,** 1961, ***1962; Dennis Lick, OT, *1975; Tim Krumrie, MG, *1981;** Matt Vanden Boom, DB, 1981; Richard Johnson, DB, 1984; Troy Vincent, DB, 1991; **Cory Raymer, C, *1994;** Tarek Saleh, DL, 1996; Ron Dayne, RB, 1997; **Aaron Gibson, OL, *1998; Tom Burke, DL, #*1998; Ron Dayne, RB,** 1997, 1998, **#*1999; Chris McIntosh, OL, #*1999; Jamar Fletcher, DB,** 1999, ***2000;** Lee Evans, WR, 2001; Wendell Bryant, DL, 2001; **Erasmus James, DL, *2004; Joe Thomas, T, #*2006**.

WYOMING: Eddie Talboom, HB, 1950; Dewey McConnell, E, 1951; Jim Crawford, HB, 1956; Mike Dirks, T, 1967; Bob Jacobs, K, 1969; Dennis Baker, OT, 1977; Ken Fantetti, LB, 1978; **Jack Weil, P, *1983; Jay Novacek, TE, *1984;** Mitch Donahue, DL, 1990; Ryan Yarborough, WR, 1992, 1993; **Marcus Harris, WR,** 1995, ***1996;** Steve Scifres, OL, 1996; Cory Wedel, PK, 1996; **Brian Lee, DB, *1997.**

XAVIER (OHIO): John Shinners, OG, 1968.

YALE: Amos Alonzo Stagg, E, *1889; Charles Gill, T, *1889; Pudge Heffelfinger, G, *1889, *1890, *1891; Thomas McClung, HB, *1890, *1891; William Rhodes, T, *1890; John Hartwell, E, *1891; Frank Hinkey, E, *1891, *1892, *1893, *1894; Wallace Winter, T, *1891; A. Hamilton Wallis, T, *1892; Vance McCormick, QB, *1892; William Hickok, G, *1893, *1894; Frank Butterworth, FB, *1893, *1894; Philip Stillman, C, *1894; George Adee, QB, *1894; Fred Murphy, T, *1895, *1896; Samuel Thorne, HB, *1895; Clarence Fincke, QB, *1896; John Hall, E, *1897; Burr Chamberlin, T, *1897, *1898; Gordon Brown, G, *1897, *1898, *1899, *1900; Charles DeSaulles, B, *1897; Malcolm McBride, B, *1898, *1899; George Stillman, T, *1899, *1900; Albert Sharpe, HB, *1899; James Bloomer, T, *1900, G, *1903; Herman Olcott, C, *1900; George Chadwick, HB, *1900, *1902; Perry Hale, FB, *1900; William Fincke, QB, *1900; Henry Holt, C, *1901, *1902; Thomas Shevlin, E, *1902, *1904, *1905; Ralph Kinney, T, *1902, G, *1904; James Hogan, T, *1902, *1903, *1904; Edgar Glass, G, *1902; Foster Rockwell, QB, *1902, *1904; Charles Rafferty, E, *1903; Ledyard Mitchell, HB, *1903; Roswell Tripp, G, *1905; Howard Roome, HB, *1905; Guy Hutchinson, QB, *1905; Robert Forbes, E, *1906; Horatio Biglow, T, *1906, *1907; Hugh Knox, HB, *1906; Paul Veeder, FB, *1906; Clarence Alcott, E, *1907; Thomas A. D. Jones, QB, *1907; Edward Coy, FB, *1907, *1908, *1909; William Goebel, G, *1908; Hamlin Andrus, G, *1908, *1909; John Kilpatrick, E, *1909, *1910; Henry Hobbs, T, *1909; Carroll Cooney, C, *1909; Stephen Philbin, HB, *1909; Douglass Bomeisler, E, *1911, *1912; Henry Ketcham, C, *1911, *1912; Arthur Howe, QB, *1911; Nelson Talbott, T, *1913; Harry LeGore, HB, *1914; Clinton Black, G, *1916; George Moseley, E, 1916; Charles Comerford, E, 1916; **Tim Callahan, G, *1920; Malcolm Aldrich, HB, *1921; Century Milstead, T, *1923; William Mallory, FB, *1923; Dick Luman, E, *1924;** Winslow Lovejoy, C, 1924; Raymond Pond, HB, 1924; John Joss, T, 1925; Herbert Sturhahn, G, 1925, 1926; Sidney Quarrier, T, 1927; **Bill Webster, G, *1927; John Charlesworth, C, *1927;** Frederick Linehan, G, 1930; **Clint Frank, HB,** 1936, **#*1937; Larry Kelley, E, *1936;** Spencer Moseley, C, 1942; **Paul Walker, E, *1944;** Ben Balme, G, 1960; Dick Jauron, HB, 1972; Rich Diana, HB, 1981.

The College Football Hall of Fame

Players

Name, College, Year Inducted (* indicates division entry)

Earl Abell, Colgate, 1915; Alex Agase, Purdue/Illinois, 1946; Harry Agganis, Boston University, 1952; Frank Albert, Stanford, 1941; Ki Aldrich, Texas Christian, 1938; Malcolm Aldrich, Yale, 1921; Marcus Allen, Southern California, 1981; Joe Alexander, Syracuse, 1920; Lance Alworth, Arkansas, 1961; Alan Ameche, Wisconsin, 1954; Knowlton Ames, Princeton, 1889; Warren Amling, Ohio State 1946; Bob P. Anderson, Army, 1959; Bobby Anderson, Colorado, 2006; Dick Anderson, Colorado, 1967; Donny Anderson, Texas Tech, 1965; Hunk Anderson, Notre Dame, 1921; Jon Arnett, Southern California, 1956; Doug Atkins, Tennessee, 1952

Bob Babich, Miami (Ohio), 1968; Everett Bacon, Wesleyan (Conn.), 1912; Reds Bagnell, Penn, 1950; Johnny Bailey, Texas A&M-Kingsville*, 1989; Hobey Baker, Princeton, 1913; John Baker, Southern California, 1931; Moon Baker, Northwestern, 1926; Terry Baker, Oregon State, 1962; Harold Ballin, Princeton, 1914; Bill Banker, Tulane, 1929; Vince Banonis, Detroit, 1941; Mike Barber, Marshall*, 1988; Stan Barnes, California, 1921; Charles Barrett, Cornell, 1915; Bert Baston, Minnesota, 1916; Cliff Battles, West Virginia Wesleyan, 1931; Sammy Baugh, Texas Christian, 1936; Maxie Baughan, Georgia Tech, 1959; Kirk Baumgartner, Wis.-Stevens Point*, 1989; James Bausch, Wichita State/Kansas, 1930; Ron Beagle, Navy, 1955; Terry Beasley, Auburn, 1971; Gary Beban, UCLA, 1967; Hub Bechtol, Texas Tech/Texas, 1946; Ray Beck, Georgia Tech, 1951; John Beckett, Oregon, 1916; Chuck Bednarik, Penn, 1948; Forrest Behm, Nebraska, 1940; Bobby Bell, Minnesota, 1962; Ricky Bell, Southern California, 1976; Joe Bellino, Navy, 1960; Marty Below, Wisconsin, 1923; Al Benbrook, Michigan, 1910; Cornelius Bennett, Alabama, 1986; Jeff Bentrim, North Dakota State*, 1998; Charlie Berry, Lafayette, 1924; Angelo Bertelli, Notre Dame, 1943; Jay Berwanger, Chicago, 1935; Lawrence Bettencourt, St. Mary's (Cal.), 1927; Fred Biletnikoff, Florida State, 1964; Bennie Blades, Miami (Fla.), 2006; Doc Blanchard, Army, 1946; Tony Blazine, Ilinois, Wesleyan*, 1934; Al Blozis, Georgetown, 1941; Ed Bock, Iowa State, 1938; Lynn Bomar, Vanderbilt, 1924; Douglas Bomeisler, Yale, 1912; Albie Booth, Yale,

1931; George Bork, Northern Illinois*, 1963; Fred Borries, Navy, 1934; Bruce Bosley, West Virginia, 1955; Don Bosseler, Miami (Fla.), 1956; Vic Bottari, California, 1938; Murry Bowden, Dartmouth, 1970; Ben Boynton, Williams, 1920; Terry Bradshaw, Louisiana Tech*, 1969; Charles Brewer, Harvard, 1895; Johnny Bright, Drake, 1951; John Brodie, Stanford, 1956; George Brooke, Swarthmore/Penn, 1895; Al Brosky, Illinois, 1952; Bob Brown, Nebraska, 1963; George Brown, Navy/San Diego State, 1947; Gordon Brown, Yale, 1900; Jim Brown, Syracuse, 1956; John Brown Jr., Navy, 1913; Johnny Mack Brown, Alabama, 1925; Tay Brown, Southern California, 1932; Tom Brown, Minnesota, 1960; Ross Browner, Notre Dame, 1977; Tel Bruner, Centre*, 1985; Buck Buchanan, Grambling*, 1962; Brad Budde, Southern California, 1979; Paul Bunker, Army, 1902; Chris Burford, Stanford, 1959; Kurt Burris, Oklahoma, 1954; Ron Burton, Northwestern, 1959; Dick Butkus, Illinois, 1964; Robert Butler, Wisconsin, 1913; Kevin Butler, Georgia, 1984

George Cafego, Tennessee, 1939; Red Cagle, Louisiana-Lafayette/Army, 1929; John Cain, Alabama, 1932; Brad Calip, East Central*, 1984; Ed Cameron, Washington & Lee, 1924; David Campbell, Harvard, 1901; Earl Campbell, Texas, 1977; Jack Cannon, Notre Dame, 1929; John Cappelletti, Penn State, 1973; Frank Carideo, Notre Dame, 1930; Charles Carney, Illinois, 1921; J.C. Caroline, Illinois, 1954; Bill Carpenter, Army, 1959; Hunter Carpenter, Virginia Tech/North Carolina, 1905; Charles Carroll, Washington, 1928; Harry Carson, South Carolina State*, 1975; Anthony Carter, Michigan, 1982; Tommy Casanova, Louisiana State, 1971; Edward Casey, Harvard, 1919; Tony Casillas, Oklahoma, 1985; Rod Cason, Angelo State*, 1971; Howard Cassady, Ohio State, 1955; Guy Chamberlin, Nebraska Wesleyan/Nebraska, 1915; Sam Chapman, California, 1937; Bob Chappuis, Michigan, 1947; Paul Christman, Missouri, 1940; Joe Cichy, North Dakota State*, 1970; Dutch Clark, Colorado College, 1929; Paul Cleary, Southern California, 1947; Zora Clevenger, Indiana, 1903; Jack Cloud, William & Mary, 1949; Gary Cochran, Princeton, 1897; Josh Cody, Vanderbilt, 1919; Don Coleman, Michigan State, 1951; Charlie Conerly, Mississippi, 1947; George Connor, Holy Cross/Notre Dame, 1947; Bill Cooper, Muskingum*, 1960; William Corbin, Yale, 1888; William Corbus, Stanford, 1933; Jimbo Covert, Pittsburgh, 1983; Hector Cowan, Princeton, 1889; Edward Coy, Yale, 1909; Brad Crawford, Franklin*, 1977; Fred Crawford, Duke, 1933; John David Crow, Texas A&M, 1957; Jim Crowley, Notre Dame, 1924; Larry Csonka, Syracuse, 1967; Tom Curtis, Michigan, 1969; Slade Cutter, Navy, 1934; Ziggie Czarobski, Notre Dame, 1947

Carroll Dale, Virginia Tech, 1959; Gerald Dalrymple, Tulane, 1931; John Dalton, Navy, 1911; Charles Daly, Harvard/Army, 1902; Averell Daniell, Pittsburgh, 1936; James Daniell, Ohio State, 1941; Tom Davies, Pittsburgh, 1921; Anthony Davis, Southern California, 1974; Ernie Davis, Syracuse, 1961; Glenn Davis, Army, 1946; Harold Davis, Westminster (Pa.)*, 1956; Robert Davis, Georgia Tech, 1947; Pete Dawkins, Army, 1958; Tom Deery, Widener*, 1981; Joe Delaney, Northwestern State*, 1980; Steve DeLong, Tennessee, 1964; Vern Den Herder, Central (Iowa)*, 1970; Kevin Dent, Jackson State*, 2006; Al DeRogatis, Duke, 1948; Paul DesJardien, Chicago, 1914; Aubrey Devine, Iowa, 1921; John DeWitt,

Princeton, 1903; Buddy Dial, Rice, 1958; Chuck Dicus, Arkansas, 1970; Don Dierdorf, Michigan, 1970; Mike Ditka, Pittsburgh, 1960; Glenn Dobbs, Tulsa, 1942; Bobby Dodd, Tennessee, 1930; Holland Donan, Princeton, 1950; Joseph Donchess, Pittsburgh, 1929; Keith Dorney, Penn State, 1978; Tony Dorsett, Pittsburgh, 1976; Nathan Dougherty, Tennessee, 1909; Bob Dove, Notre Dame, 1942; Nick Drahos, Cornell, 1940; Paddy Driscoll, Northwestern, 1916; Morley Drury, Southern California, 1927; Fred Dryer, San Diego State*, 1968; Joe Dudek, Plymouth State*, 1985; Dick Duden, Navy, 1945; Bill Dudley, Virginia, 1941; Randy Duncan, Iowa, 1958

Kenny Easley, UCLA, 1980; Walter Eckersall, Chicago, 1906; Turk Edwards, Washington State, 1931; William Edwards, Princeton, 1899; Ray Eichenlaub, Notre Dame, 1914; Steve Eisenhauer, Navy, 1953; Lawrence Elkins, Baylor, 1964; Carl Eller, Minnesota, 2006; Bump Elliott, Michigan/Purdue, 1947; Pete Elliott, Michigan, 1948; Dave Elmendorf, Texas A&M, 1970; John Elway, Stanford, 1982; Frank Emanuel, Tennessee, 1965; Steve Emtman, Washington, 2006; Ray Evans, Kansas, 1947; Thomas Everett, Baylor, 2006; Albert Exendine, Carlisle, 1907

Nello Falaschi, Santa Clara, 1936; Tom Fears, Santa Clara/UCLA, 1947; Beattie Feathers, Tennessee, 1933; Bob Fenimore, Oklahoma State, 1946; Doc Fenton, Louisiana State, 1909; Bob Ferguson, Ohio State, 1961; John Ferraro, Southern California, 1947; Wes Fesler, Ohio State, 1930; Bill Fincher, Davidson/Georgia Tech, 1920; Bill Fischer, Notre Dame, 1948; Hamilton Fish, Harvard, 1909; Robert Fisher, Harvard, 1911; Allen Flowers, Davidson/Georgia Tech, 1920; Charlie Flowers, Mississippi, 1959; George Floyd, Eastern Kentucky*, 1981; Danny Fortmann, Colgate, 1935; Bill Fralic, Pittsburgh, 1984; Sam Francis, Nebraska, 1936; George "Sonny" Franck, Minnesota, 1940; Ed Franco, Fordham, 1937; Clint Frank, Yale, 1937; Rodney Franz, California, 1949; Tucker Frederickson, Auburn, 1964; Benny Friedman, Michigan, 1926; John Friesz, Idaho*, 2006

Roman Gabriel, North Carolina State, 1961; Bob Gain, Kentucky, 1950; Arnold Galiffa, Army, 1949; Willie Galimore, Florida A&M*, 1956; Hugh Gallarneau, Stanford, 1940; Kenny Gamble, Colgate*, 1987; Edgar Garbisch, Washington & Jefferson/Army, 1924; Mike Garrett, Southern California, 1965; Charles Gelbert, Penn, 1896; Forest Geyer, Oklahoma, 1915; Jake Gibbs, Mississippi, 1960; Paul Giel, Minnesota, 1953; Frank Gifford, Southern California, 1951; Chris Gilbert, Texas, 1968; Walter Gilbert, Auburn, 1936; Harry Gilmer, Alabama, 1947; George Gipp, Notre Dame, 1920; Chet Gladchuk, Boston College, 1940; Bill Glass, Baylor, 1956; Rich Glover, Nebraska, 1972; Marshall Goldberg, Pittsburgh, 1938; Gene Goodreault, Boston College, 1940; Walter Gordon, California, 1918; Paul Governali, Columbia, 1942; Jim Grabowski, Illinois, 1965; Randy Gradishar, Ohio State, 1973; Otto Graham, Northwestern, 1943; Red Grange, Illinois, 1925; Bobby Grayson, Stanford, 1935; Charlie Green, Wittenberg*, 1964; Darrell Green, Texas A&M-Kingsville*, 1982; Hugh Green, Pittsburgh, 1980; Jack Green, Tulane/Army, 1945; Tim Green, Syracuse, 1985; Joe Greene, North Texas, 1968; Bob Griese, Purdue, 1966; Archie

Griffin, Ohio State, 1975; William Grinnell, Tufts*, 1934; Jerry Groom, Notre Dame, 1950; Ralph Guglielmi, Notre Dame, 1954; Merle Gulick, Toledo/Hobart, 1929; Ray Guy, Southern Miss, 1972; Joe Guyon, Carlisle/Georgia Tech, 1918

John Hadl, Kansas, 1961; Edwin Hale, Mississippi College, 1921; L. Parker Hall, Mississippi, 1938; Jack Ham, Penn State, 1970; Bob Hamilton, Stanford, 1935; Tom Hamilton, Navy, 1926; John Hannah, Alabama, 1972; Vic Hanson, Syracuse, 1926; Pat Harder, Wisconsin, 1942; Tack Hardwick, Harvard, 1914; T. Truxton Hare, Penn, 1900; Chick Harley, Ohio State, 1919; Tom Harmon, Michigan, 1940; Howard Harpster, Carnegie Mellon, 1928; Wayne Harris, Arkansas, 1960; Edward Hart, Princeton, 1911; Leon Hart, Notre Dame, 1949; Bill Hartman, Georgia, 1937; Jim Haslett, Indiana (Pa.)*, 1978; Frank Hawkins, Nevada*, 1980; Michael Haynes, Arizona State, 1975; Homer Hazel, Rutgers, 1924; Matt Hazeltine, California, 1954; Ed Healey, Holy Cross/Dartmouth, 1919; Pudge Heffelfinger, Yale, 1891; Mel Hein, Washington State, 1930; Don Heinrich, Washington, 1952; Ted Hendricks, Miami (Fla.), 1968; Garney Henley, Huron (S.D.)*, 1959; Chad Hennings, Air Force, 2006; Wilbur Henry, Washington & Jefferson, 1919; Clarence Herschberger, Chicago, 1898; Robert Herwig, California, 1937; Willie Heston, San Jose State/Michigan, 1904; Herman Hickman, Tennessee, 1931; William Hickok, Yale, 1894; John Hicks, Ohio State, 1973; Dan Hill, Duke, 1938; Art Hillebrand, Princeton, 1899; Frank Hinkey, Yale, 1894; Carl Hinkle, Vanderbilt, 1937; Clarke Hinkle, Bucknell, 1931; Elroy Hirsch, Wisconsin/Michigan, 1943; James Hitchcock, Auburn, 1932; Terry Hoage, Georgia, 1983; Frank Hoffmann, Notre Dame, 1931; James J. Hogan, Yale, 1904; Brud Holland, Cornell, 1938; Don Holleder, Army, 1955; Bill Hollenback, Penn, 1908; Mike Holovak, Boston College, 1942; Pierce Holt, Angelo State*, 1987; E.J. Holub, Texas Tech, 1960; Paul Hornung, Notre Dame, 1956; Edwin Horrell, California, 1924; Les Horvath, Ohio State, 1944; Jim Houston, Ohio State, 1959; Arthur Howe, Yale, 1911; Dixie Howell, Alabama, 1934; John Huarte, Notre Dame, 1964; Cal Hubbard, Geneva/Centenary (La.), 1926; John Hubbard, Amherst, 1906; Pooley Hubert, Alabama, 1925; Sam Huff, West Virginia, 1955; Weldon Humble, Louisiana-Lafayette/Rice, 1946; Ricky Hunley, Arizona, 1983; Jackie Hunt, Marshall*, 1941; Joel Hunt, Texas A&M, 1927; Ellery Huntington, Colgate, 1913; Don Hutson, Alabama, 1934

Cosmo Iacavazzi, Princeton, 1964; Jonas Ingram, Navy, 1906; Cecil Isbell, Purdue, 1937

Harvey Jablonsky, Army/Washington-State Louis, 1933; Bo Jackson, Auburn, 1985; Keith Jackson, Oklahoma, 1987; Vic Janowicz, Ohio State, 1951; John Jefferson, Arizona State, 1977; Darold Jenkins, Missouri, 1941; Jackie Jensen, California, 1948; Herbert Joesting, Minnesota, 1927; Billy Johnson, Widener*, 1972; Bob Johnson, Tennessee, 1967; Gary Johnson, Grambling*, 1974; Jimmie Johnson, Carlisle/Northwestern, 1905; Ron Johnson, Michigan, 1968; Brent Jones, Santa Clara*, 1985; Calvin Jones, Iowa, 1955; Gomer Jones, Ohio State, 1935; Stan Jones, Maryland, 1953; Lee Roy Jordan, Alabama, 1962; Frank Juhan, Sewanee, 1910; Charlie Justice, North Carolina, 1949

Mort Kaer, Southern California, 1926; Joe Kapp, California, 1958; Alex Karras, Iowa, 1957; Ken Kavanaugh, Louisiana State, 1939; Edgar Kaw, Cornell, 1922; Dick Kazmaier, Princeton, 1951; Stan Keck, Princeton, 1921; Chip Kell, Tennessee, 2006; Larry Kelley, Yale, 1936; Wild Bill Kelly, Montana, 1926; Doug Kenna, Army, 1944; George Kerr, Boston College, 1940; Henry Ketcham, Yale, 1913; Leroy Keyes, Purdue, 1968; Glenn Killinger, Penn State, 1921; Billy Kilmer, UCLA, 1960; John Kilpatrick, Yale, 1910; John Kimbrough, Texas A&M, 1940; Frank Kinard, Mississippi, 1937; Terry Kinard, Clemson, 1982; Steve Kiner, Tennessee, 1969; Phillip King, Princeton, 1893; Nile Kinnick, Iowa, 1939; Harry Kipke, Michigan, 1923; John Kitzmiller, Oregon, 1930; Barton Koch, Baylor, 1930; Walt Koppisch, Columbia, 1924; Ron Kramer, Michigan, 1956; Alex Kroll, Yale/Rutgers, 1961; Charlie Krueger, Texas A&M, 1957; Malcolm Kutner, Texas, 1941; Ted Kwalick, Penn State, 1968

Steve Lach, Duke, 1941; Myles Lane, Dartmouth, 1927; Willie Lanier, Morgan State*, 1966; Johnny Lattner, Notre Dame, 1953; Hank Lauricella, Tennessee, 1951; Lester Lautenschlaeger, Tulane, 1925; Elmer Layden, Notre Dame, 1924; Bobby Layne, Texas, 1947; Langdon Lea, Princeton, 1895; Roosevelt Leaks, Texas, 1974; Eddie LeBaron, Pacific, 1949; Jim LeClair, North Dakota*, 1971; James Leech, VMI, 1920; Darrell Lester, Texas Christian, 1935; Jerry LeVias, Southern Methodist, 1968; D.D. Lewis, Mississippi State, 1968; Leo Lewis, Lincoln (Mo.)*, 1954; Bob Lilly, Texas Christian, 1960; Augie Lio, Georgetown, 1940; Floyd Little, Syracuse, 1966; Gordie Lockbaum, Holy Cross*, 1987; Gordon Locke, Iowa, 1922; Neil Lomax, Portland State*, 1980; Chuck Long, Iowa, 1985; Mel Long, Toledo, 1971; Frank Loria, Virginia Tech, 1967; Ronnie Lott, Southern California, 1980; Don Lourie, Princeton, 1921; Richie Lucas, Penn State, 1959; Sid Luckman, Columbia, 1938; Johnny Lujack, Notre Dame, 1947; Pug Lund, Minnesota, 1934; Jim Lynch, Notre Dame, 1966

Ken MacAfee, Notre Dame, 1977; Robert MacLeod, Dartmouth, 1938; Bart Macomber, Illinois, 1916; Dicky Maegle, Rice, 1954; Ned Mahon, Harvard, 1915; Johnny Majors, Tennessee, 1956; Ronnie Mallett, Central Arkansas*, 2006; William Mallory, Yale, 1923; Vaughn Mancha, Alabama, 1947; James Mandich, Michigan, 1969; Gerald Mann, Southern Methodist, 1927; Archie Manning, Mississippi, 1970; Edgar Manske, Northwestern, 1933; Ed Marinaro, Cornell, 1971; Dan Marino, Pittsburgh, 1982; Vic Markov, Washington, 1937; Bobby Marshall, Minnesota, 1906; Jim Martin, Notre Dame, 1949; Ollie Matson, San Francisco, 1951; Ray Matthews, Texas Christian, 1927; John Maulbetsch, Adrian/Michigan, 1916; Pete Mauthe, Penn State, 1912; Robert Maxwell, Chicago/Swarthmore, 1905; Mark May, Pittsburgh, 1980; George McAfee, Duke, 1939; Napoleon McCallum, Navy, 1985; Don McCauley, North Carolina, 1970; Thomas McClung, Yale, 1891; Bill McColl, Stanford, 1951; Jim McCormick, Princeton, 1907; Tommy McDonald, Oklahoma, 1956; Jack McDowall, North Carolina State, 1927; Hugh McElhenny, Washington, 1951; Gene McEver, Tennessee, 1931; John McEwan, Army, 1916; Banks McFadden, Clemson, 1939; Bud McFadin, Texas, 1950; Mike McGee, Duke, 1959; Edward McGinley, Penn, 1924; John McGovern, Minnesota, 1910; Thurman McGraw, Colorado State, 1949; Tyrone

McGriff, Florida A&M*, 1979; Mike McKeever, Southern California, 1960; Reggie McKenzie, Michigan, 1971; George McLaren, Pittsburgh, 1918; Jim McMahon, Brigham Young, 1981; Dan McMillan, Southern California/California, 1921; Bo McMillin, Centre, 1921; Bob McWhorter, Georgia, 1913; Roy Mercer, Penn, 1912; Don Meredith, Southern Methodist, 1959; Frank Merritt, Army, 1943; Bert Metzger, Notre Dame, 1930; Wayne Meylan, Nebraska, 1967; Lou Michaels, Kentucky, 1957; John Michels, Tennessee, 1952; Abe Mickal, Louisiana State, 1935; Creighton Miller, Notre Dame, 1943; Don Miller, Notre Dame, 1924; Eugene Miller, Penn State, 1913; Fred Miller, Notre Dame, 1928; Rip Miller, Notre Dame, 1924; Wayne Millner, Notre Dame, 1935; Century Milstead, Wabash/Yale, 1923; John Minds, Penn, 1897; Skip Minisi, Penn/Navy, 1947; Lydell Mitchell, Penn State, 1971; Dick Modzelewski, Maryland, 1952; Alex Moffat, Princeton, 1883; Ed Molinski, Tennessee, 1940; Cliff Montgomery, Columbia, 1933; Wilbert Montgomery, Abilene Christian*, 1976; Donn Moomaw, UCLA, 1952; William Morley, Columbia, 1901; George Morris, Georgia Tech, 1952; Larry Morris, Georgia Tech, 1954; Bill Morton, Dartmouth, 1931; Craig Morton, California, 1964; Monk Moscrip, Stanford, 1935; Brick Muller, California, 1922; Johnny Musso, Alabama, 1971

Bronko Nagurski, Minnesota, 1929; Billy Neighbors, Alabama, 1961; Ernie Nevers, Stanford, 1925; Marshall Newell, Harvard, 1893; Harry Newman, Michigan, 1932; Ozzie Newsome, Alabama, 1977; Gifford Nielsen, Brigham Young, 1977; Dwayne Nix, Texas A&M-Kingsville*, 1968; Tommy Nobis, Texas, 1965; Leo Nomellini, Minnesota, 1949

Andrew Oberlander, Dartmouth, 1925; Davey O'Brien, Texas Christian, 1938; Ken O'Brien, UC Davis*, 1982; Pat O'Dea, Wisconsin, 1899; Bob Odell, Penn, 1943; Jack O'Hearn, Cornell, 1914; Robin Olds, Army, 1942; Elmer Oliphant, Army/Purdue, 1917; Merlin Olsen, Utah State, 1961; Dennis Onkotz, Penn State, 1969; Bennie Oosterbaan, Michigan, 1927; Charles O'Rourke, Boston College, 1940; John Orsi, Colgate, 1931; Win Osgood, Cornell/Penn, 1894; Bill Osmanski, Holy Cross, 1938; John Outland, Kansas/Penn, 1899; George Owen, Harvard, 1922; Jim Owens, Oklahoma, 1949; Steve Owens, Oklahoma, 1969

Alan Page, Notre Dame, 1966; Joe Palumbo, Virginia, 1951; Jack Pardee, Texas A&M, 1956; Babe Parilli, Kentucky, 1951; Ace Parker, Duke, 1936; Jackie Parker, Mississippi State, 1953; Jim Parker, Ohio State, 1956; Walter Payton, Jackson State*, 1974; Vince Pazzetti, Wesleyan/Lehigh, 1912; Chub Peabody, Harvard, 1941; Robert Peck, Pittsburgh, 1916; Bob Pellegrini, Maryland, 1955; Stan Pennock, Harvard, 1914; George Pfann, Cornell, 1923; H.D. Phillips, Sewanee, 1905; Loyd Phillips, Arkansas, 1966; Mike Phipps, Purdue, 2006; Pete Pihos, Indiana, 1946; Erny Pinckert, Southern California, 1931; John Pingel, Michigan State, 1938; Jim Plunkett, Stanford, 1970; Arthur Poe, Princeton, 1899; Fritz Pollard, Brown, 1916; George Poole, Mississippi/North Carolina/Army, 1948; Marvin Powell, Southern California, 1976; Merv Pregulman, Michigan, 1943; Eddie Price, Tulane, 1949; Ron Pritchard, Arizona State, 1968; Greg Pruitt, Oklahoma, 1972; Larry Pugh, Westminster (Pa.)*, 1964; Peter Pund, Georgia Tech, 1928

Garrard Ramsey, William & Mary, 1942; John Rauch, Georgia, 1948; Gary Reasons, Northwestern State*, 1983; Bill Redell, Occidental*, 1963; Rick Redman, Washington, 1964; Claude Reeds, Oklahoma, 1913; Mike Reid, Penn State, 1969; Steve Reid, Northwestern, 1936; William Reid, Harvard, 1899; Bob Reifsnyder, Navy, 1958; Mel Renfro, Oregon, 1963; Pug Rentner, Northwestern, 1932; Scott Reppert, Lawrence*, 1982; Glenn Ressler, Penn State, 1969; Bob Reynolds, Stanford, 1935; Bobby Reynolds, Nebraska, 1952; Randy Rhino, Georgia Tech, 1974; Jerry Rhome, Southern Methodist/Tulsa, 1964; Jerry Rice, Mississippi Valley*, 2006; Willie Richardson, Jackson State*, 1962; Les Richter, California, 1951; Pat Richter, Wisconsin, 1962; Jack Riley, Northwestern, 1931; Dave Rimington, Nebraska, 1982; Charles Rinehart, Lafayette, 1897; Jim Ritcher, North Carolina State, 1979; Richard Ritchie, Texas A&M-Kingsville*, 1976; Calvin Roberts, Gustavus Adolphus*, 1952; J.D. Roberts, Oklahoma, 1953; Paul Robeson, Rutgers, 1918; Dave Robinson, Penn State, 1962; Jerry Robinson, UCLA, 1978; Tracy Rocker, Auburn, 1988; Ira Rodgers, West Virginia, 1919; Johnny Rodgers, Nebraska, 1972; Edward Rogers, Carlisle/Minnesota, 1903; George Rogers, South Carolina, 1980; Johnny Roland, Missouri, 1965; Joe Romig, Colorado, 1961; Aaron Rosenberg, Southern California, 1933; Dan Ross, Northeastern*, 1978; Kyle Rote, Southern Methodist, 1950; Joe Routt, Texas A&M, 1937; Mike Rozier, Nebraska, 2006

Red Salmon, Notre Dame, 1903; Barry Sanders, Oklahoma State, 1988; Alex Sarkisian, Northwestern, 1948; George Sauer, Nebraska, 1933; George Savitsky, Penn, 1947; James Saxton, Texas, 1961; Gale Sayers, Kansas, 1964; Jack Scarbath, Maryland, 1952; Hunter Scarlett, Penn, 1908; Bob Schloredt, Washington, 1960; Joe Schmidt, Pittsburgh, 1952; Wear Schoonover, Arkansas, 1929; Dave Schreiner, Wisconsin, 1942; Germany Schultz, Michigan, 1908; Dutch Schwab, Lafayette, 1922; Marchy Schwartz, Notre Dame, 1931; Paul Schwegler, Washington, 1931; Clyde Scott, Navy/Arkansas, 1948; Freddie Scott, Amherst*, 1973; Richard Scott, Navy, 1947; Tom Scott, Virginia, 1952; Henry Seibels, Sewanee, 1900; Ron Sellers, Florida State, 1968; Lee Roy Selmon, Oklahoma, 1975; Harley Sewell, Texas, 1952; Bill Shakespeare, Notre Dame, 1935; Donnie Shell, South Carolina State*, 1973; Murray Shelton, Cornell, 1915; Tom Shevlin, Yale, 1905; Bernie Shively, Illinois, 1926; Jeff Siemon, Stanford, 2006; Monk Simons, Tulane, 1934; O.J. Simpson, Southern California, 1968; Billy Sims, Oklahoma, 1979; Mike Singletary, Baylor, 1980; Fred Sington, Alabama, 1930; Frank Sinkwich, Georgia, 1942; Jerry Sisemore, Texas, 1972; Emil Sitko, Notre Dame, 1949; Joe Skladany, Pittsburgh, 1933; Duke Slater, Iowa, 1921; Billy Ray Smith, Arkansas, 1982; Bruce Smith, Minnesota, 1941; Bruce Smith, Virginia Tech, 2006; Bubba Smith, Michigan State, 1966; Clipper Smith, Notre Dame, 1927; Emmitt Smith, Florida, 2006; Ernie Smith, Southern California, 1932; Harry Smith, Southern California, 1939; Jim Ray Smith, Baylor, 1954; Riley Smith, Alabama, 1935; Vernon Smith, Georgia, 1931; Neil Snow, Michigan, 1901; Gary Spani, Kansas State, 1977; Al Sparlis, UCLA, 1945; Clarence Spears, Knox/Dartmouth, 1915; W.D. Spears, Vanderbilt, 1927; William Sprackling, Brown, 1911; Bud Sprague, Army/Texas, 1928; Steve Spurrier, Florida, 1966; Harrison Stafford, Texas, 1932; Amos Alonzo Stagg, Yale, 1889; Bill Stanfill, Georgia, 1968; Max Starcevich, Washington, 1936; Roger Staubach, Navy, 1964; Walter Steffen, Chicago, 1908; Joe Steffy, Tennessee/Army, 1947; Herbert Stein, Pittsburgh, 1921; Bob Steuber, DePauw/Missouri, 1943;

Mal Stevens, Washburn/Yale, 1923; Ben Stevenson, Tuskegee*, 1930; Vincent Stevenson, Penn, 1905; Jim Stillwagon, Ohio State, 1970; Pete Stinchcomb, Ohio State, 1920; Brock Strom, Air Force, 1958; William Stromberg, Johns Hopkins*, 1981; Ken Strong, New York University, 1928; George Strupper, Georgia Tech, 1917; Harry Stuhldreher, Notre Dame, 1924; Herb Sturhahn, Yale, 1926; Joe Stydahar, West Virginia, 1935; Bob Suffridge, Tennessee, 1940; Steve Suhey, Penn State, 1947; Pat Sullivan, Auburn, 1971; Frank Sundstrom, Cornell, 1923; Lynn Swann, Southern California, 1973; Clarence Swanson, Nebraska, 1921; Bill Swiacki, Holy Cross/Columbia, 1947; Jim Swink, Texas Christian, 1956

Eddie Talboom, Wyoming, 1950; George Taliaferro, Indiana, 1948; Fran Tarkenton, Georgia, 1960; Jack Tatum, Ohio State, 1970; John Tavener, Indiana, 1944; Bruce Taylor, Boston University*, 1969; Chuck Taylor, Stanford, 1942; Joe Theismann, Notre Dame, 1970; Aurelius Thomas, Ohio State, 1957; Joe Thompson, Geneva/Pittsburgh, 1906; Lynn Thomsen, Augustana (Ill.)*, 1986; Samuel Thorne, Yale, 1895; Jim Thorpe, Carlisle, 1912; Ben Ticknor, Harvard, 1930; John Tigert, Vanderbilt, 1903; Gaynell Tinsley, Louisiana State, 1936; Eric Tipton, Duke, 1938; Clayton Tonnemaker, Minnesota, 1949; Bob Torrey, Penn, 1905; Willie Totten, Mississippi Valley*, 1985; Randy Trautman, Boise State*, 1981; Brick Travis, Tarkio/Missouri, 1920; Charley Trippi, Georgia, 1946; Edward Tryon, Colgate, 1925; Jerry Tubbs, Oklahoma, 1956; Bulldog Turner, Hardin-Simmons, 1939; Howard Twilley, Tulsa, 1965

Joe Utay, Texas A&M, 1907

Norm Van Brocklin, Oregon, 1948; Brad Van Pelt, Michigan State, 1972; Dale Van Sickel, Florida, 1929; H. Van Surdam, Wesleyan (Conn.), 1905; Dexter Very, Penn State, 1912; Billy Vessels, Oklahoma, 1952; Ernie Vick, Michigan, 1921

Hube Wagner, Pittsburgh, 1913; Doak Walker, Southern Methodist, 1949; Herschel Walker, Georgia, 1982; Bill Wallace, Rice, 1935; Adam Walsh, Notre Dame, 1924; Cotton Warburton, Southern California, 1934; Bob Ward, Maryland, 1951; Charlie Ward, Florida State, 2006; Andre Ware, Houston, 1989; William Warner, Cornell, 1902; Joe Washington, Oklahoma, 1975; Kenny Washington, UCLA, 1939; Jim Weatherall, Oklahoma, 1951; George Webster, Michigan State, 1966; Herman Wedemeyer, St. Mary's (Cal.), 1947; Harold Weekes, Columbia, 1902; Roger Wehrli, Missouri, 1968; Art Weiner, North Carolina, 1949; Ed Weir, Nebraska, 1925; Gus Welch, Carlisle, 1914; John Weller, Princeton, 1935; Percy Wendell, Harvard, 1912; Belford West, Colgate, 1919; Bob Westfall, Michigan, 1941; Babe Weyand, Army, 1915; Buck Wharton, Penn, 1896; Arthur Wheeler, Princeton, 1894; Byron White, Colorado, 1937; Charles White, Southern California, 1979; Danny White, Arizona State, 1973; Ed White, California, 1968; Randy White, Maryland, 1974; Reggie White, Tennessee, 1983; Don Whitmire, Navy/Alabama, 1944; Frank Wickhorst, Navy, 1926; Ed Widseth, Minnesota, 1936; Paul Wiggin, Stanford, 1956; Dick Wildung, Minnesota, 1942; Bob Williams, Notre Dame, 1950; David Williams, Illinois, 1985; Doug Williams, Grambling*, 1977; Froggie Williams, Rice, 1949; Bill Willis, Ohio State, 1944; Bobby Wilson, Southern Methodist, 1935; George Wilson, Washington, 1925; Harry Wilson, Army/Penn State, 1927; Marc Wilson, Brigham Young, 1979; Mike Wilson, Lafayette, 1928; Kellen Winslow,

Missouri, 1978; Albert Wistert, Michigan, 1942; Alvin Wistert, Boston University/Michigan, 1949; Whitey Wistert, Michigan, 1933; Alex Wojciechowicz, Fordham, 1937; Barry Wood, Harvard, 1931; Andy Wyant, Bucknell/Chicago, 1894; Bowden Wyatt, Tennessee, 1938; Clint Wyckoff, Cornell, 1895

Tommy Yarr, Notre Dame, 1931; Ron Yary, Southern California, 1967; Lloyd Yoder, Carnegie Mellon, 1926; Buddy Young, Illinois, 1946; Charles Young, Southern California, 1972; Harry Young, Washington & Lee, 1916; Steve Young, Brigham Young, 1983; Waddy Young, Oklahoma, 1938; Jack Youngblood, Florida, 1970; Jim Youngblood, Tennessee Tech*, 1972; Paul Younger, Grambling*, 1948

Gust Zarnas, Ohio State, 1937.

Coaches

Joe Aillet 1989; Bill Alexander 1951; Eddie Anderson 1971; Ike Armstrong 1957; Chris Ault* 2002

Charlie Bachman 1978; Earl Banks 1992; Harry Baujan 1990; Thomas Beck* 2004; Matty Bell 1955; Hugo Bezdek 1954; Dana X. Bible 1951; Bernie Bierman 1955; Bob Blackman 1987; Earl "Red" Blaik 1964; Bobby Bowden 2006; Frank Broyles 1983; Earle Bruce 2002; Paul "Bear" Bryant 1986; Harold Burry* 1996; Jim Butterfield* 1997; Wally Butts 1997

Charlie Caldwell 1961; Walter Camp 1951; Len Casanova 1977; Marino Casem* 2003; Frank Cavanaugh 1954; Jerry Claiborne 1999; Dick Colman 1990; Don Coryell* 1999; Carmen Cozza 2002; Fritz Crisler 1954

Duffy Daugherty 1984; Bob Devaney 1981; Dan Devine 1985; Doug Dickey 2003; Gil Dobie 1951; Bobby Dodd 1993; Michael Donahue 1951; Terry Donahue 2000; Vince Dooley 1994; Gus Dorais 1954; Pat Dye 2005

Bill Edwards 1986; LaVell Edwards 2004; Rip Engle 1973; Forest Evashevski 2000

Dick Farley* 2006; Don Faurot 1961; Hayden Fry 2003; Joseph Fusco* 2001

John Gagliardi* 2006; Jake Gaither 1975; Sid Gillman 1989; Ernest Godfrey 1972; Ray Graves 1990; Andy Gustafson 1985

Edward Hall 1951; Jack Hardin 1980; Richard Harlow 1954; Harvey Harman 1981; Jesse Harper, 1971; Roger Harring* 2005; Percy Haughton 1951; Woody Hayes 1983; John W. Heisman 1954; Robert Higgins 1954; Paul Hoernemann* 1997; Babe Hollingberry 1979; Frank Howard 1989; Marcelino Huerta* 2002

Bill Ingram 1973

Don James 1997; Morley Jennings 1973; Biff Jones 1954; Howard Jones 1951; Tad Jones 1958; Lloyd Jordan 1978; Ralph "Shug" Jordan 1982

Andy Kerr 1951; Roy Kidd* 2003; Chuck Klausing* 1998; Frank Kush 1995

Frank Leahy 1970; George Little 1955; Lou Little 1960

Slip Madigan 1974; Fred Martinelli* 2002; Dave Maurer 1991; Vernon "Skip" McCain* 2006; Charlie McClendon 1986; Herb McCracken 1973; Dan McGugin 1951; John McKay 1988; Allyn McKeen 1991; Tuss McLaughry 1962; John Merritt 1994; Dutch Meyer 1956; Jack Mollenkopf 1988; Bernie Moore 1954; Scrappy Moore 1980; Ray Morrison 1954; Darrell Mudra* 2000; Arnett "Ace" Mumford* 2001; George Munger 1976; Clarence "Big-gie" Munn 1959; Bill Murray 1974; Frank Murray 1974; Ed "Hook" Mylin 1974

Earle "Greasy" Neale, 1967; Jess Neely 1971; Don Nehlen 2005; David Nelson 1987; Robert Neyland 1956; Billy Nicks* 1999; Homer Norton 1971

Frank "Buck" O'Neill 1951; Tom Osborne 1998; Bennie Owen 1951

Ara Parseghian 1980; Joe Paterno 2006; Doyt Perry 1988; Jimmy Phelan 1973; Tommy Prothro 1991

John Ralston 1992; Harold "Tubby" Raymond* 2003; Bob Reade* 1998; Charlie Richard 2004; E.N. Robinson 1955; Eddie Robinson* 1997; Knute Rockne 1951; Dick Romney 1954; Bill Roper 1951; Darrell Royal 1983; Adolph Rutschman* 1998

Henry "Red" Sanders 1996; George Sanford 1971; Glenn "Bo" Schembechler 1993; Ron Schipper* 2000; Francis Schmidt 1971; Ben Schwartzwalder 1982; Clark Shaughnessy 1968; Buck Shaw 1972; Edgar Sherman* 1996; Andy Smith 1951; Carl Snavely 1965; Jim Sochor* 1999; Amos Alonzo Stagg, 1951; Gil Steinke* 1996; Dick Strahm* 2004; Jock Sutherland 1951; Barry Switzer 2001

Jim Tatum 1984; Grant Teaff 2001; Frank Thomas 1951; Lee Tressel* 1996

Thad "Pie" Vann 1987; Johnny Vaught 1979

Wallace Wade 1955; Lynn "Pappy" Waldorf 1966; Glenn "Pop" Warner 1951; Frank "Muddy" Waters* 2000; George Welsh 2004; Frosty Westering* 2005; E.E. "Tad" Wieman 1956; John Wilce 1954; Bud Wilkinson 1969; Henry Williams 1951; George Woodruff 1963; Warren Woodson 1989; Bowden Wyatt 1997

Bill Yeoman 2001; Fielding "Hurry Up" Yost 1951; Jim Young 1999

Bob Zuppke 1951

About the Author

Christopher J. Walsh has been an award-winning sports journalist since 1990, and currently covers University of Alabama football for the *Tuscaloosa News*. Previous beats include the Green Bay Packers, Arizona Cardinals, and Tampa Bay Buccaneers in the National Football League, and Major League Baseball's Arizona Diamondbacks. The writer/columnist has been twice nominated for a Pulitzer Prize and in 2005 helped the *Tuscaloosa News* earn a First Amendment Award (formerly Freedom of Information Award) from the Associated Press Managing Editors. In 2006, he received the Alabama Sports Writers Association's highest honor, the Herby Kirby Memorial Award. He's won numerous awards from the Associated Press Sports Editors, Alabama Managing Editors, and Alabama Press Association. Previous books include *Crimson Storm Surge: Alabama Football Then and Now*, *No Time Outs: What It's Really Like to be a Sportswriter Today*, and *Where Football is King: A History of the SEC*.